THE ZONE
TRUE TALES FROM THE HEARTLAND

MARK ZIMMERMAN

THE ZONE: TRUE TALES FROM THE HEARTLAND
Copyright © 2021 Mark Zimmerman
Zimco Publications LLC
Website: zimcopubs.com
Email: info@zimcopubs.com

ISBN Paperback: 978-0-9858692-9-8

All rights reserved.

All Text and Photographs by the Author Unless Otherwise Noted

No part of this book may be reproduced or transmitted in any form or by any means — electronic or manual, including photocopy, scanner, email, CD or other information storage and retreival system — without written permission from the author, except for personal use or as provided to the news media and book sellers.

Printed in the United States of America.

The text in this book, which is published to inform and entertain, should be used for general information and not as the ultimate source of educational or travel information. Every effort has been made to ensure the accuracy and relevence of information in this book but the author and publisher do not assume responsibility for any errors, inaccuracies, omissions or inconsistencies within. Any slights of people, places, or organizations are strictly unintentional.

The names of organizations and destinations mentioned in this book may be trade names or trademarks of their owners. The author and publisher disclaims any connection with, sponsorship by or endorsement of such owners.

Content related to this publication can be found on the publisher's website at: zimcopubs.com

> Dedicated to All the Victims
> of Unintended Consequences
> Perpetrated Throughout History
> By Employees of the
> Good Intentions Paving Company.

Also by Mark Zimmerman
and available from Zimco Publications LLC:

Mud, Blood & Cold Steel
The Retreat From Nashville-December 1864

Iron Maidens and the Devil's Daughters:
U.S. Navy Gunboats versus Confederate Gunners and Cavalry
on the Tennessee and Cumberland Rivers, 1861-65

Guide to Civil War Nashville, 2nd Edition

God, Guns, Guitars & Whiskey:
An Illustrated Guide to Historic Nashville, Tennessee, 2nd Edition

Gone Under:
Historic Cemeteries and Burial Grounds
of Nashville, Tennessee, 2nd Edition

Land of the Free, Home of the Brave
Our Founding Documents and Concise History of the USA

www.zimcopubs.com

USER AGREEMENT: Do not fold, spindle, or mutilate. Void where prohibited. Not for internal usage. Please dispose of properly. Drink responsibly. Slow children at play. Remove child before folding. Once used rectally the thermometer should not be used orally. Do not eat. This product not intended for use as dental drill. Avoid pouring on crotch. Do not allow children to play in dishwasher. Do not iron while wearing shirt. This product moves when used. Patent pending. Harmful if swallowed. Slippery when wet. Potentially hazardous situation. Do not wash dishes in the urinal. Caution: Children can't fly. Contents under pressure. May cause drowsiness. Contains peanuts and peanut by-products. Do not tip or rock vending machine. Take the bus. Do not use for breast augmentation. You don't have to go home, but you can't stay here. Touching wires causes instant death-$200 fine. Please do not feed the animals. No heavy petting on the first date. Baby on board. Do not try this at home. Professional stunt driver. Paid commercial spokesman. Eat or use by expiration date. No U-turns. Get off my lawn! Two drink minimum. Zipper may harm you. Machine wash cold. Do not look directly at the sun. Must be 18 years old or older. Don't delay, now more than ever. Past performance does not guarantee future results. Dishwasher safe. Do not eat the yellow snow. Employees must wash hands before leaving. Take only as directed by doctor. Leave the driving to us. Do not hold wrong end of chainsaw. Use only with adult supervision. Costume does not enable flight. Harmful if swallowed. Limit one per customer. Viewer discretion advised. Talk to me dirty, make me write bad checks. Coffee may be hot. Based on a true story. Names changed to protect the innocent. Never let the facts get in the way of a good story. Don't tug on Superman's cape. Warning: Absolutely no brown ones. Any other use of this telecast or any pictures, descriptions, or accounts of the game without the NFL's consent is expressly prohibited. No bills over $20 accepted. Shown to be an effective decay-preventive dentifrice when used in a conscienciously applied program of oral hygiene and regular professional care. The moose says you're closed; I say you're open. Be the ball. Empty when full. Righty tighty. Keep your head down. Do not overinflate. Keep off the grass. Right turn on red. Do not use without permission. No loitering. No colors allowed. Aim carefully. Stop making sense. No wake. Stand up straight. Get out of jail free. Don't tread on me. Enforced by radar. Cut along dotted line. Official documents inside. Do not remove tags under penalty of law. No parking zone. Remove all items from pockets. Stand up straight. Close your mouth while eating. No drinks or food items allowed inside. Keep to the right. No public restrooms. Do not block driveway. Members only. Limit one per customer. Keep your hands to yourself. Violators will be towed. Punishable by up to five years in prison. High voltage! Only your hairdresser knows for sure. Four enough, six too many? Be all you can be. Death to tyrants! Remember the Alamo! Slower traffic use right lane. No horseplay allowed. No wooden nickels. 23-Skidoo. No guts, no glory. No talking to the driver. Not for the prevention of sexually transmitted diseases. Keep hands and heads inside windows. No jake brakes. No diving in the pool. No reproduction or further use of this publication without the written permission of the publisher.

☐ I agree with these rules and regulations before reading any further.

THE ZONE: TRUE TALES FROM THE HEARTLAND

TABLE OF CONTENTS

Introduction	3
Overtime on the Frozen Tundra: The Strangest NFL Game Ever	5
BOOM Town: Largest Gunpowder Factory in World Goes Up in Smoke	12
The Life and Times of Dr. Robert Hartley, PhD	19
To Infinity and Beyond: AEDC-Cold War Aerospace Testing Grounds	24
The Flying Crowbar and Other Nuclear-Powered Aircraft	35
Decisions, Decisions	41
Getting High and Staying There	42
State Capitol - Temple of Democracy	49
Nazi Saboteurs and the Fountain of Youth	60
Ironclad Gunboats Battle Confederate Horse Cavalry	66
Watching Atomic Bomb Blasts from the Vegas Strip, Baby	75
Rockford: Sock Monkeys, Suicide, the Mafia, and Santa Claus	80
When Duke Lost the Rose Bowl…at Duke Stadium	87
Roadside Attraction: Space Shuttle Fuel Tank…Stranded	88
War Games Dangerous But Saved Countless Lives	90
Building the Bomb: Clinton Engineer Works	99
Nineteen Fifty Sixty	110
Who's Who? Know Your Composers, Explorers, Gangsters, Painters	111
Peaceful Succession of American Power	121
The Kings of Curmudgeon	127
Our Universe: Really Big and Full of Nothing	132
Oshkosh: The Wild Blue Yonder and the Flat Black Ice	136
More Civilized and Humane Methods of Executing the Condemned	142
The History of Rock 'n Roll	152
Hendrix vs. Jones: Nashville's Vibrant R&B Scene	153
The Lonesome Highway	158
General Jackson's Iron Balls	159
Welcome to the Body Farm	166
Having a Ball with Spheres	170

(continued)

TABLE OF CONTENTS

Men Behaving Badly —
   Carmack Whacked: Martyr of Political Assassination 178
   Murder During Wartime: Three Generals Slain With Impunity 181
   Sevier vs. Tipton Feud: Battle of the Lost State of Franklin 184
   The Black Patch War: Possum Hunters vs. Hillbillies 186
   The Coal Creek War: Free Miners vs. National Guard 189
   The Hoo Doo War: Vigilantism Turns To Vengeful Range Warfare 192
   The War of the Regulation: Foreshadow of the Revolution 194
   Remember the Raisin! The Battle and Massacre of River Raisin 196
   Fort Sanders: Knoxville Campaign Ends with Debacle 198
   The Wabash: Greatest Indian Victory Over U.S. Army 201

Scoundrels, Bushwhackers, and Partisan Rangers 204

Vincennes: Historic Old Town on the Wabash 218

Saturn V: The Most Powerful Machine On or Off Earth 222

Las Vegas: Where Everything Is Too Much But Never Enough 228

Evansville: WWII Arsenal of Democracy 233

Utopian Dreams: Heaven Can Wait 238

The Shadow Knows! 246

Muncie, Indiana 247

Sycamore Shoals: Victory at Kings Mountain and the Great Leap Westward 252

The Gridiron General 258

The Great Humanitarian Blamed for the Great Depression 262

Olustee: The Sunshine State's Civil War Battlefield 264

The Deep Zone and Other Regions of the Underworld 267

The '60s a-Go-Go! A Concise History 275

H.R. Gross: The Congressman Who Didn't Want to Spend Money 286

Where Are They Now? Historic Ships, Aircraft & Spacecraft 288

Four Top Ten Boomer Rankings 292

Introduction

Quicksand and Blasting Caps

One frosty morning a long time ago in the Upper Midwest, a child was born at Swedish-American Hospital, half Swiss-German and half Scots-Irish. Despite the confusion, the boy grew up to be All-American. He sported exceptionally long fingers and toes. He would be a concert pianist or pro basketball player, adults speculated. His little-league baseball team was called the Question Marks, because nobody could think of a suitable name. He earned his letter in 9th-grade football only because he didn't quit the team despite his (well-deserved) lack of playing time. He had fun-loving friends. His parents were great, despite being adults. He had a wild imagination and a whole lot of curiosity.

The young man grew up in a two-story house on a one-block street paved with bricks. On the corner was a small church with a steeple beside a green lawn with two or three giant oak trees. Behind the manse stood three fruit trees—apple, pear, and cherry. Lightning bugs blinked at night. He annoyed the neighbors, sometimes terrorizing them. He tormented his younger brother for no good reason; he's still waiting for payback. His favorite movie was *The Wizard of Oz*, shown once a year on TV (the movie looked a lot better on a color set). During the summer, kids could wander off during the day, as long as they were home by dinnertime — when the street lights turned on. As a toddler, he was a hellion, but a bookish nerd once in school. The grade school was three blocks away, a fortress-looking building with attached gymnasium. On the way to school was a little shop with big windows and glass display cases filled with every imaginable kind of candy and confection. Behind the school, guys played softball on the asphalt lots. Next to the school was a small pizza joint where the juvenile delinquents, the greasers, wore black leather jackets and played pinball.

At school, safety drills were conducted in case there was a nuclear attack. Get under your desk and put your hands over your head. Even kids knew that wouldn't do any good during an atomic blast. Grown-ups must have thought we were stupid.

Baby Boomers are the television generation. Despite the threat of nuclear annihilation, our three worst childhood fears, stoked by cartoons and public service announcements, were quicksand, blasting caps, and abandoned refrigerators. Never saw any quicksand or blasting caps, and there were better hiding places than old, rusty refrigerators. But there *were* black widow spiders, Gila monsters, and flesh-eating piranhas. And Frankenstein, Dracula, the Mummy, the Creature from the Black Lagoon, and Jack the Ripper. Parents told us to turn off those "weirdo" TV shows such as *The Twilight Zone* and *Alfred Hitchcock*. Then a new show came on called *The Outer Limits*. The "control voice" told us "they" had taken over our TV set — do not attempt to adjust it yourself. They were out there, somewhere, and they were coming to get you. No wonder we're neurotic. But we also had Saturday morning cartoons, which introduced us to classical music without us knowing it. Bugs Bunny, Daffy Duck, Elmer Fudd, the Roadrunner and Wiley Coyote, Rocky and Bullwinkle battling Boris and Natasha, plus the Jetsons and the Flintstones. Good stuff.

Fifty years have passed. The old neighborhood has changed. Today, the grade school is boarded over, rotting and decaying. Same for the candy store. The pizza parlor — a vacant lot. The church lost its steeple; the building is some sort of "community center." The lawn is an parking lot. The fruit trees are gone. The sidewalks are crumbling, literally. The old brick house still stands; it has been maintained fairly well. It can be purchased today for about $40,000. The old neighborhood is located in one of the worst crime and drug areas in the Upper Midwest.

Where there is a will, there is a way. People, especially Americans, can do anything they want if they put their minds to it. A lot of money doesn't hurt either, but that isn't always necessary. Wonderful things can be accomplished when it doesn't matter who gets the credit. Since World War Two, the United States of America has been an incredibly powerful and affluent country. Victims of our own success. Stupidity and corruption are tolerated because we can afford it. People used to wonder where their next meal was coming from; now there is too much food — obesity is our major health problem. "May you live in interesting times," the old saying goes. Growing up a Baby Boomer in Middle America has been an interesting experience. Hope you enjoy this book. I certainly enjoyed writing it.

Mark Zimmerman
January 2021

"WIDE RIGHT!"

The Strangest NFL Game Ever

The winter weather was brutal on the frozen tundra of Lambeau Field that day after Christmas back in the 1960s. The Green Bay Packers fought through the weather, injuries and adversity, and won that postseason contest on the last play of the game. No one will ever forget the famous Ice Bowl in which Green Bay quarterback Bart Starr dug in his cleats just enough to sneak the ball over the goal line and defeat the Dallas Cowboys.

But we're not talking about the Ice Bowl. We're talking about the divisional playoff game two years earlier between the Packers and the Baltimore Colts. The game nobody remembers. The game that wasn't scheduled. The one that shouldn't have been played. The first overtime game in Green Bay history, a victory based on a field goal that many people, especially the fans in Baltimore, swear did not pass through the goalposts. And for all practical purposes, Starr, the Hall of Famer who won five NFL titles, did not play. Neither did the Colts' star quarterback Johnny Unitas. Or his backup.

The game played on Sunday, December 26, 1965 in Green Bay was one of the strangest, weirdest contests ever staged in National Football League history. It also was the longest game in NFL history up to that point. And three obscure Packers, thrust into the spotlight, were instrumental in that victory.

The Western Divisional playoff was necessitated when Green Bay and Baltimore ended the 1965 season with identical 10-3-1 records (the Pack beat the Colts twice that season, but there were no tiebreaker rules back then). This was when the NFL consisted of two conferences of seven teams each, playing 14 regular-season games. There were no overtime games except in the postseason.

Over in the Eastern Conference, the Cleveland Browns, behind the running of Hall of Famer Jim Brown, easily captured their title with an 11-3 record.

In the mixed-up West, the Packers and Colts sparred for the lead. The Packers won their first six games that season (including one against the Colts) before losing badly to arch-enemy Chicago, which won nine of their last ten games. The next week, the Packers lost again, this time to Detroit, while the Colts beat the Bears. In week eleven, Green Bay lost to the Rams, and the Colts tied the Lions. A week after that, Green Bay closed the gap with a 24-19 win over the Vikings, while the Colts fell to Chicago, losing the game and their star quarterback, Unitas, to a torn ligament in his right knee. The Packers won in Baltimore, 42-27, on December 12th, with golden boy Paul Hornung scoring five touchdowns. And then the Colts lost their capable backup quarterback, Gary Cuozzo, to a separated-shoulder injury.

On the final weekend of the regular season, the Colts used newly acquired third-string quarterback Ed Brown to beat the Rams on a game-winning field goal by kicker Lou Michaels. All the Packers had to do to win the division was beat the hapless 49ers, but Green Bay faltered at San Francisco, with the 49ers tying the game with only a minute left to play. A divisional playoff was slated for the day after Christmas, in Green Bay at the newly christened Lambeau Field. The founder of the Packers, Curly Lambeau, had died earlier that year, so the New City Stadium had been renamed in his honor.

Fortunately, the forecast for heavy snow never materialized. The start of the game was delayed 30 minutes due to television requirements. The conditions that day were severe but not nearly as bad as the Ice Bowl would be, two years later. The temperature at 2:00 pm, at the start of the game, was 23 degrees but the raw winds drove the chill factor down to 12 degrees (the wind-chill factor at the Ice Bowl was 48 below zero). The turf was soggy but fairly firm after tons of hay and the protective tarpaulin were removed. Green Bay fans, sitting on metal bleachers with their every frosty breath visible, were not strangers to this type of bone-chilling weather. Even so, many of the 50,484 fans in attendance retreated to their cars in the parking lot at halftime to warm up a little. Many wore ear-flap hats and battery-heated socks and gloves, left over from deer hunting or ice fishing season. Despite the cold and the wind, the *Milwaukee Sentinel* described the weather as "ideal considering the time of the year."

The cold and the wind made passing treacherous. At the NFL

Championship three years earlier, at Yankee Stadium, winds had gusted 30 to 40 mph. Green Bay star fullback Jimmy Taylor carried the ball 31 times for 85 yards and a touchdown. The ground was concrete and the contact between players and the turf was brutal. Taylor played much of the game banged up, and with blood in his mouth from cuts. The Packers prevailed in that slugfest, 16-7. They routinely practiced under harsh conditions; their head coach was the legendary disciplinarian Vince Lombardi.

The Colts, led by head coach Don Shula, were a nine-point underdog. Shula decided to use Tom Matte, normally their tailback, as their starting quarterback (Unitas was in a full-leg cast; Cuozzo's arm was in a sling; and Brown was ineligible for postseason play). Matte had played quarterback in college at Ohio State under Woody Hayes. But he hadn't thrown many passes, since Hayes strongly emphasized the running game. Matte had thrown two passes in his pro career. He went into the game wearing a plastic wristband listing the Colts' offensive plays.

The Packers won the toss and received the opening kick-off. Then everything went south. On the first play from scrimmage, Starr dropped back and tossed a 10-yard pass to tight end Bill Anderson, who fumbled after a hit by Lenny Lyles. The ball was scooped up by Colts linebacker Don Shinnick, who trudged 25 yards into the end zone for six points. Along the way, Starr tried to take out one of Shinnick's escorts, Jim Welch, and sustained what turned out to be painful bruised ribs. Starr was taped up and tried to continue, but he couldn't raise his hand above shoulder-level (however, he did continue to serve as the holder on field-goal attempts). In 31 seconds of play the Colts had somewhat evened the odds.

"What happened," said Anderson later, "was that the ball hit me in the shoulder, instead of the stomach. Out of the corner of my eye, I saw a defender coming in to hit me, and I was trying to get the ball down into my stomach in time. I didn't quite make it. If there was a tunnel handy, I'd have crawled into it and run out of the stadium and kept on running."

Anderson, a University of Tennessee product, had played six years for the Redskins, retired to become an assistant coach at Tennessee, then a year later signed back with the Skins. He was picked up by the Packers in August 1965 to back up the starting tight end. Although used sparingly in 1965, Anderson did catch the winning touchdown pass in a 24-19 victory over the Vikings that season.

With Starr sidelined, Lombardi sent in his second-stringer, reliable Zeke Bratkowski, balding at 34, a ten-year veteran backup quarterback who had played for the Bears and the Rams. He had joined the Packers midway through the 1963 season. Bratkowski had already won two games for Green Bay that season in relief of Starr, including the first win against the Colts (back when Unitas was healthy).

Bratkowski had been a stand-out All-America quarterback for the Georgia Bulldogs, played for the Bears, served two years in the U.S. Air Force, rejoined the Bears, and then went to the Rams. A competent passer, Zeke never did manage to break into the starter's role. His nickname in Green Bay was Uncle Zekie.

The first half was a defensive struggle between the Pack and the Colts, and two quarters of futility for both offenses. Taylor was one of the finest and toughest running backs in NFL history, but this was not one of his best games. He dropped three passes and he failed to gain the end zone from a yard out, twice, once fumbling but luckily regaining the ball. On one series, the Packers had three tries to move the ball three yards into the end zone but failed. The Colts mounted a 67-yard drive that ended with a short field goal by Michaels. The lights were turned on at halftime with the score 10-0, Colts. The hometown fans were stunned at the turn of events.

In the second half, perhaps inspired by Lombardi's locker-room speech, the Packers began to move the ball. Bratkowski connected on a 33-yard pass to split end Carroll Dale, who fell at the two-yard line. Dale had been grabbed by Jerry Logan while the ball was in the air but still managed to catch the ball. Two plays later, Hornung followed guard Jerry Kramer into the end zone, narrowing the score to 10-7.

The Colts stopped another Green Bay drive with an interception at the 18-yard line, and early in the fourth quarter they stopped yet another drive with an interception at the eight.

Despite the two interceptions, this was Zeke's biggest game ever. He completed 22 of 39 passes for 248 yards. Anderson, the goat on the first play, caught eight passes that day, more than anyone else. Often, he managed to slip into the middle of the field vacated by blitzing middle linebacker Dennis Gaubatz to give Bratkowski a chance for a completion.

With 6:50 left in the game, Bratkowski dropped back to pass and was hit by defensive tackle Billy Ray Smith for a loss. The yellow flag was thrown. The referee declared that Smith had hit Bratkowski in the helmet with his open left hand, much to Smith's protestations. This gave the Pack first down at the Colt 43. Eight plays later, the green-and-gold were at the 15. On fourth down with 2:00 left in regulation, Lombardi sent in Don Chandler to try a field goal to tie the game.

Up until the 1965 season, the kicking duties had been handled by Hornung, a wonderfully versatile player, backed by lineman Jerry Kramer, when needed. That all changed when Lombardi opted for Chandler, a kicking specialist and a stand-out at the University of Florida. He played for the Giants, and ironically, played in the NFL's first and only overtime game up to that point, a loss against the Colts in 1958. During the 1965 season, Chandler kicked a 90-yard punt, still the fourth longest in NFL history. Dour, lanky, and balding, Chandler was a native Iowan who hailed from Oklahoma, where he owned a ranch and construction company.

This was the moment every kicker lived for, practiced for, and dreaded. Starr held the ball. The 22-yard kick was into a 15-mph wind. Chandler booted the chip shot, then threw up his hands and turned away. The ball sailed high and to the right and field judge Jim Tunney threw up his hands and called it good. Baltimore players looked on in disbelief—they insisted the kick was wide right. But the back judge and referee agreed with Tunney's call. The ball had sailed high, over the vertical field-goal posts, so the call was subjective. There was no instant replay or review by league officials. The score was now tied, 10-10.

Late in the game, the Packers had the ball again when Taylor caught a pass at midfield and appeared to fumble. According to sportswriter James Tackach, "while the officials separated the players, the clock continued to run. The fourth quarter ended with Shula trying to get his Colts one more play." The game would go into sudden-death overtime. This would be the second overtime game in NFL history (sudden-death, because the first team to score would win the game). Needless to say, nobody left their seats.

The Packers won the coin toss and elected to receive; the Colts would have the wind at their backs. Neither team could get anywhere on their next two possessions, but then the Colts found themselves at the Packer 47 with Michaels lined up to kick the winning score, seven minutes into overtime.

Michaels had kicked a 50-yarder that season, so he had the leg. But Buzz Nutter's snap was off and by the time the holder aligned the ball, Michaels kicked it "pitifully short."

Green Bay took over at their own 20 and ground it out. Anderson's last catch of the day, an 18-yarder, moved the ball to midfield. Several plays later, Dale snagged a Bratkowski pass and tumbled out-of-bounds at the Colt 26. The ball was advanced to the 18 by 13:39 into overtime when Chandler trotted onto the field for a 25-yard field-goal attempt to win the game. Eleven Colts crowded the line in an effort to block the kick. Bill Curry centered the ball to Starr the holder, and Chandler propelled the pigskin through the uprights. This time, there was no doubt. The anxious crowd erupted into a wall of noise. Lombardi let out a whoop, and the Packer players danced on the sidelines.

"The usually sophisticated Green Bay football fans pulled out all the stops that reached near-hysteria as their team ran off Lambeau field," wrote the *Milwaukee Sentinel* reporter.

Just like that, Chandler, Bratkowski, and Anderson injected themselves into the Packer fans' hall of fame (Chandler and Bratkowski would be officially voted into the Packer Hall of Fame in later years).

Fans poured out of the stands and into the taverns and beer joints surrounding the stadium. Beer and warm pretzels awaited them. Workmen began covering the field with tons of hay and tarps, in preparation for the next weekend's championship game with the Browns.

It had been a long haul in Titletown that year. According to press coverage, the Packers "were addicted this season to doing things the hard way."

"This game was typical of the season," said Lombardi afterward. "We did just what we had to do." Chandler said he was relaxed and confident when he made the winning kick, but his hands were visibly shaking while resting afterward in the locker room. All-Pro tackle Forrest Gregg said it had been one of the toughest games he'd ever played. Anderson, one of the heroes of the game, said he had been hit in the head during that first play from scrimmage and couldn't really remember much of anything. "It was all a little hazy the rest of the way," he later noted.

For the record, the Colts won the ground game, 143 to 112 yards, but the Packers had 23 first downs to nine, 250 passing yards to 32, and 362 total yards to 175. The Colts never crossed midfield during the second half. And the advantage of the only numbers that really counted, as shown on the mechanical Pabst Blue Ribbon scoreboard, belonged to the green and gold.

On that same day, in sunny, warm San Diego, the Buffalo Bills beat the San Diego Chargers, 23-0, to win their second consecutive American Football League title.

Coach Shula praised his team, especially Matte (who completed only five passes but ran for 57 yards), and downplayed the field-goal controversy, but Colts owner Carroll Rosenbloom said, "We didn't deserve to lose. There was no justice out there today."

Michaels, the Colt kicker, said Chandler's 4th-quarter field goal to tie the game had been at least three feet wide-right. Other Colts claimed as much. Michaels publicly challenged Chandler to state that his kick was good. Chandler responded, "It wasn't a real good kick, and I couldn't tell."

The Packers would go on to beat the Browns the next weekend for the NFL Championship, the first of three consecutive titles. The next two seasons they would win the first two Super Bowls.

The Colts, led by quarterback Matte, demolished the Dallas Cowboys, 35-3, in the Playoff Bowl. Matte was named the game MVP. His plastic wristband made the NFL Hall of Fame, even if he didn't.

During the subsequent off-season, the NFL Rules Committee passed two new changes for the 1966 season. Two officials now would be required to stand at the goal line to observe field-goal attempts. And the goalpost uprights were extended from ten feet above the crossbar to 20 feet above, to make it easier to judge kicks.

After his NFL career ended a year later, Anderson spent three decades teamed with John Ward as part of Tennessee football's beloved radio-broadcast team. Anderson had played for the Tennessee Volunteers in 1955-57 and was a co-captain in 1957. He died in 2017 at age 80.

Chandler helped the Packers win Super Bowls I and II (he kicked four field goals against the Raiders in the latter game). In his 12-season NFL career, Chandler played in 154 regular season games, kicked 660 punts for a total of 28,678 yards, 248 extra points on 258 attempts, and 94 field goals on 161 attempts. He died at his home in Tulsa, Oklahoma in 2011 at age 76.

Bratkowski coached for the Packers and several other NFL teams until the mid-1990s. He is the father of former Jacksonville Jaguars offensive coordinator Bob Bratkowski. Zeke died in November 2019 at age 88.

Note: The author can testify that the facts of this game are true. He should know, because he was there. But he remembers the weather being much colder than it actually was.

Sources: www.packershistory.net; Sports Illustrated; George Strickler, Chicago Tribune Press Service; Green Bay Packers Media Guide; www.pro-football-reference.com.

BOOM Town

Largest Gunpowder Factory in World Goes Up in Smoke

During World War I, U.S. government contractors, working at breakneck speed, built the world's largest smokeless-gunpowder plant, as well as a company town, in Hadley's Bend near Nashville, Tennessee. The project set construction speed records, but the ultimate demise of the project was nearly as spectacular. The factory provided a source of employment for thousands of Nashvillians, many of them women, at a time when men were off to war. The war had raged since 1914, although the United States did not enter until 1917. The arrival of American soldiers in France, along with the tremendous industrial output of the United States, was the determining factor in concluding the bloody world war in which millions were killed. The ammunition for the big artillery guns, along with the newfangled automatic machine guns, required a tremendous amount of smokeless gunpowder. In 1917, the American government contracted with E.I. du Pont de Nemours & Company (commonly known as Dupont) to build a gunpowder manufacturing facility. Dupont would be in timely competition with the Nitro Plant in Charleston, W.Va., being built at the same time by the Thompson-Starrett Company.

On January 12, 1918, the announcement was made that Dupont would build a manufactory at Hadley's Bend that would produce nearly one million pounds of gunpowder a day (nine similar units, each producing 100,000 pounds per day), a capacity 75 times greater than any existing plant. The plant site would be three miles long by 1.5 miles wide, the largest industrial site in Tennessee. The power plant would use 68 boilers, each rated at 825 horsepower. In full production, the plant would require each day 4,500 tons of coal, 100 million gallons of water, 1.5 million pounds of nitrate of soda, and 675,000 pounds of sulphur.

Hadley's Bend was chosen due to its isolation, security, and availability of water and coal. In 1918, Hadley's Bend was a rural area of small farms, pastureland, and woods. The bend is nearly surrounded by the Cumberland River, northeast of downtown Nashville. The Hermitage, home of former President Andrew Jackson, lies nearby. The most remarkable feature was Vaucluse, the once stately two-story brick mansion of Dr. Jack Hadley. Vaucluse was built of brick walls two feet thick and sported wallpaper imported from France, originally intended for Jackson's Hermitage. Dr. Hadley had served as a surgeon during the War of 1812. He and his wife Amelia had 13 children, but only two survived into adulthood. During the Civil War, Confederate artillerymen positioned themselves in the bend to fire upon moving Federal railroad trains across the river. At Hadley's Bend a ferry was operated for 40 years without incident by Uncle Charley. In 1917 the government paid the Hadley heirs about $100 an acre for the 3,300-acre estate. The mansion was used as construction offices and was torn down in 1924. It is said that some of the wood and stone carvings were sent to the homes of Dupont company officials in Delaware.

Also in Hadley's Bend was Soldier's Rest, the home of General Thomas Overton (1755-1825). He served in the Revolutionary War and as Inspector of Revenue in North Carolina, the same position held by his brother, Judge John Overton, in Tennessee. He was one of General Jackson's seconds in the duel with Charles Dickinson. General Overton is buried near his homeplace, in the small cemetery at the center of Old Hickory Village. A monument there pays homage to the families who lived in Hadley's Bend and who were forced to move to make way for the gunpowder plant: Bondurant, Dismukes, Donelson, Gleaves, Hadley, Jackson, Jones, and Overton.

Mason and Hanger Co. was chosen as the main contractor to build the company town. Hadley Avenue would divide the construction, with the permanent village to the east and temporary housing for construction workers to the west. The barracks and tar structures of wood frames covered with rubberoid (an asbestos compound) comprised the Colored and the Mexican villages west of the avenue. In the Mexican Village, 41 large barracks housed 3,000 workers. The permanent village was built between Hadley Avenue and the river, designed to house management officials and composed of substantial one and two-story frame houses. The home styles came out of a pattern book Dupont used for factory housing at their Hopewell plant in Virginia. The ten styles were known as Denver, Florence, Ketchum, Haskell, Bay Tree, Arlington, Davis, Cumberland, Georgia, and Welford, and resembled houses in old Northern mill towns.

By the second week in February, nearly 1,200 workers were on-site. One hundred thousand would eventually work at the plant during the course of the year, coming from Texas, Louisiana, Arkansas, Mississippi, Alabama, Georgia, Kentucky, and Indiana. The men were transported to Nashville,

issued authorization and payroll cards, assigned housing quarters, given a meal-book, and sent to the proper work superintendent. On July 1st, the U.S. Department of Labor took over control of all war-production construction hiring. At peak construction, 40,000 men were employed at one time. Even elderly Confederate veterans from the Old Soldier's Home two miles away volunteered to work.

The first step was to build a macadam road and a railroad spur into the bend. The closest main road was Lebanon Road, five miles away. Seven and a half miles of railroad track were laid in 30 days from the Central Tennessee Railroad at Hermitage Station to the plant. This required moving 2.5 million cubic yards of earth.

Railroad cars reaching the plant with materials were efficiently unloaded, including nearly 4,000 carloads of lumber, 2,400 of stone, 1,182 of sand, 558 of ice, 402 of sewer pipe, 383 of brick, 290 of cement. Of the total of 13,509 railroad carloads of materials, only two failed to reach their destination on time. Transport was handled by 200 men using 70 trucks and 80 horse or mule teams. At peak construction, 300 train cars of material were received and unloaded in one day.

Each day, a special train of 14 coaches known as the Powder Puff Special brought female workers to the plant. An average of 18,000 employees were brought to the plant from Nashville each day by rail. Fifteen thousand workers lived on the reservation. The average salary was $4 to $5 per day, with the largest payrolls reaching $4 million per month.

The railroad was not enough. Workers also arrived from Madison on ferries making three-minute trips across the Cumberland River. A pontoon bridge was built, soon to be replaced by a suspension bridge, 1,800 feet long and 91 feet above the water.

During the construction of the plant, a horrific train accident—the deadliest in U.S. history—occurred just outside Nashville. Many of the victims were workers, most of them African-American, headed to jobs at the gunpowder plant. The locomotives, each traveling at 50 mph on the same track and running behind schedule, collided head-on at Dutchman's Curve, about five miles west of Union Station, in an explosion heard for miles. It happened on July 9, 1918 at 7:30 in the morning. It was the deadliest railroad accident in U.S. history, with 101 persons killed and about one hundred injured. Within days, news about the war knocked the rail disaster off the front pages.

When completed, Old Hickory (originally named Jacksonville) consisted of 348 management homes, 1,125 bungalows, 167 two-story block apartments, 84 one-story block apartments, 284 bunkhouses, 41 washhouses, two hotels, two dining halls, three YMCAs, five schools, one grand kitchen, 10 mess halls, three short-order restaurants, several commissaries, a bank, a post office, two drugstores, two shoe shops, two bakeries, a passenger and a freight depot, hundreds of fuel houses and boxes, a fire department, 20 hose reel houses, two sewage pumping stations, a heating plant, nine community garages, restrooms, searchlight tower, ice house, and dozens of other utility buildings. The construction required more than 5,000 new architectural drawings on the equivalent of 18 acres of blueprint paper. Eighty-five million board-feet of lumber, wallboard, and Cronolite would be used.

The building of housing facilities set all-time construction records. To facilitate speedy construction, a planing mill plant and a sheet metal mill were constructed on the reservation. In four days in September, more than four million board-feet were laid for houses in the village, an average of about 308 board feet per carpenter per day, close to a world's record. In one instance, a six-room bungalow was built ready for occupancy in nine hours. A two-story block apartment building containing 36 rooms was built in 29.5 hours. The 800-pupil school building, containing 1.2 million board feet of lumber, was destroyed by fire in October; it was rebuilt in ten days.

The army of laborers required frequent, ample feeding. In the month of August, 1.1 million meals were served, as many as served in the Panama Canal Zone in six months of peak construction. The Old Hickory commissaries employed 100 cooks and 1,800 assistants.

The site required two sewage treatment plants using 50 miles of pipe and 543 manholes. The water system (large enough to service a city the size of Boston) featured two covered reservoirs, 13 large water pumps, and 227 fire hydrants. The project included the largest refrigeration plant in the world, capable of producing 3.2 million pounds of ice per day. The Post Office

employed 46 clerks and handled 9,000 pieces of mail each way and sold $250 in stamps each day.

The speed of plant construction broke all records for similar operations. Ground was broken on March 8th. The first unit of the sulfuric acid plant began continuous operation 84 days later. On June 1st, a ceremony was held to mark the occasion. Old Hickory supervisors invited state and local government leaders to attend, and a contingent of Dupont company officials came down from Delaware to participate. The wife of an assistant resident engineer broke a bottle of wine to dedicate the unit, while a band played "The Star Spangled Banner." Governor Thomas C. Rye threw the switch that turned on the machinery for the first time.

The nitric acid plant went online June 10th, followed by the first unit of the guncotton purification plant on June 23rd. The first guncotton was nitrated that day. The first powder was granulated on July 2nd, or 116 days after breaking ground.

In March, Major Wood, the government dispersing officer at Old Hickory, was relieved and sent to the Nitro Plant in West Virginia. Former co-workers promised to send him a box of powder manufactured in Tennessee for use on the Fourth of July at Nitro. This was quite a joke for Major Wood. But the workers at Old Hickory met the "impossible" deadline, just barely. At the July 4th banquet at Nitro, Major Wood good-naturedly presented the box of powder to the assembly and nearly started a riot. Incredulous Nitro workers blamed their second-place status on government red-tape, but in the end the powder box incident prompted the Nitro workers to step up their own productivity.

On September 28th, the project was hit hard by the Spanish influenza pandemic, which was inflicting more deaths around the world than the fighting in Europe. Old Hickory was a dense concentration of people working and living together, thus facilitating the spread of the disease. Temporary hospitals were quickly set up and scheduled meetings and gatherings cancelled. One in four at the plant contracted the disease, and most of the 1,300 who died from the disease in Nashville came from the plant. The basement of the Nashville YMCA, converted into a temporary morgue, overflowed with bodies. Through 1919, more than 548,000 Americans died from the influenza. Worldwide, 20 million to 40 million people died in the worst pandemic since the Black Death of 1350.

World War I ended with the armistice signed on Nov. 11, 1918. At that time, the Old Hickory plant was 93 percent completed and 96 days ahead of schedule. The plant was producing 700,000 pounds of gunpowder per day. When Dupont turned the plant site over to the U.S. government in 1919, it charged $1 for constructing the plant (the government had paid all the costs of construction). Over the previous year, Dupont had charged the government one percent of product value to operate the plant. (Fifteen years after the war, the government investigated war profiteering by the so-called "merchants of death," but no charges were brought against Dupont.) As it turned out, none of the gunpowder produced at Old Hickory was ever sent overseas or used in wartime. Within a matter of months, the plant site and village became a virtual ghost town.

The U.S. government sold the plant in December 1920 for $3.5 million to the Nashville Industrial Corporation (NIC), which had been organized specifically to bid on the purchase. NIC then began the job of selling off surplus equipment and attracting new industry to the site.

The acid-plant machinery was shipped to Chile to make dynamite for the mining of nitrate fertilizers used in the U.S. Another unit was used for making drugs and medicines; yet another sent to Alabama for making dynamite used in mining and excavating. Other acid plants ended up in Mexico, used in the refining of oil into gasoline and to be used in a fertilizer plant. The cotton purification unit was sent to a Louisiana kraft paper mill. Steam boilers from the power plant furnished steam for coal mines, electric light plants, paper mills, packing houses, cotton oil plants, and salt refineries. The huge mixers were used for roofing and insulating materials and even foodstuffs. Electric generators were sent to the Southwest. In 1923, the Dupont Fibersilk Company bought 500 acres near the site and constructed a Rayon plant.

On Aug. 11, 1924, the government reserve of gunpowder totaling 45 million pounds either exploded or were consumed in a raging fire at the old plant site, clearing a 40-acre tract and destroying 50 buildings owned by the NIC. The gunpowder "explosion" was muted and muffled. One-half of what remained of the old plant was destroyed. It had cost $22.5 million to manufacture the powder, whose postwar value was set at $450,000. The gunpowder was being stored as a reserve by the U.S. government, with half of it set aside for roadbuilding by the Department of Agriculture.

Several thousand rounds of small-arms ammunition cooked off and were expended, mostly against brick walls. No one was severely injured. The fire was the largest U.S. government loss since the Great War, and left a "white-hot tangle of debris." According to the *Washington Post*: "The flames originated in solvent recovery house No. 8, in the northeast end of the powder storage area, and leaped from building to building until finally they died out. The power house, considered the most valuable building of the plant, escaped the flames by a scant 20 yards."

Rayon, or artificial silk, production began at Old Hickory in January 1925 and continued for 25 years. Total production was more than one billion pounds and was used in a variety of clothing lines and upholstery fabrics. In the late 1950s Rayon production was phased out and Dacron production began, along with other products. In 1957, the construction of Old Hickory Lock and Dam by the U.S. Army Corps of Engineers inundated the northeast quadrant of the old factory site.

During the 1960s, the last significant vestige of the old gunpowder plant came tumbling down when the nine power-plant brick smokestacks were demolished. Known as "the sentinels," the 200-foot-tall stacks had been used by aircraft pilots as landmarks. The smokestacks were in two rows (five in one and four in another), about 200 feet apart, with the power plant in-between. Each one cost $11,000. Fifteen feet in diameter, they required foundations 20 feet deep. They were made of hollow bricks and the strongest mortar available. The reason the stacks hadn't been demolished earlier is that the cost of demolition could not be recouped by salvaging the bricks. The mortar was so strong that when the stacks came down every brick was broken. Today, the old powder plant site is occupied partially by a large auto auction lot. Residential renovators are being attracted to the village of Old Hickory, where many of the permanent homeplaces still stand. Efforts are underway to preserve the charm of the old "factory-town" community.

Sources: Dupont Technical Library; Dixon Merritt, Mason & Hanger Company; David Brand Thesis, Vanderbilt University, "Fill the Empty Shell: The Story of the Government Munitions Project at Old Hickory, Tennessee 1918-1919" May 1971.

The Life and Times of Dr. Robert Hartley, PhD

Dr. Robert Hartley practices psychology in downtown Chicago, treating an eclectic collection of troubled patients. He is married to a beautiful brunette named Emily (Harrison), who teaches third grade. They reside at the Thorndale Beach North apartments (No. 523), 5901 North Sheridan Road in Edgewater, 20 miles north of Bob's office. Their neighbor is Howard Borden, a navigator for a major airline. Bob works downtown on the 7th floor of the Rimpau Medical Arts Center, 430 North Michigan Avenue, with a bunch of health care professionals, including his best friend, Dr. Jerry Robinson, an orthodontist who has a prominent nose. Also urologist Bernie "Tup" Tupperman and arrogant plastic surgeon Phil Newman, who's a pretty good tennis player. The receptionist is a single, 29-year-old redhead named Carol Kester, a native of Davenport (or Collinsville), Iowa.

Bob and Emily live on the fifth floor of a high-rise apartment building (Bob is terrified of buying a house). Bob likes to grill out on their balcony, where Howard has chained down their furniture so it won't blow away. Bob usually takes the elevated train to and from work, although sometimes he uses a car parked in the garage of their apartment complex.

Bob is a psychologist (he doesn't like to be called a shrink), but he's not really much of a people-person or extrovert. Once, a stranger greets him with a cheerful "Good morning!" Bob replies tersely, "Same to you, fella." Bob's best patient is Elliot Carlin, a unmarried real estate mogul who wears a toupee. He is neurotic, anti-social, and mal-adjusted. Bob also sees colleague Dr. Frank Walburn as a patient. Dr. Walburn's receptionist, a gorgeous but wacky blond in a mini-skirt, later serves as young Dr. Frankenstein's vivacious assistant.

Bob also treats Mr. Petersen, a former Marine with an inferiority complex (he's terrified of disappointing his wife), and Mrs. Bakerman, a grocery store clerk who spends most of her time in Bob's office knitting and proclaiming to others, "Isn't that nice?!"

Emily is an only child. Her parents are Junior and Aggie Harrison of Seattle. Bob's parents are Herb and Martha Hartley. Both Junior and Herb served in World War Two. Junior claims to have been a bellygunner on a B-17, but he must be fibbing, because he's way too big for that. Bob served in the Korean War and took the boat there (details on his war service are sketchy). Bob's mother is high maintenance. At first her name is Eleanor but later we learn it is actually Martha. Bob's father is a laconic, patient man who ties fishing flies, avoids work, and knows how to handle Martha.

    Bob and Emily have been married four or five years and have no children or pets, although there was much interest in starting a family, at least at the beginning of their marriage (both married late in life). They were supposed to vacation in Mexico and work on starting a family, but Bob was whacked on the back by a patient — the big guy who became the sergeant at the Hill Street precinct — and Bob can't stand up straight. Bob and Emily finally do make it to Mexico (despite Emily's fear of flying), but there is no talk of starting a family anymore. Emily began teaching the third grade five years before their marriage, although later she accepts a full-time job with the school board as an advisor. Emily's favorite dessert is blueberry cheesecake. She loved to ride horses before she married, but Bob is afraid of horses.

    Bob does not like any fuss shown over his birthday. He made the mistake of buying a blender (actually a blender-izer) for Emily on their fifth wedding anniversary. This scene was later borrowed by comedian Jerry Seinfeld for one of his sitcom plots. Also, Jerry did a skit about his favorite yellow shirt, borrowed from a scene in which Emily brashly uses Bob's favorite yellow shirt as a cleaning rag prior to Bob's mother making a visit.

    Carol's family back in Iowa owns a lumberyard. One day Carol meets a new guy who drives "one of those new Japanese sportscars" (presumably the new Datsun 240Z) and gets back from lunch two hours late. A patient cancels his appointment with Bob, and Bob tells Jerry he has a theory about cancellations. Jerry launches into a harangue about Carol's tardiness; Bob never does reveal his theory about cancellations. The new boyfriend, who is separated but not legally divorced, asks Carol to move in with him although apparently they are already cohabitating. Bob and Emily host a dinner with Carol and her new boyfriend, Roger Dixon, and Bob talks Roger into getting back together with his wife of eight years and two months, Delores (Spanish for pain), who is Italian and fixes spaghetti about twice a week.

    Carol goes into the hospital to have a tattoo of a butterfly removed from her posterior (which everybody mysteriously seems to know about) and falls for her doctor, Dr. Scott Rivers, who is twice her age. It doesn't work out. We learn that Howard is afraid of going to the dentist alone, and that the mere mention of surgery "makes his skin crawl." Later, Carol does get married to a guy who really isn't very interesting.

    In the very beginning, we learn that Bob does not like chicken, even if prepared with bourbon. He doesn't like Mexican food, but he's okay with Chinese and little Swedish meatballs. He's a steak and potatoes kind of guy. On their wedding night, Emily prepared filet mignon by boiling it. She

recreates the dinner every anniversary, although now she broils the steak. Bob does like martinis, and Scotch and soda. He serves brandy to his dinner guests, the "same brandy Napoleon served to his generals." Bob also likes Crown beer, the "queen of beers."

Bob objects to Emily making a dinner reservation under the name Dr. Hartley because he's not a medical doctor. She replies that the normal wait would be two hours; Bob relents.

Divorced and father of a young son, Howard apparently eats out a lot and at the Hartleys as he usually has nothing in his refrigerator. He is often out of town flying (lots of turbulence over Omaha and the Rocky Mountains) and brings back souvenirs for his friends. He likes to visit Pittsburgh for some reason. Howard learned to fly during the war. Howard is quite the ladies' man; hosts stewardesses (e.g., Mary Ellen and Inga) at his apartment; and attends many parties (he goes to costume parties dressed as an airline navigator). He has a younger sister Debbie, who is only 22, attractive, and works at a pharmacy. One summer, at a self-help seminar, she ran naked through the woods. Apparently, however, she does not drink alcohol. Howard's brother, Gordon Borden, is a game warden. In an earlier life, he was neighbor Margaret Hoover's husband Arthur. In the beginning, Margaret is often occupied with Emily when Bob gets home from work. Then Margaret moves or dies, because she is never seen or heard from again.

Emily buys Bob a nifty new film camera with a strobe light and he can't stop taking "candid" photos. He mistakenly calls a time-delay shutter a time exposure. Emily's afraid to take a shower, but Bob assures her that he won't risk getting his camera wet.

Bob attended the University of Illinois, Class of 1952, sat in the back of the class, and wore a brush haircut (in high school he wore a ducktail). His professor, Dr. Eugene Albert, was the chief influence of his professional life. Later, Bob consults Dr. Albert and learns from him that psychology is "nothing but a crock" and that the only thing that matters in life is golf. Bob's IQ is 129 and Emily's is 151, a fact that troubles Bob greatly. Jerry's IQ is 136.

At one point, Bob takes a full-time job as a psychologist for Logger's Casualty Insurance Company with an office on the 18th floor overlooking Contemplation Pond. As an inducement to join, the company president offers him twice his current salary, a Mercedes with a chauffeur, and a Gucci leather paperweight that cost $35. An actuary tells Bob he'll live to be 77. The job doesn't work out because Bob tells middle management that there are more important things to life than working like a hump for Loggers.

Emily makes it clear that she didn't marry Bob for his looks, except perhaps his "shy, sweet smile." Bob dumbfounds her by claiming that he was considered extremely good-looking in high school, primarily because of his hair. One of his male patients, whose "problem" is being exceedingly attractive to women, tells Bob that Bob has no idea what it's like to be extremely good looking. Bob dropped Naomi for Emily but he wanted to marry Nancy (now Nancy Brock) during college. Chuck Brock is married to Nancy but later gets divorced, changes his name to Don Fedler, becomes a technical writer for pharmaceutical magazines, and becomes engaged to Carol. For some reason, he has bad feet and wears sandals. It doesn't work out.

Bob comes home from work and almost always finds Howard at home with Emily. Apparently, Bob never catches on. At one point, Jerry and Emily are doing volunteer work together and Jerry falls in love with Emily. Jerry is seeing Dr. Walburn because of his infatuation. Emily is attracted to a handsome tennis pro, but she never wavers or wanders. An attractive patient of Bob's loses a lot of weight and becomes obsessed with him; Bob discounts her "love" because it's just an occupational hazard. Emily gets jealous, however. Another female patient gets all mushy about Bob when he convinces her to quit smoking. On a trip to Peoria to watch the Bears-Packers game in a motel room (the game is blocked out in Chicago), Bob is pursued by an attractive, amorous woman named Janene who turns out to be a prostitute. Together, they win a dance contest trophy (Bob's feet are a blur during the Saber Dance). They agree to be just friends.

Bob successfully treats a pitcher for the Chicago Cubs, but Jerry is annoyed that Bob does not introduce them. Bob claims that Jerry would bother the pitcher with baseball talk and "that's not why he's here." Then the patient shows up and gives Bob an autographed baseball intended for Bob's nephew. Jerry overhears and explodes, stating that he knows Bob has a niece but no nephew. Actually, Bob has neither. Bob has a younger sister, Ellen, who has not yet married Howard Borden, much less given birth to any children. Ellen works for a local newspaper, writing restaurant reviews. She's attractive but not very interesting.

Jerry grew up in an orphanage and went to college at William & Mary. Jerry claims he has a half-brother who is a salesman who doesn't like visiting New York City because he gets mugged there. Later, we learn that Jerry's brother is of Cuban descent who also happens to be a dentist.

Emily has a fear of flying so she usually travels by train. Bob says travel by train is safer than flying, but Howard warns, "unless a plane falls on it." Emily went to college at Northwestern. On a trip to Ann Arbor she made the pilot stop the plane so she could get off. The thing she fears most about flying is "the part where you're off the ground." Howard has a fear of mice, ever since as a child he saw one trapped in his sink.

Bob loves to play golf and tennis, and he loves to watch sports. He doesn't bet on sports although Jerry does. Jerry also owns a yacht with another dentist for tax purposes. He has a business manager and a tax man. Emily learns tennis so she can play in an office tournament with Bob, much to his chagrin. It doesn't work out. Howard also plays golf; he grew up caddying. Howard doesn't play tennis, however.

On Bob's 40th birthday, Emily buys him an expensive wristwatch and gives it to him that morning in bed. She wakes him up gently by kissing his ear. Bob wakes up and tells Emily he just had a dream about a beautiful woman kissing his ear. Emily smiles and says, "That was me!" Bob replies, "No it wasn't." Bob has a habit of being brutally honest; Emily doesn't mind.

Emily is not a morning person. Once when Bob has to get up at 5:00 am to be on a TV show, she serves him bacon and eggs, minus the eggs. The bacon is uncooked and raw. The coffee is cold. Bob points this out and Emily replies, "Give me a break, Bob."

After four years of success, Bob and Emily move up to a swankier apartment; Howard remains their neighbor. Their lives become much less interesting. Emily becomes obsessed with her looks and loses interest in being a supportive wife. Bob and Emily end up moving to a small town in Oregon, where Bob teaches college. Eventually, Bob leaves Emily and moves to Vermont, where he operates a bed-and-breakfast and is married to a gorgeous woman who wears tight sweaters. Later, he wakes up in bed with Emily back in Chicago, claiming he had a bad dream about running a B&B in Vermont. Must have been the Chinese take-out, Emily dead-pans.

Source: The Bob Newhart Show, CBS-TV, 1972-78.

TO INFINITY AND BEYOND

**Arnold Engineering Development Complex:
Cold War Aerospace Testing Grounds**

The Cold War against Communist aggression required the United States to develop the latest technology in weaponry, especially in aerospace applications. Testing of these advanced systems required the most accurate simulations possible. Much of that testing was accomplished at Arnold Engineering Development Complex (AEDC) near Tullahoma in Middle Tennessee. What began as Camp Peay in the early 1900s evolved into Camp Forrest during World War II and eventually became Arnold Air Force Base and AEDC, now the world's largest flight-simulation test facility. (Recently the name was changed from center to complex).

During the past seven decades, technological advances tested and verified at AEDC have helped put men on the moon, established America's air dominance, saved lives on the battlefield, and added pinpoint precision to battling the war on terrorism. "AEDC played a tremendous role in the U.S. winning the Cold War," stated David Hiebert, AEDC historian. Testing at AEDC is one of the very first stages in the development of futuristic flight systems. The main principle under which the complex operates is anticipating what the country's aeronautical needs will be many years into the future.

AEDC's 4,000-acre reservation (built in 1950-51 within the 40,000-acre air force base) contains sprawling and towering high-tech test facilities such as aerodynamic and propulsion wind tunnels, rocket and turbine engine test cells, space chambers, arc heaters, and ballistic ranges to provide data and analysis for military flight systems, space and missile systems, and commercial airliners. Tests have ranged from firing huge rocket engines to bombarding satellites with radiation to shooting chickens into aircraft cockpit canopies. It should be noted that no actual aircraft test flights are conducted at AEDC.

Twenty-seven of the test facilities at AEDC have capabilities unmatched elsewhere in the U.S.; fourteen are unique in the world. Although managed by the U.S. Air Force Materiel Command (704th Mission Support Group), AEDC is operated with a largely civilian contractor workforce of about 3,000.

AEDC conducted test firings of the Saturn IVB engine in an altitude rocket test cell simulating conditions at 100,000 feet. Tests were also run on the Service Propulsion Engine. During Apollo XVI, the fifth mission to land on the moon, a wobble in the engine was detected, jeopardizing the flight. AEDC tests conducted years earlier determined that the mission could be safely continued, resulting in two records—the capture and return of the largest moon rock and the longest lunar rover trip.

When the space shuttle *Columbia* was destroyed during re-entry in 2003, ballistic tests at AEDC helped get the shuttle program back into space. On an underground ballistic impact range, testing called for pieces of insulating foam from the external fuel tank to be shot from 150 to 2,255 feet per second down an 86-foot barrel at various angles, with video cameras capturing 20,000 frames per second to document the impacts.

A more famous AEDC ballistic device is the Range S-3 "Chicken Gun," which uses pressurized helium as propellant to shoot chicken carcasses against aircraft canopies and engine intakes to develop data and analysis of deadly in-flight bird strikes.

Scale models of experimental aircraft are tested for airflow and other aerodynamic factors in the wind tunnels. The Propulsion Wind Tunnel 16T can simulate airflow up to Mach 1.6 and altitudes up to 76,000 feet (Mach 1 is the speed of sound or 768 miles per hour). The models, which contain numerous sensors, can cost up to $3 million to build. Many weeks and even months of preparation are undertaken for each test, which can last as little as 15 seconds. The test chambers are prepared in a separate building, then rolled on railroad tracks to the appropriate wind-tunnel facility. The four electric motors that power the wind-tunnel complex are among the largest in the world and consume enormous amounts of electricity (one of the reasons for locating AEDC in the TVA region was the availability of power). The Lockheed Martin F-35 Lightning II (a joint strike-force jet fighter that can be used by all of the military services) is being tested at Propulsion Wind Tunnel 16T (so named because it's 16 feet square). Boeing's F/A-18E/F Super Hornet, the NASA Space Shuttle, the B-2A Spirit stealth bomber, and the

Global Hawk unmanned aerial vehicle have also been tested there.

The von Karman Gas Dynamics Facility (VKF) is composed of three wind tunnels which can produce airflows up to Mach 5.5 (4,081 mph), altitudes up to 105,000 feet, and temperatures up to 1440 degrees F. Virtually every high-speed flight vehicle has required testing in Tunnels A, B and C, from re-entry and tactical vehicles and space capsules to the X-planes and winged vehicles.

Such sophisticated test facilities can be expensive. One newer facility replaced its steel components with non-rusting stainless steel, requiring 70 percent of all the stainless steel produced in the U.S. that year.

The Engine Test Facility operates nine test cells for atmospheric inlet and altitude testing. Altitude Test Cells C-1 and C-2 comprise the Aeropropulsion

Systems Test Facility (ASTF), which tests large military and commercial engines in true mission environments. ASTF has helped establish AEDC as the air force's center of expertise in turbine engine testing. Test cells C-1 and C-2 are each 28 feet in diameter and approximately 45 feet in length and are capable of testing up to Mach 2.3 and altitudes up to 75,000 feet. Either cell can provide engine inlet temperatures of up to 350 degrees and accommodate engines producing up to 100,000 pounds of thrust.

The J-6 Rocket Motor Test Facility is the largest of its kind in the world, testing solid-propellent rockets in a horizontal position. One hundred rocket motors have been tested there over the past 16 years. Exhaust from the test chamber is led through giant ducts to a concrete chamber 250 feet in diameter by 100 feet high where millions of gallons of water are released to contain the rocket exhaust gases in a matter of seconds. The huge amounts of water needed for cooling at AEDC come from Woods Reservoir, created in the 1950s by damming the Elk River.

J-6 is located a quarter-mile away from the rest of the center, shielded by a huge concrete barrier. Safety is always emphasized at AEDC—jet-engine and rocket testing can be extremely dangerous. In 1985, the nearby J-5 facility was destroyed when a Peacekeeper Missile test went awry and exploded, throwing debris a great distance. The blast would have been even larger except that there was only three seconds left of the solid propellant during the test. Four employees were killed ten days later in the test cell as they cut up the unexpended rocket fuel and it somehow ignited into a massive fire. The J-5 facility was rebuilt within a year and the J-6 site was built ten years later. A fire broke out at the J-4 facility when a liquid-propelled rocket usually tested vertically was tested horizontally; fuel leaked out and ignited. Back in 1971, two men died when they entered an offline furnace that had filled with deadly argon gas, which is clear and odorless. Overall, 16 employees have died at AEDC in the past 70 years; most were due to routine industrial accidents, such as falls.

Three monuments can be found at AEDC: one honoring those who have died at AEDC; one saluting Medal of Honor recipients; and one marking the June 25, 1951 dedication of the center by President Harry S Truman, who noted that "the scientists who work here will explore what lies on the other side of the speed of sound." As if to note AEDC's military significance to the nation, most of Truman's speech concerned the Korean War, which had begun exactly one year earlier. The occasion also fell on the birthday of AEDC's namesake and the father of modern aviation, General Henry "Hap" Arnold. A driven and far-sighted visionary, Gen. Arnold was unable to attend—his sixth heart attack claimed his life in 1950. His widow, however, was in attendance.

The military site near Tullahoma began in 1926 as Camp Peay, a state National Guard training facility covering 1,000 acres and named for Tennessee Governor Austin Peay. State guard maneuvers were conducted annually. In June 1941, Major General George S. Patton brought his "Hell on Wheels" armored division from Fort Benning, Ga. to Middle Tennessee for maneuvers. En route, each of his two columns measured 60 miles long. Patton wanted to demonstrate the mobility and power of armor in a large-scale operation and he certainly accomplished that feat. Maneuvering along the banks of the Duck River, at times in the dark without lights and under radio silence, his tankers accomplished their objectives in eight hours instead of the planned two days. He paid soldiers a $50 bounty for each "enemy" VII Corps commander captured. Reportedly, when some tanks ran out of fuel, Patton paid for the needed quantities out of his own pocket.

After Pearl Harbor, in 1942, Camp Peay was turned into a federal induction center and renamed Camp Forrest, in honor of Gen. Nathan Bedford Forrest, the Civil War cavalry commander. Eighty years before, the Tullahoma Campaign in the summer of 1863 was a strategically brilliant, relatively bloodless affair in which the Federal army pushed the Confederates out of Middle Tennessee. The campaign is not well-known due to the fact that it occurred at the same time as the surrender of Vicksburg and the battle at Gettysburg. The campaign would have accomplished even more except for the incessant rain—one Yankee noted that "Tulla" was Greek for mud, and that "homa" was Greek for more mud. Likely, Tullahoma was named for a Choctaw Indian chief. Although Forrest was much better known for other battles and campaigns, he was a master of aggressive tactics, outwitting the enemy, and moving his mounted infantry at lightning speed. During the 1930s, famed German tank commander Erwin Rommel studied Forrest's tactics. (There's a legend that he actually visited Tennessee, but that's not true. Rommel's son swore his father never visited the U.S.) It is almost certain that Patton also studied the tactics of Forrest. Patton would go on to defeat Rommel's Afrika Corps in North Africa; many of the German soldiers captured in North Africa would be sent to prisoner-of-war camps in America, including Camp Forrest.

During the war, an estimated 250,000 soldiers passed through Camp Forrest, with no less than 50,000 present at any time. Including war maneuvers conducted in 1943 in Middle Tennessee, it is estimated that one million soldiers were trained in the area before shipping out for the European theater.

Camp Forrest cost $36 million to build, covered ten square miles, contained 1,300 buildings, 55 miles of roads, and five miles of railroad track. More than 20,000 workers were required for the construction. Camp Forrest was responsible for training eleven infantry divisions, two Ranger battalions, medical and supply units, signal corps units, and Army Air Corps personnel, in addition to housing prisoners of war. Although there were barracks, many troops lived in tents. Twelve thousand civilians were employed at the camp, running the post exchange, the laundry, the motor pools, and the induction center. The town of Tullahoma grew from 4,500 to 75,000 during the war.

Both the Second and Fifth U.S. Army Ranger battalions trained at Camp Forrest in 1943. They also trained in Florida, New Jersey, and Great Britain. On June 6, 1944, the Rangers led the way at Omaha Beach during D-Day, scaling the cliffs of Point du Hoc in an incredible display of bravery.

William Northern Field was built at Camp Forrest and used to train Army Air Force crews to fly the Consolidated B-24 Liberator four-engine bomber.

In October 1941, weeks before Pearl Harbor, a disassembled W.1X jet engine and a team of experts were flown in the bomb bay of a B-24 from Great Britain to America. General Hap Arnold had witnessed tests of the jet engine developed in England and determined that the United States needed to start development of its own. The only U.S. Air Force general to wear five stars, Arnold played a key role in the Army Air Forces during World War II, supervising the air war against Nazi Germany. Arnold had led the drive before the war to build wind tunnels at Wright Field in Dayton, Ohio. In October 1942, an XP-59A aircraft developed by Bell Aviation and General Electric took to the skies at Muroc, California. Unfortunately, jet-engine development did not progress fast enough for the U.S. to benefit from jet-powered aircraft during WWII.

The situation in Germany was different, however. In addition to working on atomic weapons (which did not materialize), German scientists had developed a twin-engine jet fighter, the Me262, which flew 100 mph faster than any Allied aircraft; the V-1 guided missile; and the V-2 liquid-propelled rocket with explosive payload. As the Allies moved through France and then into Germany, officers were astounded at the advanced technology they witnessed and confiscated.

General Arnold asked an old friend, Dr. Theodore von Karman, a top U.S. aeronautical scientist, to lead an advisory group to work on air force guidelines for the next 20 years. Arnold noted that the Allies would eventually win the war, not through scientific or technological brilliance but through numbers and brute force. He wanted to change that.

In the spring of 1945, von Karman and about ten other scientists, including Dr. Frank L. Wattendorf, visited captured flight facilities in Germany and Austria. Dr. Wattendorf was to report on gas turbine propulsion, wind tunnels, and propulsion facilities. What they saw amazed them. The BMW

Phil Tarver-AEDC

plant in Munich had a jet-engine test facility in full operation with plans underway to double its capacity; a 26-foot diameter sonic wind tunnel was under construction at Oetztal, Austria, to be powered by hydraulic turbines; and a small hypersonic battery of tunnels capable of operation through Mach 10 (7,700 mph) was under construction at Kochel, Germany.

Wattendorf left Germany prematurely due to the death of his father. Over the Atlantic, in the bucket seat of a C-54, he wrote the "Trans-Atlantic Memo," calling for the construction of a new Army Air Force center in the U.S. to test high-speed aerodynamics, propulsion systems, and component parts. "The scope of the German plans makes it essential that our own plans be certainly not less ambitious in the light of our future security," he wrote in the memo, which was to become a blueprint for AEDC.

Dr. Von Karman approved of the recommendations but proposed the name Supersonic Pilotless Aircraft Development Center. Later, in December 1945 when the advisory group's report, "Toward New Horizons," was issued, the name Air Engineering Development Center was adopted.

The first major shipment of German equipment to the U.S. was made in October 1945 and consisted of the Oetztal eight-meter sonic wind tunnel, hydraulic drive system, and fan blades. Next were the Kochel wind tunnels (the actual parts came from all over Germany) and working drawings; and then the jet-engine testing facility at Munich. Delivery was delayed due to the U.S. Navy testing of their own experimental jet engine in Germany. The BMW equipment from Munich was used to build the Engine Test Facility, the first operational plant at AEDC. Transporting the machinery required 58 railroad cars, two barges, and truckloads totaling 450 tons. Some of that equipment is still in use today.

After the war, scientific expertise was in high demand, not only by the U.S. but by the Soviet Union. Under Project Paper Clip, German scientists were recruited on a contract basis, with eight eventually working at AEDC.

The late 1940s saw much delay in developing the test center due to politics and government bureaucracy. In 1946 Camp Forrest was declared surplus, and all property was either sold and shipped or demolished. Nothing but roads, brick chimneys, and concrete foundations remained until the construction of AEDC. Also that year, Sverdrup & Parcel of St. Louis won the contract to develop AEDC. In 1947, the Army Air Forces became the U.S. Air Force, a military service of its own (Arnold Air Force Base would become the first new base built by the USAF). In 1948, the initial recommendation of Moses Lake, Wash. for the site was rejected by Secretary of the Air Force Stuart Symington and Commanding General Carl Spaatz for "strategic reasons." All other sites were re-examined, with Camp Forrest being the final recommendation due to the availability of land (defunct Camp Forrest), power (Tennessee Valley Authority), water (Elk River), and the influence of Tennessee Senator Kenneth McKellar of the Appropriations Committee. One hundred million dollars were earmarked for the construction of the center, which was renamed in 1950 in memory of General Arnold.

In 1952, PeeWee, a wind tunnel only one foot long, began operation, anticipating any problems which might arise for the actual 16-foot-long test tunnels. The next year, the Falcon guided missile was tested at nearly five times the speed of sound. In 1954, the first engine, a J47 turbojet for the B-47 bomber, was tested at a simulated altitude of 30,000 feet.

In the beginning there were three main facilities at AEDC:
- The Engine Test Facility (ETF) composed of the BMW Munich equipment.
- The Von Karman Facility (VKF) with the Kochel hypersonic system.
- The Propulsion Wind Tunnel (PWT) with speed range from Mach 0.9 to 3.5, now designated an International Historic Mechanical Engineering Landmark.

At the request of the U.S. Air Force, General Leif Sverdrup created the Arnold Research Organization (ARO) to operate the facility. The first commander was Major General Franklin Carroll.

"Virtually every modern aircraft's design, engine and weapons system,

Rocket test cell (right) behind concrete barrier, with exhaust ducting leading to cleansing chamber next to water tank, with Woods Reservoir in background. AEDC.

missile, space vehicle, and probe have been tested in the center's three major test complexes," according to historian Darlene M. Merryman of Motlow State Community College.

The journey to space began for AEDC on March 27, 1957, when the aerodynamic loads a rocket would experience at escape velocity (25,000 mph) were measured in AEDC's von Karman Gas Dynamics Facility. The following year, engineers in the Engine Test Facility test-fired their first solid-propellant rocket motor for the third-stage of a space vehicle. In 1959, the first wind tunnel tests were performed on a model that would evolve into the Saturn V rocket.

During the 1960s, AEDC conducted some 55,000 hours of test support for the Apollo program, involving 25 of the center's then 40 test facilities. These tests included simulated re-entry tests, which evaluated thermal protection materials. From 1960 to 1968, AEDC conducted more than 3,300 hours of wind tunnel tests, representing more than 35 percent of all of NASA's Apollo wind tunnel tests. From 1965 to 1970, 340 rocket engines were fired in the single largest test program ever conducted at the center, to evaluate the Saturn V upper stages.

In the 1990s, AEDC opened its doors to commercial customers. AEDC also operates the Hypervelocity Wind Tunnel at White Oak, Md. and the National Full-Scale Aerodynamics Complex at Mountain View, Calif.

Aircraft, jet engines, and rockets tested at Arnold Engineering Development Complex (partial listing):

- Lockheed Martin F-35 Lightning II
- Boeing F/A-18E/F Super Hornet
- B-2A Spirit stealth bomber
- RQ-4 Global Hawk unmanned vehicle
- NASA Space Shuttle
- Evolved Expendable Launch Vehicle
- X-33 reusable launch vehicle
- F-22A Raptor
- F-14 Tomcat
- F-15 Eagle
- F-16 Fighting Falcon
- B-1 Lancer
- Atlas space launch vehicle
- X-43 reusable launch vehicle
- National Aerospace Plane
- X-37 orbital test vehicle
- GP7200 turbofan engine (Airbus A380)
- PW6000 (Airbus 318)
- Trent 1000 (Boeing 787)
- XF7-10 (Japanese P-X)
- Advanced Turbine Engine Gas Generator
- Minuteman and Peacekeeper ICBMs
- Mercury space capsule
- Project Gemini
- Saturn V upper-stage rocket engines
- F-105 Thunderchief
- C-141 Starlifter
- C-5 Galaxy cargo plane
- A-10 Thunderbolt II
- Navy Tomahawk cruise missile
- Patriot Air Defense Missile
- F-117A Nighthawk stealth fighter
- International Space Station
- X-15 test rocket
- XB-70 Valkyrie
- Global Positioning System (GPS)
- Mars Science Laboratory
- Boeing 787 Dreamliner

The University of Tennessee Space Institute (UTSI) is a graduate education and research institution located adjacent to Arnold Engineering Development Complex. UTSI was established in 1964 as part of the University of Tennessee and has become an internationally recognized institution for graduate study and research in engineering, physics, mathematics, and aviation systems.

UTSI supports AEDC in maintaining "state of the art" expertise in both technical and managerial ranks. About 500 AEDC employees have earned graduate degrees at the Institute, including 40 doctorates. In addition, thousands have participated in the continuing education programs offered by UTSI. The faculty and students have worked on a variety of research and technology development projects with AEDC personnel. More than 2,000 graduate degrees—including more than 250 doctorates—have been awarded through UTSI, a large number of them to Tennesseans. For years, UTSI has served Tennessee industry by offering an off-campus master of science degree program in Engineering Management (Industrial Engineering) at industrial locations. In addition, UTSI serves the cause of national defense by offering an MS degree program in Aviation Systems at naval bases in Maryland and California, primarily to navy test pilots.

During WWII, eleven prisoner-of-war camps were built in Tennessee, including Camp Crossville, the Memphis Armed Service Forces Depot, and Camp Campbell (now Fort Campbell). On May 12, 1942, Camp Forrest received its first assignment of German prisoners of war from North Africa. Later, Italian and Japanese prisoners were added. The POWs were sheltered in small, four-man huts and used as labor at hospitals, bakeries, kitchens, and automotive shops as well as agricultural workers. Camp Forrest received more than 22,000 POWs during the war, with the last prisoner leaving the camp on April 13, 1946.

Camp Campbell was a specialized POW camp, housing Germans who were dedicated "anti-Nazis." Although united against Hitler, these prisoners continuously argued among themselves.

Security at the camps was less than maximum. The prisoners were treated relatively well and many took up residence in the U.S. after the war. Reportedly, however, about four prisoners were shot by guards and killed trying to escape. In November 1942, two prisoners jumped off a train bound for Camp Forrest and were apprehended a few days later. An Afrika Corps prisoner walked out of Camp Forrest and caught the 9:25 train to Nashville, where he went bar hopping with an unsuspecting GI on leave before being snatched during a routine security check.

Nationwide, only 1,583 of the 356,560 POWs in the U.S. managed to escape or walk away, and of those only 22 were never recaptured.

In 1945, the U.S. government initiated the Intellectual Diversion Program to enlighten Germans on the American way of life. Many of the POWs were impressed with what they saw in America and later became U.S. citizens.

Prior to becoming a prisoner-of-war camp, Camp Forrest was the first civilian internment camp in the U.S., housing 600 Germans and 200 Italians from January to November 1942. The civilians (aliens and not U.S. citizens) were rounded up and shipped under armed guard to the camp, where they were segregated into gangs of 225 men and housed in small huts infested by black widow spiders. The internees wore all-green clothing. They complained that the grounds were frequently quite muddy. The internees published a camp newspaper called *The Latrine,* printed in English. There was much speculation in camp when it was learned that the civilian internees would be relocated and replaced by prisoners of war. Eventually, the internees were dispersed to several camps in North Dakota and Texas.

A monument at the Chattanooga National Cemetery marks the burials of 186 prisoners of war from both world wars (105 are Germans from WWII).

Sources: AEDC-"Beyond the Speed of Sound"; Personal Tour-2010; www.arnold.af.mil/News/Commentaries/Display/Article/804839/the-history-behind-german-wind-tunnels-at-aedc; High Mach-AEDC.

THE FLYING CROWBAR
and other Nuclear-Powered Aircraft

During the 1950s, the U.S. government tried to develop aircraft and spacecraft propelled by atomic power, i.e., nuclear reactors, and came amazingly close to creating both a Mars rocket and the most horrific Cold War weapon ever conceived. Today, NASA is looking at using nuclear rocket engines to send astronauts to Mars.

The atomic age held the promise of untold benefits to society—publications such as *Popular Mechanics* claimed that Americans would be flying their own atomic-powered aircraft by at least the turn of the century. Seventy years later, we're still driving Fords and Buicks. Nuclear powerplants had their heyday, with 98 nuclear power reactors built in 30 states, operated by 30 different power companies. The U.S. Navy routinely and safely operates 11 nuclear-powered aircraft carriers and more than 100 atomic-powered submarines, many of which carry nuclear warheads. But popular approval of nuclear energy tanked following the Three Mile Island accident in 1979 and few power reactors have been built since then.

At the beginning of the Cold War, the U.S. Air Force believed it possible to power heavy, long-range strategic bombers with nuclear reactors. Because the power generated by a reactor could function indefinitely, it was thought that the added weight of the nuclear reactor and its radiation shielding would be offset by the elimination of conventional fuel tanks. The aircraft would still be powered by jet engines, but instead of burning fuel, the engines would be propelled by blasts of super-heated air passing through a nuclear reactor core. Such an aircraft could stay aloft for weeks, limited only by the needs of the crew.

From July 1955 to March 1957, the USAF flew two modified B-36 bomber aircraft 47 times testing massive radiation shielding. The bombers carried aloft a three-megawatt test reactor, but no testing of a nuclear propulsion reactor actually took place. By 1961, the U.S. had spent $7 billion on these projects.

At the same time, the Soviet Union also was researching the feasibility of nuclear-powered aircraft, likely in response to what they perceived as U.S. success. In the summer of 1961, the Soviets flew a modified Tu-95 Bear bomber (nicknamed the Swallow) with a nuclear reactor onboard but with no nuclear propulsion.

More importantly, in the fall of 1957, the Soviets successfully launched the first ICBM (intercontinental ballistic missile) and the first artificial manmade satellite (Sputnik). Missiles soon became the preferred method of delivering nuclear warheads for both the U.S. and the Soviets. Also, scientists were never able to design an aircraft light enough and still protect the crew adequately from nuclear radiation. Eventually, in the 1960s, efforts to build a nuclear-powered bomber were abandoned.

During the Sixties, a major objective of the Cold War was to be the first nation to land men on the Moon and return them safely. This expensive contest (capitalism versus communism) was eventually won by the U.S. in July 1969, thus fulfilling President John F. Kennedy's proposal in May 1961 to land a man on the Moon before the end of the decade (and beating the Russians).

What most newsmen and historians failed to report was that Kennedy also proposed in a special address to Congress that month that the U.S. "accelerate development of the Rover nuclear rocket. This gives promise of some day providing a means for even more exciting and ambitious exploration of space, perhaps beyond the moon, perhaps to the very end of the solar system itself."

The U.S. Air Force funded secret, small-scale studies of nuclear-thermal rockets at Oak Ridge National Laboratory in Tennessee from 1947 to 1949. Project Rover began in 1955 under the USAF and the Atomic Energy Commission (AEC) at the famed Los Alamos Scientific Laboratory site in New Mexico. Land was set aside at the Nevada Test Site near Las Vegas for the testing of engines.

Project Rover consisted of three principal phases: Kiwi (1955 to 1964), Phoebus (1964 to 1969), and Pewee (1969 to the project's cancellation, at the end of 1972). Nuclear reactors for Project Rover were assembled at Los

Alamos' Pajarito Site. For each engine there were actually two reactors built, one for "zero-power critical" experiments conducted at Los Alamos and another used for full-power testing at the Nevada Test Site (now the Nevada National Security Site).

In 1958, test facilities were constructed at Jackass Flats, a valley named for the wild donkeys which grazed there. The facilities were joined by a network of roads and the Jackass and Western Railroad ("the world's shortest and slowest"). In August 1960 the AEC and the National Aeronautics and Space Administration (NASA) established the Space Nuclear Propulsion Office. From 1957 through 1970, the Space Nuclear Propulsion Office conducted nuclear reactor tests at the Nevada Test Site (Area 25).

In 1961, NASA and the AEC embarked on a second nuclear-rocket program known as NERVA (Nuclear Engine for Rocket Vehicle Application). Taking advantage of the knowledge acquired as scientists designed, built, and tested Project Rover research reactors, NERVA scientists and engineers worked to develop practical rocket engines that could survive the shock and vibration of a space launch. From 1964 to 1969, Westinghouse Electric Corporation and Aerojet-General Corporation built various NERVA reactors and rocket engines.

On Dec. 8, 1962, Kennedy and other federal officials flew over the Nevada Test Site and then toured the Nuclear Rocket Development Station.

In 1969, NERVA's success prompted NASA-Marshall Space Flight Center director Wernher von Braun to propose sending 12 men to Mars aboard two rockets, each propelled by three NERVA engines. The mission would launch in November 1981 and land on Mars in August 1982.

From 1964 to 1969, NERVA tested the operation of several NRX (Nuclear Reactor Experimental) and XE 1,100-megawatt reactor engines. In 1966, the NRX-A4 engine systems test was the first to demonstrate that a nuclear-powered rocket could start and operate on its own and perform reliably over a wide range of conditions. It ran for almost two hours and 30 minutes at full power. In 1968-69, a nuclear engine was tested numerous times in conditions simulating the vacuum of space.

Basically, the nuclear reactor in a rocket is used to provide a source of continuous supercharged heat (up to 4,370 degrees). The concept of a nuclear-powered rocket engine is that the spacecraft would be propelled by pumping liquid hydrogen from a tank through the core of the reactor, where it would be superheated and expand significantly, providing exhaust thrust out the combustion nozzle. The reactor core would consist of carbon-uranium rods whose radioactivity would be fine-tuned by the turning of control rods. The control rods were covered on one side by borax to absorb neutrons and on the other side by beryllium to reflect neutrons.

A nuclear rocket could make the trip to Mars in as little as four months, and a trip to Saturn in as little as three years (as opposed to seven years conventionally), according to Los Alamos Laboratory. The nuclear rocket would be at least twice as efficient as a chemical rocket, but the nuclear rocket engine could be used only in space, not for lift-off. The rocket would have to be launched into space by conventional chemical rocket engines.

From 1959 to 1964, the Kiwi reactor development program built and tested eight prototype reactors ranging from 100 to 1,000 megawatts. Gaseous hydrogen was used as both propellant and coolant. In 1959, Kiwi A was the first full-power reactor tested for use in a rocket engine. Five years later, Kiwi B-4E was operated at full power of 1,000-megawatts. It used uranium carbide as fuel instead of uranium oxide. In 1965, a Kiwi reactor was deliberately destroyed at maximum radioactivity to determine a "worst case" launch accident scenario.

Phoebus (named for the Greek sun chariot god) reactors were the more powerful and technically advanced versions of the Kiwi B-4 reactors. The Phoebus 2A reactor engine generated about twice the specific impulse (thrust per unit flow of propellant) achieved by the best conventional chemical rockets. Phoebus 2A contained 4,000 fuel elements and was the most powerful nuclear rocket engine ever built. It delivered 5,000 megawatts of thermal power and 250,000 pounds of thrust. The Phoebus 2A test conducted in June 1968 was limited to 80 percent of full power due to the overheating of a pressure vessel clamp.

During the Project Rover/NERVA programs, scientists conducted 22 major tests of nuclear-thermal-rocket engines. Project Rover/NERVA was terminated in 1973 due to changing national priorities. Some experts believe that the U.S. would already be landing astronauts on Mars if the NERVA nuclear rocket program had not been abandoned.

In 2000, NASA created Project Prometheus to develop nuclear-powered systems for long-duration space missions. This project was NASA's most serious consideration of nuclear power for space missions since the cancellation of Project Rover/NERVA. In 2005, NASA canceled the Prometheus Project as a result of budget constraints.

Perhaps the most interesting and horrific application of nuclear-powered flight was the Pluto Project (named for the Roman god of the underworld), designed to create a nuclear-powered ramjet cruise missile armed with nuclear warheads. Most people associate cruise missiles with the German V-1 buzz bomb used against London during World War II or the U.S. Tomahawk missile used in recent years for "surgical" strikes.

In 1961, the U.S. military chose Chance Vought Aircraft to design a

Tory II-A test vehicle of the SLAM ramjet

supersonic low-altitude missile (SLAM) under Project Pluto, which was being conducted at Lawrence Livermore Radiation Laboratory in California.

The resulting prototype (which never flew) was the size of a locomotive, 88 feet in length, six feet in diameter and weighed 61,000 pounds. The vehicle was shaped like a missile but with a ramjet scoop attached along its length. The nuclear-fueled ramjet, unshielded against radiation, was rated at 35,000 pounds of thrust. It could haul and deliver up to 26 nuclear warheads.

The Ling-Temco-Vought (LTV) SLAM would be launched through the use of conventional booster rockets and then initiate its ramjet engine. The missile would then cruise over the ocean at low altitude until directed by military officers to its targets, supposedly over the Soviet Union. SLAM would use its guidance system to hug the contours of the earth (about 1,000 feet high at Mach 3) while delivering its payload, then terminate its mission by diving deep into the ocean.

In its Tory II-C configuration, the SLAM ramjet produced over 500 megawatts of power in five minutes of continuous operation during a test conducted in May of 1964.

Scientists had to develop new materials for the SLAM that could withstand tremendous temperatures, shocks and vibrations, and radiation. Coors Porcelain Company, whose owner later turned to brewing beer, developed new types of ceramics for the project.

Due to its high durability and relatively low complexity, the SLAM vehicle was dubbed the "Flying Crowbar" by scientist Ted Merkle, the director of the Pluto Project at Livermore. Merkle was a dedicated supervisor, hard-driving and impatient, especially with "people who didn't know how to do things."

Testing the unmanned vehicle presented its own set of obstacles. One facility at the Nevada test site (Site 401) stored 1.2 million pounds of air which had to be preheated to 943 degrees and delivered at a pressure of 316 psi to simulate ramjet inlet diffuser conditions. For a five-minute, full-power test, as much as a ton of air per second had to be forced over 14 million one-inch steel balls in four huge steel tanks raised to 1,350 degrees by oil-burning heaters. A two-mile stretch of fully-automated railroad ran from the static test stand to the disassembly building, where the reactor was taken apart and examined by remote control. Scientists worked in a tin shed and watched their work over closed-circuit television.

All of the parameters for successful flight of the SLAM were met by designers. The concept was totally feasible. However, officials began to have doubts about actually creating and using SLAM for several reasons, the most significant being the worst-case scenario — a rogue missile.

If guidance of a successfully launched SLAM was lost, the cruise missile could fly for an indeterminate time, perhaps weeks or months, spewing a trail of intense radiation and destructive, deadly shock waves everywhere it went. The sound of the missile would reach 150 decibels, louder than the launch of a Saturn V rocket. Flying low at Mach 3, the missile could not be shot down. It would be the Doomsday Machine.

The program was terminated in July 1964 by the Defense and State departments as too costly ($50 million per missile) and "too provocative." It was believed by many that if the U.S. deployed a missile of such awesome power against which there was no known defense, then the Soviets would be compelled to do so, according to Chance Vought. The advent of ICBMs, which could reach targets much faster, also doomed the project. SLAM came to be known as "slow, low, and messy." At the end of the project, Chance Vought had 177 engineers and scientists involved in the program full time, in addition to 350 people at Livermore and 100 more at Site 401. The total cost for Project Pluto was $260 million.

On March 1, 2018, Russian President Vladimir Putin announced that the 9M730 Burevestnik (NATO reporting name: SSC-X-9 Skyfall) experimental nuclear-powered, nuclear-armed cruise missile was under development for the Russian Armed Forces.

Sources: National Atomic Testing Museum, Las Vegas, Nevada; Ralph C. Merkle at www.merkle.com.

decisions, decisions
don't delay – now more than ever

Bikini or One-Piece	Menthol or Regular
Mountains or Beach	George or Jack
Blond or Brunette	Ice or Neat
Hot Dog or Hamburger	*Time* or *Newsweek*
Bourbon or Scotch	Manual or Automatic
Revolver or Pistol	Marilyn or Jayne
Heaven or Hell	Army or Navy
Ford or Chevy	Jack or Arnie
Spring or Fall	Star Trek or Star Wars
Football or Baseball	Digital or Vinyl
Mary Ann or Ginger	Mercury or Evinrude
Sailboat or Motorboat	A&W or Hines
Coke or Pepsi	Your Place or Mine
Mac or PC	Mars or Hershey's
Ali or Frazier	8-Track or Cassette
Trout or Catfish	Bacon or Sausage
Paper or Plastic	Cash or Credit
Coffee or Tea	Chunky or Creamy
Sports Bar or Tavern	Domestic or Imported
Harley or Honda	Owl or Early Bird
North or South	DC or Marvel
Horse or Mule	Suspenders or Belt
Ferrari or Lamborghini	1st Class or Economy
Steak or BBQ	Smoking or Non-Smoking
Venus or Mars	Mallet or Blade
Life or *Look*	Cup or Mug
Dog or Cat	Color or B&W
Blade or Electric	Sweet or Unsweet
Boxers or Briefs	Firm or Soft
Necktie or Bowtie	AC or DC
Beatles or Stones	Cake or Pie
Schlitz or Colt 45	Frankenstein or Dracula
Superman or Batman	Dodgers or Yankees
Your Money or Your Life	Sci-Fi or Fantasy
Convertible or Sedan	Draft or Bottle
Acoustic or Electric	Cadillac or Lincoln

Getting High and Staying There

In 1988, Tennessee fans eagerly anticipated the start of the new football season. In 1987, the Volunteers had compiled a 10-2-1 record, beat Indiana in the Peach Bowl, and finished 14th in the nation. However, the Vols started the '88 season by losing the first three games, to Georgia, Duke, and LSU. Diehard fan and WSIX-Nashville radio personality Duncan Stewart took it personally and vowed to stay atop the station's outdoor billboard until the Big Orange won a game. He set up living quarters 38 feet above Division Street in front of the sign which read "WSIX Go Big Orange!" He conducted his afternoon radio talk show atop the billboard platform, sitting in a director's chair, wearing a Vols ballcap and waving a UT flag at passersby. The stunt generated a tremendous amount of publicity, and questions about Stewart's sanity. He watched each Vols game on a small portable TV set. Then the Vols lost to Auburn and Washington State. Five and Uh-Oh. Then Stewart, 42, injured himself climbing up the ladder in high winds. He was relegated to living in a tent at the bottom of the billboard, walking on crutches, and taking painkillers. Soon he was back up the billboard. It was two weeks until the Alabama game ("the third Saturday in October"), and the Vols weren't likely to beat the Crimson Tide. They didn't, losing at home, 28-20. Stewart had first climbed the billboard on September 20th, three days after Tennessee lost to LSU. Finally, on Oct. 22nd, Tennessee managed to beat Memphis State, 38-25, in an away game, snapping that season's six-game losing streak, the worst opening losing streak in the program's 92-year history. After 33 days atop the billboard, Stewart descended his ladder for the last time as fans cheered below. "This morning when I woke up, I just had a good feeling Tennessee would win today," said Stewart. "Now that the losing streak is over, I think Tennessee will win the rest of its games and salvage the season." Just so. The Vols won the last five games of the 1988 season to go 5-6. The next season the Vols went 11-1, won the Cotton Bowl, and finished 5th in the nation.

For some people, their dream is to get high and stay high as long as they can. During the crazy 1920s, pole-sitting became a popular fad, a test of endurance, a means of getting attention, and a quest for setting records. The fad was started by stunt actor and former sailor Alvin "Shipwreck" Kelly. He sat atop a flagpole on a small platform for more than 13

William Ruppert, 14, of Maryland, sat atop a pole for 23 days in 1929.

hours. From then on, records were continually set for "King of the Pole" until in 1929 Shipwreck decided to reclaim the title. He sat atop a flagpole for 49 days in Atlantic City, New Jersey, setting a new record. The following year, however, his record was broken by Bill Penfield in Strawberry Point, Iowa, who sat on a flagpole for 51 days and 20 hours before a thunderstorm forced him down. Pole-sitting died out as a fad with the advent of the Great Depression, to be replaced by other tests of endurance such as dance marathons and going days and weeks without eating meat.

Pole-sitting dates back 2,000 years when the all-time record was set by St. Simeon Stylites the Elder (388-459 AD) of Antioch, who devoted his life to sacrifice and contemplation. As a pathway to peace and meditation, Simeon sat on a small platform atop a column for 36 years. The columns he used ranged from 10 to 50 feet high. He preached daily to the people below. Simeon died on his pillar, which today is enclosed by the oldest surviving Byzantine church, and he was declared a saint.

Alfred Lord Tennyson memorialized Simeon the Stylite in an 1833 poem, and Guinness World Records awarded him the world's record for pole sitting. Following the example of Simeon, other "stylites" began living on pillars.

Fast-forward to 1946 when Marshall Jacobs, 37, of Ohio married his fiancée Yolanda Cosmar atop a flagpole with a roost.

Richard "Dixie" Blandy was a Creole born and raised in Vieux Carre, Louisiana. He was 5-4 tall. He worked in the circus, as a boxer, house painter, merchant marine, riveter, steeplejack, flagpole painter, and salesman. In

1933, he claimed the title as champion flagpole sitter during 77 days and nights at the Chicago World's Fair. He died in 1974 when the pole on which he was sitting collapsed.

Flagpoles eventually were passed over in favor of small huts, capsules, and other tiny accommodations atop one or two utility-type poles. In 1959, 17-year-old Mauri Rose Kirby spent 211 days in a nine-square-foot box atop a pole at the South Wind Drive-In in Indianapolis, Indiana. The businessowner thought the stunt would attract good publicity. Kirby's box contained a telephone, sleeping bag, and an electric heater which proved less than ideal in subzero temperatures. "I remember one night a man called me on the phone we installed on top of the pole and threatened to kill me if I didn't come down. Then there was this idiot who came by every morning and rammed the pole with his pickup truck and laughed while I swayed back and forth in the air," she said in a 1983 article in the *Indianapolis Star*. "I'm glad it's over. I'd never do it again or advise anybody else to do it," she said.

In the early 1960s, Peggy Townsend of Gadsden, Alabama, suffered a broken leg at age 13 when run over by an automobile. She spent the next two years in traction, a full bodycast, and a hospital bed. Two years later, Townsend called a local disc jockey to request a record; the DJ said he would play it if she would bring him a cup of coffee. The DJ had a photo of Mauri Rose Kirby on his desk. He asked Townsend if she knew anybody who would be willing to break Kirby's pole-sitting record. Townsend said she would, that the two years in the hospital had prepared her for another feat of endurance. The stunt was announced without naming the participant. Townsend's boyfriend, Jerry Clark, told her that the participant must be an idiot. "Well," Townsend said to him, "you are looking at the idiot." Several local businesses sponsored the stunt, including radio station WGAD, and promised her two cars if she broke the record of 211 days.

In December 1963, Townsend climbed the 50-foot pole to her new accommodations, a six-foot-square by seven-foot-tall canvas cottage. She had a telephone, television, radio, chair, and sleeping bag. Thunderstorms and snowstorms were a major problem. Clark, her boyfriend, gave her an electric blanket, meals home-cooked by his sister, and eventually, an engagement ring. When the teenager developed an abscessed tooth, a dentist was hauled up the pole to remove the tooth. There were electrical and plumbing problems, but the youthful Townsend persevered through it all.

Whenever the WGAD "girl on the flagpole" called the radio station to request a song, it became an instant hit. Local bestsellers were "Popsicles and Icicles" by the Mermaids and "If I Am a Fool for Loving You" by Jimmy Clanton. Finally, after 217 days, Townsend was lowered to the ground. Six months later she became Mrs. Jerry Clark.

It's been said many times that teenage daughters don't listen to their mothers. In October 1986, Mauri Rose Kirby's daughter, 18-year-old Mellissa Sanders, began her occupancy of a 6x7x9 cottage atop two 43-foot-tall poles at the newly opened South Pole restaurant in Indianapolis. The businessowner thought it'd be great to set a new world's record. The pole-house was equipped with heat, air conditioning, carpeting, a telephone, a television, and a stereo. Sanders and her pet, Pole Cat, came down on March 24, 1988 after 516 days aloft. She spent the entire year of 1987 (and then some) in her cubicle. She broke the record for pole-sitting (488 days) set by Mark Sutton of Victoria, British Columbia.

Sanders endured a 70mph snowstorm and having to bathe in a plastic kiddie pool. She talked all night on the phone. Waiting for her to come down from her perch were her record-setting mother and her finacé, Keith Seal of Monterey, Calif. They met after Seal read an article about Sanders and telephoned her. They announced their engagement in August 1987, before meeting. "We've been engaged and we haven't even gone on a date yet," Seal said, although he had climbed up the roost to personally meet Sanders.

In 1979 in Fayetteville, North Carolina, H. David Werder spent 113 days atop a 14-foot pole in a 1957 Volkswagen Beetle that served as a sign for a car repair shop. He was trying to break the pole-sitting record of 399 days set in 1976 in San Jose, California, by Frank Perkins. The Volkswagen leaked and Werder caught pneumonia and came down.

Five years later, Werder could be found living in a ramshackle hut 30 feet above the corner of Gulf-to-Bay Boulevard and U.S. 19 in Clearwater, Florida. He resided in the hut of plywood and giant cable spools for more than 439 days, temporarily and unofficially setting a world record.

"He successfully waged war against the Sanitation Department, Planning and Zoning, the Police Department, the Fire Department and any other bureaucratic entity that chose to tilt at his windmill," said Clearwater police spokesman Wayne Shelor, a former reporter who helped monitor Werder's exploits for the *Clearwater Sun*.

Officials had unsuccessfully tried to evict Werder because NFL Super Bowl XVIII was coming to Tampa Bay along with thousands of tourists, and the pole-house was considered an eyesore.

He vowed to stay up until the price of gasoline went down to 50 cents a gallon, until there was peace in the Middle East, until the federal government raised the speed limit to 65 mph, until all POWs and MIAs were accounted for in Vietnam, and until Tampa Bay hosted the Super Bowl.

Drunks had tried to climb the pole, and one lush even tried to unscrew the bolts holding up the pole. Werder threw his lucky horseshoe at him and sent him to the hospital. Werder said one more unloosened bolt would have ended the stunt for good.

After much persuasion, Werder agreed to come down. But a supporter tipped police that Werder had a gun and would use it. Police sharpshooters were poised on nearby roofs. But the bearded pole-sitter peacefully descended in a fire truck lift. He wore a silver jumpsuit and a white plastic hat. He flashed a thumbs-up sign and kissed the ground.

Years later, Werder ran for mayor and then for Congress. By the way, Oakland beat up Washington in Super Bowl XVIII in Tampa.

Endurance is one thing; height is another. Imagine climbing up a spindly vertical tower for three hours with 90 pounds of equipment on your back and your belt in high winds. Working on cellphone, radio, and television towers is the deadliest job in the United States, according to a trade publication, experiencing 10 times more deaths than construction workers. From 2003 to 2011, fifty to one hundred workers were killed climbing the towers.

The KVLY-TV tower is a 2,063-foot-tall television-transmitting mast in Blanchard, North Dakota. It is used by Fargo station KVLY-TV Channel 11. Completed in 1963, it was the tallest structure in the world for ten years. It remains the fourth-tallest structure in the world (since the construction of the Tokyo Skytree and the Shanghai Tower), the tallest structure in the Western Hemisphere, and the tallest broadcasting mast in the world. In comparison, the Empire State Building is 1,454 feet tall, including antenna.

Five miles to the southwest is the KRDK-TV mast at 2,060 feet high. In South Dakota is the KDLT tower at 1,999 feet tall.

Staying aloft for lengthy periods of time takes determination and endurance. Doing it while constantly moving demands an aircraft and two slightly daft pilots.

Dick Rutan and Jeana Yeager flew the innovative Rutan Model 76 *Voyager* around the world without stopping or refueling. The flight took off from the Edwards Air Force Base runway in the Mojave Desert on Dec. 14, 1986, flew westward 26,366 miles at an average altitude of 11,000 feet, and landed back on the same runway slightly more than nine days later. The astonishing flight more than doubled the old distance record set by a Boeing B-52 strategic bomber in 1962.

The *Voyager*, designed by Rutan's brother Burt, featured twin booms, a forward canard, and wide graceful wings made of carbon fiber. The aircraft weighed only 939 pounds empty but carried 7,000 lbs. of fuel in 16 tanks, which required constant adjustments to maintain the aircraft's balance. After barely making it off the ground, the crew and aircraft ran into mechanical and weather-related problems, not to mention the rigors of staying awake for extended periods of time in a very cramped space. "I got to really hate this airplane. I felt not only was it not going to work, but I would probably die in

it," Rutan said of the *Voyager*. "Yes, it had terrible flying qualities, but it had to make it around the world. Burt knew that it must have major compromises to make it around the world."

Hanging from the ceiling of the McCarran International Airport in Las Vegas, Nevada, is a conventional-looking Cessna 172 two-seater aircraft with a unique history. Back in the day, to promote the Hacienda Hotel, Robert Timm, a slot machine repairman and WWII bomber pilot, suggested an endurance flight. Mechanical problems thwarted the first three attempts, which lasted up to 17 days. A new engine and new co-pilot, John Cook, were tried on the fourth attempt. Modifications to the Cessna included a 95-gallon Sorenson belly tank, an accordion-style folding copilot's door, a foam pad in place of the co-pilot's seat, and plumbing that came through the firewall to allow inflight oil changes.

Timm and Cook took off from McCarran Field the afternoon of Dec. 4, 1958. To verify that they did not secretly land during the flight, officials in a car speeding down the runway painted white stripes on the tires as the plane flew just above them.

Assistants in a Ford truck with a fuel tank and pump in the back refueled and resupplied the aircraft. The Cessna would meet the truck on a closed section of road in the desert near Blythe, California. An electric winch lowered a hook to snag the refueling hose, and one of the men filled the belly tank while standing outside on a retractable platform. It took about three minutes to fill the tank. The procedure was performed 128 times.

Time took its toll. "We had lost the generator, tachometer, autopilot, cabin heater, landing and taxi lights, belly tank fuel gauge, electrical fuel pump, and winch," Cook wrote in his journal. The engine gradually lost power as carbon built up on the spark plugs and in the combustion chambers. Disaster nearly struck on the night of January 9th, their 36th day aloft, when Timm fell asleep at the controls and awoke more than an hour later to find the Cessna flying through a canyon on autopilot.

Finally, it was time to land. The two men had stayed aloft in their small plane for 64 days, 22 hours, and 19 minutes. They had flown more than 150,000 miles, equivalent to about six times around the world, and basically never went anywhere. Needless to say, they needed a soapy shower and a hot meal, perhaps a drink or two.

Talking about cramped quarters, astronauts Frank Borman and James Lovell spent 14 days sitting in the Gemini 7 space capsule in which they could barely move. Each man had an 8x6 inch window to look through. Their compartment measured about 80 cubic feet, in which they had to perform all types of bodily functions. Lovell said the trip was like "living in a men's room." Borman said, "Gemini was a tough go. It was smaller than the front seat of a Volkswagen Bug. It made Apollo seem like a super-duper, plush touring bus."

At least they had each other. Astronaut Al Worden spent three days of the Apollo 15 mission alone in the command module while his two buddies walked on the moon. On the far side of the moon Worden was 2,235 miles from his crewmates and 250,000 miles from Earth. Alone in space.

In early 2016, American astronaut Scott Kelly returned to Earth after 340 days aboard the International Space Station, setting the U.S. record for consecutive days in space. Four Russian cosmonauts have spent more than a year in space. In 1994-95, cosmonaut Valeri Polyakov logged 438 days aboard the Mir space station.

The largest single object ever sent into space, SkyLab in 1973, could not be rescued in time and was slated to re-enter the atmosphere and crash to Earth in 1979. Unfortunately, mission control could not greatly affect or accurately predict where it would crash and how many pieces would hit the ground. The odds were 1 in 152 that debris would hit any human. Opportunists advertised SkyLab hardhats and prediction maps for sale, even repellent. On July 11, 1979, after 35,000 orbits, the spacecraft, 83 feet long and weighing 84 tons, finally plunged to earth over the Indian Ocean and western Australia and did not hit anyone. About two dozen pieces of the spacecraft were recovered in Australia, which fined NASA for littering.

Sources: www.propublica.org; www.aopa.org; www.oca.org; nasa.org.

STATE CAPITOL – TEMPLE OF DEMOCRACY

Greek Revival Masterpiece • Civil War Fortress • Engineering Landmark
Reconstruction • Monument to Women's Suffrage • Hail to Old Glory

The Tennessee State Capitol, a hilltop temple of democracy on America's first frontier, was built 1845-59 in Nashville and still serves as the seat of state government. The General Assembly meets there, the governor's office is located there, gala ceremonies are conducted there, and special-interest groups protest there. The Tennessee State Capitol is steeped in history, serving as a fort for Unionists during the Civil War, the backdrop for naming the American flag Old Glory, the decisive battleground in securing women's right to vote, gunfire during Tennessee's readmission into the Union, at least one accidental death, and an art gallery of sculptures and monuments to great men and women and their causes. Capitol Hill is designated a National Historic Landmark.

The capitol's esteemed architect, William Strickland of Philadelphia, is buried within its walls, and President and Mrs. James K. Polk are buried on the grounds in a tomb designed by Strickland. The chairman of the Capitol Commission, Samuel D. Morgan, the man most responsible for preserving the integrity of the building during its 16 years of construction, is also interred within its walls.

It is one of the few state capitols topped by a tower (forty others have domes). The capitol is also a National Historic Civil Engineering Landmark for being the first to use structural iron roof trusses.

The state capitol and grounds form the nucleus of a history-rich tourist district consisting of the War Memorial Plaza, War Memorial Building, State Military Museum, the Bicentennial Capitol Mall State Park, and the

Tennessee State Museum. The State Supreme Court and State Library and Archives also are located nearby.

The Tennessee State Capitol, a Greek Revival temple by design, sits atop Campbell's Hill, 200 feet above the Cumberland River, which flows six city blocks to the east. The four-acre site, originally known as Cedar Knob, was the home of attorney George W. Campbell. Although Tennessee became the 16th state in 1796, Nashville wasn't designated the permanent capital until 1843. Knoxville, Kingston, and Murfreesboro served at times as the state capital, and in Nashville the legislature met at the Davidson County Courthouse.

Representing the city, Mayor Powhattan Maxey bought the tract for $39,000 and offered it to the state for free, a major inducement for locating the capital in Nashville. Campbell's house was moved south of Cedar Street (now Charlotte Avenue) and served as home to Military Governor Andrew Johnson during the Federal occupation of Nashville during the Civil War. The house, along with many grand but dilapidated townhouses surrounding the capitol, were torn down during 20th-Century construction and urban renewal projects.

Campbell had not been the only occupant on the hill. The Holy Rosary Cathedral was located at the northeast corner of the plot. According to the historical marker: "Near here in 1820 the first Catholic Church in Tennessee was built by Irish Catholic workers then building a bridge over the Cumberland River. In 1830 a brick structure known as Holy Rosary Cathedral succeeded the frame building. Here Bishop R.P. Miles, first Bishop of Tennessee, was installed Oct. 15, 1838. When St. Mary's Cathedral was built in 1847, Holy Rosary Church became St. John's Hospital and Orphanage. The site was sold to the state in 1857."

It was with great and unprecedented fanfare, including elaborate Masonic ritual and political speechifying, that the cornerstone for the magnificent new capitol was laid on July 4, 1845. Tennessee's favorite son and national hero Andrew Jackson had died just a month before, while Old Hickory's protégé James Knox Polk had been inaugurated earlier that year as the eleventh U.S. President. At that time, Tennessee's third and future President, Andrew Johnson of East Tennessee, was serving in the U.S. House of Representatives.

Created by the General Assembly in 1844, the Tennessee Capitol Commission considered several architects before selecting William Strickland. A native of New Jersey, Strickland was one of the young nation's most prestigious architects. As a teenager he apprenticed to Benjamin Latrobe, architect of the U.S. Capitol. He won a design competition for the Second Bank of the U.S. in Philadelphia. He supervised the restoration of the tower over Independence Hall. In 1832 he designed the Merchant Exchange in Philadelphia, which features a choragic tower. He designed the sarcophagus

Tennessee State Capitol.

for George Washington's tomb at Mount Vernon. Several of his plans were rejected, however, including Washington monuments in Philadelphia and the District of Columbia, and an enlargement of the U.S. Capitol.

At the invitation of the Capitol Commission, Strickland visited Nashville and submitted plans, which were accepted. On June 18, 1845, he signed a contract for the project at a salary of $2,500 a year.

Strickland estimated the building would cost $340,000 ($90,000 less if convict labor was used) and would take three years to construct. There is some evidence that Strickland intentionally low-balled the cost estimate. As it turned out, the construction lasted 16 years and cost three to four times the estimate.

Commissioners did not receive any compensation for their duties. During the 16 years of construction (1844-1859), one million dollars in legislative appropriations passed through the Capitol Commission, and from all historical evidence the funds were expended honestly. The meager annual appropriations from the legislature and the use of convict labor caused continuous controversy and frequent delays. Nevertheless, the project was one of the most ambitious of the era. The State of Ohio began its statehouse in 1839 and took 22 years to complete and cost $1.3 million.

The Tennessee State Capitol measures 236 feet by 109 feet, with a unique tower bringing its height to 206 feet. The floor plan is somewhat deceiving from the exterior. The base is a rusticated vaulted stone crypt. The next level up was originally known as the basement; it now houses state offices. The next level up is the main level, housing the Senate and House chambers and the State Library Room. This high-ceilinged main level features two rows of windows, giving the illusion from the exterior that it is actually two stories. The building is surrounded by stone terraces.

There are porticoes at each of the four main facades. The east facade, facing the river, is the historic main entrance. The east and west porticoes each feature six Ionic stone columns. The larger north and south porticoes each feature eight columns. Each carved stone column is 36 feet tall and 4.5 feet in diameter.

The square rusticated base of the tower is 42 feet tall. The slender circular tower above it is 37 feet tall. The tower is based on the Choragic Monument built in Athens, Greece about 334 B.C. by Lysicrates, a great choral leader. The Tennessee tower is twice the size of the original Greek monument, also known as the Lantern of Diogenes. The columns of the tower are of the Corinthian order, with acanthus leaves. The cornice is topped by delicate acroteria. Strickland created a large wooden model of the tower during the construction phase which can be seen at the nearby State Museum.

Strickland also designed the Wilson County Courthouse (1848) in Lebanon with a choragic tower. That building does not survive. But Strickland could create other designs. In 1849 he designed the First Presbyterian Church in downtown Nashville in the Egyptian Revival style, unusual for a Christian church of the period. This magnificent twin-towered brick church survives as the Downtown Presbyterian Church, and is designated a National Historic Landmark.

Although capitol plans called for a magnificent stone building, it was not to be too elaborate. Cornerstone ceremony speaker Edwin Ewing stated that, "Plainess, durability, and convenience are to be studied as more in accordance with republican institutions." Capitol Commissioner John Bass wanted "nothing too elevated or grand for the State of Tennessee."

The capitol was built entirely of stone. Efforts during construction to hold down costs by substituting brick interior work were rejected, probably at the insistence of Chairman Morgan. The interior walls and columns were made from East Tennessee marble. Architect Strickland noted that there are "no examples of any buildings in the United States, either public or private, in which the walls are constructed of rubbed or polished stones on the interior, indeed, there are very few buildings in Europe of this handsome and permanent class."

The limestone for the capitol was hauled from a quarry owned by Samuel Watkins less than a mile west of the hilltop site (where Charlotte Avenue now intersects with the interstate highway loop). The stone was described as "a stratified limestone, full of fossils, some of it very hard, of a slightly blueish-gray tint, with cloud-like markings." Unfortunately, this type of Tennessee limestone would prove to be relatively soft and filled with phosphate veins which would hold water, freeze in the wintertime, and crack the stone. Several extensive remodeling and renovation projects would be required over the years because of this weakness.

Tomb of President and Mrs. James K. Polk at Tennessee State Capitol.

Located conveniently close to the state penitentiary, the quarry was worked by convict labor totaling about 120 men (convicts were not allowed to work at the building site). The commission deemed it necessary to hire on "15 able-bodied negro men" at $18 per month. Another one hundred men worked at the site and at other duties. The men worked six-day weeks extricating the stone from the quarry, cutting and rubbing stone, and sawing and rolling stone. Stonecutters were paid $2.50 a day; laborers $1 day.

To get started, eight thousand yards of stone and material were removed from the top of Campbell's Hill. The foundation of the capitol was built of stone seven feet thick; the upper walls are 4.5 feet thick. Each stone weighed six to ten tons (20,000 pounds) and was moved by wooden derricks and block and tackle. The stones were so expertly cut and fitted that the average mortar joint is less than 3/16ths of an inch.

There were several problems and distractions during the construction phase. More than two years after commencement, the capitol building had risen only to the floor line of the main level.

In November 1847, Strickland complained: "There are many idle and mischievous boys and young men who indulge in writing pasquinades and vulgar words upon the walls of the State Capitol, and otherwise scarifying the building." (The word pasquinade refers to a statue in ancient Rome on which abusive Latin verses were posted.) In response, the legislature passed a law making it a misdemeanor "to deface the State House."

A cholera epidemic struck Nashville in 1849. Strickland moved to the boarding house of Mrs. Mary Ann Schaub at 924 Jefferson Street (the structure still stands). Strickland's dog Babe died at the time and was buried in the yard, noted by a marker. At the time, the boarding house was "out in the country" even though it could be seen from Capitol Hill.

President Polk died of cholera in 1849 shortly after leaving office. Strickland designed his tomb, which was located at Polk Place, his residence not far from the capitol site. After Mrs. Polk died in the 1890s, the heirs sold off Polk Place, and the tomb was moved to its current site at the capitol. Polk Place does not survive.

The capitol was roofed and enclosed during 1852. Three thousand sheets of copper weighing 27 tons were ordered from C.G. Hussey & Co. of Pittsburg for the roof. The 210 tons of round and flat iron bars for the roof trusses were produced by Cumberland Iron Works of Stewart County, Tennessee.

On Oct. 3, 1853, the General Assembly met in the new but far-from-finished building for the first time. Referring to the new structure, outgoing Governor William B. Campbell told the legislature: "May your proceedings be characterized by similar order, harmony, and dignity."

Historian and State Capitol Curator James Hoobler described the interior of the capitol: "The interior included space on the ground floor for the governor's office, the State Archives, offices of the secretary of state, the treasurer, and the register of land, as well as the Tennessee Supreme Court, a federal district court, and the Repository of the Official Weights and Measures. The main floor contained the assembly halls for the House of Representatives and the Senate, legislative committee rooms, and the State Library, which is considered the finest room in the capitol. The library features cast-iron stacks, surrounding galleries, and a cast-iron spiral staircase connecting the various stack levels. Wood & Perot Company provided the decorative iron work in the library, as well as the iron work for the staircases in the main building and the cupola tower." T.M. Brennan ironworks of Nashville produced the foliated ornamental iron on the tower.

The south crypt held furnaces and fuel while the north crypt was used as the State Arsenal and held 8,000 pieces of weaponry.

Lighting fixtures were provided by Cornelius and Baker of Philadelphia, which had provided fixtures for the U.S. Capitol and 11 state capitols. Four gasoliers were needed—one for each legislative chamber, one for the main hall, and one for the library. The fanciful House gasolier featured 48 burners and bronze figures of Indians, American eagles, buffalo, corn, tobacco leaves, and cotton blossoms. The Senate chamber gasolier had 30 burners. The gasoliers were converted to electricity in 1895.

On April 7, 1854, architect Strickland died unexpectedly at the City Hotel, where he was residing. The funeral conducted in the House chambers the next day drew 2,000 to 3,000 people. By his prior wishes, he was interred in

a vault in the northeast corner of the capitol. (The inscription on the vault is incorrect—he was age 66 when he died.) Strickland's eldest son, Francis, 36, was named architect. He had already been working with his father on the project for many months without compensation.

On March 19, 1859, with no ceremony, the final stone was laid on the lower terrace. The capitol grounds were still unfinished, described in one report as being "in a most chaotic state, a mere mass of huge broken rocks, together with various dilapidated out houses, altogether a disgrace to the State and city." A civil engineer was hired, and stabilization and landscaping plans adopted. Unfortunately, disaster struck again as the Civil War disrupted those plans. Chairman Morgan, a secessionist, was busy establishing a factory to make percussion caps for the Confederate army. Governor Isham Harris and the state legislature, meeting for several months as the governing body of a Confederate state, fled Nashville for Memphis as the Federal army approached.

On Feb. 25, 1862, Nashville became the first capital of a Confederate state to fall to invading Federal forces. After the mayor surrendered the city (no shots having been fired by either side), Federal troops marched from the river up Cedar Street to hoist the Stars and Stripes atop the capitol. Troops encamped on the rough grounds. Vandals broke into the State Library room in the capitol and unwrapped the 3,500-year-old Egyptian mummy displayed there, searching unsuccessfully for treasure. At least one of the capitol's rooms was used as a military barracks.

The capitol played a significant role in the story of the American flag becoming known as Old Glory. Captain William Driver (1803-1886), a veteran merchant ship's captain from New England who had sailed around the world twice, retired to Nashville in 1837. In 1824 his wife had sewn a large 10 x 17 American flag to fly on her husband's ship. When he first saw it, he called it Old Glory. In Nashville, Capt. Driver, a staunch Unionist, flew his beloved flag over the street in front of his home on holidays and on his birthday, March 17. Originally it bore 24 stars, but ten more were added in 1860, reflecting the growth of the nation, along with an anchor sewn on the canton. When the Confederates took over Nashville, he hid the flag within a quilt.

When Federal soldiers captured Nashville in 1862, Driver retrieved his cherished flag and climbed above the capitol's east entrance and hoisted Old Glory up the mast. He remained to guard it all that night. Too fragile to fly for long, he retrieved it the next day. Soldiers and civilians then began to refer to the American flag as Old Glory, and the name stuck.

Although Driver strongly favored the Union, three of his sons fought for the Confederacy, and one was killed at the Battle of Perryville in Kentucky. Captain Driver is buried at the City Cemetery in Nashville, where the American flag flies 24 hours a day by special Congressional approval.

Today the original Old Glory is stored at the National Museum of American History, Smithsonian Institution, Washington, D.C., although it is not normally on pubic display. In 2006, the faded and fragile Old Glory was returned to Nashville for the first time in 100 years for a temporary exhibition at the Tennessee State Museum.

Andrew Johnson, a former governor of Tennessee, had been the only U.S. Senator from a Southern state not to resign after his state had seceded. He was named by President Lincoln as military governor of Tennessee. Fearful that Confederates would retake the city, Johnson ordered defensive works constructed and the capitol fortified. A wooden stockade, turrets, and bales of cotton were assembled on the terraces. Parrott rifles, heavy siege artillery with rifled barrels, were positioned on the terraces pointing outward at the occupied city and its residents. The guns were never fired in anger, but were fired several times in honor of Federal victories or elections.

Like many buildings in Nashville, the capitol was temporarily used as a military hospital following the battle at Murfreesboro, Tenn. (Stones River), which ended on Jan. 2, 1863.

After the war, in 1866, the legislature was ready to vote on the 14th Amendment, granting citizenship to blacks, when several opposing legislators attempted to flee and block passage by denying a quorum. Armed guards fired on the legislators, who halted and returned to the session. The legislation passed, paving the way for Tennessee to become the first Confederate state admitted back into the Union (it had been the last to leave). A sculpture off the main-level staircase commemorates this vote. The lower marble staircase railing is chipped from one of the bullets fired from the upper stairs.

One of the biggest post-war events was the highlight of Nashville's Centennial—the unveiling on May 20, 1880 of the equestrian statue of General Andrew Jackson in the terraced garden on the east side of the capitol grounds. The bronze statue by Clark Mills was the first equestrian statue in the U.S. and a bold design, considering that the entire sculpture is supported only by the horse's hind legs. It is the first of three castings and the artist's proof. Identical statues can be found in Jackson Square in New Orleans and Lafayette Park in Washington, D.C. (a replica also stands in Jacksonville, Florida).

A month later, Capitol Commission Chairman Samuel D. Morgan—the driving force behind the construction and completion of the Tennessee State Capitol—died. On Christmas Eve 1881 his remains were interred in a tomb in the southeast corner of the building.

By 1885 stone in parts of the building was "rapidly deteriorating and going to decay," but repair work was put off. However, the water closet located in the crypt was totally replaced at the cost of $2,000 after being described as producing "a stench in the nostrils of decency" and deemed a nuisance by the State Board of Health.

In 1890, a civilian died after falling from an upper portico at the capitol, prompting the installation of safety railings.

The turn of the century saw the building of a south stonework entrance and a major repair effort. Stone on the building was scrubbed with wire brushes and covered with a mixture of boiling paraffin wax and linseed oil. Surfaces were patched with "granitoid," made from Portland cement concrete. The entire building was electrified.

In 1909 a statue of Sam Davis, the "Boy Hero of the Confederacy," by sculptor George J. Zolnay was erected at the southwest corner of the capitol grounds. Before being hanged as an alleged spy by Federal troops in 1863 because he would not name his accomplices, Davis spoke his last words, "I would die a thousand deaths before I would betray a friend."

At the turn of the century, Marathon Motors of Nashville produced newfangled horseless carriages. To prove how rugged the vehicles were made, the company conducted a public demonstration by driving a motorcoach up the numerous steps on Capitol Hill.

The final dramatic showdown over the 19th Amendment giving women the right to vote played out in 1920 in the Tennessee State Capitol. Both sides established headquarters at hotels near the capitol, and handed out propaganda literature. Suffragists, identified by wearing yellow roses, needed one more state to ratify the amendment and Tennessee was their last chance. The Senate approved, but the vote in the House was thought to be evenly split. Harry Burn, the youngest legislator, was against ratification and wore a red rose until he received a note from his mother urging him to vote in the affirmative. His "yea" for the amendment was the deciding vote.

By the 1950s the capitol building itself was in need of extensive repair and restoration. The original exterior Bigby limestone was replaced with 90,000 cubic feet of Oolitic limestone from Indiana during a four-year project. All of the terrace stonework was replaced, as well as all 28 Ionic columns and the entire entablature, including the pediments and parapets of the porticoes. A 50-ton guy derrick mounted on a steel tower was used to renovate the capitol's lantern tower. The copper roof and all doors and windows were replaced.

In 1957 interior work was performed. The crypt level was excavated and transformed into offices. Limestone floors were replaced with marble from Carthage, Missouri. New heating, air conditioning and electrical systems were installed. The 300-foot-long Motlow Tunnel was built beneath the south side of the capitol, offering convenient access from Charlotte Avenue. In 1974, Legislative Plaza was completed, with a subterranean state office building beneath a large urban plaza.

In 1984, James Hoobler, director of the Tennessee Historical Society, reported to state officials deteriorating conditions inside the capitol. The leaking roof and exterior stonework were repaired. The State Library and Supreme Court chambers were restored to their original state of elegance. The project was finished four years later.

The interior of the capitol serves as a defacto art gallery. Portraits of Strickland, Morgan, and Presidents Jackson, Polk, and Johnson can be found on the first floor along with the portraits of former governors. Ceiling frescoes painted in 1858 by German immigrants John Schleicher and Theo Knoch depict Westward Expansion surrounded by Muses of Literature, Sculpture, Music and Painting; an American Eagle surrounded by 31 stars (the number of states at the time); Justice; Liberty; and the State Seal.

The governor's reception room contains murals painted by Jirayr H. Zorthian during the 1938 remodeling—the First Tennesseans; Hernando de Soto; Fort Prudhomme 1682; Fort Loudoun 1756; Watauga Association 1772; Founding of Nashville 1779-80; Nashville 1855; Battle of the Bluffs at Fort Nashborough 1781; the State of Franklin 1784; and Agriculture and Commerce from the State Seal.

Behind the speaker's podium in the House chamber is the original

Tennessee marble wallscreen with vertical Roman spears, signifying strength in unity. The columns in the House gallery are made of Nashville limestone nearly 22 feet tall.

The former State Library Room contains an ornate, cast-iron winding staircase. Cast-iron portrait medallions on the railings depict William Shakespeare, Joseph Addison, Dante, U.S. Senator Ephraim Foster, Sir Walter Scott, Lord Byron, George Washington, Benjamin Franklin, Thomas Jefferson, Patrick Henry, Andrew Jackson, Daniel Webster, Henry Clay, John Milton, James K. Polk, Washington Irving, William Hickling Prescott, U.S. Sen. Felix Grundy, Gov. William Carroll, U.S. Sen. Hugh Lawson White, Joseph Story, John Bell, and John C. Calhoun.

Ceiling portraits painted by Schleicher and Knoch in 1859 depict Dr. Gerard Troost, Dr. Phillip Lindsley, James Kent, Dr. James Priestley, Rev. Charles Coffin, Henry Wadsworth Longfellow, Matthew Fontaine Maury, and William Hickling Prescott.

Busts on the main level portray Jackson, Polk, Johnson, John Sevier, Cordell Hull, Nathan Bedford Forrest, Admiral Albert Gleaves, Admiral David Farragut, Matthew Maury, Cherokee linguist Sequoyah, noted author Mary Murfree, and Sampson Keeble, a Nashville barber and the first African-American to serve in the Tennessee Legislature, 1873-1874.

Source: Mark Zimmerman, God, Guns, Guitars & Whiskey: An Illustrated Guide to Historic Nashville, Tennessee-2nd Edition.

NAZI SABOTEURS
and the
Fountain of Youth

More than a dozen years ago, a crew from a utility company discovered a fascinating object while surveying an overgrown field on the outskirts of Washington, D.C. — a large slab of granite with an inscription honoring six Nazi spies executed by the U.S. government in 1942. The field was in an area called Blue Plains, an old burial ground or potter's field. The monument indicated it had been placed there by the National Socialist White People's Party. Further research indicated the monument had been there, hidden in obscurity, since at least 1986. In 2010, the stone was removed by the park service and now sits in a storage facility in suburban Maryland. Nobody knows whether the stone actually marked the burial site of the executed Nazi saboteurs because the site was kept a secret.

The six German spies were executed by electric chair — one right after the other — on Aug. 8, 1942, on the directions of President Franklin D. Roosevelt following a quick military trial. There were actually eight saboteurs, but two received leniency for their cooperation with federal authorities and served brief prison terms before being deported back to Germany.

The Germans, all of whom had spent considerable time in the United States before the war and could speak English well, had been trained for the sabotage mission under the auspices of Operation Pastorious, named for the leader of the first German migration to America in 1683. The operation was enthusiastically backed by Adolph Hitler, who resented the U.S. industrial support of Great Britain at the beginning of the war. In charge of the operation was Lt. Walter Lippe of the Abwehr-2 (Intelligence 2), a vain and boisterous egotist who had been deported from the U.S. for his involvement in the Bund, an organization of German sympathizers who supported the Third Reich. The saboteurs were taken to aluminum and magnesium plants, railroad shops, canals, locks, and other facilities in Germany to familiarize them with the vital points and vulnerabilities of the types of targets they were to attack. Maps were used to locate those American targets, spots where railroads could be most effectively disabled, the principal aluminum and magnesium plants, and important canals, waterways, and locks. After training in explosives and sabotage techniques at a secret camp in Germany, the eight agents (four others flunked out) gathered on the west coast of France for transport to the U.S. aboard two U-boats (submarines). Due to their reckless conduct during the overland journey to France, the operation was nearly discovered and aborted. One team of four led by George Dasch was landed on Long Island on June 13, 1942. After burying their supplies and explosives in the sand dunes, one of the team ran into an unarmed coastal patrolman who accepted money as a bribe to keep quiet. By the time the patrolman reached his station and reported the strange incident, the saboteurs had left the scene.

A second team of German saboteurs was landed four days later at Ponte Vedra Beach, just south of Jacksonville, Florida. The submarine, U-254, grounded on the sandy shore, parallel to the coastline, and labored to free itself. Despite landlubbers hearing the drone of diesel engines offshore and even smelling the exhaust fumes, the German sailors managed to right the submarine and escape. The saboteurs headed inland. The Florida team was led by Edward Kerling, 32, who had lived in the U.S. for 11 years, working as a chauffeur for wealthy residents of a New York suburb. Also landing there were Herbert Haupt, 22, a would-be Luftwaffe pilot who liked flashy jewelry; Werner Thiel, 35, a former toolmaker who had worked in Fort Myers; and Hermann Otto Neubauer, 32, who after returning to Germany had been wounded by artillery fire on the Russian front. Having changed into civilian clothes, the Florida group took the bus to Jacksonville and stayed at the Mayflower and Seminole hotels, then traveled by train to Cincinnati, with two going on to Chicago and the other pair to New York City.

Meanwhile, Dasch, the leader of the Long Island group, confessed to a comrade that he was having second thoughts. It has been speculated that Dasch never really intended to go through with the sabotage operation; he was not a devout Nazi party member. In addition, the agents were carrying close to $175,000 in cash with them and had savored samples of what that money could buy for them in America. Regardless, Dasch called the local office of the FBI and told them he was a newly arrived German who would meet with officials in Washington, D.C. the next week. The call was basically ignored. Five days later, Dasch called the FBI headquarters from a hotel in DC. This time, he was picked up by special agents and thoroughly interrogated. Dasch cooperated, thinking that he was now an international hero. The other three agents were quickly arrested — one week after landing.

Of the Florida group, Kerling and Thiel were arrested in New York City on June 23rd, and Neubauer and Haupt were arrested in Chicago on June 27th. The military trial was conducted July 8 to August 4, 1942. All eight were convicted and sentenced to death, with two death sentences later commuted.

FBI Director J. Edgar Hoover enthusiastically promoted the capture of the saboteurs as brilliant counter-espionage work by his agency, neglecting to mention that Dasch had nearly begged the FBI for a week to arrest him, and then he fully cooperated.

In late 1944, another Nazi sabotage operation was attempted. Two agents, William Curtis Colepaugh and Erich Gimpel, were landed as spies from a German submarine on the coast of Maine in a desperate attempt to secure information. They, too, were quickly apprehended by the FBI before accomplishing any part of their mission.

Interestingly, no acts of deliberate sabotage in the U.S. during World War II can be attributed to foreign agents, only to vandalism, resentment, relief from boredom, labor strife, or the "curiosity of children."

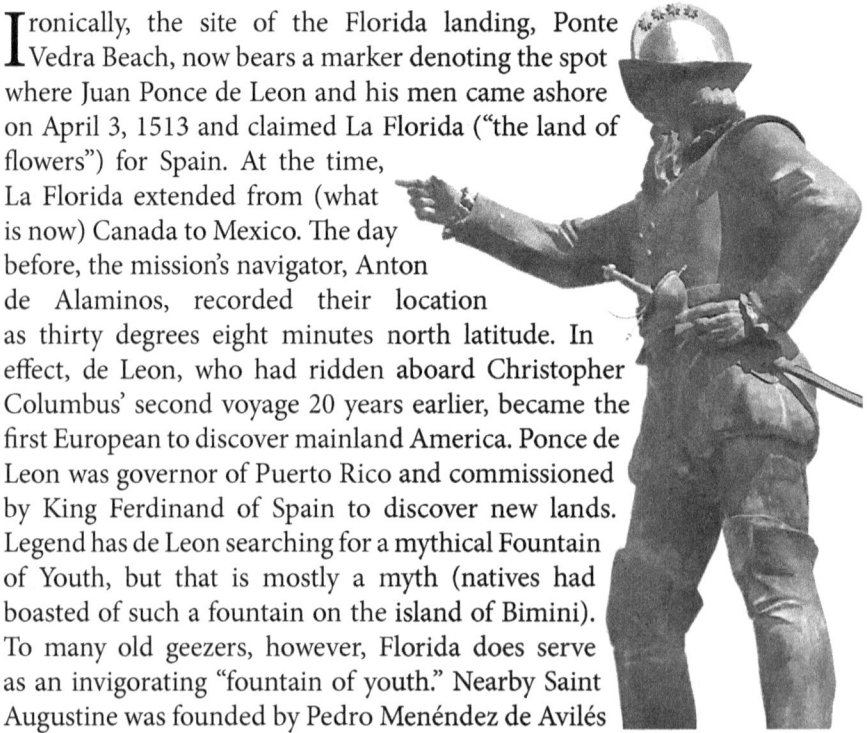

Ironically, the site of the Florida landing, Ponte Vedra Beach, now bears a marker denoting the spot where Juan Ponce de Leon and his men came ashore on April 3, 1513 and claimed La Florida ("the land of flowers") for Spain. At the time, La Florida extended from (what is now) Canada to Mexico. The day before, the mission's navigator, Anton de Alaminos, recorded their location as thirty degrees eight minutes north latitude. In effect, de Leon, who had ridden aboard Christopher Columbus' second voyage 20 years earlier, became the first European to discover mainland America. Ponce de Leon was governor of Puerto Rico and commissioned by King Ferdinand of Spain to discover new lands. Legend has de Leon searching for a mythical Fountain of Youth, but that is mostly a myth (natives had boasted of such a fountain on the island of Bimini). To many old geezers, however, Florida does serve as an invigorating "fountain of youth." Nearby Saint Augustine was founded by Pedro Menéndez de Avilés in 1565; the grand fort there, Castillo de San Marcos, can be visited today. Ponte Vedra Beach is a small but affluent community, home to numerous golf professionals and other sports celebrities, and TPC Sawgrass, host of The Players Championship.

It is not known whether Juan played golf, but in 1521, he was mortally wounded by natives on the gulf coast of La Florida, taking an arrow in the thigh that was poisoned with the sap of the manchineel tree. He died in Cuba and was buried in the Cathedral of San Juan Bautista in Puerto Rico. Today, 30 percent of Puerto Rico's population is descended from de Leon and his wife, according to one historian.

Believe it or not, goose-stepping worshippers of Adolf Hitler's Third Reich were not uncommon in the U.S. during the 1930s. Fascist leaders such as Hitler in Germany and Benito Mussolini in Italy were praised for their nationalism and efficient governance. Hitler sympathizers organized as The Bund, operating in the Midwest, particularly Chicago and Cincinnati, and the Northeast. Members were American citizens of German descent. The Bund was formed in 1936 and elected a German-born American citizen named Fritz Julius Kuhn as its leader (Bundesführer).

The Bund established a number of training camps, in New Jersey, New York, Wisconsin, and Pennsylvania. The Bund held rallies with Nazi insignia and the Hitler salute and attacked the Roosevelt administration. The Bund displayed the American flag alongside the flag of Nazi Germany, and declared that George Washington was "the first Fascist" who did not believe democracy would work. One infamous rally in New York City attracted 20,000 attendees.

In 1939, Kuhn was investigated in New York for tax evasion, arrested, tried, and convicted. He served time in prison and was eventually deported.

Following Pearl Harbor and Hitler's declaration of war against the U.S., the Bund found it difficult to effectively operate. The House Committee on Un-American Activities was active in denying any Nazi-sympathetic organization the ability to operate freely during World War II. In December 1942, fifty leading German-Americans (including Babe Ruth) signed a "Christmas Declaration by men and women of German ancestry" condemning Nazism, which appeared in ten major American daily newspapers.

One week after Pearl Harbor, 33 German spies, many of them U.S. citizens, either pleaded guilty or were convicted of espionage following an extensive investigation by the FBI. The prison sentences totaled more than 300 years. The operation was made possible by the work of one double-agent.

Flag of the German-American Bund

The leader of the spy ring was Frederick J. Duquesne, a native of South Africa who became a U.S. citizen in 1913. Four years later, he was arrested for involvement in fradulent insurance claims related to the sinking by fire of a British steamship. By 1940, Duquesne was operating Air Terminals Co. in New York City.

William Sebold was a naturalized U.S. citizen who worked in industrial and aircraft plants throughout the U.S. and South America after leaving his native Germany in 1921. During a return trip to Germany in 1939, Sebold was persuaded by high-ranking members of the German Secret Service to spy on America. Sebold received espionage training in Hamburg (including how to work a shortwave radio), but not before secretly visiting the American consulate in Cologne and telling officials there that he wanted to cooperate with the FBI.

Sebold returned to New York City in February 1940 as Harry Sawyer, a diesel engineering consultant. He was to meet with various Nazi spies, pass along instructions to them from Germany, receive messages in return, and transmit them back in code to Germany.

Lab engineers with the FBI built a secret shortwave radio transmitting station on Long Island. Special agents pretending to be Sebold sent authentic-sounding messages to his German superiors for some 16 straight months. More than 300 messages were sent, and another 200 were received from the Nazis.

The FBI set up an office for Sebold, complete with hidden microphones and cameras behind one-way mirrors. Sebold met with a series of spies wishing to send secret national defense information to the Gestapo. In Sebold's office, Duquesne explained how fires could be started at industrial plants. On one occasion, Duquesne provided Sebold with photographs and specifications of a new type of bomb being produced in the United States. He claimed that he secured that material by secretly entering the Dupont plant in Wilmington, Delaware. Duquesne, who was vehemently anti-British, submitted information dealing with national defense in America, the sailing of ships to British ports, and technology. He also regularly received money from Germany in payment for his services.

When enough evidence had been gathered, the suspected spies were rounded up and prosecuted. Of the 33 suspects, 19 pleaded guilty and the others were found guilty by jury trial in Brooklyn in December 1941. Duquesne received an 18-year prison sentence.

One of the spies was Paul Bante, a German native who served in the German army during World War I. He came to the U.S. in 1930 and became a naturalized U.S. citizen in 1938. A former member of the German-American Bund, Bante claimed that Germany put him in contact with one of their operatives, Paul Fehse, because of Bante's previous association with a Dr. Ignatz T. Griebl. Before fleeing to Germany to escape prosecution, Dr. Griebl had been implicated in a Nazi spy ring with Guenther Gustave Rumrich, who was tried on espionage charges in 1938.

Bante assisted Fehse in obtaining information about ships bound for Britain with war materials and supplies. Bante claimed that as a member of the Gestapo his function was to create discontent among union workers, stating that labor strikes would assist Germany.

Sebold met Bante at the Little Casino Restaurant, which was frequented by several members of the spy ring. During one such meeting, Bante advised that he was preparing a fuse bomb, and he subsequently delivered dynamite and detonation caps to Sebold. Bante was convicted and received 18 months in prison for his "service."

Hartwig Richard Kleiss was another spy. According to the FBI: "Born in Germany, Kleiss came to this country in 1925 and became a naturalized citizen six years later. Following his arrival in the United States, he was employed as a cook on various ships.

"Kleiss obtained information for Germany, including blueprints of the *SS America* which showed the locations of newly installed gun emplacements. He included information about how guns would be brought into position for firing. Kleiss also obtained details on the construction and performance of new speedboats being developed by the United States Navy, which he submitted to Sebold for transmittal to Germany.

"Kleiss had originally chosen to stand trial. However, after cross-examination, he changed his plea to guilty on a charge of espionage and received an eight-year prison sentence."

Sources: Jessie-lynne Kerr, Florida Times-Union; Joan Irene Miller thesis, Portland State University; David A. Taylor, Smithsonian Magazine; Chicago Daily Times archives; www.fbi.gov/history/famous-cases/duquesne-spy-ring.

Ironclad Gunboats Battle Confederate Horse Cavalry

Kelley v. Fitch at Bell's Bend, Tennessee

The Ultimate Clash of Cavalry v. Navy

On Tuesday, Nov. 29, 1864, at noon, the villagers of Dover, Tennessee, witnessed an amazing sight—the tinclad gunboat *USS Moose* leading a continuous procession of 60 steamers loaded with blueclad soldiers churning and chugging its way up the Cumberland River. The convoy was escorted by the City Class ironclad *Carondelet*, the river monitor *Neosho*, and the tinclads *Volunteer, Peosta, Fairplay, Silver Lake, Brilliant, Springfield, Reindeer,* and *Victory.* As promised, the convoy was delivering to Nashville the 10,000 veteran XVI Corps troops of Major General Andrew Jackson Smith. The well-traveled soldiers, known as Smith's Guerrillas, had journeyed by land from western Missouri and then by river from St. Louis. The flotilla included the steam transports *Albert Pearce, Havana, James Raymond, Julia, Lilly Martin, Maggie Hayes, Victory, Marmora, Camelia, Silver Cloud, Arizona, J.F. McComb, Mercury, Financier, Lilly, New York, Lady Franklin, Pioneer, Magnet, Prima Donna, Wananita, America, Thomas E. Tutt, Mars, Omaha, Olive, Silver Lake, Kate Kearney, Spray, Mollie McPike,* and *Prairie State.* When the mighty flotilla reached Nashville without incident the next day, commanding General George Thomas engaged in an unusual show of emotion by hugging General Smith heartily. Smith's reinforcements were desperately needed at Nashville as the Yankees were waiting for the arrival of the Confederate Army of Tennessee under General John Bell Hood.

Navy Lt. Commander LeRoy Fitch, who was standing in for the sick 10th

District chief James Shirk, now commanded two ironclad gunboats, the heavy gunboat *Peosta,* and at least eight tinclad gunboats, "the greatest fleet of gunboats ever to appear on the Cumberland during the war," according to historian Byrd Douglas. Fitch was notified of his new assignment by Acting Rear Admiral Samuel Phillips Lee, who had assumed command of the Mississippi Squadron at a brief ceremony on November 1st at Mound City aboard the flagboat *Black Hawk,* replacing Rear Admiral David Dixon Porter, who went to the North Atlantic Blockading Squadron.

Meanwhile, 18 miles south of Nashville at Franklin, Hood had caught up with the small army of General John Schofield, which had been trying to reach the safety of the Nashville fortifications. In a spectacular frontal assault over two miles of open ground against fortified fieldworks, Hood's valiant soldiers suffered horrendous casualties, especially in its officer corps. Twelve Confederate generals were either killed, wounded, or captured.

The next day, on Thurs., Dec. 1st, Schofield managed to fall back to Nashville and its fortifications. Hood's soldiers followed. The Confederates set up a four-mile siege line that fell about three miles short of encircling the southern part of Nashville (the northern half of Nashville was enclosed by a giant bend in the Cumberland River). Brigadier General James Chalmers' division of 1,500 troopers was positioned at the extreme left flank of the Confederate line while Forrest took the bulk of his cavalry, under orders from Hood, to raid U.S. positions at nearby Murfreesboro.

On December 2nd, Lt. Colonel David Campbell Kelley and the 26th Tennessee Battalion of 300 men set up field artillery at two positions on bluffs overlooking the river opposite the grist mills at Bell's Bend. The artillery consisted of two 10-pound Parrott rifles of Lt. H.H. Brigg's section of Capt. T.W. Rice's artillery, plus two 12-pounder howitzers from Walton's battery. The site, known as Davidson's Landing, was four miles by land west of downtown Nashville and 17 miles downriver. Between Bell's Bend and Nashville were staging areas at Davidson Island and Hyde's Ferry. Two miles downriver from Bell's Bend was the Hillsboro Landing. Beyond that was the infamous Harpeth Shoals. Kelley's batteries were in excellent position to contest any Federal gunboats and blockade the river. The confrontations in the next few days would constitute the heaviest engagements of Confederate cavalry versus U.S. Navy gunboats during the war. Unfortunately for the Confederates, Hood's army arrived one day too late to contest the arrival of Smith's massive convoy.

Kelley was a Methodist minister and physician who commanded cavalry under Forrest. He was not a chaplain, a rank he disdained. After many engagements during the war, Kelley was a fearless and experienced fighter against Federal river gunboats.

Meanwhile, Thomas was worried that Hood might try to ford the Cumberland above Nashville and get behind his lines. He instructed Fitch to direct a patrol up the river 100 miles to Hartsville consisting of the *USS Springfield* (Acting Volunteer Master Edmund Morgan) and the U.S. Army gunboat *Newsboy*.

On Sat., Dec. 3, 1864, while U.S. gunboats conducted routine patrols below Nashville, the rebel batteries at Bell's Bend fired upon two transports, the *Prairie State* and the *Prima Donna,* and drove them to the riverbank. Kelley's men captured 56 of the crew, 200 horses and mules, and many sacks of grain. The steamers were taken several miles downriver to Hillsboro Landing. At about this time, the naval supply steamer *Magnet* ran the batteries and was hit several times. Her captain, named Harrol, grounded his boat and managed to hightail it back to Nashville to report the batteries to Lt. Commander Fitch. At 12:45 am on December 4th, Fitch responded by leading an attack column consisting of the *USS Carondelet* (commanded by Acting Volunteer Master Charles Miller), the tinclad *Fairplay* (Acting Volunteer Lt. George J. Groves), the flagboat *Moose* (Acting Volunteer Master Washington C. Coulson), the *Reindeer* (Acting Volunteer Lt. Henry Glassford), and the *Silver Lake* (Acting Volunteer Ensign J.C. Coyle). The *Neosho* and the *Brilliant* were left at Hyde's Ferry to protect the Federal right flank. It should be noted that during the military maneuvers around Nashville during December 1864 that the City Class ironclad *USS Cincinnati* was stationed at Clarksville and did not participate.

The *Silver Lake* was typical of a U.S. Navy tinclad gunboat. The 236-ton sternwheeler, constructed at California, Pa. in 1862, was 155 feet long with a beam of 32 feet and a six-foot draft. Her two boilers and two steam engines produced six knots of speed. The tinclad was armed with six 24-pound brass Dahlgren howitzers.

That night was "cool, cloudy, and devoid of natural light," according to historian Jack Smith, "and hence the Confederates did not spot the Yankee craft..." At 12:45 am on December 4th, the ironclad *Carondelet* opened up with grapeshot and canister against Kelley's lofty field artillery batteries. The *Fairplay* was slightly below the upper battery, the *Moose* directly opposite it, the *Reindeer* 50 yards above, and the *Silver Lake* trailing. The Confederates responded with volleys that were "rapid and warm." The *Carondelet* steamed past, turned hard about, and churned back past the batteries. After 20 minutes of sharp exchanges, Kelley's gunners drew back. The ironclad lobbed shells at the Confederate positions until 2:30 am and withdrew.

One Yankee sailor later wrote about "the thundering of the mighty guns, the shells screeching through the air back and forth, from one side to the other; sometimes bursting in the air, sometimes in the water, throwing the

USS Neosho at Bell's Bend. (Library of Congress)

water high in the air."

The *Carondelet* fired 26 rounds. The *Fairplay* fired 37 rounds and received two hits (the shells did not explode and caused minor damage). The *Moose*, which almost collided in the narrow channel (80 yards wide) with the *Reindeer*, was hit three times while expending 59 rounds. To avoid the collision, the *Reindeer's* captain ran the bow of his boat into the bank so the current would swing the stern downstream, and then chugged upriver to get back into position. The *Silver Lake*, only lightly engaged, fired six rounds of canister. Amid the noise, smoke, and confusion, Kelley's batteries retreated, either to regroup or for want of ammunition. Fitch attributed the silencing of the rebel guns to the gunnery skills of the *Moose's* crew and Acting Volunteer Master Coulson. The tinclad flagboat was lucky. One enemy shell nearly hit the gunpowder magazine and did not explode, while another would have torn through the bottom of the *Moose* if not deflected by a deck beam.

The *Carondelet* and *Fairplay* reached the two captured transports downstream at Hillsboro Landing and thwarted attempts by the Confederates to torch them. After hasty repairs, all five of the U.S. gunboats returned to Nashville safely with the *Prairie State* and *Prima Donna*. Fitch reported to Thomas that he had fought with Buford's brigade of Forrest's cavalry, part of a strong Confederate left flank ending at the river. In fact, the Confederate line did not reach the river; Buford and Forrest were at Murfreesboro; and the men he fought were commanded by Kelley, the "devil's parson." The major consequence of the duel at Bell's Bend were orders by Federal officials to stop all river traffic between Clarksville and Nashville. In essence, the Confederates had created a blockade.

In a later report to Chalmers, his superior, Lt. Col. Kelley stated that the Confederate officers and men assigned to the captured U.S. transports at Hillsboro Landing commenced to looting the boats and consuming confiscated whiskey "too freely." The men in question were Company B of the 3rd Tennessee Cavalry commanded by Captain James G. Barbour. Kelley said he found it necessary to clear the boats of looters "myself with a drawn sabre." Kelley personally stood guard for two hours to prevent the return of the plunderers. He posted Capt. Chandler to act as guard, caught some sleep, and then went off to look for the "lost squadron" after he awoke. The company was called upon to go back and protect the captured boats but "such was the delay occasioned by drunkenness that the boats had been removed before I could reach them." Chandler said he set fire to the boats but "someone hidden on board extinguished them." Kelley admitted that "Capt. Chandler had evidently been drinking, but I am not prepared to say that this prevented his executing orders." This correspondence was contained in a copy of a manuscript letter in General Chalmers' papers at the National Archives found by Nashville historian Paul Clements and brought to the attention of the Battle of Nashville Trust.

Fitch   Kelley

The *Carondelet*, a City Class casemate ironclad with 13 gunports, was the most famous of all the Western river gunboats, having participated in 15 engagements, including a duel with the Fort Donelson batteries and another duel with the Confederate ironclad *CSS Arkansas*. Despite its fame, the *Carondelet* was also known as one of the slowest gunboats on the rivers.

The *Neosho* ironclad was one of only two gunboats of its kind during the Civil War. Built in 1863 by James Eads at a cost of $195,000, the 523-ton behemoth was 180 feet long, 45 feet wide, and drew only four feet of water. With a crew of 100, she could make 12 knots at top speed but was difficult to maneuver. Low-board to the water, the distinguishing characteristics were a cylindrical rotating turret in the bow fitted with two 11-inch Dahlgren smoothbores and protected with iron plating six inches thick, the enclosed paddlewheel at the stern, and the wooden pilothouse superstructure and single chimney in-between. Fake gunports were painted on the iron turret to confuse the enemy. Along with the *USS Osage*, the *Neosho* was the only river monitor powered by paddlewheel.

The *Neosho*'s guns, 13 feet long and each weighing nearly eight tons, used a 15-lb. powder charge to fire a 166-lb. solid shot or a load of canister balls.

A planned reconnaissance down the river on December 5th was postponed by the ominous sound of heavy cannon fire in the distance that Fitch speculated might be the beginning of a major Confederate assault on the city. He therefore kept his gunboats close at hand. The noise was actually Confederate assaults against railroad blockhouses south of the city.

Commanded by Acting Volunteer Lieutenant Samuel Howard, the strange-looking *Neosho* led a convoy of transports and gunboats downstream from Nashville on Tuesday, Dec. 6, 1864 at 9:30 in the morning. Following behind her, in order, were the *Metamora* transport, the tinclads *Moose* and

Reindeer lashed together, the *Prima Donna* and *Arizona* transports, the *J.F. McComb* and *Mercury* sidewheeler transports, the tinclad *Fairplay,* the transports *Financier, Lily, New York* and *Lady Franklin,* the tinclad *Silver Lake,* transports *Pioneer* and *Magnet,* and finally the *Carondelet.*

By this point in time, Kelley had positioned three batteries of field artillery on the south banks of the river opposite Bell's Mills, having added two more 12-pounder howitzers. Because Kelley made a practice of actively repositioning his guns and firing many salvos, U.S. Commander Fitch reported that he was facing at least 14 rebel guns instead of the actual six.

At 11:15 am, the middle battery opened on the *Neosho* at the point-blank range of 20 to 30 yards. The *Neosho* responded with deadly canister loads from its two powerful Dahlgrens. Despite the pounding, the *Neosho* remained at station; the Confederate barrage blew away all of the ironclad's wooden superstructure like a blast of wind. The U.S. flag fell to the deck. Amid the conflagration, Quartermaster John Ditzenbach and civilian pilot John H. Ferrell climbed out onto the deck and attached the flag to a shortened but upright spar. For their bravery, Ditzenbach and Ferrell were awarded the Medal of Honor. Ferrell is one of only a handful of civilians ever so honored. A native of Tennessee, Ferrell had been residing in Illinois when hired by the U.S. Navy. He survived the war and died in 1900.

USS Neosho pilot John Ferrell's official Medal of Honor citation (June 22, 1865) reads:

"Served on board the U.S. Monitor Neosho during the engagement with enemy batteries at Bells Mills, Cumberland River, near Nashville, Tenn., 6 December 1864. Carrying out his duties courageously during the engagement, Ferrell gallantly left the pilothouse after the flag and signal staffs of that vessel had been shot away and, taking the flag which was drooping over the wheelhouse, make it fast to the stump of the highest mast remaining although the ship was still under a heavy fire from the enemy."

The December 6th firefight lasted for two and a half hours with Kelley "doing good work and thoroughly enjoying himself with his guns on the river bank." The firepower of the rebel batteries was too much for the convoy; at 3:10 pm all but the *Neosho* and *Carondelet* retired upriver. The two ironclads took a break but returned to Bell's Bend at 4:30 in the afternoon. The *Carondelet* tied fast to the north bank just upstream from the batteries and commenced to firing its starboard and stern guns. The apparently indestructible *Neosho* steadied itself in the channel opposite the middle battery, drew a bead on the Confederate gunners, and disabled two of the rebel 12-pounder artillery pieces. The afternoon exchange lasted only an hour. Similar to the situation at Johnsonville, the Federal gunboats were forced to elevate their guns to aim at the Confederates on the bluffs and their shells flew harmlessly overhead.

A City-Class Federal ironclad gunboat — all seven were identical. This is the *USS Cairo*. The *USS Carondelet* looked exactly the same. (Library of Congress)

Afterwards, it was determined that the *Neosho* had been hit at least 100 times that day with only superficial damage. "Some six or eight men in the turret of the *Neosho* were somewhat bruised and scratched in the face by a shell striking the muzzle of one of the guns and exploding." Other injuries were too trivial to mention. It could have been much worse. An unexploded Confederate shell was found in the *Neosho's* gunpowder magazine.

December 7th was spent coaling and repairing the damages to the ironclads and tinclads. On December 8th, the two ironclads along with the *Moose* and *Reindeer*, lashed together, steamed downriver to Davidson's Landing and for 90 minutes leisurely shelled a brick house believed to be occupied by Confederate soldiers.

As it turned out, at the time of Fitch's bitter fights with Kelley's batteries, the U.S. convoy could not have made the trip to Clarksville anyway—the water level at Harpeth Shoals had fallen so much in the previous week that no boats could have gotten through!

Bitter winter weather, low water, and other considerations limited gunboat activity until a thaw in the weather on December 14th foretold the movement of Federal troops out of their fortifications the next day to do battle.

Thomas' Federal armies moved out of their fortifications around Nashville on Thursday, Dec. 15, 1864 and brought the fight to Hood's waiting troops. The U.S. 6th Cavalry Division under General Richard Johnson was late moving out the Charlotte Pike against the Confederate left flank due to dense fog and entanglements with U.S. infantry troops. Finally, Johnson moved out and engaged with Chalmers' cavalry near the Belle Meade plantation. Kelley had moved four guns back a half-mile from the river and fired at the *Neosho* on the Cumberland River and at the advancing U.S. horsemen. After dark,

Kelley retreated southeastward to Brentwood; Fitch reported erroneously that U.S. cavalry had captured Kelley's guns. During the two-day Battle of Nashville, Thomas drove Hood back to the point where a concentrated attack on Shy's Hill collapsed most of the Confederate resistance and forced a rout. Only a determined stand by relatively fresh troops on the Franklin Pike prevented the total destruction of the Confederate Army of Tennessee. Thus began the tragic 10-day, 100-mile fighting retreat of Hood's army in an effort to safely cross the Tennessee River in northern Alabama. During this time, the bulk of Forrest's command disengaged at Murfreesboro and linked up with the army at Columbia, and then fought effectively as the retreating army's rear guard. It was estimated that 10,000 horses perished in the harsh winter conditions.

The Confederates could not cross the Tennessee River at Florence, Ala., but established a pontoon bridge at Bainbridge, six miles above Florence at the foot of Muscle Shoals. Due to the rainy weather, the river level was up and many officers believed that the odds of U.S. gunboats reaching the pontoon bridge "not improbable." On December 20th, Acting Rear Admiral Samuel P. Lee led a flotilla of gunboats up the Tennessee towards Florence, where the Confederates had established an artillery battery. Lee's squadron boasted more guns than Fitch had at Nashville, and included the ironclads *Neosho, Carondelet, Pittsburg,* and the timberclad *Lexington.* Even with the rising waters, the *Carondelet* and *Pittsburg* had to be left behind at Eastport, Mississippi, while the *Neosho* and the tinclads *Reindeer* and *Fairy* engaged with two four-gun rebel batteries at Florence. The Confederates stopped firing after 30 minutes and the gunboats drifted back downstream. The next day another futile engagement resulted in the *Neosho* being hit 27 times and the Federal flotilla suffering three killed and five wounded. By the evening of December 27th, all of Hood's retreating troops had crossed the Tennessee River to safety. Lee was determined to disrupt the enemy's movements and ordered the *Neosho* monitor up the river, but a "sudden and rapid fall of the river" convinced the gunboat's pilot to stop short of Little Muscle Shoals.

Hood's failed 1864 offensive was the last major combat in the Western Theater, but U.S. Navy gunboat operations continued on the Tennessee and the Cumberland with some guerrilla resistance encountered. "The guerrilla war continued, having a logic of its own, even though the military purposes were negligible," noted historian Richard Gildrie.

On April 29, 1865, almost three weeks after Robert E. Lee surrendered to U.S. Grant at Appomattox, the tinclad *Moose* successfully thwarted a Confederate attempt to cross the Cumberland River in order to burn down the town of Eddyville, Kentucky. The *Moose,* captained by the veteran riverman W.C. Coulson, all of 25 years old, heard news of the movement while moored at Tennessee Rolling Mills. The acting master of the U.S. steamer *Albiona* had sighted 16 guerrillas at Centre Furnace, two miles from the river, at the crack of dawn. Five hours later, a courier reported a force of 150 to 200 men moving north to cross the river. Put immediately to full steam downriver, the *Moose* rounded the big bend at Eddyville and interrupted two boats of Confederates shoving off the shore. "They were taken completely by surprise and offered but little resistance," reported Coulson. Upon seeing the gunboat, the Confederates jumped out of their boats into the water. The forward gun on the upper deck of the *Moose* let loose, along with small arms fire from riflemen on the tinclad. The men on the shore, most armed only with revolvers, scattered. Few others made it across the river. A landing party pursued, shot and killed four and wounded the same number. They captured six rebels, along with 19 horses and three mules. Coulson reported that the Confederate force was under Major Hopkins of Buford's command, but historian Jack Smith refutes this assertion, stating there is no record of a Major Hopkins serving under General Abraham Buford. Often, guerrilla bands would pose as well-known military units to confuse the enemy. Two of the prisoners were found to be civilians impressed as guides, and were released. Coulson did report that 60 men eventually made it north of the Cumberland. "I shall continue to cruise this vicinity, keeping a good lookout for them, and convoying transports by dangerous places." The Eddyville affair was the last major naval counter-insurgency action on the Western waters.

In 1868, David Campbell Kelley, Forrest's "Fighting Parson," took a D.D. degree from Cumberland University and served the Methodist Episcopal Church in Gallatin and other towns in the Nashville area. Kelley was one of the founders of Vanderbilt University in 1873 and served on its board of trustees from 1875 to 1891. He held several posts in the church hierarchy and ran unsuccessfully as the Prohibition Party candidate for Tennessee governor in 1890. Kelley died in Nashville on May 14, 1909. According to John E. Fisher, Kelley was "a vocal force in urging upon whites reasoned and informed views of blacks and relations between the races." Forrest said, "He displayed all the dash, energy, and gallantry which has so long made him an efficient officer."

Lt. Commander LeRoy Fitch taught at the U.S. Naval Academy for a year, commanded a gunboat in the Atlantic and Caribbean for a year, and became superintendent of the Pensacola Naval Yard with the rank of Commander. He retired to his hometown of Logansport, Indiana, due to illness and died in obscurity in 1876 at the age of 39.

Sources: Mark Zimmerman, Iron Maidens and the Devil's Daughters; Myron "Jack" Smith, The USS Carondelet: A Civil War Ironclad on Western Waters; Official Records of the War of the Rebellion.

Here's to Upshot-Knothole!

Watching Atomic Bomb Blasts From the Vegas Strip, Baby

In April 1956, a 21-year-old Elvis Presley, billed as "America's only atomic-powered singer," began a two-week run at the New Frontier Hotel in Las Vegas, appearing with Freddy Martin's orchestra and comedian Shecky Greene. Too hip for Glitter Gulch, the kid bombed, a reviewer calling his act "brash, loud, and braying."

Once the entertainers left the stage about 4:00 am, the real show was ready to begin. It was time for the Dawn Bomb Party. Armed with atomic cocktails (vodka, cognac, sherry, and champagne), partiers sought the best vantage points—high atop Binion's Horseshoe or the panoramic Sky Room at the Desert Inn. Those wanting a front-row seat grabbed some drinks and snacks and hopped a special bus to Mount Charleston for $3 a head.

The audible signal was sent out and then the flash, to the north, about 60 miles away. Celebrators wearing protective goggles gawked at "a big ball of furiously churning fire, smoke, sand and debris rapidly rising from the ground in huge, rolling waves. The afterglow remained for several minutes while the mushroom cloud continued to rise, then drift away and apart," according to an article in *Nevada Highways & Parks*.

After bearing witness to the awesome spectacle, bomb-blast gawkers might consume a couple more drinks and then head on down to the pancake house for breakfast, and then hit the sack or the slots.

"The best thing ever to happen to Vegas was the atomic bomb," said Benny Binion, owner of the Horseshoe Club casino. Promotion is everything. Once the Gateway to Boulder Dam, then Sin City, Las Vegas became known as Atomic City. In Vegas, beauty contests were held to name Miss Atomic Bomb, usually a showgirl covered only by cotton gauze in the shape of a mushroom cloud.

The craze started in 1952 with the nationwide public viewing of an atomic blast, a year after testing began on the 640 square miles of the Nevada Test Site (formerly the Nellis Air Force Base Gunnery and Bombing Range). On April 22, 1952, about 200 reporters, including live television broadcasters, gathered on News Nob, only ten miles from ground zero, to publicly witness the detonation of Charlie, a thermonuclear bomb more than three times as powerful as the bombs dropped on Japan during World War II. One newsman reported putting on his goggles and waiting for the signal that "Big Shot" had been dropped from the B-36 bomber — "A fantastically bright cloud is climbing upward like a huge umbrella…You brace yourself against the shock wave that follows an atomic explosion. A heat wave comes first, then the shock, strong enough to knock an unprepared man down. Then, after what seems like hours, the man-made sunburst fades away."

In 1951, the U.S. Sixth Army built Camp Desert Rock next to the Nevada Proving Ground to house troops exposed to atomic detonations. More than 60,000 military and civilian personnel witnessed, often at close range, one or more of the 100 atmospheric nuclear tests conducted in Nevada. Troops were stationed in trenches three miles from ground zero and basically told to keep down and cover up. After the blast, the troops were marched to ground zero to check the area. They returned to the decontamination area, turned in their film badges, and brushed each other off with brooms. Then they were checked with Geiger counters for radiation.

In 1953, Annie, the first test of the Upshot-Knothole series, was conducted for the Federal Civil Defense Administration (FCDA), which constructed "a typical American community" to see what would happen to it during an atomic blast. The village contained two wooden-frame houses, 50 automobiles, eight bomb shelters, utility stations, furniture, appliances, and even mannequins simulating residents of this desert town. The test was witnessed by more than 600 Civil Defense observers and newsmen.

The Army managed to develop a huge cannon that could shoot a nuclear projectile or shell. In May 1953, soldiers witnessed a 15-kiloton air-burst in the desert produced by an 800-lb. shell (280mm) fired from a 85-ton artillery piece. Further development of the cannon concept proved troublesome and was discontinued.

In addition to generating tourism, the Nevada Test Site also brought thousands of military personnel, thousands of jobs, and more than $176 million in federal funds to the region, two-thirds of which went back into the Las Vegas economy. For twelve years, an average of one bomb every three weeks was detonated, for a total of 235 bombs. Flashes from the explosions

were so powerful that they reportedly could be seen from as far away as Montana. Scientists claimed that the radiation's adverse effects would have dissipated and been rendered harmless by the time the shock waves reached Las Vegas. They scheduled tests to coincide with weather patterns that blew fallout away from the city. However, as the tests continued, people in northeastern Nevada and southern Utah began complaining that their pets and livestock were suffering from beta particle burns and other ailments.

In recent years, Congress has appropriated millions of dollars in payments to "down-winders" who have developed cancer due to nuclear testing fallout.

The first full-scale atomic bomb test was code-named Trinity as part of the Manhattan Project during World War II. On July 16, 1945, scientists from the Los Alamos Laboratory successfully tested the plutonium bomb at the Alamogordo Bombing and Gunnery Range in New Mexico. The bomb was mounted on top of a 100-foot-tall tower before detonation. The uranium bomb (which was not tested), named Little Boy, was dropped on Hiroshima, Japan on Aug. 6, 1945. The plutonium bomb, named Fat Man, was dropped on Nagasaki, Japan three days later. These were the only two atomic bombs used in wartime. These atomic bombs worked on the concept of nuclear fission, where atoms are split to produce vast amounts of energy.

Modern fusion weapons consist essentially of two main components: a nuclear fission primary stage (fueled by uranium or plutonium) and a separate nuclear fusion secondary stage containing thermonuclear fuel — the heavy hydrogen isotopes deuterium and tritium, or in modern weapons, lithium deuteride. Thermonuclear weapons are often called hydrogen bombs or H-bombs.

After the war, the U.S. military conducted 23 tests of nuclear weapons in the South Pacific, specifically Bikini Atoll, between 1946 and 1958, most of them atmospheric.

In November 1952, the U.S. detonated the first thermonuclear bomb or hydrogen bomb, during the Ivy Mike test at Eniwetok Atoll. This much more powerful bomb worked on the concept of nuclear fusion, fusing atoms together. This bomb actually uses a small fission bomb as a trigger device.

Ivy Mike produced a yield of 10.4 megatons of TNT—700 times more powerful than Little Boy's 15 kilotons. Ivy Mike vaporized the island and created a fireball three miles wide and a 30-mile-wide updraft. The heat and mushroom cloud terrified even veteran bomb-blast observers on ships 35 miles away.

In 1954, the Castle Bravo test produced two-and-half-times the expected yield and clouds of radioactive material. Public concern eventually led to the 1963 ban on aboveground nuclear tests. The distance of the Pacific test sites from the United States posed significant logistical problems and costs and the humid climate created havoc with sensitive testing equipment.

In May 1955, Wigwam was conducted in the Pacific Ocean approximately 500 miles southwest of San Diego, California. The device was detonated at a depth of 2,000 feet in water 16,000 feet deep. Results showed that most of the radioactivity from Wigwam was confined deep under the surface of the ocean. Additional weapon effects tests, named Operation Argus, occurred in the South Atlantic in 1958.

From 1945 until 1992, the U.S. conducted 1,054 atomic bomb tests (24 in conjunction with the United Kingdom). Eighty percent were underground (shaft or tunnel) with the remainder atmospheric (dropped from a bomber, shot from a cannon, lifted by a balloon or rocket, or set on a barge, tower, or the ground). Five tests were conducted underwater. By location, 106 tests were in the South Pacific, three in the South Atlantic, 17 at various sites in New Mexico and Nevada, and 928 tests at the Nevada Testing Site (100 atmospheric and 828 underground).

The last atmospheric test conducted at the Nevada Test Site was Little Feller on July 17, 1962, followed thereafter only by underground tests. Needless to say, there wasn't much to see compared to the atmospheric tests. Vegas concentrated more on promoting jackpots and floor shows.

On average, 12 underground tests per year were conducted at the NTS. Shaft tests were the most common (representing over 90 percent of all tests conducted) and primarily occurred on Yucca Flat or Pahute Mesa.

The tests were assigned interesting code names, such as Upshot-Knothole, Grable, Annie, Plumbbob, Nougat, Seersucker, Mink, Priscilla. One name that was rejected was Ganja, part of the Mandrel series named after types of grasses. Test series and individual tests, sometimes the device itself, were code named for the sake of national security. Names reflecting rivers, mountains, trees, cheeses, wines, fabric, animals, famous scientists, insects, and Indian tribes were used to identify nuclear tests within a series.

The majority of the underground Nevada tests were conducted by drilling vertical holes about three feet in diameter down about 1,000 feet. This process took about two months to complete. The devices would be lowered into the hole followed by a cylindrical canister containing sensors that were linked by miles of cables to sensitive diagnostic instruments housed on the surface. The hole was then plugged with gravel, sand, and coal-tar epoxy. Test results were recorded during the tiny fraction of a second during and after detonation. Everything below the plug was destroyed, of course, and a crater was created on the surface as the hole collapsed. Viewed from above, portions of the Nevada Test Site today look like the surface of the Moon.

Speaking of craters, the Plowshare Program was begun in 1958 to develop peaceful uses for nuclear explosives, such as mass excavations and other engineering projects. Twenty-six Plowshare nuclear experiments were conducted at the Nevada Test Site. The most notable experiment was the 1962 Sedan 104-kiloton thermonuclear blast, displacing 12 million tons of earth and creating a crater 1,280 feet in diameter and 320 feet deep. The detonation was equivalent to an earthquake registering 4.75 on the Richter Scale. The program was terminated in 1975 "due to waning industrial interest and mounting public concern about the environmental consequences."

Elvis returned to Vegas to recoup his career in 1969 and died eight years later in Memphis. The nation's underground testing program concluded on Sept. 23, 1992 with the last test, Divider. All nuclear testing ended in 1992. Today, the United States is the only nuclear nation neither designing nor fielding new nuclear weapons. The emphasis is on modernizing the existing stockpile.

Not too far from the Vegas Strip on East Flamingo Road sits the National Atomic Testing Museum, which offers a wealth of information, photographs, models, replicas, and artifacts. Visitors learn about aboveground and underground testing, view a replica of the Control Point where countdowns were conducted, and experience a ground-zero theater simulation of an aboveground test. Efforts are being made to move the museum to downtown Las Vegas.

Sources: National Atomic Testing Museum; Nevada Highways & Parks; Department of Energy, Nevada Operations Office.

NUTS AND BOLTS

ROCKFORD ILL.

SOCK MONKEYS, SUICIDE, THE MAFIA, AND SANTA CLAUS

Rockford, the gritty city at the top of Illinois, the nuts and bolts capital of the world, is also home to an item much more cuddly—the venerable sock monkey. Some kids probably wanted to ask Santa Claus for a sock monkey for Christmas when he was due to arrive at Rockford's North Towne Shopping Center in late 1965. Jumping out of an airplane! Promotions said Santa would arrive at 12 noon from 1.5 miles in space!

The plan was for two parachutists—first an elf-like Santa's helper and then Santa himself—to bail out of a small aircraft at 2,600 feet and float down into the center's parking lot. All in front of 5,000 adoring children and their parents. Santa and his elf helper were both experienced skydivers, from Lake Geneva, Wisconsin. They were accompanied by a pilot, of course.

Santa's helper, dressed as an elf, jumped first. He had smoke canisters attached to his legs to make his descent more visible to ground observers. When he deployed his parachute it became tangled in the smoke canisters on his legs. He tumbled a thousand feet. He couldn't untangle the main chute so he deployed the emergency chute. Unfortunately, the emergency chute got wound up with the main chute, rendering them both useless. As the ground announcer hurriedly explained that the first jumper had been just a dummy without a parachute, the victim landed three blocks southwest of the mall in the backyard of an unoccupied residence. Horrified onlookers who realized what had happened knew there was no possibility of survival. The victim was pronounced dead on arrival at the hospital.

Up in the aircraft, Santa Claus witnessed the entire horrific episode.

"You're not going to jump now!" yelled the pilot. Santa replied, "I've got to. All those kids might get hysterical if they knew what happened." He jumped out of the plane and floated safely to the parking lot, where he exchanged places with a shopping center Santa, who met with the kids still at the scene. The skyjumping Santa rushed to the hospital.

The victim was a skydiving instructor and veteran of more than 1,000 jumps. He taught parachute classes and had performed the Santa Claus jump several times. He likely packed his own chute. The Santa impersonator was also an accomplished jumper and had performed at a college homecoming in Whitewater, Wisconsin several days earlier.

Years later, a witness who said he was six years old at the time recalled, "Everyone was outside in the parking lot waiting for Santa to arrive. Then the radio DJ said over the PA system, 'Everyone look to the sky, Santa Claus is on his way,' so we counted down and sang Santa Claus is Coming to Town. Then me and my brother saw a small red dot in the sky, then red and green smoke. Closer and closer it got to us, me and my brother were so excited. But just then when we thought he would soon land ... the DJ said loudly and in a frightening voice, 'Parents, please cover your children's eyes and please leave the area. Then my Dad and Mom covered me and my brother's eyes and moved us swiftly to the car and went home! I was totally confused."

Another witness recalled, "Santa came out of the plane, and I remember the red smoke bomb tied to him as he spiralled down, down, down. I didn't realize what happened at the time, just remember some screaming. Since Santa had flying reindeer and could go up and down chimneys, I just figured the laws of gravity didn't pertain to him, and he didn't need a chute. Mom grabbed up all of us and said now that we saw Santa's Helper, we were going to (another mall) to see Santa, but instead we went home."

Only two years later, at the North Park Shopping Center in Evansville, Indiana, a helicopter delivering Santa to a crowd of 1,000 kids and parents hit power lines and crashed, killing the Santa impersonator (not a skydiver) and the pilot. Electricity was knocked out to the northwest section of the city for three hours.

Each year there are roughly two dozen fatalities involving skydivers out of more than three million jumps, according to the United States Parachuting Association. During the 1970s, the number of fatalities was about twice as many as now.

In 1932, during the Great Depression, a local newspaperman in Mesa, Arizona decided it would be a terrific idea to have Santa Claus jump out of an airplane to greet adoring kids and their parents at the annual Christmas parade, instead of just arriving in a plane like the year before. A local pilot put him in touch with a stuntman, who agreed to wear a Santa suit and jump from a plane at 3,000 feet. He would land in a nearby field and then be escorted to the parade by the local constable.

When the day arrived, the newsman-promoter found the stuntman in a local bar way too inebriated to get into an aircraft much less jump out of one. He needed to come up with another plan quick. The promoter went to a local department store and persuaded the manager to loan him a mannequin, which he dressed in the Santa suit and added the parachute. The pilot would push the mannequin out of the airplane. Santa would float down to earth in the field, where the promoter would be waiting. He would put on the Santa outfit and ride into town, with nobody the wiser. Uh-huh.

Well, of course, the parachute rig did not deploy and scores of cheering children (the largest crowd in Mesa history) watched as Santa Claus plunged 3,000 feet to his untimely death. The promoter stuck to his plan and arrived by escort at the parade. The children were hysterical, their parents enraged, and one woman went into premature labor. The parade proceeded, but the mood was somber indeed. Ironically, parents went overboard in buying Christmas presents for their children, believing it would dampen their experience. The promoter gamely tried to portray the stunt gone awry as a miracle, that Santa could fall to the ground and then miraculously survive to greet the children. Most of the townsfolk didn't buy it. He was known as "the man who killed Santa Claus" and was eventually forced to move to Colorado.

Speaking of stunts and North Towne Shopping Center, one of the more unusual stunts used to promote various commercial interests was for some daring soul to be buried alive. The attraction was to see how long the underground man could stay submerged. In 1971, Raymond "Suicide" Hayes set a world's record for being buried alive. He spent 42 days buried in a 6 x 12 concrete vault 16 feet below the pavement of the Rockford shopping center. Hayes was described as a Hollywood stuntman, daredevil, race car driver, bootlegger, and boogie-woogie piano man. At age 14, he ran away from his North Carolina home to enlist in World War II. He was taken prisoner by the Germans, the youngest American POW. After the war, he ran moonshine for his father and uncle. Beginning at age 19, he went to Hollywood and performed stunts in 150 movies over 20 years. He built Anchorage, Alaska's first race car track and earned his nickname by flipping cars in mid-air. He set a world's record by driving a snowmobile 305 miles across frozen Lake Superior. He jumped from an airplane at 30,000 feet with no parachute (another jumper tossed him one in mid-air). Hayes also experienced another milestone during his Rockford stunt—he met his future wife, Luci Petrie. People could observe Hayes in his underground crypt through a "peep pipe" and talk to him. Luci talked to Hayes several times each day, and lowered him food and Jim Beam whiskey through another pipe. A 40-year-old widow at the time, Luci said that at first she thought Hayes was a crazy blowhard, but his Southern charm and silver tongue won her over. "That man could talk the devil out of his horns," she said in a Rockford newspaper article. She was his third wife; their marriage lasted 22 years. Inside the vault, Suicide received a long-distance telephone call from the Apollo 15 astronauts, but he thought it was a joke and hung up. He also got a telegram from President Richard Nixon, a Republican. Suicide tore it up because he was a diehard Democrat. Reportedly, Hayes returned to Rockford the next winter for a stunt in which he lived in a car parked on the frozen Rock River.

Suicide eventually wore out his body and retired from stunts to operate an auto parts store. He died of a heart attack at age 66.

Nobody is sure who was the first woman to construct a monkey doll out of red-heel work socks. Supposedly, during the poverty of the Great Depression, women would make dolls for their children out of old work socks worn out by their blue-collar husbands. In 1955, Nelson Knitting Co. of Rockford, which had just merged with Forest City Knitting Co., was awarded the patent for the design of sock monkeys. Sock monkey mania began when the company decided to include sock monkey instructions with every pair of their Red Heel socks.

Here's how the company obtained the patent. Two years before, Helen Cooke of Colorado received the patent and sued another dollmaker for enfringement. The dollmaker contacted Nelson Knitting in regards to the patent. The company knew of women who had created sock monkey dolls prior to 1953 and gathered documentation. Grace Winget of Rockford testified that she made a sock monkey for her grandson in February 1951. Presented with this and other evidence, Cooke settled with the dollmaker and sold the patent to Nelson Knitting for $750. The company also paid other women for the rights, including "a Tennessee woman who was given $1,000." Rockford became the official home of the sock monkey. The patent expired in the 1970s, so now sock monkeys can be manufactured by anyone. (Nelson Knitting never actually made the dolls; they included instructions with sales of their socks.)

The annual Sock Monkey Madness Festival in Rockford, first held in 2005, celebrates the original sock monkey that helped the Nelson Knitting Company win the patent and obtain the title "Home of the Sock Monkey." Additionally, there is a 7-foot-2-inch sock monkey named "Nelson" (after the founder of the factory, John Nelson). Nelson, the super-sized sock monkey mascot created by author/crafter Dee Lindner, was sewn out of 44 Rockford red-heeled socks. Guinness World Records states that the biggest sock monkey was made in 2015 by Jody Lewis, 27, of Great Britain. Made from 66 pairs of socks, the adorable doll stands ten-and-a-half feet tall.

John Nelson came to America from Sweden in 1852 when he was 22 years old. He met his future wife on the voyage over. Five years later, he settled in Rockford as a cabinetmaker. He invented a dovetailing machine to make furniture joints. Foolishly, he sold the rights to the machine for $100. During an 1865 trip to Chicago, he observed a demonstration of an automatic sock knitting machine. He thought he could do better. With the financial backing of two Rockford businessmen and the assistance of machinist William Burson, he worked on the design and three years later obtained a patent for an automatic sock knitting machine. By 1873 the two men had developed an automatic knitting machine that produced the first truly seamless sock. The men went their separate ways in 1877, and in 1880 the Nelson Knitting Co. was established. Then he developed a knitting machine for woolen mittens.

By the time of Nelson's death in 1883, Nelson Knitting was running 120 machines around the clock, with other machines in Paris, Austria, and Canada. The Nelson family formed Forest City Knitting in 1890 and two years later built the 200-room Nelson Hotel in Rockford. By the time the U.S. entered the world war in 1917, Rockford boasted five knitting companies which could produce 180,000 pairs of socks a day, including the Uncle Sam Sock. The knitting industry continued at full production through the war and even during the Great Depression. Across the country, socks made with a brown body and tan toe, heel and top were known as Rockfords. To stand out, Nelson Knitting began knitting red yarn into the heel, producing the Rockford Red Heel. Nelson sold through Montgomery Ward while Forest City sold through Sears. During World War II, Rockford's factories worked around the clock, producing 144,000 pairs of socks each day. In 1946, Rockford workers, 60 percent of them women, knit 24 million socks. One experienced knitter could run 25 to 30 machines at a time continuously for eight hours with no breaks. Lunch was consumed while watching the machines. In 1954 came the merger of Nelson and Forest City, and then sock monkey mania. In 1966, Nelson Knitting introduced the tube sock to the world, only the latest in a series of innovations dating back to the late 1800s.

But just like wornout socks, all good things must come to an end. In 1992, after 112 years of covering feet, Nelson Knitting went out of business. The first knitting company in Rockford was also its last.

During the 1940s and 1950s Rockford was known as the Screw Capital of the World for its production of hardware (nuts and bolts); the city was also the second largest producer of furniture. At the same time, Rockford was known as Forest City for its parks and abundance of large beautiful deciduous trees.

Times have changed, however. In the early 1960s, Dutch elm disease ravaged the tree population and nearly 50,000 trees were cut down. Economic conditions took a turn for the worse. In 2018, Rockford was named the 11th most dangerous city in the country and also was named the 16th worst city in the U.S. in which to live. Rockford's violent crime rate was higher than Chicago's; its unemployment rate highest in the state; and property values half the state's norm. Despite Rockford's ranking, the executive director of Transform Rockford, which aims to turn the city into a top 25 place to live by 2025, said the community is "making progress."

In popular culture, Rockford is probably best known as hometown to the rock band Cheap Trick, which formed in 1973, sold 20 million albums, and still tours internationally. They achieved superstardom with their 1979 album, *Cheap Trick at Budokan,* a recording of their live concerts in Japan. Their big hit, "I Want You to Want Me," might just as well apply to their hometown.

During Prohibition a hundred years ago, Rockford boasted its own lively Mafia scene, much like nearby Chicago, only much smaller and actually much more stable through the years. Paul Giovingo was a major bootlegger in Rockford, rivaled by Antonio Musso of Madison, Wisconsin, who wanted to muscle in on Rockford's liquor stills and speak-easies. In 1930, Giovingo's brother Joe was murdered. A federal investigation into bootlegging known as the Freeport Liquor Case put Paul Giovingo and Musso in the pen for a couple years. During that time, Jack DeMarco, a Giovingo associate, was shot dead in his own home shortly after being released from Leavenworth. On Feb. 13, 1933, Paul Giovingo, released from prison, was driving his Chevrolet coupe through Rockford when he was ambushed by hitmen armed with shotguns and revolvers. Now Musso had the power, backed by the Milwaukee and Chicago crime families. Another Rockford criminal who failed to appreciate Musso's ascendancy was Charles Kalb, the top local bookmaker who controlled gambling on a regional basis. Musso wanted to move in and gave warning to Kalb, who ignored him. On Dec. 21, 1937, Kalb was shot and killed in his vehicle during an ambush close to his home. His wife and his bodyguard survived the attack. Nobody was ever charged for the murder. Musso was the boss of organized crime in Rockford, a title he held for the next 20 years. In 1957 and in ill health, he sent his capo Joe Zammuto to the infamous crime syndicate meeting in Apalachin, N.Y., which was raided by local police. The following year, Musso died and his top capo Jasper Calo stepped up into the role. Zammuto had most of Rockford's rank-and-file behind him and persuaded Calo to step down after Calo's house was sprayed with bullets. Eventually, Calo, a wealthy man, retired to his native Sicily and died of natural causes.

Aragona Social Club, aka Saint Mary of Mercede of Aragona, Sicily Society.

The organized crime family in Rockford never numbered more than 20 to 30 "made" members at any one time, according to the FBI. Many of them were natives of Sicily, particularly the commune of Aragona. Operating in a low-key manner and with the blessings of the Milwaukee and Chicago syndicates, Zammuto's crime family prospered well into the 1970s. Their main meeting place was the Aragona Social Club, aka the Saint Mary of Mercede of Aragona Society, on Kent Street.

The infamous Pizza Connection investigation of the 1980s involved the Rockford crime family. The Sicilian-based mafia boss Gaetano (Tano) Badalamenti headed a massive heroin importation and distribution ring thought to have smuggled thousands of kilograms of heroin into the U.S. from Europe for years. Federal investigators found that several of the drug network's operatives and distributors were residing and working in the Rockford area, and were affiliated with the Zammuto family. Joe Zammuto died of natural causes in 1990 in Rockford.

Sources: Midway Village Museum; www.thenewyorkmafia.com; https://history.rockfordpubliclibrary.org/localhistory; U.S. Parachuting Association; Rockford Register Star.

When Duke lost the Rose Bowl
...at Duke Stadium

In 2021, due to the Covid-19 pandemic, the Rose Bowl, the "Granddaddy" of all college football bowl games, was not played at the Rose Bowl stadium in Pasadena, California; it was played at AT&T Stadium in Dallas, Texas. (Alabama beat Notre Dame and went on to defeat Ohio State in the championship game.)

But that's not the only time the game was moved. Back in 1942, due to paranoia following the attack on Pearl Harbor and the threat of further Japanese military aggression, the Rose Bowl, with Oregon State and Duke set to play, was moved from the West Coast to Durham, North Carolina, site of Duke University. The highly favored Duke Blue Devils were upset by the Oregon State Beavers, 20-16, in a game played under adverse weather conditions. The teams were tied 7-7 at halftime. Oregon State head coach Lon Stiner gave an impassioned halftime speech, interrupted by an inebriated fan looking to urinate in the Beaver locker room. The 1942 Rose Bowl was the only Rose Bowl victory for the Beavers and it's the only time the two programs have played each other. Duke head coach Wallace Wade and many of the game's players ended up fighting in World War II. Oregon State left guard Frank Parker saved the life of Duke backup quarterback Charlie Haynes in Italy after Haynes had been severely wounded. Parker carried Haynes on his back to an abandoned farmhouse to get medical attention. During the Battle of the Bulge, OSU right tackle Stan Czech shared some food with a fellow soldier who had not eaten in two days. Czech soon recognized the soldier as Coach Wallace Wade. Later, Czech was taken prisoner, escaped and recaptured, and spent six months in a POW camp. Oregon State's Gene Gray flew more than 30 bombing missions over Germany.

Sidenote: Following the 1961 season, Ohio State turned down an invitation to play UCLA in the Rose Bowl. The OSU faculty voted to reject the invitation because they thought academics should take priority over sports (besides, the Buckeyes had already beaten UCLA during the regular season). Ohio State students burned effigies of faculty members, broke windows, and marched downtown to the State Capitol. Coach Woody Hayes, of all people, brought calm by supporting the faculty vote even though he disagreed with it. "Football is not worth it," he said. Minnesota went to the Rose Bowl instead, and beat UCLA. Ironically, Hayes' successful career ended when he was fired for punching a rival player at the 1978 Gator Bowl.

Sources: The Chronicle, Duke University; Los Angeles Times; Bob Greene, Wall Street Journal.

Roadside Attraction
Space Shuttle Fuel Tank...Stranded

Sitting on a side street just off the Leonard C. Taylor Parkway, nestled among the dozens of dry-docked watercraft off Green Cove Springs on St. John's River in Florida, is a curious and difficult-to-miss historical object, a relic of the 20th-Century space program. The yellowish-orange cylindrical space shuttle external fuel tank sitting on its side fascinates the observer due to its size — 154 feet long (15 stories high if stood on end) and 28 feet in diameter. It weighs 37 tons empty, and when full holds half-a-million gallons (1.5 million lbs.) of super-cold liquid hydrogen and liquid oxygen.

The tank sits on a wheeled trailer by the side of the road, accessible to anyone interested enough to stop and gawk. Up close, an object so large and so smooth and brightly and evenly colored is difficult to comprehend. There is nothing to compare it with.

The contractor for the external tank was Lockheed Martin (previously Martin Marietta) in New Orleans, La. The tank was manufactured at the Michoud Assembly Facility in New Orleans, and was transported to Kennedy Space Center by barge. The 900-mile voyage usually took six days.

Launched with the space shuttle and two rocket boosters, the fuel tank was jettisoned ten seconds after main-engine(s) shut-off (8 minutes and 30 seconds into the flight and 70 miles high). The tank was destroyed while re-entering the earth's atmosphere. A total of 136 of the giant tanks were constructed.

The Green Cove Springs tank was the third and final test tank for the Space Shuttle Program and was used for structures/stress testing at NASA's Marshall Space Flight Center in Huntsville, Alabama, between 1977 and 1980. No longer needed, it was put on display at NASA's Stennis Space Center in Mississippi. In 1997, it was moved again to Kennedy Space Center (KSC) until 2013. After the space shuttle program ended in 2011, NASA began selling off surplus equipment. The Wings of Dreams Aviation Museum in Keystone Heights, Florida, won the rights to the surplus fuel tank. With the assistance of private volunteers, the relic was transported on a 200-foot barge and two

The Space Shuttle *Atlantis* at lift-off, with the huge fuel tank and two booster rockets attached. (NASA)

tugboats from Kennedy Space Center up the intercoastal waterway, through Jacksonville and south up the St. John's River to Green Cove Springs. Then it was supposed to be towed on land the final 55 miles to the museum in Keystone Heights. However, the logistical nightmare of having to close major highways, take down power lines and other cables, and road conditions in general prevented the movement of the gigantic object, which is probably visible from space (it certainly can be Googled on a satellite map). No aviation-related object that large has been moved on land since Howard Hughes moved his Spruce Goose, a gigantic eight-engine wooden cargo seaplane, from California to Oregon 80 years ago. The Spruce Goose flew only once.

The Military Museum of North Florida, a collection of artifacts from all services and all American wars, is just across the highway and worth a look. The actual space shuttle *Atlantis* (33 space missions) can be seen at Kennedy Space Center in Florida, but the external fuel tank there is only a replica.

TOUGHEN MEN FOR DIRTY WORK

WAR GAMES DANGEROUS BUT SAVED COUNTLESS LIVES

During World War II, Middle Tennesseans witnessed the second invasion of Yankees in less than 100 years when the U.S. 2nd Army conducted war maneuvers, sometimes known as war games, within a 22-county area. Between September 1942 and March 1944 nearly one million soldiers passed through the Tennessee Maneuvers area. The location was chosen for its resemblance to Northwest Europe — woods, hilly terrain, pastures and the Cumberland River (i.e., the Rhine) and its tributaries. Training men for war is rough, tough work, but it saves lives. Over and over again, men who had abhorred training exercises credited the training with saving their lives in the chaos of actual combat. "We are here," said Lieutenant-General Ben Lear, "to toughen the men for dirty work." General Leslie McNair, speaking at his field headquarters in June 1943, said, "Maneuvers are a dress rehearsal for the grim and dirty business. When the chips are down, lessons learned in Middle Tennessee will make the going easier from the beaches to Berlin."

Up until that point, the U.S. Army numbered less than 200,000 men, and the training regimen was less than satisfactory. Enlistees learned how to fight against tanks by throwing beer cans filled with sand (grenades) at quarter-ton trucks labeled with "I am a tank" signs.

In the summer of 1941, the area around Tullahoma was used by Major

General George S. Patton, Jr. to demonstrate the utility of a newfangled war machine — the tank. Patton's "Hell on Wheels" 2nd Armored Division journeyed northward from Fort Benning, Georgia, 400 vehicles in two columns, each 60 miles long. These were light to medium tanks, Stuarts and Lees, and armored half-tracks and staff cars.

Tank of 66th Armored Regiment overturned at a bridge, June 1941.

Many of the tanks were shipped by rail from Georgia to Tennessee. Prior to the exercises, Patton addressed his officers in no uncertain terms: "I want to bring to the attention of every officer here the professional significance which will attach to the success or failure of the 2d Armored Division in the Tennessee maneuvers." He went on to explain that some military officers considered the new armored divisions a waste of manpower and resources. "Therefore it behooves every one of us to do his uttermost to see that in these forthcoming maneuvers we are not only a success but such an outstanding success that there could be no possible doubt in the minds of anyone as to the effectiveness of the armored divisions. Bear this in mind every moment."

At that time, there were 77,000 troops in Middle Tennessee. And this was before the U.S. had officially gone to war. Patton's men were the Red Force. The Blue Force was the VII Corps under General Frederick Smith, who offered a $25 bounty for the capture of Patton, who immediately offered a $50 reward for the capture of any Blue Force commander.

On June 20, 1941, Patton personally led his 2nd Armored Division "Hell on Wheels" across several fords of the Duck River, moving in the dark without lights and under radio silence, quickly surrounding and defeating his opponents in the Manchester vicinity. He led the Second Armored Division from Cookeville down Highway 70 to Lebanon, crossed the Stones River at Walter Hill, then headed southwest toward Shelbyville, where his force captured the 30th Infantry. Patton paid out his bounties. In another exercise, Patton's force accomplished its two-day objective in eight hours. Plainly, Patton and his men and machines had successfully demonstrated the effectiveness of armored infantry.

Of course, it wasn't all success. At one point, a tank ran into the townhall of tiny Bell Buckle to avoid colliding with a farm truck. To the press, Patton later explained, "The damn city hall was not on the map!"

Patton and the 2nd Division would move on to the most famous Louisiana Maneuvers, and then northwest Africa for Operation Torch in November 1942.

Camp Forrest (named for Confederate cavalry commander Nathan Bedford Forrest) was one of the largest training camps in the U.S., with never fewer than 50,000 troops there; and overall processed about one million soldier trainees. The camp was a training area for infantry, artillery, engineers, and signal organizations. It also served as a hospital center and temporary encampment area for troops during maneuvers. Tullahoma grew from 1,000 to 100,000 during the war, putting a tremendous strain on infrastructure.

The staging of the 2nd Army war maneuvers in 1942 over such an extensive area of terrain occupied by civilians in the normal course of their lives was probably unprecedented. The military received nearly unanimous consent from private property owners to proceed. Roads were clogged and worn, fences torn down, livestock scattered, and a noisy chaos inflicted on a bucolic countryside. Courts were established to determine compensation for damages, and military police pushed to work overtime. Amenities built for the soldiers included service clubs, guest houses, library, post exchanges, post office, hospital, religious services, theaters, showers, Red Cross, and Army Emergency Relief facilities. Recreation facilities included swimming, archery, tennis, a sports arena, and a 9-hole golf course.

Camp Forrest was also used to train U.S. Army Rangers, the special forces of the times. The 2nd and 5th Ranger Battalions were formed in 1943, and later led by Major J.E. Rudder and Major Max Schneider respectively. Army Rangers practiced climbing the cliffs at Carthage and Hunter's Point. They later trained in Florida, New Jersey, and Great Britain. The Army Rangers led the invasion of Nazi-occupied Europe on D-Day, gaining fame by scaling the sheer cliffs of Point du Hoc under enemy fire.

For the 1942-44 series of war maneuvers, headquarters were set up at Cumberland University in Lebanon where Cordell Hull, secretary of state and a Tennessee native, had attended law school. Nashville was the principal railhead. Supply depots were situated in Murfreesboro and Chattanooga, containing half-a-million rounds of .30-caliber blank rifle ammunition, 9,000 smoke anti-tank mines, 30,000 dummy anti-tank mines, 120,000 blocks of dummy TNT, plus tons of food stuffs and fuel for the mechanized divisions. Over the hills and valleys, farmland and small towns, Blue and Red armies engaged in weekly strategic "problems," with troops moved in and out

according to a calendar of "phases" that lasted about four weeks apiece.

Typical tasks included attacks from Manchester northward to Gallatin, assaults on bridges over the Cumberland River, crossing the Cumberland in assault boats and pontoon bridges, an armored attack on the railhead at Hartsville, an attack from Donelson to Smith and DeKalb counties, a counterattack from Chestnut Mound to Donelson, and the defense of Murfreesboro against Ranger attacks.

The Battle of the Cumberland began on Sept. 17, 1942. The local Gallatin newspaper reported, "The Blue Army penetrated red defenses of Gallatin and occupied a portion of the town from Hancock's tobacco barn and the bridge at Kelly's Tire Company, around Ed Mac's, up Muddy Run, and as far into town as Trousdale Place." Members of the 502nd Paratrooper Infantry Regiment, Co. H. set a record by marching 145 miles in 57 hours.

In addition to the weekday maneuvers, on weekends roughly 100,000 young soldiers looking for recreation converged on Nashville and other smaller towns. Maneuvers paused at noon on Thursday or Friday, when a light plane would fly over the mock battle lines, sounding a siren. Nashville officials recognized the need to create diversions for the enthusiastic young men. The USO and American Red Cross set up facilities; movie theaters and cafes were crowded; schools opened gyms for weekend dances; churches opened lounges. The Grand Ole Opry drew record crowds. The Nashville police directed many soldiers to the state capitol to sleep on the grounds. Of course, such a concentration of young men on the loose drew crowds of eager young women, including those for hire.

According to a survey of WWII sites in Middle Tennessee: "Gallatin hosted about 6,000 soldiers during the first weekend in October 1942, and the Service Center that the Army established at Trousdale Place reported that 1,700 free baths had been provided over the weekend with another 4,000 during the week. There were six dances for the soldiers, and the Daughters of the American Revolution with the United Daughters of the Confederacy hosted a buffet for over 700 men. The American Legion fed another 500, and the Service Center placed 240 soldiers in private homes for Sunday dinner. Many families took soldiers home with them after church services."

After the war, some men came back and married local girls that they had met. Some took their new brides home and some stayed in Tennessee.

Military officials asked civilians not to talk, feed, or house soldiers during the weekdays of the war maneuvers, a request that was generally ignored. Troops camped in close proximity to farmhouses during the exercises, and many families fed soldiers while they were in the area. Farmers allowed soldiers to sleep in the barns as long as they didn't smoke. As payment, soldiers often left behind money and outdated commodities that they were otherwise told to bury (coffee, sugar, lemons, apple butter, flour, condensed milk, and canned fruits). Local children would resell candy bars to the soldiers or shine their shoes for a small fee.

Soldiers visited the home of 99-year-old Frank Ross, the last living Confederate soldier in Rutherford County, where he sat in his gray uniform and regaled them with tales of the Civil War. One of the most brilliant, and relatively bloodless, campaigns of that war was the 1863 Tullahoma Campaign, which culminated about the time of the Battle of Gettysburg (and thus has not received the attention it deserved), forcing the Confederate army out of Tennessee. The weather was rainy throughout the campaign, forcing one Federal soldier to translate the town's Indian name — Tulla means mud, and homa means more mud.

Although the war games caused a lot of commotion and chaos, the benefits outweighed the costs, for the soldiers and the local residents. A resident of Coffee County said, "I'm sorry they're leaving because we never had a show around here like this before. They were fine looking boys and sure did themselves up proud."

The last phase of the Tennessee Maneuvers began on Jan. 31, 1944; further exercises were suspended due to the urgent need for replacement troops in Europe.

Congress approved $5 million in funding to repair damages after 10,000 claims had already been settled. Nine battalions of engineers were in Middle Tennessee in April 1944, repairing roads and bridges. The 1800th Battalion was composed of American engineers of German, Italian, and Japanese ancestry often mistaken for prisoners-of-war. Residents were surprised when the battalion musicians gave a public concert at Castle Heights Military Academy in Lebanon.

While the war maneuvers in Middle Tennessee only simulated war, the exercises themselves could prove deadly. Ten civilians and 268 soldiers died during the maneuvers, the vast majority due to traffic accidents. Twenty men died in 1942 when a truck skidded off an overpass in Nashville, and many others died in crashes involving jeeps, motorcycles, halftracks, and tanks. Two tanks fell off a pontoon bridge while crossing the Cumberland River during a night crossing in October 1942, and six men died. Drownings were common. Men died from lightning strikes, explosions, weapons accidents, and natural causes such as heart attacks. There were three homicides, two resulting in court-martial death sentences. A tornado in Lebanon killed one soldier when the high wind picked up a fighter aircraft and dropped it on the barracks in which the soldier was sleeping.

Perhaps the most tragic loss of life during the maneuvers came at the very conclusion, the last stormy night of maneuvers, March 22/23, 1944. The men of Co. B of the 104th Infantry Regiment, 26th (Yankee) Division, were tasked with crossing the swift, overflowing Cumberland River at Averitt's Ferry northeast of Lebanon. The river was about 50 yards wide. Crossing rivers and streams in all sorts of conditions was one of the most crucial training tasks for the soldiers to master. They would be called upon to do so in Northwest Europe. Despite the reservations of his subordinates, Lt. Col. Dwight T. Colley, a decorated World War I veteran, made the decision to go ahead and cross the rapidly flowing river.

At 2:00 am, the first of two pontoon boats, each outfitted with a small outboard motor, entered the waters, struggled against the current, then disappeared from view downstream. The second boat was loaded with 23 soldiers dressed in full combat gear and a heavy 60mm mortar. Struggling against the current, the outboard motor conked out. The boat took on water, causing the occupants to shift to one side of the boat and capsizing it. The heavily laden soldiers were swept away with the current. Two managed to climb out onto the riverbank to safety. The other 21 men drowned. They were aged 19 to 28, all from the Northeast except one from Texas and one from West Tennessee. The rescue effort involved U.S. Coast Guard vessels from Nashville, army personnel and civilian officials, and Civilian Air Patrol pilots. The boat was found four days later 27 miles downstream. The first body was found two days after that, 200 yards downstream. On April 13, one victim was found at the foot of Broadway in Nashville, 80 miles from the accident site. A subsequent Army investigation found no officers negligent.

On April 4, 1944, a memorial service for the victims was held at Fort Jackson, South Carolina, on the parade grounds with the men of the 104th Regiment at attention.

This was not the first time the raging Cumberland River had claimed the lives of Yankees trying to cross to the other side. On May 5, 1863, near Somerset, Kentucky, the 27th New Jersey Infantry Regiment was on a two-day expedition and reached the river at 3:00 p.m. after a 13-mile hike. The previous night had been stormy, swelling the river. The regiment was commanded by Capt. John T. Alexander.

One of the survivors testified later:

"To prevent the boats being washed down by the current, two ropes were stretched across like a letter V, the two uniting in one on the opposite shore. The means of propelling us consisted of six men placed in the bow of the boat, who would grab the rope, pull, let go and grab again. The upper rope was used by the infantry, while the artillery and transportation train were carried over by the lower boat. All the companies with the exception of parts of companies B, C, and L had passed over without accident. Fifty or sixty men were carried over at each trip. Captain Alexander was in command of company L. The boat that contained these companies had reached within forty feet of the opposite bank when the men at the bow lost hold of the rope and could not regain it. The boat started downstream, driven by a rapid current. The men became panic-stricken and rushed to the opposite end of the boat, which caused it to sink, and in less time that it has taken me to write this account the whole boatload was swept by the lower rope into the rapid Cumberland. Those who could swim were seized by the death grasp of those who could not swim. It was an awful sight. May God spare me from being again a spectator of such a scene. The men had on their cartridge boxes, filled with 60 rounds, and were fully armed, and equipped with tents, overcoats, blankets, etc., which hindered many from saving themselves. I saw Captain Alexander and the Orderly Sergeant go down. Company B lost three men, Company C nine, and companies L and A twenty."

Thirty-three men drowned in the river; only five bodies were recovered, including Captain Alexander. One survivor waited a day on the riverbank to recover bodies but Confederates were on the opposite side. The five were buried in the Mill Springs National Cemetery.

At Camp Forrest, William Northern Field, an airbase covering 3,325 acres, was used as a training site for crews of multi-engine B-24 Liberator bombers of the Army Air Force. During the war, Smyrna Airport became home to the B-24 Pilot Transition Combat Crew Training School. In the latter half of 1942, 700 pilots rotated through the school.

Apparently crewmen from other countries were included in the training. King Peter II of Yugoslavia visited seven of his countrymen at the base and flew in a B-24 to Nashville to dine at the Andrew Jackson Hotel. The unexpected visit prompted a female employee at the hotel to hastily fashion a Yugoslavian flag in honor of his highness.

Thirty-two Consolidated B-24 Liberator heavy bombers were housed at the base, which included five hangars and a control tower. Crews would be tested for accuracy after they dropped sand bags filled with just enough black powder to create a bang on the ground. Training in the four-engine behemoths could be nerve-wracking and in some cases deadly. In May-July 1943 and May 1944, six B-24 Liberator bombers crashed in separate incidents near the Smyrna field, killing a total of 30 crew members. Several other flyers were killed during maneuvers in accidents involving light aircraft. In July 1942, Major General Frank Mahin of Iowa, commander of the 33rd Division, was killed in a plane crash.

Nearly 75 years later, on June 2, 2016, one of the Blue Angels Navy Flight Demonstration Squadron crashed near Smyrna Airport while practicing for the Great Tennessee Airshow. Captain Jeff Kuss (USMC), age 32, of Durango, Colorado, was flying No. 6 Super Hornet fighter jet when it crashed and took his life.

Capt. Kuss was a decorated pilot who had accumulated more than 1,400 flight hours and 175 carrier landings. He was a graduate of Navy Fighter Weapons School, also known as TOPGUN. Captain Kuss served in Afghanistan and earned the Strike Flight Air Medal and the Navy and Marine Corps Achievement Medal during his time in the military. He joined the Navy Blue Angels in September 2014, and flew as Opposing Solo for the 2016 team.

Shortly after takeoff, Kuss initiated a Split-S maneuver, but he was flying too fast and too low, according to the subsequent Navy investigation. He called in over the radio that he had turned off his afterburners, but he hadn't. After his initial climb, Kuss attempted to half-roll the jet while inverted, then go into a descending half-loop, so that he would end up in the opposite direction at a lower altitude. But because his afterburners were still on, Kuss went into the split at 184 knots, when it should have been 125 to 135. He was also flying at 3,200 feet — 300 feet below the required altitude for the maneuver. A low cloud ceiling of 3,000 feet likely contributed to his initiating the maneuver below the normal altitude.

The Captain Jeff Kuss USMC Memorial was dedicated on June 9, 2018 with ceremonies featuring distinguished officials and a F/A-18C Hornet flyover by

Captain Kuss' former Marine Fighter Attack Squadron 312 (VMFA-312), the Checkerboards. The centerpiece of the memorial is a Blue Angel McDonnell Douglas F/A-18C Hornet on permanent loan from the National Naval Aviation Museum in Pensacola, Florida, weighing 21,600 lbs. Captain Kuss is buried in Durango.

Twenty-seven Blue Angels pilots have been killed in air show or training accidents. Through the 2017 season, there have been 261 pilots in the squadron's history, giving the job a roughly 10 percent fatality rate.

Their six demonstration pilots fly in more than 70 shows at 34 U.S. locations annually. Each year, an estimated 11 million spectators watch the Blue Angels at air shows. Since their formation, they have flown for more than 260 million spectators.

_{Much of the material used in this article can be found in Woody McMillin's impressive research book, "In the Presence of Soldiers: The 2nd Army Maneuvers and Other World War II Activity in Tennessee"; www.navytimes.com; "Thank God It's Only Maneuvers!" thesis, Joshua G. Savage, East Tennessee State University.}

Building the Bomb

CLINTON ENGINEER WORKS

At the dawn of the 20th Century, as legend goes, a deranged mountain man wandered into a tiny crossroads town in Bear Creek Valley in East Tennessee after weeks of going missing and related the vision he had experienced: "Bear Creek Valley someday will be filled with great buildings and factories, and they will help toward winning the greatest war that ever will be. And there will be a city on Black Oak Ridge. Big engines will dig big ditches, and thousands of people will be running to and fro. They will be building things, and there will be great noise and confusion and the earth will shake. I've seen it. It's coming."

Whether John Hendrix was a mystic or got himself into a bad batch of moonshine is debatable. He died in 1915 and never witnessed the coming of the big machines in Bear Creek Valley, but he was right. During World War II, in a race with Nazi scientists, the U.S. government built a secret city in the hills and valleys, along with several huge manufacturing plants designed to enrich the radioactive uranium that would be the fuel for the first atomic bomb used in wartime. The thousands of Tennesseans who lived in Oak Ridge, Happy Valley, and Knoxville and who worked at the X-10, Y-12, K-25, and S-50 plants for about two years never knew what they were producing until they heard the news on August 6, 1945, that a Boeing B-29 four-engine bomber named *Enola Gay* had dropped the Little Boy atomic bomb on Hiroshima, Japan, producing a huge mushroom cloud and killing 70,000 inhabitants outright.

Three days later, another B-29 dropped the Fat Man plutonium bomb on Nagasaki, Japan, and five days after that the Japanese surrendered and World War II was over. Operation Downfall, the planned invasion of the Japanese home islands which would have resulted in the deaths of hundreds of thousands of young American soldiers and up to two million Japanese, was cancelled.

At the beginning of the war, the possibility of Adolf Hitler possessing atomic weapons was unthinkable. As it turned out, Nazi Germany, whose scientists had pioneered research into nuclear fission, had given up trying to produce an atomic bomb of their own. Fortunately, many of their scientists had fled the country before the war and went to work for the Allies. Astonishingly, it took the Allies only six years from the time that nuclear fission was discovered to figure out how to fabricate a bomb, enrich enough uranium and plutonium to arm it, test it, package it, and deliver it. The odds against success were very high indeed.

In January 1939, German chemists Otto Hahn and Fritz Strassman proved that the nucleus of an uranium atom could be split by bombarding it with neutrons, i.e., uranium could be used to produce nuclear fission. Hungarian physicist Leo Szilard discovered that the fission of uranium could result in a chain reaction and tremendous release of energy, enough to produce a highly explosive bomb. Fearing the oppression of Nazi Germany and its efforts to produce an atomic weapon, Szilard escaped to the United States, where he worked for the Allies.

In August 1939, about one month before the German invasion of Poland and the start of World War II, the famous scientist Albert Einstein sent a letter of concern to President Franklin D. Roosevelt (the letter had been written by Szilard, a former student of Einstein's), which read in part:

"Some recent work by E. Fermi and L. Szilard…leads me to expect that the element uranium may be turned into a new and important source of energy in the immediate futuret…it may become possible to set up a nuclear chain reaction in a large mass of uranium, by which vast amounts of power and large quantities of new radium-like elements would be generated… This new phenomenon would also lead to the construction of bombs…"

In early 1940, two exiled German scientists living in Great Britain declared that an atomic bomb could be constructed from a few kilograms of uranium-235. Uranium-235 is the very rare isotope of uranium-238, which is found abundantly in nature (only 0.7 percent of uranium is isotope 235).

"Girls of Atomic City" at the Y-12 plant gate.

In order to make an atomic bomb, effective ways of enriching uranium and producing uranium-235 had to be developed.

In November 1941, Roosevelt was informed by scientists that a uranium bomb was feasible. Ten days later, the Japanese attacked Pearl Harbor and, subsequently, Hitler declared war on the United States. On Dec. 18th the S-1 Project was dedicated to building an atomic bomb. In January 1942, Roosevelt gave the green signal. On Aug. 13, 1942, the Manhattan Project (named for the site of its original headquarters) was created by the U.S. Army Corps of Engineers, with General Leslie Groves in command of the Manhattan Engineer District. Groves, a capable engineer, was well-suited to supervise this massive project. In addition to being highly motivated and energetic, his previous supervisory experience had been building the Pentagon, the world's largest office building, near Washington, D.C.

General Groves authorized the immediate purchase of 1,250 tons of high-grade uranium ore. The Belgian firm Union Minière had shipped the ore to the United States in 1940 from its Belgian Congo mine in order to remove it from Germany's reach. It had been sitting for two years out in the open in 2,000 steel drums on Staten Island. The other main source of uranium ore (called pitchblende) was Canada.

On Dec. 2, 1942, Fermi and other scientists produced the first operating nuclear reactor on the squash courts underneath the University of Chicago's football stadium.

Los Alamos, New Mexico was chosen as the site for the fabrication of the atomic bomb, which was known as "the device." Hanford, Wash. would be the site for the production of radioactive plutonium. Bear Creek Valley in East Tennessee, bordered on the north by Black Oak Ridge and on the other three sides by the Clinch River, was chosen as Site X, known as the Clinton Engineer Works (Clinton, Tenn. was a nearby small town), for the production of enriched uranium. (It was also used to test a plutonium-producing pilot plant.) There was plenty of electricity available from Tennessee Valley Authority (TVA) plants, especially at Norris Dam, plenty of fresh water, nearby railroad facilities, and an abundant workforce in nearby Knoxville.

At one point, the operations at Clinton Engineer Works (CEW) consumed more than one-tenth of all the electricity produced in the United States. On the other side of Knoxville, the ALCOA plant was also devouring vast amounts of energy to produce aircraft-grade aluminum. Within months, the world's largest steam power plant (at that time) would be built at the west end of the CEW reservation.

When U.S. Senator Kenneth McKellar of Tennessee, powerful chairman of the Senate Appropriations Committee, was consulted by President Roosevelt as to the feasibility of raising huge amounts of funds for the project, McKellar reportedly replied, "Yes, it can be done, and Mr. President, just where in Tennessee are we going to locate that thing?"

CEW encompassed 60,000 acres of wooded hills and valleys in both Anderson and Roane counties (each lost about one-eighth of their acreage). The reservation was 17 miles long and seven miles wide; the plants could be located in separate valleys so as not to affect each other in the case of explosion or other catastrophe. The 3,000 residents of communities such as Scarboro, New Hope, Elza, and Wheat were notified that they had a few weeks to permanently relocate so that the government could use their land for the war effort (they were financially compensated). As one might imagine, this coersion created some ill feelings among the landowners. "Many viewed Oak Ridge as a highly secret, probably wasteful, and certainly enormous federal project," according to historian Charles W. Johnson of the University of Tennessee-Knoxville.

Security and secrecy were the buzz words at CEW. The northern perimeter of the reservation was bordered with a high fence, and seven guarded gates were erected. All personnel inside the reservation were required to wear ID badges at all times, except inside their homes. Workers were told not to discuss their assignments with others; most didn't really know much about the purpose of their work anyway, except that it was vital to the war effort. Billboards warned about "loose lips" and emphasized the work ethic required to win the race with the Huns (Germans). Workers were told to explain their work to inquiring minds as putting the holes in doughnuts and the lights on lightning bugs. Government agents lived and worked among the CEW employees. Those who talked too much or asked too many questions found themselves out of a relatively high-paying job.

No security system can be perfect. George Koval, codename Delmar, was a radiation safety technician, giving him access to areas at each of the sites where the various materials for the atomic bombs were being worked. Koval was born an American citizen of Russian parents in 1913, in Sioux City, Iowa. He traveled with his family to Russia in 1932 and obtained advanced degrees from the Mendeleev Institute of Chemical Technology in Moscow. He received Soviet citizenship in 1939 and was then recruited by the GRU as a Soviet spy. Reportedly, due to information about Oak Ridge supplied by Koval, the USSR rejected enriched uranium as fuel for an atomic bomb and concentrated on plutonium. He fled the U.S. in 1949. Koval was unknown as a spy until 2007, when he was posthumously awarded a Hero of the Russian Federation, the highest honorary title bestowed on a Russian citizen, by Russian President Vladimir Putin.

The new town of Oak Ridge (which did not appear on any map until 1949) was established at the eastern end of the reservation, away from the plants, with construction beginning in the spring of 1943. Skidmore, Owings, and Merrill were the city designers; Stone and Webster of Boston were the main contractors. Land had to be cleared, roads built, along with sanitary water plants, water and sewer lines, and power lines. Workers built schools, theaters, churches, drugstores, barbershops, and grocery stores. One ingredient that was in constant, vast supply was mud. Several main east-west roads ran through the town, with all north-south streets named for states and in alphabetical order. Workers were racially segregated as was the local custom at the time. (Later, in 1955, Oak Ridge would be one of the first Southern cities to integrate their schools.) High-ranking inhabitants occupied "cemestoes" or homes prefabricated in bonded cement and asbestos. Single people lived in apartments or one of 98 dormitories. Others were housed in trailers, barracks, plywood huts, and "Victory Cottages." About 6,000 trailers from all over the eastern U.S. were brought in and located around central bathhouses. The plywood huts were 16x16, with a wood floor, undersized studs, plywood sheeting, and a potbellied stove. By the summer of 1944, Oak Ridge boasted a population of 66,000, the fifth largest city in Tennessee. By the end of the war, the city grew to 75,000. In addition to workers housed on-site, the sixth-largest bus system in the country hauled in workers from Knoxville.

The main production facilities at CEW were as follows:

- X-10, later known as the Oak Ridge National Laboratory, housed the Graphite Reactor, built as a test project for the production of plutonium.
- Y-12, located in the valley just south of Oak Ridge, used the electromagnetic separation process to enrich uranium.
- K-25, located at the far western end of the reservation, used the world's largest structure for its gaseous diffusion process of enriching uranium. A second similar plant, K-27, was built following the war.
- S-50 used the thermal diffusion process. This plant, built after the others, was located near K-25 and the power plant.

The Graphite Reactor at ORNL is the world's oldest surviving reactor (shut down in 1963), a tourist attraction and a National Historic Landmark. The reactor, so named because of the large amounts of graphite used, was built as a pilot reactor to demonstrate the viability of building large reactors to produce plutonium for a bomb. Construction at X-10 by E.I. du Pont de Nemours and Co. began on Feb. 1, 1943 and was completed in eleven months. Three thousand workers built 150 buildings at a cost of $12 million. Materials included 30,000 cubic yards of concrete and four million board feet of lumber. Workers ate their meals in a cafeteria housed under a striped circus tent; an old schoolhouse served as office space.

The reactor is a 24-foot-square graphite cube surrounded by seven feet of high-density concrete. Forty-four thousand aluminum-clad uranium slugs measuring 1x4 inches were fitted into 1,248 channels running through the cube, also known as "the Pile." The initial power production of 1,000kW was eventually increased to 4,000kW. The reactor "went critical" on Nov. 4, 1943, with Fermi at the controls. Within two months it was producing a third of a ton of irradiated uranium a day. Two months later, the first few grams of plutonium were produced. Testing was successful, and much larger production reactor facilities were built at Hanford, Wash. The Graphite Reactor produced the first electricity from nuclear energy. It was the first reactor used to study the nature of matter and the health hazards of radioactivity. And for years after the war, it was the world's foremost source of radioisotopes for medicine, agriculture, industry, and other purposes. After the war, ORNL was used to produce radioisotopes needed to unravel the human genetic code, diagnose and treat cancer, trace phosphorus in fertilizers, and many other applications. According to pioneering scientist Alvin Weinburg, postwar ORNL director, "Science couldn't continue today without (radioisotopes). If God has a golden book and writes down what it is that Oak Ridge National Laboratory did that had the biggest influence on science, I would guess that was the production and distribution of radioisotopes."

Building the bomb—time was of the essence. There was no confirmed way to enrich uranium, so three production processes were built and tested during the war, with design and construction accomplished as the projects progressed. It was a supremely stressful process. The three methods of enriching uranium (separating bomb-grade U-235 from U-238) were electromagnetic, gaseous diffusion, and liquid thermal diffusion. A fourth method, centrifical separation, was utilized only in the postwar years.

The electromagnetic separation process was invented by Noble Laureate Ernest O. Lawrence at the University of California-Berkeley and used a customized mass spectrometer known as a calutron (CALifornia University cycloTRON). In doing so, Lawrence's staff was using the world's most powerful magnet. In basic terms, the calutrons vaporized and electrically charged the uranium atoms or ions, which were then pulled around a semi-circular track by powerful magnets. Due to their difference in weight, the two isotopes of uranium would land at different spots on the receiver plates, where they accumulated and then were collected. Shaped like the letter "D," the calutrons were arranged side-by-side in an oval resembling and called a "racetrack." Although theoretically sound, the technology proved to quite vexing.

Construction began on the first Y-12 building on Feb. 18, 1943. There were nine calutron buildings—five Alpha and four Beta. The Alpha machines enriched the uranium by about 15 percent, then the Betas enriched it to the point of weapons-grade material. The formal start of mass operations was Jan. 27, 1944. Duties were assigned to the following six large companies:
- Research and development by University of California-Berkeley Radiation Lab

- Parts and equipment by Westinghouse Electric and Manufacturing Co.
- Electrical equipment and controls by General Electric
- Magnets by Allis-Chalmers Co.
- Plant construction by Stone & Webster Engineering Co.
- Plant operation by Tennessee Eastman Co.

The Y-12 plant housed 1,152 calutrons in nine major buildings that covered an area equal to 20 football fields. The plant comprised a total of 268 buildings at a cost of $500 million. Within one four-week period, 63 rail cars of concrete blocks were unloaded there. In eleven weeks, 1,585 rail cars of lumber arrived. One hundred and twenty-eight carloads of electrical equipment arrived in a two-week period. Most of these materials had to be warehoused before being used for construction.

When first turned on, the magnets in the calutrons, weighing 20 tons each, pulled nails out of the walls and wreaked havoc on metallic objects. Strange magnetic phenomena were observed. Workers on the catwalk above the powerful magnets could feel the tug of the magnetic field on the nails in their shoes. The metal innards of watches would be smashed together by the magnetic fields. Workers had to use non-ferrous tools. One worker carrying a metal plate got too close and was pinned between the heavy plate and the magnets. Told to shut off the magnets, the supervisor replied, "The war is killing 300 people an hour. If we shut down the magnet, it will take days to get re-stabilized and get production back up again, and that's hundreds of lives. I'm not going to do that. You're going to have to pry him off with two-by-fours." Eventually, the trapped worker was freed without serious injuries.

Tennessee Eastman hired and trained young women just out of high school to operate the calutrons. Sitting on stools in front of tall control panels, the "cubicle operators" would patiently monitor the controls and adjust rheostat knobs to run the calutrons efficiently. Eventually, some operators could control up to four cubicles at one time. Many of the engineers thought that they could do a better job than the women. Tennessee Eastman agreed to a one-week competition between engineers controlling the calutrons on one side of the aisle and the young ladies on the other. The females won the competition hands down. Turns out the engineers couldn't leave the controls alone, constantly fiddling with them. The women were much more patient. Every now and then an engineer would fiddle around on his own and claim to get more production out of the machine, but then it would take hours to recalibrate the controls and get the machines running at normal speed.

Due to the wartime shortage of copper, silver was used for the electrical conductors for the calutron magnets. Accordingly, 14,700 tons of silver valued at $300 million was borrowed from the U.S. Treasury at West Point, N.Y. The silver bars were shipped to New Jersey to be fashioned into billets and then shipped to a copper plant to be rolled into three-inch-wide strips, less than an inch thick and 40 feet long. Then the strips went to Allis-Chalmers in Milwaukee, where they were wound around giant steel spools insulated with wood and shipped to Oak Ridge. After the war, most of the silver was shipped back to the Treasury but not all. Four calutrons continued to operate using silver conductors (70 tons worth) as they were used to produce isotopes other than uranium for medical uses. The last of the silver was returned to the U.S. Treasury in 1970. It was determined that, after 28 years of handling and usage, only 0.0036 of one percent of the silver was unaccounted for.

"The development and use of the calutron to produce enriched uranium for the first atomic bomb that was exploded in warfare, and then to produce the full spectrum of separated isotopes for uses in peacetime, is the greatest example of beating swords into plowshares in the history of humankind," according to pioneering physicist William E. Parkins.

The K-25 plant, operated by Union Carbide at the far western end of the reservation, was built at a cost of $500 million and employed 12,000 workers. Construction began in June 1943. The U-shaped structure, consisting of 50 four-story buildings, was the largest enclosed structure in the world at the time, measuring 1,000 feet wide and half-a-mile long and covering 44 acres. Innovative foundation techniques were required to avoid setting thousands of concrete piers to support load-bearing walls. K-25 housed 1,000 diffusers in which highly corrosive uranium hexaflouride gas was pushed through barriers with microscopic openings. Producing these micro-fine barriers was problematic, and the process wasn't proven until March 1945. The process of pushing gas through barriers had to be reproduced many, many times to be effective. The pores of the barrier had to be less than one millionth of an inch, uniform in size, could not become plugged, and had to be rugged enough to withstand high-pressure uranium hexafluoride gas. Although the actual design is still classified, it is believed that the barrier was composed of sintered nickel powder. In all, the plant used 3,122 diffusers containing almost 5.2 million barrier tubes measuring 6,659 miles in length. In addition, the corrosive gas attacked the grease in the seals; therefore, new gas-tight pump seals had to be created. The material used for the seals came to be known after the war as Teflon. The plant was automated but still required 9,000 workers employed in three shifts.

Because the K-25 plant was eleven miles away from the town of Oak Ridge, another housing facility nicknamed Happy Valley was created with a population of 15,000. Half of the workforce commuted daily to the site.

A second gaseous diffusion plant, K-27, was constructed in April 1945 and came online in 1946, making the original process obsolete. This plant, along with others built at Paducah, Ky. and Portsmouth, Ohio, produced enriched uranium for Cold War atomic weapons and as fuel for nuclear-powered submarines. The Oak Ridge plant was shut down in 1964 after 20 years of faultless operation. Today, only the Paducah facility is operational; the enrichment process is now accomplished by gas centrifuges.

Due to operational difficulties, neither the Y-12 nor the K-25 plant was producing the desired amounts of bomb-grade uranium, and the clock was ticking. In a brilliant move, it was decided that enriched uranium from the K-25 plant would be used as feeder material for the Y-12 plant, greatly increasing the yield.

One of the other projects at CEW was building the world's largest steam-powered electrical generating plant on the Clinch River near the K-25 plant. Steam was a major ingredient in the thermal diffusion process for separating uranium as devised by Phillip Abelson of the U.S. Navy. Due to the excess of steam from the generating plant, General Groves ordered the H.K. Ferguson Co. to construct the S-50 thermal diffusion plant there. The facility consisted of 2,142 columns 40 feet high. Uranium from the S-50 plant, enriched only two percent, was fed into the K-25 gaseous diffusion process, which achieved 23 percent enrichment. After this was processed at Y-12 by the calutrons, the U-235 was 84 percent pure.

Fifty kilograms (about 110 pounds) of U-235 were collected during the first year of Oak Ridge operations. The first shipment of enriched uranium-235 (200 grams at 12 percent enrichment) was delivered to the scientists and fabricators at Los Alamos in March 1944. Air travel was deemed too risky. The precious enriched uranium would be transported from Oak Ridge to Los Alamos by teams of two armed plainclothes couriers riding the rails.

Before leaving Oak Ridge, the precious uranium tetraflouride, sometimes known as green salt, was placed in gold-lined nickel cylinders the size and shape of a coffee cup. Two containers were placed in a reinforced suitcase that was strapped to the arm of an Army lieutenant dressed in a business suit. Couriers transporting the uranium packages inside the reservation were told to ride in a car between CEW buildings. "If you got run over, it would be a mess to dig up the ground to recover the uranium, but in a car it would all be in one place," the officer in charge explained. Along with other armed military policemen dressed like salesmen, the couriers were driven in a Chevrolet sedan with Tennessee plates to Knoxville, where they boarded the "Southland" passenger train to Chicago. At the Windy City train station, the suitcase was transferred to another team of "traveling salesmen" who took the green salt on the Sante Fe "Chief" train to the Lamy way station in the New Mexico desert, where they were met by a car from Los Alamos. The delivery system worked without a hitch.

The scientists and engineers were fairly confident that the uranium bomb would work. They tested the plutonium bomb design on July 16, 1945 in New Mexico with the first nuclear test blast, which was successful.

The Little Boy uranium bomb was ten feet long, 28 inches in diameter, and weighed 8,800 pounds. Along the length of the interior of the bomb, a chemical explosive was used to propel a slug of uranium down a barrel into another mass of uranium, creating a nuclear chain reaction. Approximately 600 milligrams of mass (0.02 ounces) were converted into energy equaling 13 to 18 kilotons of TNT.

Over two years of production, thousands of scientists, construction workers, and operators labored with several complex and unproven technologies, using massive quantities of electrical energy generated by East Tennessee dams and reservoirs, to painstakingly produce a relatively miniscule amount of radioactive material that would be fabricated into a package shipped by boat to a tiny island in the South Pacific, secured with the blood of thousands of U.S. Marines and sailors, so that a highly sophisticated four-engine bomber could deliver the package to the Empire of the Rising Sun and force the fanatical and racist military regime, responsible for the deaths of millions of Asians, to contemplate the unthinkable—unconditional surrender. And it worked.

Although the war was over, production continued at Oak Ridge as the United States needed atomic weapons to counter the Soviet Union during the Cold War. In 1949, the security gates at Oak Ridge were torn down and the town was placed on road maps. A year later, the population of Oak Ridge, with the highest per capita number of PhDs in the world, had dropped to 30,000 residents, where it remained for the next 50 years. The city was incorporated in 1959.

Today, ORNL's High Flux Isotope Reactor, constructed in the 1960s to produce transuranic isotopes, is still the Western world's sole supplier of californium-252, an isotope instrumental in the exploration of new energy resources, medical therapy, and the detection of environmental pollutants and explosives in luggage.

It is also the site of the world's most powerful supercomputers. Frontier is a $600 million project expected to come online in 2021. The goal for Frontier is a speed of 1.5 quintillion calculations per second—up to 50 times faster than today's top supercomputers. Since 2005, Oak Ridge National Laboratory has deployed Jaguar, Titan, and Summit, each the world's fastest computer in its time.

Sources: Richard Rhodes, The Making of the Atomic Bomb; Manhattan Project archives; The Oak Ridger; American Museum of Science and Energy; Oak Ridge Historian D. Ray Smith, The Oak Ridger, 2014.

Nineteen Fifty Sixty

Atlas Shrugged, filter cigarettes, kiloton yield, transistor radio, horn-rimmed glasses, nylon runs, Tom Collins, *Twilight Zone,* bridge game, the Twist, homemade chex mix, cross-your-heart bra, harvest yellow and avocado green, *Popular Mechanics,* Wiley Coyote, switchblade, stomach ulcers, Camelot, hang ten, Jack Benny, the divorcée next door, capri pants, The Lettermen, hi-fi system with reel-to-reel tape deck, pro bowling, juvenile delinquency, Schlitz beer, McDonalds, Bozo the Clown, drive-in movies, school of design, vacation in Paris, TV dinners, *West Side Story,* Cadillac fins, turtleneck sweater, FM radio, Captain Kangeroo, Mouseketeer, hightop sneakers, green savings stamps, International Year of the …, lawn darts, Marvin Gardens, cheap Japanese junk, Stingray, electric can openers, radioactive fallout, VW Beetle, uppers, root beer stands, Chubby Checkers, Westerns, Yogi Bear, private detectives, Edsel, Disneyland, crewcuts, sit-ins, Nat King Cole, malt liquor, hootenanny, Saturday Night Specials, color television, *The Jetsons,* Tennessee Ernie Ford, communications satellites, Technicolor, *As the World Turns,* Soupy Sales, heavyweight prizefight, *House of Wax,* 45 records, hot rods and dragsters, beatniks, Elmer Fudd, bongo drums, Jack Paar, fallout shelters, uranium prospecting, chinchilla farms, computer programmer, Herb Alpert, 10-speed bicycle, Honda motorcycles, Datsun, portable dishwashers, Dick Tracy, electric toothbrush, DDT, the Pill, berets, Boris Karloff, slot cars, TV repairman, *Dragnet,* Niagra Falls, martini lunch, Mayberry, bra burning, station wagons, St. Lawrence Seaway, Mercury Seven, View-Master, Dick Clark, Boeing 707, Etch A Sketch, Mitch Miller, slide projector, Cassius Clay, *The Flintstones,* horizontal hold, polio vaccine, steel beer can opener, payola, Adam Clayton Powell, Richard Speck, *Saturday Evening Post,* Burl Ives, fluoridation, *The Sound of Music…*

Don't know Bach from Beethoven? Can't tell a Van Gogh from a Vermeer? Did Cortes discover the Pacific or was that de Soto? Nod off during high school history? Do Pretty Boy and Baby Face look the same? Here's a handy, concise guide to distinguish your Dutch Masters from your Spanish Conquistadors. Your composers from your conductors. Your backside from a hole in the ground.

Know Your Composers:

Johann Sebastian Bach (1685-1750) German. Prolific composer of Baroque-period sacred and secular music, including instrumental and vocal music, and hundreds of cantatas. His style is characterized by counterpoint and harmonies, including Italian and French rhythms, forms, and textures.

Joseph Haydn (1732-1809) Austrian. A court musician and friend of Mozart, Haydn developed Classical chamber music and was known as the "father" of the symphony and the string quartet. He tutored Beethoven. A central characteristic of Haydn's music is the development of larger structures out of short, simple musical motifs. Short in stature, he was beloved, and like

Mozart he enjoyed practical jokes.

Wolfgang Amadeus Mozart (1756-1791) Austrian. A child prodigy and master of the Classical style, Mozart composed more than 600 works of symphonic, concertante, chamber, operatic, and choral music. He loved elegant clothing, billiards, practical jokes, and a fondness for scatological humor. He wrote sacred music for Emperor Joseph II and dance music for the masses.

Ludwig van Beethoven (1770-1827) German. His three "periods" of works span the transition from the classical period to the romantic era. Suffered from deafness. Piano virtuoso. He composed symphonies, chamber music, piano sonatas, and one opera. Perhaps best known for *Symphony No. 5*.

Franz Schubert (1797-1828) Austrian. Gifted as a child but dead at age 31, Schubert produced more than 600 secular vocal works, seven complete symphonies, sacred music, operas, incidental music and a large body of piano and chamber music in the late Classical-early Romantic period. He greatly admired Beethoven.

Frederic Chopin (1810-1849) Polish. He was a virtuoso pianist of the Romantic era who wrote primarily for solo piano. Like Schubert, he was a child prodigy who died young. His innovations in style, harmony, and musical form, and his association of music with nationalism were influential throughout and after the late Romantic period.

Richard Wagner (1813-1883) German. His compositions, mostly opera, are notable for their complex textures, rich harmonies, and orchestration. His life involved political exile, turbulent love affairs, poverty, and repeated flight from his creditors. Decades later, Adolf Hitler was greatly influenced by Wagner's nationalism and anti-Semitism.

Franz Liszt (1811-1886) Hungarian. A composer, virtuoso pianist, conductor, music teacher, arranger, and organist of the Romantic era. He is widely regarded as one of the greatest pianists of all time. He was also a writer, philanthropist, and Hungarian nationalist.

Johannes Brahms (1833-1897) German. A virtuoso pianist, Brahms composed for symphony orchestra, chamber ensembles, piano, organ, and voice and chorus. His works were highly structured with deeply romanctic motifs. He is considered both a traditionalist and an innovator. He was a religious agnostic.

Gustav Mahler (1860-1911) Austro-Bohemian. A Romantic composer, he acted as a bridge between the 19th century Austro-German tradition and the modernism of the early 20th Century. A Jew who converted to Catholicism. A great operatic conductor.

George Gershwin (1898-1937) American. Pianist and painter. Composed with his brother Ira. He wrote both classical and popular music. Best known for *Rhapsody in Blue* and the opera *Porgy and Bess*. Composed film scores in Hollywood. Died young of brain tumor.

Jerome Kern (1885-1945) American. He composed musical theater and popular music. One of the most important American theater composers of the early 20th century, he wrote more than 700 songs, used in more than 100 stage works, including such classics as *Ol' Man River, Smoke Gets in Your Eyes* and *The Way You Look Tonight*.

Irving Berlin (1888-1989) American. Russian native, his family came to the U.S. when he was five. Best known for writing *White Christmas* and *Alexander's Ragtime Band*. Wrote in the American vernacular. Died at age 101.

Aaron Copland (1900-1990) American. Known as the ultimate American composer, he wrote open, slowly changing harmonies in the vernacular, evoking the pioneer spirit. He wrote *Appalachian Spring, Fanfare for the Common Man,* and *Third Symphony*. From the 1960s onward, Copland's activities turned from composing to conducting.

Leonard Bernstein (1918-1990) American. He composed in many styles, including symphonic and orchestral music, ballet, film and theater music, choral works, opera, chamber music and works for the piano. His best-known work is the Broadway musical *West Side Story*. He was a big fan of Mahler. He was a public personality during the turbulent 1960s.

Know Your Explorers:

Erik Thorvaldsson (950-1003), aka Erik the Red, Norse. He founded the first settlement in Greenland. His son, Leif Erikson (970-1020), born in Iceland, is thought to be the first European to set foot on continental North America (Newfoundland), 500 years before Columbus.

Marco Polo (1254-1324) Venetian. Merchant who traveled to Asia on the Silk Road and wrote to Europeans about the culture and workings of the Eastern world. Reaching China, he was appointed an emissary by the Kublai Khan. His books inspired Columbus and other explorers.

Vasco da Gama (1460-1524) Portuguese. He was the first European to reach India (1498) by sea, around Africa, initiating the spice trade routes between the West and the Orient. He was appointed Governor of India. Portugal maintained a commercial monopoly for several decades. It was not until a century later that other European powers, first the Dutch Republic and England, later France and Denmark, were able to challenge Portugal's monopoly and naval supremacy in the Cape Route.

Christopher Columbus (1451-1506) Genoan. Sailing for the King and Queen of Spain, he made four voyages to the Western Hemisphere, thinking he had found a western sea passage to the East Indies. He first landed in the Bahamas, then Cuba and Hispaniola. Colombia the country and the District of Columbia are named for him. Popularly known as the discoverer of the New World. Buried in Seville Cathedral.

Amerigo Vespucci (1454-1512) Italian. He sailed two voyages in 1499-1502, first for Spain and then for Portugal, reaching what is now Brazil in the New World. His writings greatly popularized the Age of Discovery although historians still debate the exact nature of his voyages. Cartographers began to apply the Latin word America to the land mass known as the New World.

Hernando Cortes (1485-1547) Spanish. The first and perhaps best known conquistador, Cortes led an expedition that caused the fall of the Aztec Empire, defeating the native leader Montezuma, and brought large portions of what is now mainland Mexico under the rule of the King of Castile in the early 16th Century. At times, he fought charges of mutiny under the Spanish governor's rule.

Hernando de Soto (1500-1542) Spanish. A conquistador, he traveled to Mexico and Peru, but is best known for leading the first European expedition deep into the territory of modern-day U.S. (through modern Florida, Georgia, Tennessee, Carolinas, Alabama, Mississippi, and most likely Arkansas). He is the first European documented as having crossed the Mississippi River. His men fought with natives; he died of fever on the west bank of the river and was buried there.

Juan Ponce de Leon (1474-1521) Spanish. Explorer and conquistador known for leading the first official European expedition to Florida and serving as the first governor of Puerto Rico. He landed along Florida's east coast, then charted the Atlantic coast down to the Florida Keys and north along the Gulf Coast, perhaps as far as Charlotte Harbor. Legend says he was searching for the Fountain of Youth. He was wounded in Florida and died of his wounds in Cuba.

Francisco Pizarro (1471-1541) Spanish. A conquistador, his expeditions led to the Spanish conquest of Peru. He captured and executed the Incan emperor Atahualpa at the Battle of Cajamarca in November 1532. Three years later he founded the city of Lima.

Vasco Nunez de Balboa (1475-1519) Spanish. A conquistador, he is best known for having crossed the Isthmus of Panama to the Pacific Ocean in 1513, becoming the first European to lead an expedition to have seen or reached the Pacific from the New World. He was arrested and beheaded by the Spanish governor of Panama, allegedly for disloyalty to the Crown.

Ferdinand Magellan (1480-1521) Portuguese. He organized the Spanish expedition to the East Indies, 1519-22, resulting in the first circumnavigation of the globe, which was completed by Juan Sebastián Elcano. He sailed Cape Horn, around South America, to the Philippine Islands, where he was killed during the Battle of Mactan. He named the Pacific Ocean. The Portuguese regarded Magellan as a traitor for having sailed for Spain. In Spain, Magellan's reputation suffered due to the unflattering accounts of his actions given by the survivors of the expedition.

Frances Drake (1540-1596) English. Most famously known for his circumnavigation of the world in a single expedition (1577-80) and was the first to complete the voyage as captain while leading the entire expedition. He claimed what is now California for the English and inaugurated an era of conflict with the Spanish on the western coast of the Americas. The Spanish branded him a pirate. He participated in the 1588 defeat of the Spanish Armada. He was buried at sea in full armor in a lead-lined coffin off the coast of Puerto Rico.

Henry Hudson (1565-1611) English. In 1607-08, Hudson made two attempts to find a rumoured Northeast Passage to China via a route above the Arctic Circle. In 1609, he landed in North America on behalf of the Dutch East India Company and explored the region around what is now New York City.

Looking for a Northwest Passage to Asia, he sailed up the Hudson River, and laid the foundation for Dutch colonization of the region. On his final expedition, Hudson became the first European to see Hudson Strait and the immense Hudson Bay. In 1611, his crew mutinied and cast Hudson, his son, and seven others adrift; they were never seen again.

Know Your Painters:

Sandro Botticelli (1445-1510) Italian. Master of the Early Renaissance, known for his religious subjects (*Madonna and Child*), mythology (*The Birth of Venus*), and portraits.

Leonardo da Vinci (1452-1519) Italian. Renaissance genius. Innovative painter, best known for *Mona Lisa* (the smiling woman) and *The Last Supper*. Developed techniques of perspective and authentic landscapes. Worked in Milan and Florence.

Michelangelo (1475-1564) Italian. Contemporary of da Vinci. One of the greatest painters and sculptors. His style resulted in Mannerism. Known for painting the ceiling of the Sistine Chapel (took four years to complete), and sculpting the statue of David. Full name is Michelangelo di Lodovico Buonarroti Simoni.

Raphael (Raffaello Sanzio da Urbino) (1483-1520) Italian. Prolific but died at age 37. Extremely influential. Clarity of form, ease of composition, and human grandeur characterize his style. Buried in Pantheon in Florence.

Rembrandt van Rijn (1606-1669) A Dutch master of the 17th Century, prolific painter, draughtsman, and printmaker. Known for portraits. *The Night Watch* is one of his most famous works.

Johannes Vermeer (1632-1675) Dutch. Specialized in domestic interior scenes of middle-class life. Obscure but rediscovered in 1800s. Reputation has become greatly enhanced.

John Whistler (1834-1903) American. Worked in Britain. Leading proponent of "art for art's sake." Most famous work was *Whistler's Mother*, sometimes known as the Victorian *Mona Lisa*.

Paul Cézanne (1839-1906) French. Bridged gap between Impressionism and

Cubism. Known for his panes of color and short brushstrokes. Like most artists, he displayed several different periods of work.

Claude Monet (1840-1926) French. Founder of Impressionism. Documented French countryside. Master of the effects of light and atmosphere. Known for *Water Lilies*.

Vincent Van Gogh (1853-1890) Dutch. Bold colors and brushwork. Most famous for *The Starry Night*. Troubled man, died of suicide. Cut off his own ear, although nobody knows why.

Henri de Toulouse-Lautrec (1864-1901) French. One of best known painters of Post-Impressionism along with Cézanne and van Gogh. Recorded details of bohemian Parisian lifestyles. Stunted in size, alcoholic. Died at age 36.

Henri Matisse (1869-1954) French. Leader of Fauvism (emotional use of dissonant colors) and along with Picasso developed new techniques of painting in the 20th Century.

Pablo Picasso (1881-1973) Spanish. Co-founded the Cubist movement and collage. Experimented in many genres but best known for abstract, surreal modern art. Controversial; temperamental womanizer.

Jackson Pollack (1912-1956) American. Alcoholic, volatile reclusive. Major artist of abstract expressionism. He poured and splashed paint onto a canvas on the floor. Died in one-car wreck.

Georgia O'Keeffe (1887-1986) American. Known as the Mother of American Modernism for her landscapes of New Mexico and depictions of flowers and animal skulls. Independent spirit, she died at age 98.

Grant Wood (1891-1942) American. Known for paintings of rural Midwest, most notably *American Gothic*. Active artist in a large number of media. *American Gothic* depicts a Midwestern farmer with pitchfork and his spinster daughter (not his wife).

Norman Rockwell (1894-1978) American. Painter, illustrator, and chronicler of popular American lifestyles. Known for covers of *Saturday Evening Post* (*Four Freedoms*). He is often criticized as being idealistic and sentimental. Lived in Stockbridge, Massachusetts.

Thomas Hart Benton (1889-1975) American. Known for Regionalism and stylized depictions of Midwestern life. Painted many murals, especially during the Depression. Wrote autobiography, played the harmonica.

Salvador Dali (1904-1989) Spanish. Surrealist artist known for bizarre images (eggs, melting clocks, and symbolism), eccentric personal behavior (cape, walking stick, long waxed moustache), and penchant for publicity. He also worked in a variety of other visual arts.

Know Your Outlaws and Gangsters:

Wild Bill Hickok (James B. Hickok, 1837-1876) was a frontier soldier, scout, lawman, gambler, and showman known for his many gunfights and his wild tales. An Illinois native and fugitive from justice at age 18, he headed west to Kansas and Nebraska, sometimes serving as a lawman. Despite his outlandish claims, Hickok reportedly killed six or seven men in gunfights. In 1876, Hickok was shot and killed while playing poker in Deadwood, Dakota Territory. His cards at the time are known as the Dead-Man's Hand — two pair, black aces and eights (his hole card is disputed). Not to be confused with William Frederick "Buffalo Bill" Cody (1846–1917), operator of a traveling Wild West Show.

Jesse James (1847-1882) was the controversial leader of the James-Younger Gang of bank and train robbers. During the Civil War, he and brother Frank were pro-Confederate guerrillas in Missouri and Kansas. The gang botched a bank robbery in Northfield, Minn. They persisted for several more years before James was shot and killed by associate Robert Ford, a new recruit who hoped to collect a reward.

Billy the Kid (Henry McCarty, 1859-1881) was an outlaw and gunfighter of the Old West who killed eight men before he was shot and killed at the age of 21. He was also known as William H. Bonney. He was charged with killing the sheriff and one deputy during the Lincoln County War in New Mexico. He was shot and killed on July 14, 1881 by Sheriff Pat Garrett.

John Wesley Hardin (1853-1895), the son of a Methodist preacher, killed his first man at age 15. By the time he was sent to prison eight years later, he claimed to have killed 42 men, but authorities attribute 27 deaths to him. Hardin was known to tell tall tales about himself. Within a year of being released from prison in 1894, he was shot and killed in an El Paso saloon.

Butch Cassidy (Robert LeRoy Parker, 1866-1908) led the notorious Wild Bunch of bank and train robbers in the Old West during the last decade of the 19th Century. Pursued by Pinkerton agency detectives, Parker and accomplice Harry Alonzo Longabaugh, aka the Sundance Kid, fled the country with Longabaugh's girlfriend Etta. They traveled to Argentina and then Bolivia, where they reportedly perished in a shoot-out with army soldiers in November 1908.

Al Capone (1899-1947), aka Scarface, was the crime boss of Chicago, 1932-39, a bootlegger during Prohibition, but sent to prison for tax evasion at age 33. A native of New York City, Capone lived the high life in the Windy City until the St. Valentine's Day Massacre brought public and law enforcement attention to the city's seven gangs. He served eight years in prison and died at age 48 in Florida.

Baby Face Nelson (Lester J. Gillis, 1908-1934) robbed banks and helped John Dillinger escape prison in Indiana. He was first arrested at age 12 for accidentally shooting a playmate. He ran with Chicago's Touhy Gang, and began robbing banks and invading homes in 1930. Associates called him Jimmy. He stood only 5-4 and weighed 133 lbs. On Nov. 27, 1934, Nelson was shot and killed in Barrington, Ill., during a gunfight with FBI special agents.

Machine Gun Kelly (George Kelly Barnes, 1895-1954), a Memphis native, kidnapped oil tycoon Charles Urschel in 1933 and collected a $200,000 ransom. Kelly was a bootlegger who used a Thompson submachine gun. He was arrested for the kidnapping the same night Dillinger escaped from prison. It was the first major case solved by J. Edgar Hoover's FBI. Kelly spent his last 21 years in Leavenworth.

John Dillinger (1903-1934) led his gang in robbing 24 banks and four police stations during the Great Depression. He escaped from jail twice. He murdered an East Chicago, Ind. policeman. He courted publicity, and the press loved him. He was known as Public Enemy No. 1. Dillinger was shot and killed by federal agents while leaving the Biograph Theater in Chicago on July 22, 1934. And no, his supposedly gigantic male member is not on display at the Smithsonian.

Pretty Boy Floyd (Charles A. Floyd, 1904-1934) robbed banks in the Western and Central states during the 1930s and gained popularity because he would also burn mortgage documents during the heists, freeing homeowners from their debt (possibly a myth). Following Dillinger's demise, Floyd became Public Enemy No. 1. He was killed in October 1934 in Ohio during a gunfight with the FBI. Like Nelson, he despised his nickname.

Ma Barker (Kate Barker, 1873-1935) was the mother of several criminals who ran the Barker-Karpis gang of Midwestern bank robbers. She traveled with her sons during their criminal activities, but it is uncertain as to her criminal involvement. She and one of her sons were killed during a shoot-out with the FBI in Florida in January 1935.

Bonnie and Clyde (Bonnie E. Parker and Clyde C. Barrow) led their gang through the American heartland robbing banks, stores, and gas stations during the early 1930s, gaining national notoriety. They reportedly murdered nine police officers and four civilians. In May 1934, they were killed in a police ambush in Louisiana in which officers fired about 130 rounds. She was 23; he was 25.

PEACEFUL SUCCESSION OF AMERICAN POWER

DESPITE ASSASSINATIONS, RIOTS, MUDSLINGING, DIRTY TRICKS, RECOUNTS, IMPEACHMENT, DEATH BY ILLNESS AND POLITICAL SHENANIGANS

Contrary to popular belief, the United States of America is a relatively old nation, guided by a supreme written law, the U.S. Constitution, and continual peaceful succession of power by officials and parties. Back in the 1770s, the thirteen British colonies declared their independence, won the war, tried but rejected the Articles of Confederation, then drew up the U.S. Constitution, which was ratified by the required number of new states. The chief executive, the President, was chosen by the Electoral College. At first, members of the Electoral College, chosen by the states, cast two votes. The highest vote-getter became President; the second highest became Vice-President. This was later changed to voting for a political party ticket consisting of one person for President and one person for Vice-President.

There have been 45 Presidents. One (Cleveland) served two non-consecutive terms. One served more than two terms (Roosevelt). Fifteen served two full terms (Truman literally didn't but close enough). Nine became President without being elected. Four Presidents were assassinated (Lincoln, Garfield, McKinley, and Kennedy) and their VPs replaced them (Johnson, Arthur, Roosevelt, and Johnson, respectively). Four Presidents died of natural causes (Harrison, Taylor, Harding, Roosevelt), replaced by their VPs (Tyler, Fillmore, Coolidge, and Truman). One President resigned (Nixon), replaced by VP Ford. Three Presidents have been impeached by the House (Johnson, Clinton, Trump), but none convicted by the Senate. Ten incumbent Presidents failed to win re-election (Adams, Quincy Adams, Van Buren, Cleveland, Harrison, Taft, Hoover, Ford, Carter, Bush). Several incumbents declined to run again for various reasons. Five Presidents won the Electoral College vote but lost the popular vote (Jackson, Hayes, Harrison,

Bush, Trump).

The President is officially elected by the members of the Electoral College. At first, the electors were chosen by the state legislatures, but later all the states gave the franchise to the citizens. The electors (there are now 538) meet at a specified date in December at their state capitals to cast their votes.

Back in the day, the Secretary of State was considered to be the logical successor to the sitting President (of course, he had be elected). Both Henry Clay and William Jennings Bryan unsuccessfully ran three times for President.

George Washington (1789-1797, Independent) The Electoral College unanimously elected him President following the ratification of the U.S. Constitution. John Adams got the next largest number of votes and was elected Vice-President. The election of 1792 produced basically the same results. After two terms, Washington voluntarily retired to his home at Mount Vernon to the astonishment of kings, despots, dictators, and emperors around the world.

John Adams (1797-1801, Federalist) beat Thomas Jefferson in 1796 in a very close election. Jefferson became VP even though he was of a different party.

Thomas Jefferson (1801-1809, Democratic-Republican) handily beat Adams in 1800 following Adams' single term. Jefferson won re-election by beating Chas. C. Pinckney by a wide margin.

James Madison (1809-1817, D-R) beat Pinckney and George Clinton handily and then won re-election against DeWitt Clinton.

James Monroe (1817-1825, D-R) beat Rufus King in a lopsided election in 1816. He won re-election in a landslide victory against John Quincy Adams.

John Quincy Adams (1825-1829, D-R) became President over Andrew Jackson, who won the popular vote, due to what Jackson called the Corrupt Bargain. Adams was elected by Congress because neither Adams nor Jackson won the minimum required number of electoral votes. Powerful Congressman Henry Clay, who had been one of the presidential candidates, threw his support to Adams, reportedly in exchange for political favors.

Andrew Jackson (1829-1837, Democrat) roundly beat single-termer Adams in the rowdy 1828 election, which featured all sorts of slanderous accusations and rumors. Jackson would serve two terms, easily besting Clay in 1832.

Martin Van Buren (1837-1841, D), Jackson's hand-picked successor, won election over William Henry Harrison, a Whig, and several others.

William Henry Harrison (1841, Whig) defeated Van Buren's re-election bid by claiming that he, Harrison, had been born in a log cabin, among other assertions. Quite elderly, Harrison died after only one month in office.

John Tyler (1841-1845, Whig) was Harrison's vice-president and strongly asserted his claim to the office after Harrison's death although there was much debate about the proper succession procedure. Tyler was disowned by his own party and declined to run for election in 1844.

James K. Polk (1845-1849, D) beat perennial candidate Clay in the 1844 election by 65 electoral votes despite barely besting Clay in the popular vote. Polk vowed to serve only one term and kept his promise.

Zachary Taylor (1849-1850, Whig), a Mexican War hero, beat Lewis Cass and Van Buren in 1848. He served little more than a year before dying of illness, thrusting his VP Millard Fillmore into office.

Millard Fillmore (1850-1853, Whig) served out the rest of Taylor's term and did not run in 1852, becoming one of several Presidents not elected to office on their own.

Franklin Pierce (1853-1857, D) handily beat Mexican War hero Winfield Scott in 1852 but only served one term, having failed to be re-nominated by his party.

James Buchanan (1857-1861, D) won in 1856 against John C. Fremont, the Republican Party's first candidate, and Fillmore. He honored his pledge to serve only one term.

Abraham Lincoln (1861-1865, Republican) won the 1860 election with 180 Electoral votes against John Breckinridge (72), John Bell (39), and Stephen Douglas (12). His election resulted in the secession of Southern states and eventually the Civil War. Four years later, Lincoln handily beat one of his former generals, George McClellan, during a wartime election. Three months into his second term, Lincoln became the first President to be assassinated. VP Andrew Johnson assumed office.

Andrew Johnson (1865-1869, D) was unpopular, especially with Congress, which impeached him and came within one vote in the Senate of convicting him. He did not run for re-election.

U.S. Grant (1869-1877, R), Civil War hero, beat Horatio Seymour 214-80 in 1868 and won re-election handily over Thomas Hendricks and three other candidates four years later.

Rutherford B. Hayes (1877-1881, R) and Samuel Tilden won 185 and 184 electoral votes respectively. Tilden got more popular votes. Hayes was elected President by Congress via the controversial Compromise of 1877, which ended Reconstruction in the South.

James Garfield (1881, R) beat out fellow Civil War officer Winfield Scott Hancock in a close election in 1880. Six months later, he was assassinated by a gunman. VP Chester Arthur became President.

Chester Arthur (1881-1885, R) served out Garfield's term and did not run for election due to ill health.

Grover Cleveland (1885-1889, D) beat James Blaine in a very close 1884 election.

Benjamin Harrison (1889-1893, R) defeated Cleveland's re-election bid in another close election (Cleveland won the popular but not the electoral vote).

Grover Cleveland (1893-1897, D) won back his place in the White House by defeating Harrison's re-election bid and became the only President to serve non-consecutive terms. Populist James Weaver got 22 electoral votes.

William McKinley (1897-1901, R) beat William Jennings Bryan in a fairly close election revolving around tariffs and monetary policy (gold vs. silver). In 1900, he beat Bryan again, by an even wider margin, but he was assassinated about one year into his second term.

Theodore Roosevelt (1901-1909, R) became President when McKinley was shot and killed. He won re-election by handily defeating Alton Parker.

William Howard Taft (1909-1913, R), Roosevelt's hand-picked successor, beat Bryan by 321-162 electoral votes. He ran for re-election in 1912 but won only 8 votes.

Woodrow Wilson (1913-1921, D) won a highly contended election against two former Presidents—Roosevelt and Taft. He beat Roosevelt 435-88, and in 1916 won a fairly close decision against Charles E. Hughes.

Warren G. Harding (1921-1923, R) prevailed over James Cox 404-127 and won 7 million more popular votes than Cox. He died two-and-a-half years later of a heart attack (some historians speculate that his wife poisoned him due to his extramarital affairs).

Calvin Coolidge (1923-1929, R), Harding's VP, became President and easily won re-election in 1924 against John Davis and Robert LaFollette.

Herbert Hoover (1929-1933, R) won election in 1928 against Alfred E. Smith, 444-87. Blamed for the Great Depression, Hoover was soundly beat for re-election.

Franklin D. Roosevelt (1933-1945, D) won the 1932 election over Hoover by a margin of 472-59. He won re-election three more times as he guided the U.S. through the Depression and World War II. He defeated Alfred Landon, 523-8, in 1936; Wendell Wilkie by 449-82 in 1940; and Thomas Dewey by 432-99 in 1944. Roosevelt served only three months into his fourth term before dying of natural causes.

Harry S Truman (1945-1953, D), Roosevelt's little-known VP, assumed the office following FDR's death. Against all odds, he won re-election over Dewey and Strom Thurman (States Rights Party) in 1948.

Dwight D. Eisenhower (1953-1961, R), hero of World War II, beat Adlai Stevenson for President in 1952 by 442-89. Four years later, he defeated Stevenson again, by 457-73.

John F. Kennedy (1961-1963, D) beat Eisenhower's VP, Richard Nixon, in 1960 in one of the closest elections in history. Two-and-a-half years later, Kennedy was assassinated.

Lyndon B. Johnson (1963-1969, D) became President following Kennedy's death and easily won election on his own in 1964, defeating Barry Goldwater, 486-52. Bogged down by the Vietnam War, LBJ declined to run for re-election.

Richard M. Nixon (1969-1974, R) won a highly contested election in 1968, 301-191, over Hubert Humphrey. Third-party candidate George Wallace captured 46 electoral votes. During the campaign, Robert Kennedy (D) was assassinated. In 1972, Nixon easily won re-election in a lopsided affair over George McGovern, 520-17. Nixon resigned in August 1974 under threat of impeachment.

Gerald R. Ford (1974-1977, R), Nixon's second VP, became President and unsuccessfully ran for re-election against Jimmy Carter in 1976.

James E. Carter Jr. (1977-1981, D) beat incumbent Ford by a 297-240 margin but served only one term, losing re-election to Ronald Reagan.

Ronald Reagan (1981-1989, R) beat incumbent Carter, 489-49, and Independent John Anderson (no electoral votes). Reagan easily won re-election in 1984 over Walter Mondale, 525-13.

George H.W. Bush (1989-1993, R), Reagan's VP, won the 1988 election over Michael Dukakis, 426-112, but lost re-election.

William J. Clinton (1993-2001, D) beat incumbent Bush by 370-168 while Reform candidate Ross Perot won 19.7 million popular votes but no electoral votes. In 1996, Clinton easily won re-election over Robert Dole, 379-159, and Perot. In 1998 he was impeached by the House but acquitted by the Senate.

George W. Bush (2001-2009, R) won election in 1980 over Clinton's VP Albert Gore Jr. in a very close contest, 271-266, in which Gore received more popular votes. Bush won a second term in 2004 by defeating John Kerry, 286-251.

Barack H. Obama (2009-2017, D) beat John McCain, 365-173, to win election in 2008. He was re-elected in 2012 by defeating Mitt Romney, 332-208. He was the only incumbent President re-elected with less votes than four years before.

Donald J. Trump (2017-2021, R) beat Obama's Secretary of State, Hilary Clinton, for election in 2016 by 304-227 electoral votes although Clinton garnered more popular votes. In 2019, Trump was impeached by the House and acquitted by the Senate.

Get off my lawn! the Kings of Curmudgeon

These days, it seems like the world is full of do-gooders, grinning salesmen, glad-handing politicians, and polite pollyannas. What we need is a golden age of grouchy, cantankerous old codgers willing to share their wisdom with the world, i.e., curmudgeons. With the aging of the population, there will be no shortage of such characters. But who will be their role models? Who were the greatest curmudgeons of all time?

First, let's define curmudgeon. The dictionary states: a person (especially an old man) who is easily annoyed or angered and who often complains. Synonyms include bear, bellyacher, complainer, crab, crank, croaker, crosspatch, fusser, griper, grouch, grouser, growler, grumbler, grump, murmurer, mutterer, sourpuss, and whiner.

One example was Senator Jesse Helms of North Carolina, a grumpy old conservative. The CBS war correspondent and TV commentator Andy Rooney seems to fit the bill. Curmudgeons are grumpy but not cruel, evil or murderous. Stalin, the Grinch, Scrooge, and Oscar the Grouch would seem to be likely candidates, but they're mostly villians and/or cartoons, not real persons like Mr. Magoo and Popeye. The Wizard of Oz was certainly grumpy and grouchy, but he wasn't real. Remember the man behind the curtain? The writer and critic H.L. Mencken was grouchy but way too intellectual. Perhaps our best examples, other than your own crazy uncle, come from the world of entertainment.

Joseph Kearns played George Wilson (Mr. Wilson!) on the TV series *Dennis the Menace* (he was also the voice of the Doorknob in the 1951 animated Disney film *Alice in Wonderland*). Ben Weaver, played by Will Wright, was the crotchedy old department store owner in Mayberry. Mr. Potter (Lionel Barrymore), the crusty old tycoon of Bedford Falls, was most definitely a curmudgeon.

Most mortifying was Sheriff Buford T. Justice on *Smokey and the Bandit*, played by the superb Jackie Gleason. Much less intimidating yet supremely in control was skinflint Jack Benny, with his violin and jalopy. "Well!"

The medical profession had its share with Dr. John Becker (Ted Danson) and Dr. Gregory House (Hugh Laurie).

More recently on television there's been Frank Barone (Peter Boyle), Martin Crane (John Mahoney), and Mike Baxter (Tim Allen). Edgy comedians George Carlin, Don Rickles, and Rodney Dangerfield were hilarious but don't quite seem to make the grade.

Three beloved characters earn the distinction of honorable mention in the pantheon of curmudgeoness — Fred G. Sanford (Redd Foxx, real name John Elroy Sanford), Archie Bunker (Carroll O'Conner), and Lou Grant (Ed Asner).

Foxx was one of the first black comics to play to white audiences on the Las Vegas Strip. His nightclub act was quite raunchy. On the *Sanford & Son* TV show, in tense situations, he would clutch his chest and shout, "'Lizabeth, I'm acoming to see you." Sanford died in 1991 at age 68 of a heart attack.

Bunker was known for his off-kilter views on current affairs, but he was often on the right track, as even liberal scriptwriter Norman Lear would acknowledge. "Stifle yourself, Edith!" he would belligerently yell at his poor wife.

Lou Grant was the stereotype of the rough-and-tumble newsroom editor who yelled at subordinates, glowered a lot, and often consulted a bottle of whiskey stowed in his desk drawer. Needless to say, such a character cannot exist in a modern newsroom (if newsrooms even still exist).

And now the best of the best. The three shining examples of high curmudgeonism are Oscar Madison/Max Goldman (Walter Matthau), Grandpappy Amos McCoy (Walter Brennan), and W.C. Fields.

Grouchy and cantankerous, but also slovenly and lustful, was Oscar Madison, the sportswriter in the *Odd Couple* movie who feuded with neurotic Felix Unger, first played on Broadway by Art Carney (Ed Norton on *The Honeymooners*) and later by Jack Lemmon, hilarious as he tried to clear his sinuses in public. Oscar was portrayed perfectly by Matthau, who also starred as Max Goldman opposite feuding neighbor John Gustafson (Lemmon) in *Grumpy Old Men*. Matthau also shines in *The Sunshine Boys* as curmudgeonly old Willy Clark, who fights and fusses with former vaudeville partner Al Lewis, played by George Burns. The two seniors in the movie were supposed to be the same age, but in reality Matthau was 24 years younger than Burns.

Mopey-faced Matthau got a great review in his first acting role, as a derelict. A reviewer crowed, "The others just looked like actors in make-up, but Walter Matthau really looks like a skid row bum!"

Walter John Matthow was born on New York City's Lower East Side to Jewish parents from Ukraine and Lithuania. He created rumors that his name was Walter Foghorn Matuschanskayasky. He is credited as such in the movie *Earthquake*. He served in World War II as a radioman-gunner on a B-24 Liberator heavy bomber based out of Norfolk, England. He flew missions during the Battle of the Bulge and ended the war as a staff sergeant.

A prolific actor, he starred in numerous stage plays, movies, and TV series and shows, and not always as a curmudgeon. He was a warmonger in *Fail Safe* and got beat up by Elvis Presley in *King Creole*. He won an Oscar (how appropriate) for his supporting role in *The Fortune Cookie*.

Matthau played the role of Mr. Wilson in the 1993 movie *Dennis the Menace* and the coach in *Bad News Bears* (1976). He is probably best known by modern audiences as Max Goldman in *Grumpy Old Men* in which he assaults Jack Lemmon with a frozen fish and gets cussed out by an even older curmudgeon, Gustafson's father, played by Burgess Meredith, age 95. "Damn kids!" he swears, referring to Matthau and Lemmon. "It's butt cold out here and I'm fresh outta beer." Goldman drives like a maniac, plays practical jokes on his neighbor, calls others bonehead and schmuck, and complains that passing gas is like farting razor blades.

Limping along in his denim bib overalls and slouch hat and complaining in his old-man screeching voice was Brennan as Amos McCoy, the grandpa on the TV series *The Real McCoys* (1957-63). The show was about a West Virginia family that moves to a farm in California. Grandpappy often quarreled with a fellow senior neighbor over checkers and horseshoes. Amos claimed to have fought with Teddy Roosevelt's Rough Riders in the Spanish-American War (Brennan was four years old at the time). In one episode, Amos clashes with used car salesman San Fernando Harry, played by Jesse White, who later played the Maytag appliance salesman in TV commercials, a curmudgeon in his own right.

Despite being an ornery old cuss, Brennan was one of only three actors to ever win three Academy Awards. Brennan played Judge Roy Bean opposite Gary Cooper in *The Westerner* and Old Man Clanton opposite Henry Fonda in *My Darling Clementine*. In 1962 at age 68, he recorded "Old Rivers" as a single that went to No. 5 on the Billboard chart.

Yes, Brennan had false teeth and no, the limp was not real. When discussing upcoming movie roles with directors, he would inquire, "With or without?" referring to his dentures.

Brennan appeared in more than 230 film and television roles during a career that spanned nearly five decades. He also garnered much attention for his ultraconservative views (he fought hard to keep prayers in public schools).

"Get away from me, kid. You bother me." With a swift kick behind his back, the old codger got rid of the toddler so he could concentrate on his bottle of booze and the nifty broad with the fancy hat. His enticements were rebuffed not once but twice. He flipped on his hat and twirled his cane as he sauntered away. "If at first you don't succeed, try, try again. Then quit. No use being a damn fool about it."

Such was the life of W.C. Fields (1880-1946), the master of all curmudgeons, on stage and screen as in real life. "Start out each day with a smile and get it over with," he advised.

A professional juggler at age 15, he was one of the greatest pantomimists and comedians in the world. His career spanned burlesque, vaudeville, the legitimate stage, silent pictures, talkies, radio, books, and recordings. God only knows what he would have thought about television (*The W.C. Fields Variety Hour!* brought to you by Pepto-Bismo).

Fields was a natural confidence man. "Never give a sucker an even break." He was also an alcoholic. "Whilst traveling through Afghanistan, we lost our corkscrew. Had to live on food and water for several days."

Despite his disdain for the human race, children, and dogs, Fields actually was a sympathetic character, a lovable rogue.

Born William Claude Dukenfield (aka Charles Bogle, Otis Criblecoblis, Mahatma Kane Jeeves) in Darby, Pa., he had a violent relationship with his hot-tempered father, and his education stopped at grade school. Fields adopted a costume of scruffy beard and shabby tuxedo and entered vaudeville as a genteel "tramp juggler" in 1898, using the name W.C. Fields. He was renowned as the world's greatest juggler. He performed a wild billiards act on the Ziegfeld Follies and worked hard to polish his comedy act.

Fields was always nattily dressed in top hat, cutaway coat and collar, spats, and cane, similar to the comic strip character Ally Sloper (which may have been inspired by Charles Dickens' Mr. Micawber, whom Fields later played on film).

Fields married a fellow vaudevillian and chorus girl, who assisted in his acts (and got blamed when they flopped) and taught him how to read. He had extramarital affairs and fathered an illegitimate son.

In 1936, heavy drinking precipitated a decline in his health. By 1938 he was suffering from delirium tremens. After a year off from work, Fields began making radio broadcasts in his familiar snide drawl, which became very popular. He joined the ventriloquism act of Edgar Bergen and his dummy Charlie McCarthy, whom Fields would refer to as a "woodpecker's pin-up boy" or a "termite's flophouse." The dummy would reply, "Is it true, Mr. Fields, that when you stood on the corner of Hollywood and Vine, 43 cars waited for your nose to change to green?"

A staunch atheist, Fields collected books and studied theology. Caught once reading a Bible, Fields said he was "looking for loopholes."

Fields spent the last 22 months of his life in a sanitorium and in 1946, on Christmas Day—the holiday he said he despised—he had a massive gastric hemorrhage and died, aged 66. He was cremated, and contrary to popular belief, his interment marker does not say, "I'd rather be in Philadelphia." There is no epitaph. By the way, January 29th is National Curmudgeons Day, held on the great man's birthday.

REALLY BIG
and full of nothing

"The fact that the universe is comprehensible is a miracle," said Albert Einstein. The universe is a really big place, I think we all can agree. But how big is it really? Can we even comprehend how big it is? Back in the day, the ancients gazed at all the stars in the night sky and imagined they were lights on the inside of a huge dome. But we know the universe is bigger than that. Let's find out how big, shall we.

Let's start with building a scale model of our solar system and progress from there, but first a general overview and some standards.

Our solar system consists of eight planets, including Earth, and some debris revolving around the Sun, which is actually a star. Our solar system sits towards the end of a spiral of stars in a galaxy known as the Milky Way. The galaxy consists of 200 billion stars, most separated by huge amounts of space. And there are 100 billion galaxies in the universe, most of them also separated by huge amounts of space.

The standard measurement of distance in space is the light-year, the distance light travels in one year. Light travels at 186,000 miles per second, so a light year is a distance equal to six trillion miles. In reality, it takes almost 8.5 minutes for sunlight to reach Earth, and it takes more than five hours to reach the edge of the solar system. In our scale model, in which the Sun is the size of a basketball, light moves only two inches per second or about 10 feet per minute. For reference, remember that a football field is 100 yards long.

Revolving around the Sun are the four relatively small inner planets — Mercury, Venus, Earth, and Mars. Each would be about the size of a BB or the head of a map pin. (One million Earths could fit inside the volume of the Sun.) Earth would be 31 yards from the Sun and Mars 47 yards. Then there are the four huge gaseous planets — Jupiter, Saturn, Uranus, and Neptune.

Between Mars and Jupiter lies the Asteroid Belt. Asteroids are minor planets, more than 750,000 of them with diameters larger than three-fifths of a mile and millions of them smaller.

Jupiter is five times further from the Sun than Earth is from the Sun. In our model, that's 162 yards. Jupiter is about the size of a ping pong ball. Saturn is 300 yards away. By the time we get to Neptune, we're a half-mile or 8.8 football fields away from our basketball Sun. Then there's the Kuiper Belt, a region of icy debris that extends far beyond the orbit of Neptune.

(In 2006, Pluto was reclassified as a dwarf planet because it's smaller than Earth's moon and exists in the Kuiper Belt. In reality, Pluto is 3.6 billion miles from the Sun and takes 248 years to make one revolution.)

Researchers have found mathematical evidence suggesting there may be a "Planet X" deep in the solar system. This hypothetical Neptune-sized planet orbits our Sun in a highly elongated orbit far beyond Pluto. The object, which researchers have nicknamed "Planet Nine," could have a mass about 10 times that of Earth and orbit about 20 times farther from the Sun on average than Neptune. Planet Nine may take between 10,000 and 20,000 Earth years to make one full orbit around the Sun.

That's just our own solar system, a small portion of our galaxy.

Now if we were to place the nearest star (Alpha Centauri) on our scale model of our solar system it would be 4,300 miles away from our basketball Sun. In reality, that's 4.3 light-years distant. If our basketball Sun was located in Chicago, the nearest star would be located in Frankfurt, Germany.

If we expanded our basketball-sun model to include the entire Milky Way galaxy, we would have to make our model 100 million miles wide. This means that to make a model of our galaxy where our Sun is the size of a basketball, our model would reach from the Sun to a point some 10 million miles beyond the Earth. The Sun is one of more than 200 billion stars in the Milky Way. It orbits some 25,000 light-years from the galactic core, completing a revolution once every 250 million years or so.

And that's just our own galaxy.

The closest galaxy to our own is Andromeda, which is 2.5 million light-years away. On our scale model, the nearest galaxy would be 2.5 billion miles from our basketball-sun.

In reality, the edge of the universe is thought to be at least 15 billion light-years away from us in all directions. So, our model of the universe in which our Sun is the size of a basketball would be 30 trillion miles in diameter.

At least 95 percent of the stars in our universe are smaller than our Sun, but there are some that are much larger, as much as 400 times larger. Compared to our basketball, such a star would be a sphere that reaches from one goal line of a football field to the other.

How about traveling in the other direction, getting really small?

Some experts speculate that we human beings are right at the middle of the size spectrum, from subatomic particles to the edge of the universe. If we can imagine the outer edges of the universe, then we can also get very small.

If you stretched out all the DNA strands from all the cells in your body, it would measure twice the diameter of our solar system. The human body consists of some 10 octillion atoms (1 followed by 28 zeroes), an amount roughly a million times larger than the number of stars in the visible universe. An atom is the smallest unit of ordinary matter that forms a chemical element. Every solid, liquid, gas, and plasma is composed of molecules composed of atoms. Atoms are extremely small, typically around 100 picometers across. A picometer is one-trillionth of a meter, which is 39 inches.

The basic structure of the atom became apparent in 1911, when Ernest Rutherford showed that most of the mass of an atom lies concentrated at its center, in a tiny nucleus. Rutherford postulated that the atom resembled a miniature solar system, with light, negatively charged electrons orbiting the dense, positively charged nucleus (protons and neutrons), just as the planets orbit the Sun.

The smallest thing that we can see with a regular microscope is about 500 nanometers. A nanometer is one-billionth of a meter. So the smallest thing that you can see with a light microscope is about 200 times smaller than the width of a hair. Bacteria are about 1,000 nanometers in size.

The most powerful microscopes are called atomic force microscopes, because they can see things by the forces between atoms. So with an atomic force microscope you can see things as small as a strand of DNA or even individual atoms. These microscopes use computers to help convert the information from "tapping" on the sample to make a three-dimensional view of the object. So with the world's most powerful microscope, scientists have been able to see DNA.

Reaching the subatomic level, things become very strange, beyond the comprehension of most people, including the author. There are many subatomic particles — protons, neutrons, electrons, six flavors of quarks, six types of leptons, 12 gauge bosons, and the Higgs boson.

More than 200 subatomic particles have been detected—most of them highly unstable, existing for less than a millionth of a second—as a result of collisions produced in cosmic ray reactions or particle accelerator experiments.

The atom is composed mostly of empty space. The center nucleus is calculated to be roughly one-ten-thousandths (0.0001) the diameter of the atom.

If you ponder the vastness of outer space and the emptiness of atomic space, one realizes that the recognizable universe we live in is about 99.99 percent nothing!

But hold on — nothing (seemingly empty space) might actually be something, according to mathematicians and physicists.

Nobel Laureate and physicist Paul Dirac of England was a profound mathematician who had a brilliant visual imagination. In 1928, he produced Dirac's Equation, which unifies Einstein's theory of special relativity and the theories of quantum (subatomic) mechanics. Stated very plainly, his theory holds that nothingness or empty space is actually full of matter and anti-matter called virtual particles.

Dirau's Equation (simplified) $I \gamma \cdot \partial \Psi = m \Psi$

"Nothingness is, in fact, a seething mass of virtual particles appearing and disappearing trillions of times in the blink of an eye," said Professor Jim Al-Khalili of the University of Surrey. In accordance with the Big Bang Theory, the laws of quantum mechanics can be applied to the entire cosmos. In the beginning, there was matter and anti-matter colliding and resulting in nothingness, except that for every billion particles, one particle of matter was left over, plus a lot of background radiation. "Our universe is just the quantum world inflated many, many times," said Al-Khalili. "Nothing has really shaped everything."

What does the cosmos have in store for us?

According to science, the universe is 13.7 billion years old. The universe is expanding, and the rate of expansion is accelerating. One hundred billion years from now, residents of Earth will only be able to see stars in their own galaxy. Everything beyond the Milky Way will be invisible.

But, in about 5 billion years from now, our Sun will expand into a red dwarf star so gigantic that it will engulf Mercury, Venus, and the Earth.

However, scientists have just discovered a giant black hole at the center of the Milky Way so monstrously heavy and dense that its gravity is sucking everything into it, including light rays.

Sleep tight.

Sources: Dr. David H. Hathaway, NASA/MSFC; "Everything and Nothing: The Amazing Science of Empty Space, XIVE-TV; The Royal Swedish Academy of Sciences.

OSHKOSH

the
WILD BLUE YONDER
and the
FLAT BLACK ICE

Oshkosh (pop. 67,000) lies in the central Wisconsin basin on either side of the Fox River and nestled between Lake Butte des Mortes and massive Lake Winnebago. Most people know the town from the children's clothing manufacturer Oshkosh B'Gosh or perhaps Oshkosh Corp, manufacturer of heavy-duty specialty trucks. Back in the day, the 47 sawmills in Oshkosh provided the lumber to rebuild Chicago following the Great Fire of 1871. The town boasts a branch of the University of Wisconsin, two chocolatiers, and world-class sailboating and fishing. The chase scene in the 2009 movie *Public Enemies* was filmed in downtown Oshkosh. The town boasts an equal number of churches and taverns. It's the home of U.S. Senator Ron Johnson and former Marvel Comics editor Mark Gruenwald, who was cremated after his untimely death in 1996 and, according to his wishes, had his ashes mixed with ink for the first printing of the trade paperback compilation of Squadron Supreme.

However, for one week each year in late July, Wittman Regional Airport in Oshkosh becomes the busiest airport in the world, hosting the annual EAA AirVenture celebration. In 2019, the event drew 10,000 aircraft and 642,000 attendees (including 2,772 from 93 other countries). The event was covered by more than 850 members of the media. During an 11-day period the control tower at Wittman supervised an average of 127 takeoffs and landings per hour. More than 860 businesses set up exhibits, while 5,500 volunteers ran the event.

More than 3,000 people flew in the EAA's Ford Tri-Motor Tin Goose, an airliner built in 1929, and 669 enjoyed the thrill of riding in the Boeing B-17 Flying Fortress "Aluminum Overcast." The latest in military jet aviation also performed for crowds, including the F-22 Raptor fighter and the A-10 Thunderbolt "Warthog."

AirVenture drew more than 1,000 home-built aircraft, 939 vintage aircraft, more than 100 seaplanes, 62 aerobatic planes, and 400 military warbirds.

EAA stands for Experimental Aircraft Association. It was founded in 1953 by Paul H. Poberezny, who served as the organization's president from 1953 to 1989 and then as chairman of the board until 2009. The first gathering was in September 1953 as a small part of the Milwaukee (Wisconsin) Air Pageant. Fewer than 150 people registered as visitors. EAA's fly-in grew quickly in its first few years and by the late 1950s it had outgrown its facilities. In 1959, the event moved to Rockford (Illinois) Municipal Airport, where it would stay for the next decade.

By 1969, it was apparent that the EAA Fly-In Convention had simply become too large for the Rockford facility. Sites were studied for a new home. Aviation legend Steve Wittman, who had been an EAA member since the association's founding, suggested the Oshkosh airport. Oshkosh featured acreage surrounding the airport to handle the annual influx of airplanes, vehicles, and tents. There were two lengthy runways (east/west and north/south) which did not cross, allowing greater traffic movement.

Throughout the 1970s and 1980s, the convention exploded into national prominence. Attendance jumped into six figures each year and the event became one of sport aviation's top gatherings. The name changed to EAA AirVenture Oshkosh in 1998. No airshow of such magnitude can escape aviation accidents, some deadly. In 2010 a twin-engine business jet crash-landed at AirVenture, causing major damage and injuring the pilot. The next year, an F-16 Fighting Falcon warbird overran the runway, collapsing the nose gear. In 2007, the pilot of a P-51 Mustang was killed when he collided with another P-51 during a landing. The other pilot was not injured. Two years earlier, the pilot of an F-51D fighter was killed in a crash while

performing a stunt routine. In 2006, a passenger in an aircraft was killed when the propeller of a Grumman Avenger warbird struck his aircraft during take-off maneuvers. Numerous air crashes have occurred over the years involving aircraft en route to the Oshkosh airshow.

The EAA Aviation Museum displays many historic aircraft, the personal artifacts of astronaut Frank Borman, and both the *"Bonzo"* aircraft racers designed, built, and flown by the airport's namesake, Steve Wittman (1904-1995). Despite poor vision in one eye, Wittman was flying by age 20, performing stunts and joyrides, and then worked as a test pilot. He flew his first air race in Milwaukee in 1926. He competed in transcontinental races and the Thompson Trophy races in his airplanes *Chief Oshkosh, Bonzo, Buttercup,* and *Buster.* During WWII, he trained pilots for the Army Air Corps. He managed the Oshkosh airport for 38 years and was instrumental in creating the EAA and bringing its annual event to Oshkosh in 1970. At age 90, Wittman was still demonstrating aerobatics in aircraft he had designed. In 1995, Wittman and his second wife were killed in an air crash near Stevenson, Alabama en route from their Florida home to Oshkosh. He is a member of the National Aviation Hall of Fame.

Lake Winnebago is 30 miles long and 12 miles wide, covers 206 square miles, and reaches only 21 feet at its deepest. Anglers vie to land one of the region's best sporting fish — the famous muskellunge or "muskie," which can grow to be six feet long and weigh 60 pounds. During the winter, Lake Winnebago freezes over and ice fishermen in portable shacks, some quite modern and elaborate, congregate to form villages on the frozen lake. Vehicles can be driven out onto the ice. At certain times during the winter, the lake produces what is called ice shoves, frozen ice boulders that pile up on the shore. Ice shoves can reach 40 feet high. A 35-foot-high wall of ice was reported at one lakeside supper club. In 2017 ice shoves buried the docks at the Oshkosh yacht club. In 1977 a tavern was destroyed.

With steady winds and wide-open expanses, Winnebago is a sailor's delight. Regattas test the speed and skill of men (and women) and their boats. On one occasion, an intrepid crew battled a windstorm in a small sailboat fixed with a lead keel to see if the boat would capsize. It didn't — the wind blew out the sails first.

Sailing is not limited just to the summertime. During the coldest of winter, when the huge lake freezes over, strange-looking boats glide on steel runners or skates at speeds up to 100 mph. Iceboating is a sport hundreds of year old; it is believed that mankind first exceeded 100 mph on an iceboat in Europe.

Iceboating is fast and exhilarating and dangerous. Iceboats can travel much faster than the speed of the wind. The official iceboat speed record

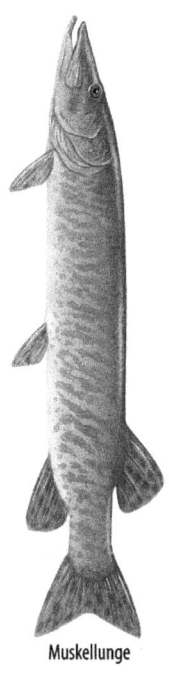

Muskellunge

set by John D. Buckstaff remains the one set on Lake Winnebago way back in 1938. The record is 143 miles an hour. Iceboats feature a mast and boom and mainsail like regular sailboats but ride on a long narrow beam transected by a wide outrigger resting on metal runners or blades. Traditionally the third runner is mounted in the rear and is used to steer. Veteran iceboater Dave Lallier said, "Driving these old stern steerers is like driving a forklift at 85 mph. They get pretty squirrelly." There was a time when massive iceboat freighters transported hay and chickens across Lake Winnebago.

Newer designs in the 1930s placed the steering runner up front in the bow. Iceboats can be quite small, designed for one sailor, or run to 40 feet in length with a five-man crew in a stern cockpit. Modern iceboats even have enclosed, streamlined cockpits. The largest iceboat in the world is *The Deuce,* a 54-foot behemoth built in the 1930s and recently restored. The iceboat hit 104 mph with a five-man crew.

"Iceboating is 11 months planning, two weeks fixing, and two weeks waiting for decent ice. Somewhere in there, you might get to sail," said Chuck Nevitt of Oshkosh in an article by Dan Egan in the *Milwaukee Journal-Sentinel.* Some believe that Nevitt, then age 27, set the world's speed record back in 1947 during a race. The Coast Guard veteran piloted his 42-foot Flying Dutchmen between two buoys set two miles apart. It took 53 seconds, and that included a tack he made in the middle of the course that added about a quarter-mile to the distance. "They figured somewhere in there I was doing 150 mph. Maybe 155," Nevitt said, insisting he didn't care about breaking the record set by his friend Buckstaff. "It doesn't make a damn bit of difference to me," he said.

There currently is no official world speed record for iceboats, according to the Guinness World Records website.

Jesuit missionary Claude Allouez was the first documented iceboater in North America, rigging a sail to a canoe in the Green Bay area. Iceboating became popular in the U.S. in the late 1800s as a sport for the Eastern elite. Iceboaters would race their vessels against locomotives chugging along the Hudson River. The boats were the fastest things on Earth at the time. The sport drifted west to Wisconsin, Minnesota, and Michigan. Lake Winnebago became one of the sport's hot spots because it is big and relatively shallow, which makes for more consistently thick ice. Lakes dotting southern Wisconsin, such as Lake Geneva, have been popular for boaters.

Boaters in Oshkosh can use Miller's Bay in Menominee Park for mooring. The bay is sheltered by Monkey Island, which was used by pryotechnicians to stage 4th of July fireworks shows. One 4th of July back in the 1960s something went awry and the entire fireworks display ignited at once. Pryotechnicians could be seen diving into the bay as the once-in-a-lifetime conflagration of fireworks illuminated the night sky.

Keeping watch, as always, in Menominee Park was Chief Oshkosh, or at least the 10-foot-tall bronze statue of the Menominee tribal leader. The statue depicts a tall, barechested young warrior atop a nine-foot-tall granite pedestal. His tombstone reads: "A man of peace, beloved by all." The statue was designed by the Italian sculptor Gaetano Trentanove and cost $12,500 in 1911 ($300,000 in today's dollars).

Oshkosh (the word means claw) was known to be an alcoholic in his later life. (During the 20th Century there was a Chief Oshkosh Beer brand.) Shortly before his death, he weighed over 400 pounds. He died in Keshena, Wisconsin, in a drunken brawl on Aug. 29, 1858. In 1926 the Menominee allowed Oshkosh's remains to be moved to Menominee Park.

"The statue doesn't look anything like him," said Jeffrey Behm, an anthropology professor at the University of Wisconsin-Oshkosh in a 2016 article on the Oshkosh Community News Network. "I mean he was a short, muscular man; he wasn't this tall Nordic-looking Indian."

The chief wasn't really peaceful and wasn't beloved by all, even members of the tribe or his own family. Some claimed he was too accommodating to the white settlers.

In fact, Oshkosh did not become chief by birth or through acclamation of the Menominee people. Instead he was picked to serve in that role at a treaty signing in 1827 after federal officials determined that it was too difficult to negotiate with the tribe because there was nobody clearly in charge.

Although the chief's remains were moved from the Menoninee tribal reservation in 1926 and reburied in Oshkosh with great ceremony, some

Sources: Brian Zimmerman; Wisconsin Historical Society

experts doubt that the chief ever left the reservation. There's speculation that the remains of a woman were buried at the Menoninee Park site.

"Whatever Oshkosh's faults were, he led his people capably during one of the most difficult periods of their history and kept the tribe in their native Wisconsin," wrote biographer Scott Cross, the archivist at the Oshkosh Public Museum. Chief Oshkosh's greatest legacy may be the tribal reservation itself.

Menominee Reservation is located 65 miles due north of Oshkosh, consisting of 235,000 acres of forest land. In the early 1800s, the tribe occupied lands covering 10 million acres. Less than half of the tribe's 8,700 members live on the reservation due to the lack of employment opportunities.

The Menominee forest, which occupiesw most of the reservation and stands out in satellite photos as a rectangular patch of green against the surrounding land, is the mainstay of the local economy and has been remarkably productive. According to Menominee Tribal Enterprises, the business arm of the tribe, the forest has yielded over two billion board feet of lumber, twice what was originally there, and yet "there is more forest volume standing today than when timber harvesting began."

Sources: Much of the text on Chief Oshkosh derives from a 2016 article by Miles Maguire on the Oshkosh Community News Network. A source for iceboating is a 2003 article by Dan Egan of the Milwaukee Journal-Sentinel.

More Civilized and Humane Methods of Executing the Condemned

Throughout the ages, civilized societies have searched long and hard for more efficient, effective, and humane methods of executing persons convicted for capital offenses. Some argue that in a civilized society the government shouldn't have the power to kill its own citizens even for the most heinous crimes. But most citizens have supported the death penalty as a suitable means of justice.

The Code of King Hammurabi of Babylon in 1800 B.C. codified the death penalty for 25 different crimes. Probably the earliest method was stoning, followed by crucifixion, impalement, burning at the stake, garroting, beheading, and firing squad. Modern methods include electrocution (the electric chair), asphyxiation (the gas chamber), and lethal injection.

Until the 1890s, hanging was the primary method of execution used in the United States. Hanging is still used in Delaware and Washington, although both have lethal injection as an alternative method. The last hanging to take place was that of Billy Bailey, a convicted double-murderer, on Jan. 25, 1996 in Smyrna, Delaware. He chose hanging instead of lethal injection.

During the reign of Henry VIII in England, as many as 72,000 people were executed. Some common methods of execution at that time were boiling, burning at the stake, hanging, beheading, and drawing and quartering. Executions were carried out for such capital offenses as marrying a Jew, not confessing to a crime, and treason.

Public hangings became a popular method of execution for persons committing capital crimes in England about 1,000 years ago. The hangman, lord of the gallows, was an important job, more than just putting a hood over

Execution of George Atzerodt, David Herold, Lewis Powell, and Mary Surratt on July 7, 1865, at Fort McNair in Washington, D.C.

the condemned's head and pulling a lever. The knot on the noose had to be tied correctly. The rope had to be boiled and pulled to eliminate stretching. The well-constructed knot is lubricated with wax or soap "to ensure a smooth sliding action." The prisoner is weighed and trial runs are conducted with sandbags of similar weight. This is to determine the length of drop necessary to ensure a quick death by breaking the neck. If the rope is too long, the inmate could be decapitated, and if it is too short, strangulation could take as long as 45 minutes. Immediately before the execution, the prisoner's hands and legs are secured, he is blindfolded, and the noose is placed around the neck, with the knot behind the left ear. The trap-door is opened and the prisoner falls through.

Hangings were spectacles, meant to impress upon the masses that crime does not pay. A clean jerk produced applause. An inmate convulsing and screaming in pain while suffocating to death spoiled the show. If the inmate had strong neck muscles, weighed relatively little, if the drop was too short, or the noose had been wrongly positioned, the fracture-dislocation was not rapid, with death resulting from slow asphyxiation. If this occurs, the face becomes engorged, the tongue protrudes, the eyes pop, the body defecates, and violent movements of the limbs occur.

In England, Henry Pierrepoint assisted at 35 hangings and carried out 70 executions himself, and didn't bungle a one. He persuaded his older brother Tom and son Albert to follow in his footsteps. Henry Pierrepoint was sacked in July 1910 because he arrived for the execution of Frederick Foreman in Chelmsford "considerably the worse for drink."

Albert Pierrepoint was by far the most prolific hangman of the 20th Century, presiding at the hangings of 433 people, including 16 women, in his 24 years of service. The most notable took place in December 1945, when he hanged 11 staff members from the Belsen concentration camp, including camp commandant Josef Kramer, the "Beast of Belsen." He is also credited with the quickest hanging on record when he executed James Inglis in seven seconds on May 8, 1951 at Strangeways in Manchester.

The first recorded execution in the colonies was that of Captain George Kendall in the Jamestown colony of Virginia in 1608. He was charged with being a spy for Spain. In 1612, Virginia Governor Sir Thomas Dale enacted the Divine, Moral and Martial Laws, which provided the death penalty for even minor offenses such as stealing grapes, killing chickens, and trading with Indians. During the Salem witch trials of the early 1690s, 17 women and two men were hanged, although it is estimated that thousands were hanged throughout the colonies.

On July 7, 1865, four civilians, including one woman, were publicly hanged before a restricted audience in Washington, D.C. for complicity in the shooting of President Abraham Lincoln. The assassin, actor John Wilkes Booth, was shot and killed by Federal troops 12 days after he shot Lincoln.

In June 1882, Charles Guiteau, who was obviously mentally ill, was hanged for the assassination of President James Garfield. Guiteau was hanged privately indoors. His malfunctioning brain was preserved, and today sits in the National Museum of Health and Medicine. His body was boiled in a chemical solution and reduced to a skeleton.

Today, an I.Q. of 70 is the baseline number frequently used to qualify someone for capital punishment.

The largest mass execution in American history took place on Dec. 26, 1862. The U.S. Government hanged 38 Dakota Indians (sometimes called Santee Sioux) for murder and rape during the Dakota War. This occurred during the American Civil War. Lincoln commuted the death sentences of nearly 300 other convicted tribesmen.

On Oct. 20, 1865, Champ Ferguson, a Cumberland Plateau guerrilla charged with 53 murders during the Civil War, was hanged in Nashville, Tennessee in front of his wife and children. His supporters, including General Joseph Wheeler, testified that Ferguson was a captain in the Confederate army and should be paroled. Ferguson was one of only two Confederates officially executed by the Federals, the other being Henry Wirz, commandant of the notorious Andersonville (Georgia) prison camp.

On June 19, 1953, Julius and Ethel Rosenberg became the only two American civilians executed for espionage during the Cold War. They were convicted of giving information about the atomic bomb to the USSR.

Rainey Bethea was the last person in America to be executed publicly, in 1936. He was convicted of the rape and murder of a 70-year-old woman. The sheriff in charge of the hanging in Owensboro, Kentucky, was a woman, which attracted media coverage. Twenty thousand spectators came to view the hanging. The sheriff turned the job over to a male associate, but the media circus so embarrassed Kentucky officials that they stopped public executions. Other states quickly followed suit.

Twenty-eight states allow the death penalty. There are 2,591 convicts sitting on death row, including 57 women. California has 724 prisoners on death row, Florida 346, Texas 214, Alabama 172, Pennsylvania 142.

The death penalty was outlawed at the state and federal level by a 1972 Supreme Court decision that cancelled all existing death penalty statutes. A 1976 decision allowed states to reinstate the death penalty, and in 1988 the government passed legislation that made it available again at the federal level.

In 2020, the Federal Bureau of Prisons put 10 inmates to death, more than all the states combined that executed prisoners. That year, Texas executed three inmates, while Alabama, Georgia, Missouri, and Tennessee each put one prisoner to death. On Jan. 13, 2021, Lisa Montgomery became the first female inmate to be put to death by federal authorities in nearly 70 years. She was convicted in 2007 for the 2004 murder of a woman who was eight months pregnant.

There have been 1,526 executions in the U.S. since 1976, the vast majority by lethal injection (1,346), followed by 163 by electrocution, 11 in the gas chamber, and three each by hanging and firing squad.

Fifty-six percent of those executed were white, 34 percent black. Of the total, 1,245 executions were in the South, including 570 in Texas. This compares with 190 in the Midwest, 87 in the West, and four in the Northeast.

According to data collected by the Death Penalty Information Center, 78 people were sentenced to death in federal cases between 1988 and 2018, but only three were executed.

It is estimated that three percent of all executions are "botched," i.e., they deviated from the execution protocol. Most involve failures to locate a vein for lethal injection due to the age, health, or drug addiction of the condemned, or malfunctions or human error during electrocutions.

No longer used, beheading by sword or axe had a long history in Europe. The Greeks and the Romans considered beheading a less dishonorable and less painful form of execution than other methods in use at the time. With an axe, the executioner could use a high block or a low block. The guillotine was a French invention and was not adopted by Great Britain or its colonies. One of the reasons is that it was deemed appropriate that the condemned's body should remain basically intact for proper burial.

By his own choosing, convict Ronnie Gardner was executed by firing squad in Utah in 2010. The inmate was bound to a chair with leather straps across his waist and head. The chair is surrounded by sandbags to absorb the inmate's blood. A black hood is pulled over the inmate's head. A technician locates the inmate's heart with a stethoscope and pins a circular white cloth target over it. Standing in an enclosure 20 feet away, five shooters are armed with .30-caliber rifles loaded with single rounds. One of the shooters is given a blank round 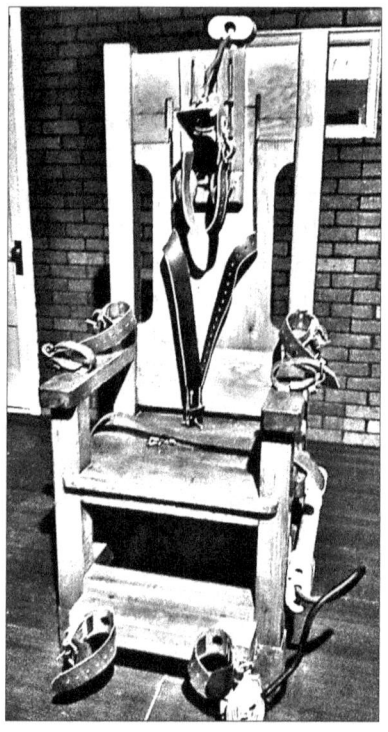 (nobody knows which one). Each of the shooters aims his rifle through a slot in a canvas barrier and fires at the inmate.

New York built the first electric chair in 1888, seeking a more humane method of execution than hanging. Thomas Edison, advocate of direct-current (DC) electricity, and George Westinghouse, inventor of alternating-current (AC) electricity, fought with each other, trying to accuse the other's method as being unsafe. Edison made sure the New York electric chair used alternating current, thereby inferring that his DC method was safer. The first electrocution did not go well. William Kemmler, a drunk who killed his common-law wife with a hatchet, was strapped in and the current applied. He was determined dead and the current turned off. "Great God, he is alive!" somebody cried. The current was turned on for four more minutes to end his life. Westinghouse was horrified. "They could have done a better job with an ax," he told reporters.

Before electrocution, the condemned is shaved and strapped to a chair with belts that cross his chest, groin, legs, and arms. A metal skullcap-shaped electrode is attached to the scalp and forehead over a sponge moistened with saline. The sponge must not be too wet or the saline short-circuits the electric current, and not too dry, as it would then have high resistance. An additional electrode is moistened with conductive jelly (Electro-Creme) and attached to a portion of the prisoner's leg that has been shaved to reduce resistance to electricity. The prisoner is then blindfolded. After the execution team has withdrawn to the observation room, the warden signals the executioner, who pulls a handle to connect the power supply. A jolt of 500 to 2000 volts is applied for about 30 seconds. The current surges and is then turned off, at which time the body is seen to relax. The doctors wait a few seconds for the body to cool down and then check to see if the inmate's heart is still beating. If it is, another jolt is applied. This process continues until the prisoner is dead. The prisoner's hands often grip the chair and there may be violent movement of the limbs which can result in dislocation or fractures. The tissues swell. Defecation occurs. Steam or smoke rises and there is a smell of burning.

U.S. Supreme Court Justice William Brennan once offered the following description of an execution by electric chair:

"...the prisoner's eyeballs sometimes pop out and rest on [his] cheeks. The prisoner often defecates, urinates, and vomits blood and drool. The body turns bright red as its temperature rises, and the prisoner's flesh swells and his skin stretches to the point of breaking. Sometimes the prisoner catches fire....Witnesses hear a loud and sustained sound like bacon frying, and the sickly sweet smell of burning flesh permeates the chamber." According to the deputy chief medical examiner of Cook County, Illinois: "The brain appears cooked in most cases."

Pedro Medina was electrocuted in Florida in 1997. A crown of foot-high flames shot from his headpiece, filling the execution chamber with a stench and thick smoke. A switch was thrown to prematurely end the two-minute cycle of 2,000 volts. After the execution, prison officials blamed the fire on a corroded copper screen in the headpiece of the electric chair, but experts hired by the governor later concluded that the fire was caused by the improper application of the sponge to the head.

In May 1946, a convicted murderer, Willie Francis, age 17, survived execution by electric chair when the device, nicknamed Gruesome Gertie, malfunctioned at the Louisiana State Penitentiary. The electric chair had been set up improperly by a drunken prison guard. After subsequent legal appeals were rejected, Francis was electrocuted in May 1947.

In 1924, the use of cyanide gas was introduced in Nevada as a more humane method of execution. The condemned person is strapped to a chair in an airtight metal chamber. Underneath the chair is a pail of sulfuric acid. A long stethoscope is affixed to the inmate so that a doctor outside the chamber can pronounce death. The warden gives a signal to the executioner, who flicks a lever that releases crystals of sodium cyanide into the pail. The subsequent chemical reaction releases deadly hydrogen cyanide gas. The prisoner is instructed to breathe deeply to speed up the process.

Most prisoners, not surprisingly, try to hold their breath. The eyes pop, the skin turns purple, and the victim drools. Oxygen is cut off to the brain. An exhaust fan sucks the poison air out of the chamber, and the corpse is sprayed with ammonia to neutralize any remaining traces of cyanide. A half-hour later, technicians enter the chamber, wearing gas masks and rubber gloves. They ruffle the deceased's hair to release any trapped cyanide gas before removing the body.

The gas chamber.

In January 1957, Jack Graham was executed in the Colorado gas chamber for mass murder. On Nov. 1, 1955, he killed 44 people aboard United Airlines Flight 629 near Longmont, Colo., using a dynamite time bomb. Graham planted the bomb in his mother's suitcase, who was killed along with 43 other people, in an apparent attempt to claim $37,500 worth of life insurance money.

In 1977, Oklahoma became the first state to adopt lethal injection as a means of execution. It would be five more years until Charles Brooks became the first person executed by lethal injection in Texas on Dec. 2, 1982.

Today, all of the states that have the death penalty use this method. The condemned person is bound to a gurney and a member of the execution team positions several heart monitors on the skin. Two needles (one is a back-up) are then inserted into usable veins, usually in the inmate's arms. Long tubes connect the needle through a hole in a cement block wall to several intravenous drips. The first is a harmless saline solution that is started immediately. Then, at the warden's signal, a curtain is raised exposing the inmate to witnesses in an adjoining room. Then, the inmate is injected with sodium thiopental, an anesthetic which puts the inmate to sleep. Next flows pavulon or pancuronium bromide, which paralyzes the entire muscle system and stops the inmate's breathing. Finally, the flow of potassium chloride stops the heart. Death results from anesthetic overdose and respiratory and cardiac arrest while the condemned person is unconscious. If the drugs are injected into a muscle instead of a vein, or if the needle becomes clogged, extreme pain can result. Many prisoners have veins damaged from intravenous drug use, and it is sometimes difficult to find a usable vein, resulting in long delays while the inmate remains strapped to the gurney.

Timothy McVeigh killed 168 people by igniting a bomb at the Federal building in Oklahoma City, Okla. on April 19, 1995. He was caught, tried, and convicted of mass murder on June 2, 1997. He was executed by lethal injection on June 11, 2001. His request for a nationally televised execution was denied.

On Sept. 15, 2009, efforts to execute convicted murderer and rapist Romell Broom in Ohio were stopped after more than two hours when the executioners were unable to find a usable vein in Broom's arms or legs. During the failed efforts, Broom winced and grimaced with pain. After the first hour's lack of success, on several occasions Broom tried to help the executioners find a usable vein. Ohio Governor Ted Strickland ordered the execution to stop, and announced plans to attempt the execution again after a one-week delay so that physicians could be consulted for advice on how the man could be killed more efficiently. The executioners blamed the problems on Broom's history of intravenous drug use. On April 14, 2020, Broom's execution was postponed to March 16, 2022.

In 1987 in Alabama, Doyle Lee Hamm went on a crime spree culminating in the murder of a motel clerk. After conviction and imprisonment, he developed lymphatic cancer. In February 2018 technicians tried for more than two hours to find a suitable vein to use to execute him. Finally, approaching a midnight deadline that prohibited further attempts, the execution was called off. Shortly thereafter, with the threat of litigation, Alabama reached a confidential settlement, the terms of which preclude a second execution attempt.

Federal executions by lethal injection are conducted at the U.S. Penitentiary in Terre Haute, Indiana. The United States military has executed 135 people since 1916. The most recent person to be executed by the military is U.S. Army Private John A. Bennett, executed on April 13, 1961, for child rape and attempted murder. Since the end of the Civil War in 1865, only one person has been executed for a military offense — Private Eddie Slovik, who was executed on Jan. 31, 1945, after being convicted of desertion.

On Aug. 8, 1942, six German nationals were executed by electrocution, one after the other, at the District of Columbia jail after being sentenced to death for sabotage by a military commission. The Germans landed on the East Coast by submarine and intended to blow up U.S. military installations. The saboteurs were caught before they caused any damage.

In 1945, the U.S. Army executed 14 German prisoners of war by hanging at the prison in Fort Leavenworth, Kansas. The POWs, members of the German military, had been convicted by general court-martial for the murders of fellow Germans believed by their fellow inmates to be collaborating as confidential informants with the United States military authorities. While the murders had been committed in 1943 and 1944, the executions were delayed until after the end of hostilities in Europe due to fears of German retaliation against Allied POWs. The hangings were carried out in a warehouse elevator shaft which had been converted into a temporary gallows. The 14 Germans were subsequently buried in the Fort Leavenworth Military Prison Cemetery.

The U.S. Army executed 35 soldiers during World War I by hanging, all for offenses relating to murder or rape. The U.S. Army executed 98 servicemen following courts martial for murder and/or rape in Europe during WWII. The remains of those servicemen were originally buried near the site of their executions.

Eighteen of those military executions were carried out at Shepton Mallet (built in Somerset County, England, in 1610). Executions by hanging were normally carried out at 1:00 am; shooting executions were carried out around 8:00 am. The British method of hanging was used. There was no standard drop and no hangmen's coiled noose, but an exactly calculated drop using a British-style eyelet noose. U.S. Army regulations required that a condemned prisoner at execution "will be dressed in regulation uniform from which all decorations, insignia, or other evidence of membership therein have been removed. Likewise, no such evidences will appear on any clothing used in burial." The deceased was left hanging for one hour, as was the norm in England.

In 1949 the remains of the executed soldiers were re-interred in Plot E, a private section specifically built to hold what the military refers to as "the dishonorable dead." Plot E is detached from the four main cemetery plots for the honored dead of World War I at the Oise-Aisne American Cemetery and Memorial in France. Plot E is located across the road, deliberately hidden from view, surrounded by hedges and hidden in thick forest. Officially, Plot E does not exist; it is not mentioned on the American Battle Monuments Commission website or in any guide pamphlets or maps. The plot is accessible only through the back door of the superintendent's office. The 96 white grave markers are the size of index cards and have nothing on them except sequential grave numbers engraved in black. Two bodies were later disinterred and allowed to be returned to United States for reburial. No U.S. flag is permitted to fly over Plot E.

There have been no military executions since 1961, although the death penalty is still a possible punishment. Five people are currently awaiting execution under military justice. All executions, if carried out, will be by lethal injection, including Nidal Malik Hasan, a former U.S. Army Major convicted of killing 13 people and injuring more than 30 others in the Fort Hood mass shooting on Nov. 5, 2009. Hasan is incarcerated at the prison at Fort Leavenworth.

Long stays on death row have become increasingly common. The Fair

Punishment Project estimated in March 2017 that about 40 percent of condemned prisoners have spent more than 20 years on death row.

Carey Dean Moore spent 38 years on death row by the time of his execution in 2018. He was sentenced to death in 1980 for the murders of two cab drivers.

Brandon Jones was executed in Georgia on Feb. 3, 2016, just short of his 73rd birthday. He was the oldest person executed in the state's history. Jones was originally convicted and sentenced to death in October 1979. He spent 36 years and four months on death row. His initial conviction had been overturned because jurors had consulted a Bible during deliberations. He was retried in 1997 and again convicted and sentenced to death.

Michael Selsor was first sentenced to death in Oklahoma on Jan. 30, 1976, for murder and was imprisoned for 36 years and 3 months prior to his execution on May 1, 2012. Although his sentence had been reduced to life in prison when Oklahoma's death penalty was overturned in 1976, he was re-sentenced to death for the same crime in 1998.

Manuel Valle was executed in Florida on Sept. 28, 2011. The U.S. Supreme Court delayed his execution for several hours, and Justice Breyer dissented from the decision allowing it to go forward. Breyer wrote that Valle's 33 years on death row was a cruel and unusual punishment. He claimed that the goals of due process (not executing an innocent man) and timely executions may be irreconcilable.

Texas executed Rolando Ruiz on March 7, 2017. Ruiz's lawyers had urged the Supreme Court to consider the constitutionality of subjecting him to extended solitary confinement on death row. A quarter-century elapsed since Ruiz committed a contract murder in 1992, two days after he turned 20 years old. Ruiz has lived for more than two decades under a death sentence, spent almost 20 years in solitary confinement, received two eleventh-hour stays of execution, and received four different execution dates.

Gary Alvord, a Florida prisoner who at the time of his demise had spent more years on death row than any other condemned prisoner in the country, died on May 19, 2013, of natural causes. Alvord was 66 years old and had been sentenced to death for murder almost 40 years before, on April 9, 1974.

On April 19, 2018, Alabama executed 83-year-old Walter Moody, the oldest person and only octogenarian put to death in the U.S. since executions resumed in 1977. Moody's execution stemmed from his 1996 conviction for the murder of a federal judge. Between 1977 and 2000, only ten prisoners aged 60 or older were executed. From 2010 to 2019, 45 were executed (23 since 2015).

Sources: Much of the information in this chapter comes from Wikipedia, www.capitalpunishmentuk.org, and the Death Penalty Information Center. Also, Wall Street Journal.

The History of Rock 'n Roll

A-wop-bom-a-loo-mop-a-lomp-bom-bom
"Tutti-Frutti," Little Richard, 1955

Dooby dooby doo wah, doo wah, doo wah
"Ooby Dooby," Roy Orbison, 1956

Louie Louie, oh no, me gotta go
"Louie, Louie," The Kingsmen, 1963

Ha manie f^$@# mumble &% aarhh grumble-mumble?
"Blowin' In The Wind," Bob Dylan, 1963

One, Two, Three, Fa!! Yaaaaa, Yaaaaaa, Ya!
"I Saw Her Standing There," The Beatles, 1964

Do wah diddy diddy dum diddy do
"Do Wah Diddy Diddy," Manfred Mann, 1964

Doe doe di doe doe ditta di da doe
"Funk #48," The James Gang, 1969

Rap appa tap ruffa rut don riffle doh riff raff roh roo dip doo dang
A lot of them, James Brown, 1960s

AaaaaaYeeeeAHhhhhh! AaaaaaYeeeeAHhhhhh!
"Immigrant Song," Led Zeppelin, 1970

Eh-Yowwwwaaaaaaahhhhhh!!
"Won't Get Fooled Again," The Who, 1971

Bring me a doctor, I have a hole in my head
"Making Flippy Floppy," Talking Heads, 1983

I like a good beer buzz early in the morning
"All I Wanna Do," Sheryl Crow, 1994

Y'all cowards couldn't rap this dope with a Zig-Zag
"I Don't Like To," Shad, 2007

THE ZONE: TRUE TALES FROM THE HEARTLAND

Years ago, *Rolling Stone* magazine ranked Jimi Hendrix (1942-1970) as the greatest rock guitarist of all time. Perhaps best known for his psychedelic, electrified version of *The Star-Spangled Banner* at the 1970 Woodstock music festival, Hendrix could coax sounds out of a guitar like no other. He could play his guitar behind his back or with his teeth. "His riffs were a pre-metal funk bulldozer, and his lead lines were an electric LSD trip down to the crossroads..." wrote reviewer Tom Morello. Tragically, Hendrix died of a drug overdose at age 27 following only four years of rock stardom.

It might surprise some boomers and stoners that Hendrix himself claimed that he learned how to play star-spangled guitar during his brief tenure in Nashville, Tennessee, home of country music. Furthermore, on one occasion, Hendrix challenged a local blues guitar legend to a cutting match at a local nightclub, and lost.

"That's where I learned to play really...Nashville," Hendrix was quoted.

A native of Seattle, he was born Johnny Allen but was renamed by his father Al as Jimmy Marshall. By the summer of 1958, Al had purchased Jimmy a five-dollar, second-hand acoustic guitar from one of his friends. For the rest of his life, Hendrix and his guitar were inseparable. He even slept with it. In 1961, Hendrix enlisted in the U.S. Army because he figured he was going to get drafted sooner or later anyway. He chose the Screaming Eagles of the 101st Airborne Division, based at Fort Campbell, Kentucky. Hendrix found Army life gave him little time to pursue his artistic talents. About a year in, he was injured during a jump and was honorably discharged. During his Army stint, he played beer joints in nearby Clarksville, Tenn., and partnered with a fellow Eagle and bass guitarist, Billy Cox. In 1962, Hendrix and Cox headed to Nashville. Jimmy and Billy caused quite a stir in Music City USA, which boasted a lively rhythm-and-blues scene along Jefferson Street and in a small section of downtown at Fourth and Cedar. Known as Jimmy, aka Marbles (because some thought he had lost his), Hendrix worked backup in bands, a little studio work, and played alongside Cox in their band, the King Kasuals, at Club Del Morocco on Jefferson Street. Some of the first video footage of Hendrix is a 1965 clip of him backing Buddy & Stacy on "Shotgun" on *Night Train,* a popular local TV show hosted by Hoss Allen. Hendrix was an eccentric showman who was ahead of his time, and most people thought he was slightly off-kilter.

Jimmy and Billy also played the regional Chitlin' Circuit of black clubs, backing up various acts. "The idea of playing guitar with my teeth came to me in a town in Tennessee. Down there you have to play with your teeth or else you get shot. Those people were really hard to please."

Hendrix and Cox were arrested once in Nashville, which was at the forefront of the Sixties civil rights movement. Cox was quoted, "Every Sunday we would go down to watch the race riots. We took a picnic basket because they wouldn't serve us in the restaurant." Jimmy shared a room with Cox over Joyce's House of Glamour, a beauty parlor next door to the Del.

Soul acts came to play in Nashville before segregated black and white crowds at venues such as the Ryman Auditorium, the Sulphur Dell baseball stadium, Centennial Park, and the War Memorial Auditorium. One act featured Sam Cooke, Solomon Burke, Jackie Wilson, B.B. King, and Chuck Jackson. "I got a little job playing in the backup band," Hendrix recalled. "I learned a lot playing behind all those names every night." Hendrix also played clubs in Printers Alley, such as the Jolly Roger. Hendrix played in the band backing Marion James, Nashville's Queen of the Blues, formerly known as House Rockin' James. She had a national top-ten hit, "That's My Man," in 1966, and recorded CDs over the years, including *Northside Soul* (2012).

One of the regulars on the *Night Train* house band was a fiery blues guitarist named Johnny Jones, also a regular at Club Baron on Jefferson Street. A native of Tennessee, Jones lived in Memphis and moved to Chicago, where he played with Junior Wells and Freddie King before tiring of the harsh winters and moving to Nashville. Legendary music promoter Ted Jarrett pulled Jones out of a house band in Clarksville, where he was then backing female impersonators, and gave him gigs backing Nashville R&B hitmakers Gene Allison and Earl Gaines.

Jones became a local legend who played in the King Kasuals with Hendrix and Cox. He was Jimmy's mentor. On Tuesday nights, Jones and his band The Imperials played for the soldiers in Clarksville. That's where Hendrix saw Jones and latched on, hoping to inject some real blues into his guitar playing.

"I had that mud on my feet," Jones told the *Nashville Scene*. "I brought that swagger, that feel—that's what Jimi wanted…I had what he had to have. I had that lowdown smell of Mississippi in (my guitar style)."

At one point, according to legend, Hendrix decided to take on his mentor. He hauled his guitar and amp from Club Del Morocco on down to Club Baron and challenged Jones to a blues duel. Both put on quite a show, swapping licks. The enthusiastic crowd applauded the most for Jones. A self-assured player, Jones nevertheless thought Hendrix had actually won, that Hendrix lost the Jefferson Street showdown because his amplifier was inferior and he couldn't play loud enough.

Jefferson Street boasted numerous R&B music venues and nightclubs from 1945 to 1970. There was Club Baron, Club Del Morroco, Sugar Hill Club, Club Stealaway, the New Era, the Club Revillot, Maceo's, Deborah's Casino Royale, Ebony Circle, Pee Wee's, and Behind the Green Door. Little Richard played at Club Revillot when he was "just scuffling," and still singing the original bawdy lyrics to "Tutti Frutti."

The Del Morocco was a plush dinner club owned by Theodore "Uncle Teddy" Acklen, with the Blue Room patronized by Jackie Robinson, Joe Louis, Roy Campanella, Count Basie, and other visiting celebrities. The downstairs music stage played host not only to Hendrix and his band but to Rudy Richardson, who dyed his hair with shoe polish and had diamonds embedded in his navel, and Ironing Board Sam, who played an electric keyboard attached to an ironing board.

Jefferson Street was hot but so was Fourth Avenue downtown. The New Era Club was the place to see chartbusters like Aretha Franklin, B.B. King, Jerry Butler, and Joe Tex. The New Era was owned for many years by William Sousa "Soo" Bridgeforth, an elder of the North Nashville community and one-time owner of the Birmingham Black Barons, a team for which Charley Pride once pitched. The club sat where the historic Municipal Auditorium now stands. Fats Domino played at Grady's when he was in town and Bessie

Smith sang "Empty Bed Blues" at the old Bijou Theater, which also hosted Jerry Jackson's weekly vaudeville revue.

Etta James recorded her *Rock The House* live album at Nashville's New Era Club in 1963. Earl Gaines played the Ryman Auditorium with the Top Ten Revue of 1955. Frank Howard & the Commanders sang up a storm and Bubba Suggs performed "So What" on the organ.

The Elks Lodge on Jefferson Street, formerly Club Baron.

Gene Allison grew up in Nashville singing with local gospel groups. He went on to record "You Can Make It If You Try," which was covered by the Rolling Stones.

Sweet Clifford, aka Clifford Curry, recorded for Nashville's Excello label, hitting it big with "She Shot a Hole in My Soul." Saxophone player Hank Crawford led Little Hank & the Rhythm Kings at the Subway Lounge in Printer's Alley. Little Willie John, Roscoe Shelton, Arthur Gunter, Gene Allison, and Christine Kittrell also performed in Nashville.

Night Train debuted in October 1964 and featured Otis Redding, Clarence "Gatemouth" Brown, and Percy Sledge as guest stars. The show boasted a house band led by musical director Bob Holmes and showcasing the fiery blues licks of Johnny Jones. Local talents such as Jimmy Church, the Spidells, the Hytones, and the Avons were regulars, and Jimi Hendrix appeared while he was still a backing guitarist.

In 1967, Robert Knight scored a crossover hit with the original "Everlasting Love," recorded in Nashville.

All good things must come to an end. In the 1950s, a federally funded urban renewal project did away with the historic black downtown district, and in 1970 Jefferson Street fell victim to a major interstate highway project. Changes in musical tastes and the business of music publishing and production also helped to quash the once-vibrant Nashville R&B scene. The only venue still standing on Jefferson Street is Club Baron, now the Elks Lodge.

Jimmy Hendrix left Nashville for New York City, changed the spelling of his name, and found fame and fortune in London, England, as leader of the Jimi Hendrix Experience. He starred at the Monterey and Woodstock music festivals. Singles such as "Hey Joe," "Purple Haze," and "All Along the Watchtower" were huge hits; studio albums *Are You Experienced* and *Electric Ladyland* both went double-platinum. He reunited with Cox to form the Band of Gypsys, but he died tragically in 1970 at age 27 of an accidental drug overdose. The Rock and Roll Hall of Fame describes Hendrix as "arguably the greatest instrumentalist in the history of rock music."

Johnny Jones replaced Hendrix in the King Casuals in 1968 and retired in the late 1970s, but then in the 1990s he restarted and accompanied the likes of Earl Gaines, Roscoe Shelton, Charles Walker, and others at local clubs. He released his debut album under his own name, *I Was Raised on the Blues,* in 1999. He said he had to have time with his guitar every day; it was therapy.

Promoter Ted Jarrett died in 2009. Jones played at a tribute concert to Jarrett at The Place, veteran bandleader Jimmy Church's nightclub on Second Avenue. He also performed at the ninth annual Jefferson Street Jazz and Blues Festival that same year shortly before his death at age 73.

"He (Jones) was the premier blues guitarist in Nashville for more than 50 years," said Michael Gray, an editor at the Country Music Hall of Fame.

According to music critic Ron Wynn, Johnny Jones incorporated into his style the angular, tight fills, fluid lines and dashing harmonies that punctuated the vocals of B.B. King and T-Bone Walker, plus the equally explosive guitar work of Wayne Bennett, whose sound was a key element in the Joe Scott band arrangements underscoring Bobby "Blue" Bland's fiery vocals.

Nashville's R&B legacy was celebrated by a special exhibit at the Country Music Hall of Fame and Museum in 2005. A two-disc album also was released. The National Museum of African-American Music is slated to open downtown in the near future, not far from Jimi Hendrix's star on the Music City Walk of Fame.

Sources: Articles and obituaries in The Nashville Scene magazine and The Tennessean newspaper by Randy Fox, Daniel Cooper, Ron Wynn, and Michael Gray and the Country Music Foundation website.

The Lonesome Highway

GENERAL JACKSON'S IRON BALLS

In November 1814, about 215 Middle Tennesseans under the command of Colonel John Cocke, former Montgomery County sheriff, boarded flat-bottom boats for a treacherous journey down the Cumberland, Ohio and Mississippi rivers to join Major General Andrew Jackson's 7th U.S. Infantry Regiment in New Orleans. In addition to troops, guns, powder, and supplies, the militiamen also transported cannonballs cast at ironmaster Montgomery Bell's Cumberland Furnace in Dickson County. The cannonballs were used to good effect during the Battle of New Orleans on Jan. 8, 1815.

Historically, Tennessee has not been known as an industrial state, but by 1796 (the year Tennessee became a state) a stone stack was in blast at Cumberland Furnace. Built by pioneer James Robertson, the "Father of Middle Tennessee," the furnace took advantage of slave and immigrant labor, abundant iron ore deposits and timberland, and navigable rivers. The furnace was bought in 1804 by Bell, the state's first capitalist and industrialist, who by 1820 was producing 300 tons of hollow-ware (pots, pans, etc.), 50 tons of pig iron, and six tons of machinery.

During the 19th Century and well into the 20th Century, a total of 87 identifiable blast furnaces, ironworks, and forges operated in 14 counties along the Western Highland Rim, which extends from the Land Between the Lakes near Kentucky, south along the Tennessee River to Iron City at the Alabama border. During the last quarter of the 19th Century, Tennessee ranked fifth in the nation in iron production. It has been estimated that these industries mined 8.56 million gross tons of iron ore and produced more than four million tons of pig iron from 1797 to 1930.

The production of ironware was a complicated and tedious process, but the demand for durable goods on the frontier was insatiable, and the smelting of iron ore and forging of pig iron made many men very wealthy. On the other hand, the furnace workers often toiled under severe conditions and received little compensation; most of them were African-American slaves.

By necessity, the blast furnaces needed to be located near iron ore deposits (the type known as brown hematite), where the ore had to be mined and cleaned and hauled to the furnace in two-wheeled ox-driven carts. These deposits were located close to the surface or in "banks." Limestone was used in the process as "flux." Under great heat, the limestone drew the impurities out of the iron ore. The limestone, which is ubiquitous in Middle Tennessee, had to be quarried and crushed and hauled to the furnace. Lime kilns can be seen today in Erin. The purified, crushed limestone was used across the nation for water purification. The other main ingredient was charcoal (actually charred wood), which was needed to produce the great temperatures (2800 degrees F) needed to melt the ore. Many men were employed to cut timber (usually during the colder months) to make charcoal, which was produced by a skilled artisan called a collier. The collier would prop the timber into a conical stack, inserting smaller pieces of wood between the larger logs to reduce the air spaces as much as possible. Then the entire tepee-shaped stack was covered with leaves, dust, and dirt, with several air holes left at the ground level. The wood was burned or charred very slowly over the course of two weeks, the collier living in a crude hut nearby to constantly monitor the air intake and combustion. The result was charcoal. It took a cord of wood (four-foot-long sticks piled four feet high and eight feet long) to yield 33 bushels of charcoal, and 165 bushels of charcoal to make a ton of cold-blast iron. In later years, the charcoal was replaced with coal and then with coke (a refinement of coal).

The blast furnace was a rectangular stack of limestone rocks, wider at the base that at the top. The Bear Spring Furnace, which can be seen today near Dover, was typical — 37 feet high, 38 feet square at the base, and 25 feet square at the top. The open hearth was six foot, four inches high. The stack was built in 1873 of rusticated limestone, without mortar.

The three main ingredients were loaded into the blast furnace from the top on a structure called the bridge. Locating the furnace next to a hill or cliff made building a bridge easier. The ingredients in the furnace required a blast of air to produce critical temperatures, hence the name blast furnace. The air was blasted by bellows or drums powered by either a waterwheel or a steam engine. In later years, hot air would be recirculated to provide a hot blast, which was more efficient.

When the furnace was in blast, the melted and purified iron ore would be directed into a trench formed in the ground with sand. Numerous smaller trenches branched off from this main trench, which reminded the pioneers of piglets feeding at the mama sow, hence the name pig iron. These crude bars of pig iron would then be shipped to forges to be beaten into wrought iron and formed into farm tools, pots and pans, nails, and other durable goods. Products such as cannon tubes and cannonballs had to be cast, by pouring molten iron into forms.

Great Western Furnace, near Dover.

Although there were many ironmasters who operated furnaces and forges along the Western Highland Rim, the most prominent was Bell (1769-1855), a native of Pennsylvania whose family's fortunes were destroyed by the British during the Revolutionary War. As a boy he apprenticed to a tanner, but he hated the work. At the age of 20, he moved with his widowed sister and her six children to Lexington, Kentucky, where he prospered as a hat maker. He saved enough money to buy Robertson's ironworks at Cumberland Furnace and promptly built a iron ore empire. He constructed a second furnace and obtained a government contract to produce iron products, cannon shot, gunpowder, and whiskey. Cannonballs fired by General Jackson's forces at New Orleans came from Bell's works. Thus, Bell was able to exact some revenge against the British for destroying his family's wealth 40 years earlier.

Since they were located on the frontier, Cumberland Furnace and other large iron manufacturing sites had to be self-sufficient plantations, with a magnificent house (the Big House) serving the ironmaster while the workers and slaves lived in cabins or huts. The plantation would also include a kitchen, smokehouse, warehouse, blacksmith shops, stables, and usually a water-powered grist mill. At one point, Bell owned 14 furnaces and forges, 50,000 acres of land, 300 slaves, and 400 mules. Around 1820, Bell came up with an interesting method of powering a new forge. At a place called the

Narrows of the Harpeth River, the river forms a hairpin turn around a high ridge of limestone and passes within 100 feet of itself. Using only manpower, crude tools, and black powder, Bell constructed a tunnel (16 feet wide by 8 feet high) through the solid rock that connected the river with itself, with a 16-foot difference in elevation. The water falling through this diversion tunnel was then used to power a waterwheel, which was directly linked to a trip-hammer to beat pig iron into usable metal. Although Bell had the vision and money (many locals called him a fool to attempt the excavation) to build Pattison (Patterson) Forge, it was Samuel W. Adkisson (1801-1875), a teenaged mathematician, who designed the project. And it was the brute strength and stamina of many black slaves, whose names are unknown to this day, to carve the tunnel out of solid rock. Today the tunnel is designated a National Historic Civil Engineering Landmark. There is a second tunnel located about 200 feet away from the first, purposely left unfinished.

Although he died a miser and a "man of mystery," Bell did leave a legacy. He is known to have fathered at least one child, a daughter who married his nephew James L. Bell. The couple had two daughters and two sons. At the time of his death in 1855 at age 86, Bell left $20,000 for the establishment of a private free school for boys. Today that school is the prestigious Montgomery Bell Academy in Nashville.

Also, before his death, Bell began freeing his slaves at a great financial cost to himself. In 1853-54, through the auspices of the American Colonization Society, he sent at least 88 of his freed slaves to the Liberian colony in West Africa, paying for their passage and six months of expenses. Unfortunately, the colonization project produced only mixed results for the freedmen.

Another antebellum iron plantation was located at Cedar Grove Furnace, the only remaining double-stack furnace, located near the Tennessee River in the southern portion of the Western Highland Rim. This furnace was probably the first in Tennessee to use the "hot blast" method in which the air blast was heated before being blown into the furnace, thus increasing the efficiency of the process and requiring less raw materials. The plantation covered 8,800 acres and "employed" about 100 workers. In 1833 the furnace was producing 40 tons of pig iron a week. The pigs were hauled by ox carts two miles to the river, where they were loaded into wooden flat-bottomed boats about 65 feet long which could carry several tons. In 1850, rebuilt and under new ownership, Cedar Grove Furnace was producing 1,800 tons of iron. In 1862, the operation was shut down by Federal river gunboats lobbing shells into the factory. The ironmaster was ambushed and shot to death shortly thereafter. By 1883, all that remained was the double-stack furnace.

Another famous iron plantation was near Brownsport in Decatur County on the west side of the Tennessee River. According to an 1874 Bureau of

Agriculture report:

"The amount of iron ore in this county is considerable. The ore (limonite) is singularly free from flint, sand, sulphur and phosphorus. Near Brownsport Furnace is a bank from twelve to twenty feet in thickness, and resting upon a limestone bed. This bank is capped with a cherty mass, and there is an unusually small proportion of dead matter. Brownsport Furnace is the only one in operation in the county. It is three miles from the Tennessee River. This furnace has been in operation forty years, and has now a capacity of 6,000 tons of pig metal per annum, or from eighteen to twenty tons per day. The stack is forty feet high and twelve feet between bosh. It blows with three tuyers (nozzles), is hot blast and has all the modern improvements. It has a vertical engine, with twenty-four inch cylinder, and a blowing cylinder sixty inches in diameter. Sand rock for hearths is convenient, and the ore is dug within one hundred yards of the trundle head. For making a ton of iron 120 bushels of charcoal are used (2,688 cubic inches to the bushel). Coal costs seven and a half cents per bushel delivered. Ore delivered costs $2.00 per ton. About two and a quarter tons of ore make a ton of iron. The hauling of the pig iron to the river costs $1.25 per ton. Limestone is delivered at $1.00 per ton. The iron made is only suitable for castings, most of it being consumed for light castings, such as require strength and toughness. About 200 hands are kept employed."

The Williamson Furnace was built in 1832 near Fernvale along the Caney Fork of the South Harpeth River in Williamson County. It is somewhat of a modern mystery why the furnace was located there since there are no iron ore deposits in the immediate vicinity.

The owners of the Sugar Creek Furnace in Hickman County learned that they had made a big mistake—the closest iron ore deposits were nine miles away! Eventually the cost of hauling ore to the furnace became prohibitive and the operation was shut down.

Because the ironworks required a lot of capital and manpower, the industry was often hit hard by financial downturns and changed ownership often. Then again, some sites worked the nearby ore deposits until they were depleted or too difficult to mine. Competition from elsewhere in the U.S. iron belt and even overseas closed many of the ironworks. Many of the Highland Rim ironworks were destroyed during the Civil War when the Federal army and navy moved through the area encompassing the Highland Rim. A few survived, rebuilt, and prospered after the war, some remaining in operation well into the 20th Century.

The iron industry on the Western Highland Rim has its share of folklore and legend. At the Brownsport Furnace, it is said that a slave facing punishment decided to run to the bridge and throw himself into the hot blast furnace rather than face the cruelty of his master. In 1917, during a tour of his Southern holdings, William J. Wrigley delighted the children of Waynesboro by handing out free chewing gum in the public square.

Anthony W. Van Leer, a Pennsylvania native, bought Cumberland Furnace and by 1860 was producing more than 1,800 tons of pig iron with a work force of 93 men and seven women. After the war, in 1880, VanLeer's granddaughter, Mary Florence, reopened the furnace in partnership with her husband, a former Federal officer named Captain James P. Drouillard. The site was producing 20 tons of pig iron a day with 250 employees. The furnace was finally shut down by the government in 1942. In 1988 the village of Cumberland Furnace was named a historic district by the National Register of Historic Places.

The Woods-Yeatman operation included furnaces at Carlisle and Bear Spring, a bloomery or forge at Randolph, and the Cumberland Rolling Mill, which also included a nail factory. Operations ceased at Bear Spring in 1901.

The Great Western Iron Works between the Tennessee and Cumberland rivers opened in 1855 and in a 34-week period produced 1,350 tons of iron. The furnace closed the following year, however, due to lack of ore and a slave insurrection by the furnace crew. The last ironworks in Stewart County went out of production in 1927.

Today, the only remnants of the vast ironmaking operations on the Western Highland Rim are a few preserved limestone stacks (Bear Spring and Great Western), traces of ore pits, and scattered pieces of blue-colored slag stones lying on the ground.

Bullets for longarms such as muskets and rifles and for handguns were made from lead, either balls cast in a handheld mold or conical blunt-tipped bullets manufactured in mass (the celebrated Minié ball was actually a conical-shaped projectile, not a ball). Shotguns or scatter-guns used shells filled with small pellets or "shot" instead of bullets. An ingenious method was devised in the late 1700s to create precisely sized spherical projectiles called shot in mass numbers. The facility built to accomplish this was a shot tower. A slender tower usually of brick or stone was built into the side of a tall riverside bluff. Heated into molten metal, lead would be poured through specifically sized screens and allowed to drop a considerable distance down a shaft and into containers filled with water. During the fall (about 150 feet was required), the lead would naturally form into perfect spheres and then be quenched or solidified by the water. A good frontier example is the Jackson Ferry Shot Tower (1807) in the Virginia state park near Max Meadows. Seventy-five feet of the shaft was dug into the riverside bluff, necessitating the building of a 75-foot tower of stone 2.5 feet thick. The thick walls kept the interior consistently cool, which aided the process.

The Phoenix Shot Tower in Baltimore, Md. was the tallest structure in the U.S. from 1828 to 1846 at 234 feet tall. The Sparks Shot Tower in Philadelphia was the first in the U.S., built in 1808. The first shot tower was built in 1782 in Bristol, England.

The Bliemeister method has supplanted the shot tower method since the early 1960s. In this process, molten lead is dripped from small holes and dropped approximately one inch into a hot liquid, where it is then rolled along an incline and then dropped another three feet. The temperature of the liquid controls the cooling rate of the lead, while the surface tension of the liquid and the inclined surface(s) work together to bring the small droplets of lead into highly regular balls of lead in spherical form. The size of the lead shot is determined by the diameter of the hole used to drip the lead, ranging from approximately 0.018 inches (0.46 mm) for No. 9 lead shot to about 0.025 inches (0.64 mm) for No. 6 or 7 shot, while also depending on the specific lead alloy that is used. The roundness of the lead shot depends on the angle of the inclined surfaces as well as the temperature of the liquid coolant. Various coolants have been used, from diesel fuel to antifreeze and water-soluble oil. After the lead shot cools, it is washed, then dried, and small amounts of graphite are added to prevent clumping. Lead shot larger than about No. 5 tends to clump badly when fed through tubes, even when graphite is used. Lead shot smaller than about No. 6 tends not to clump when fed through tubes when graphite is used.

Jackson Ferry shot tower in southwest Virginia.

Double-aught (00) buckshot is 0.33 in. in diameter. Birdshot ranges roughly from 0.2 to 0.1 inches in diameter. In recent years, lead shot has been discontinued from usage due to possible contamination of wildlife (lead poisoning).

Sources: Michael T. Gavin, Tennessee Civil War National Heritage Area, MTSU; Encyclopedia of Tennessee History and Culture.

WELCOME TO THE BODY FARM

Science and technology have fostered many advances in the art of identifying and capturing murderers. The dead can speak, but only to those trained in the science of corpse decomposition. Outside the University of Tennessee-Knoxville training hospital is an acre of wooded land bordered by fencing topped by razor wire. Inside can be found a landscape both horrifying and highly scientific — multiple dead bodies exposed to the elements, decomposing and decaying. Welcome to the Body Farm.

The Body Farm, made famous in Patricia Cornwell's bestselling crime fiction, is the brainchild of Dr. William Bass, the Tennessee state forensic anthropologist. Dr. Bass is a scientist who studies the human skeleton, specifically those unearthed from earlier, even ancient, times. As a forensic anthropologist, he assists law enforcement in examining the remains of victims, sometimes victims of murder. In investigating such cases, Dr. Bass came to realize that the decaying of human flesh had not been seriously studied since the 13th Century. New research was needed.

It all started back on Friday, Dec. 15, 1864, during the Civil War, when more than two weeks of nerve-racking suspense exploded into earth-shattering violence. The decisive Battle of Nashville ended the next day when Federal troops charged up Compton's Hill to confront the Confederate soldiers crouched around its crown. The attack was bloody and overwhelming. The Confederates had several options — throw down your weapon and run, surrender, or fight to the death. Most ran, but one of the Army of Tennessee's bravest officers, Lt. Colonel William Shy of the 20th Tennessee, chose to make a stand. The next morning on that scarred hill, burial details found the body of Col. Shy felled by a single gunshot to the middle of the brow. Reports of the officer being stripped of clothing and bayonetted to a tree are most likely false. The slain officer was taken to the porch of the Compton farmhouse. Shy was 26 years old at his death. His parents rode from their family home near Franklin to accept the body. Colonel Shy was buried in the family graveyard on Del Rio Pike in Franklin. From that point on, Compton's Hill has been known as Shy's Hill.

Fast-forward 113 years to December 1977, where on the morning of Christmas Eve, the new owners of an antebellum estate on Del Rio Pike discovered that the grave of Colonel Shy had been disturbed, dug out and down three to four feet. Grave robbers in search of relics, the owners thought. The sheriff's department was contacted but did not investigate until after the holidays. There didn't seem to be any emergency or need to hurry. What they found just below the disturbed earth, however, was disconcerting — what appeared to be the body of a recent murder victim. The body was in bad shape but some pink flesh was evident. He was dressed in a tuxedo. His head was missing. The local coroner was called in. Authorities theorized that, in a plot deserving of an episode of Alfred Hitchcock, the killers had tried to bury the body in an existing grave but had been interrupted for some reason.

The sheriff's department decided to call in Dr. Bass at UT-K for a closer look. What he found were the loose bones of a skeleton with some flesh attached, minus the head and dressed in formal attire. One of the hands was still inside a white glove. Dr. Bass speculated that the victim might have been a waiter at a local restaurant or a bridegroom who may have dissed some in-laws.

The coffin underneath was found to be made of cast iron and had a large jagged hole in it. After most of the remains had been recovered and laid out on a piece of plywood, Dr. Bass was lowered down into the grave by his ankles and examined the inside of the coffin. Nothing but a thin layer of goo.

Dr. Bass took the remains to the Tennessee Bureau of Investigation and then back to his office at the university, a former locker room underneath the football stadium.

The doctor and his students determined that the victim was male, 5-9 to 6-0 tall, and middle to late-20s in age. A cause of death could not be determined. Then the press got hold of the story, probably encouraged by that old chestnut of a headline — "Headless Body in Topless Bar." The plot thickened when deputies looked further into the dark, dank coffin and found a skull, actually 17 pieces of it that had to be glued back together. It was obvious now the cause of death — a large caliber gunshot wound two inches above the left eye. Clues began to accumulate. The teeth of the victim showed no signs of any dental work or care. The clothing was found to be made entirely from natural fibers with no labels. The shoes were square-toed. Dr. Bass and the technicians at the TBI lab came to realize that the recent murder victim was actually Colonel Shy himself. Instead of killers trying to stuff a body into the coffin, the ghouls had actually tried to pull the officer's body out of the coffin.

Dr. Bass had miscalculated the time of death by more than 100 years. He was embarrassed, especially since the story was broadcast worldwide to a fascinated audience. The truth emerged. Colonel Shy, a young man from a prominent family, had been embalmed and buried not in his uniform but in his best clothes. The cast-iron coffin had been hermetically sealed, slowing down decomposition.

"Personally, I was embarrassed. Scientifically, I was intrigued; above all, I was determined to do something about it," Dr. Bass wrote in his 2004 book *Death's Acre*. The faulty conclusion in the Shy case had been due mostly to presumptions and ignorance about the science of body decomposition. No research had been conducted on the subject since the Chinese official Sung Tz'u wrote *The Washing Away of Wrongs* about 750 years ago.

Early in his career in Kansas, Dr. Bass worked a case in which he asked a farmer if a cow could be killed and laid in the field in order to study how the carcass decomposed. Nothing came of the request, but the methodology lingered in the doctor's mind. During his tenure at UT-K, Dr. Bass was consulted many times by law enforcement to examine the remains of victims. Unfortunately there were no facilities to house the deceased. The agriculture school had farms outside of town. On one of them was a three-sided shed suitable for temporarily housing the dead. The only problem was that the inmates working on the penal farm next door took to sightseeing at the macabre shed. Nothing was disturbed, but...

Then the Shy case came along and prompted Dr. Bass to advocate not only the Body Farm but the building of a world-class forensic anthropology research center. Such research was necessary but could be construed by some as "gruesome, disrespectful, even shocking." There was an acre of land available next to the UT Medical Center. In 1981, the researchers laid out their first donated body onto a small concrete pad built for this purpose. The body was covered with a small woodframe of wire mesh to keep out the larger rodents. Then it was wait and observe, document and interpret. Today the Body Farm contains dozens of donated bodies in various stages of decomposition under various environmental conditions. Data collected on the farm has been instrumental in identifying culprits in many murder cases.

Today, the UT Forensic Anthropology Research Facility includes the Body Farm and a large state-of-the-art research building. Research there has determined:

- Decomposition rates: The sequence does not vary, but the timing can. A mathematical formula was derived to determine decomposition rates based on accumulated degree days.
- Differential decomposition: A particular part of a corpse decomposing

too quickly tells scientists that an additional variable is at play at that location (i.e., trauma), even if no trace of it still remains.
- Decomposition variables: Studies conducted to determine how different conditions affect decomposition — sunlight vs. shade, inside a building vs. outside, shallow vs. deep burial, submerged vs. surface burials, clothed body vs. naked, etc.
- Forensic entomology: Studies of grave insects. This data and knowledge of an individual insect species' life cycle can provide a separate method of calculating time since death.
- Burials: On average, decomposition progresses at approximately one-eighth the speed of a body that remains on the surface.
- Chemical analysis of soil samples: Biochemicals are produced in a predictable manner during the different stages of decomposition. By analyzing soil under an actively decomposing corpse, the time since death can be accurately determined.

Based on this and other research projects, forensic science has progressed in leaps and bounds, providing criminal investigators with much more information concerning the fate of the victim. This, in turn, has lead to a higher conviction rate in murder cases. FBI special agents involved in crime scene recovery have studied at the Body Farm for the past 20 years.

Over the past 45 years, the Body Farm has received the remains of about 70 unidentified victims. They have worked to resolve these cold cases for the past 10 years and so far have been able to successfully identify 20 individuals.

"All of the research that we do out here is to benefit law enforcement and to move forensic science forward in areas such as grave recognition and how best to excavate burials," said Dawnie Wolfe Steadman, current director of the Forensic Anthropology Center at UT-K, who manages the research facility. To duplicate real-life scenarios, donors are left to decompose in various states—partially clothed, wrapped in plastic, placed in a car trunk, or in a garbage bin. "These are all things we can test," Steadman said, "and directly help law enforcement figure out their cases better."

Today, there are six other body farms at university research centers across the country.

In the early 2000s, Dr. Bass formed an alliance with Jon Jefferson, veteran journalist, writer, and documentary filmmaker, and they have published several fictional books on forensic anthropology.

Colonel Shy was reburied in a new coffin with full military honors several weeks after the graverobbing incident. The ghouls who opened Col. Shy's grave have never been prosecuted.

Sources: Death's Acre-Inside the Legendary Forensics Lab, The Body Farm, Where the Dead Do Tell Tales by Dr. Bill Bass and Jon Jefferson. G.P. Putnam's Sons, 2003. Also, online blog of Jen Danna, scientist and author of scientific crime fiction.

Having a ball with spheres

In geometry—the physical manifestation of mathematics—can there be a more perfect example of a shape than that of a sphere? An object formed by an infinite number of points equidistant from one fixed point? The celestial spheres were the fundamental entities of the cosmological models developed by Plato, Aristotle, Ptolemy, and Copernicus. The apparent motions of the fixed stars and planets were treated as embedded in rotating spheres made of an aetherial, transparent fifth element (quintessence). Since the fixed stars did not change their positions relative to one another, it was argued that they must be on the surface of a single starry sphere.

Technically, a ball is the enclosed area of a sphere. Of all the solids having a given volume, the sphere is the one with the smallest surface area. The distance from the center to the surface is the radius. Twice the radius is the diameter. A measurement all the way around the ball is called the circumference.

How accurate can experts manufacture a sphere or a ball? One of the most accurate human-made spheres was a fused quartz gyroscope for the Gravity Probe B experiment, and differs in shape from a perfect sphere by no more than 40 atoms (less than 10nm) of thickness. If one of these spheres were scaled to the size of the Earth, the greatest imperfections would measure only eight feet high. Conversely, if the actual Earth were shrunk to the size of a billiard ball it would appear to be very smooth, but reportedly some people could still feel or detect the roughness caused by mountains and ocean trenches. In 2008, Australian scientists created even more perfect spheres, approximately the size of ping pong balls, accurate to 0.3 nm.

Balls. There are all kinds of balls. Snowballs, dirtballs, meatballs, pinballs, beach balls, cannon balls, masquerade balls, sausage balls, popcorn balls, and so on.

Mozart loved the feel of smooth rolling balls, e.g., billiard balls. He would think about symphonies while bouncing balls off the billiard table cushions.

There's attractive comedienne Lucille Ball of *I Love Lucy* fame. Ball State University in Muncie, Indiana, named for the Ball brothers of New York who came to the Midwest to manufacture glass.

Atoms, eyeballs, highballs, speedballs, fireballs, Minié balls, and the balls of your feet aren't really balls or spheres. In the case of atoms, they are depicted that way to illustrate mathematical formulae.

Did you ever want to "open the ball" on someone who annoys you? Go balls-out? The terms derive from a centrifugal governor on an engine. The faster the engine runs, the faster the rotation of a connecting shaft, and the further outward its attached metal balls twirl, until their weight holds down a connecting rod which limits the fuel intake of the engine, thus governing it.

If you drop the ball, you have screwed up. Get the ball rolling by making the first move; get something out of mothballs. Random results is how the ball bounces. Everything is the whole ball of wax. Your spouse is the ole ball and chain. Band leader Mitch Miller used to tell members of sing-alongs to "follow the bouncing ball."

Knoxville, Tennessee holds two distinctions regarding balls and spheres. The Women's Basketball Hall of Fame boasts the world's largest basketball, 30 feet in diameter and weighing ten tons. Nearby, the 26-story Sunsphere, a 75-foot diameter globe of glass treated in 24k gold built for the 1982 World's Fair, has become the city's symbol.

Each new year begins with the dropping of the ball in New York City's Times Square. The tradition was begun in 1907-08 by *New York Times* publisher Adolph Ochs to supplant the usual fireworks show. The first ball was constructed of wood and iron, and lit with 100 incandescent light bulbs. By New Year's Eve 2008, the ball displayed its fifth new design. Manufactured by Waterford Crystal with a diameter of six feet and weighing 1,212 pounds, the ball used 9,576 energy-efficient bulbs that consumed the same amount of electricity as 10 toasters. The display also uses computerized lighting patterns.

The disco ball or glitter ball originated in the Roaring Twenties and saw a big resurgence during the disco dancing craze of the 1970s. The retro Dive Motel in Nashville features a disco ball in every room and a large one in the Dive Bar.

Then there's ball pits, generally a shallow basin 2.5 feet deep filled with hollow multi-colored plastic balls. Kids love to play in them, sort of like burrowing in a pile of leaves or a snowpile. Ball pits are disappearing due to germs—researchers found more than 31 different types of bacteria in ball pits they tested. In one overly dirty ball pit, the scientists discovered that a single ball contained 712,000 micro-organisms. They didn't say how long it took to count that many.

It's amazing how many sports, indoors and out, utilize a round ball of various size and material. Competitors have been using balls in sports ranging back to ancient times, ranging from bowling balls to marbles. What we do to balls in the name of competitive sports is ghastly — we throw them, kick them, hit them with bats, clubs, paddles, mallets, and racquets, roll them on the ground or lanes, tap them, smash them against walls, poke them with sticks, break them, and flick them with our fingers.

The football started out round but then became elongated (the shape is a prolate spheroid). On Nov. 6, 1869, Rutgers faced Princeton in a game that was played with a round ball, usually regarded as the first game of American college football. The football eventually became enlongated to facilitate the forward pass, codified in 1906, and used extensively in the 1930s. It also spelled the end of the drop-kick. The earliest footballs were made out of a pig's bladder, hence the nickname pigskin. Back in the day, white footballs were used at night for visibility. In the NFL, the ball must be inflated to an air pressure between 12.5 and 13.5 psi and weigh 14 to 15 ounces.

In an NFL game, the home team must provide 36 footballs for an outdoor game or 24 for an indoor game. Twelve new footballs, sealed in a special box and shipped by the manufacturer, are opened in the officials' locker room two hours and 15 minutes before the game. These balls are specially marked with the letter "K" and are used exclusively for the kicking game. The NFL introduced them to prevent teams from doctoring footballs to increase the distance of kicks. Since 1941, Horween Leather Company has been the exclusive supplier of leather for NFL footballs. Wilson, the official supplier for the NFL, makes about 700,000 footballs per year for all uses. Wilson consumes 20,000 feet of cowhide per week. One cowhide can make as many as 20 footballs.

The heaviest sports ball resembles a cannon ball, but it's not fired out of a gun. The shot put is a field-and-track event. The shot weighs 16 pounds (8.8 lbs. for women), can be used indoors or outdoors, and can be made of cast iron, solid steel, stainless steel, brass, or synthetic materials.

As for basketball, the Spalding NBA Official Game Ball costs $250, consists of full-grain leather inflated at 8psi, and measures 29.5 inches in circumference (size 7). It's only for indoor use. However, for the 2021-22 season, Wilson will take over as the official ball after a 40-year hiatus. The first purpose-built basketballs were made from panels of leather stitched together with a rubber bladder inside. A cloth lining was added to the leather for support and uniformity. A molded version of the early basketball was invented in 1942. In the late 1990s, synthetic composite materials were introduced. In 2018, nearly $214 million worth of basketballs were sold in the U.S. alone. The most common ball is orange with black ribs, covered with

4,118 pebbles (2.5mm in diameter). Balls now come in a variety of solid and multiple colors.

The iconic soccer ball is a black-and-white patterned spherical truncated icosahedron design. Many different designs of balls exist, varying both in appearance and physical characteristics. The inside of the ball consists of a latex or butyl rubber bladder which enables the ball to be pressurized. The ball's cover is made of leather, synthetic leather, polyurethane or PVC panels. The ball is 8.7 inches in diameter.

Balls used in ten-pin bowling typically have holes for two fingers and the thumb. Balls used in five-pin bowling, candlepin bowling, duckpin bowling, and kegel have no holes, and are small enough to be held in the palm of the hand. Same for bocce balls and croquet balls. Bowling balls were made of lignum vitae (hardwood) until the 1905 introduction of rubber balls. Polyester ("plastic") balls were introduced in 1959 and, despite developing less hook-generating lane friction than rubber balls, by the 1970s plastic dominated over rubber, which then became obsolete with the early-1980s development of polyurethane ("urethane") balls. Reactive resin balls of the 1990s use additives in urethane surface materials to create microscopic oil-absorbing pores that increase "tackiness," which enhances traction.

Pro bowling balls weigh 12 to 16 pounds and cost up to $250. They can incorporate various core designs, i.e., balls have various solid shapes serving as their cores to enhance hooking. The fingerholes are usually custom-drilled to fit individuals. Bowling balls come in all colors, multi-colors, translucent, and even clear.

Baseballs are composed of a rubber or cork center wrapped in yarn and covered by two peanut-shaped pieces of white horsehide or cowhide bound by 108 hand-woven red-dyed stitches. Early baseballs came in all shapes and sizes and materials. Baseballs have been known to be live or dead during certain periods based on how well batters abuse it. For example, the 1920s were the age of the live ball with batting averages improving. The official ball of the National League, formed in 1876, was the A.G. Spalding. In 1934, the National League and American League came to a compromise and standardized the baseball. They agreed on a cushion cork center; two wrappings of yarn; a special rubber cement coating; two more wrappings of yarn; and, finally, a horsehide cover. In 1974, covers switched from horsehide to cowhide. Two years later, the Major Leagues began using Rawlings balls.

Today, several dozen baseballs are used in a typical professional game, due to scratches, discoloration, and undesirable texture that can occur during the game, not to mention foul balls and homeruns. Back in 1920, a batter was hit in the head and killed with a discolored ball difficult to see in the twilight conditions. Today, the alum tanning of white cowhide is done in Tullahoma,

Tennessee. Then the balls are manufactured in Puerto Rico, about 80,000 each year. Eighty-eight inches of cotton thread and 316 yards of yarn are used in each ball. Major League Baseball teams rub their baseballs in a special mud from the Delaware River in New Jersey. The mud gives the ball its off-white appearance and allows pitchers to have a better grip and more control over the ball.

Of course, some pitchers also doctor their own baseballs, illegally. They have scratched, scraped, and cut the cover, and added spit, tobacco juice, tar, wax, petroleum jelly, and shoe polish to the ball to affect its flight. In 1920, each team was allowed to designate up to two pitchers who could throw spitballs. After 1920, the use of the spitball was banned with the exception of a group of 17 existing spitballers, who were grandfathered in and allowed to throw the pitch legally until they retired.

Back in the day, golf balls were made of small rubber bladders filled with liquid, wrapped with yards of rubber twining, and covered with a thin balata shell. Amateur golfers could easily mishit and cut "smiles" into the covers with bad shots and eventually rip the cover clean off the ball. Most duffers carried high-quality unblemished golf balls to be used only on the putting greens. Low-quality or marked balls would be used by golf courses for their driving ranges.

Centuries ago, the first golf balls were made of wood and then later a leather ball stuffed with bird feathers called a featherie. The first mass-produced golf balls were molded out of the sap of the Malaysian sapodilla tree and called gutties. Golfers soon observed that for some reason gutties with nicks and imperfections flew truer than smooth balls. Golf ball manufacturers thus began etching, carving and chiseling different textures into guttie surfaces, trying to find the pattern most conducive to stable flight. Eventually it was discovered that dimples or indentations worked best. Today's golf balls have 300 to 500 dimples each (the record number is 1,070). A dimpled ball has half the drag of a smooth ball. Dimples also allow golfers to apply spin, usually backspin, to the ball. That's why a golfer can hit the ball past the pin on the green and it will roll back to the cup.

A guy named Coburn Haskell discovered quite by accident that a ball wound with rubber bands bounced rather well. Soon balls were made from wound cores covered with a new material, the sap of the Balata tree.

All balls used the 1908 Taylor dimple pattern until the early 1970s, when all different varieties of dimple patterns were introduced and tested. Then some golfers experimented with yellow or green colored balls.

Today, some professionals still use a wound ball, but most golfers use a solid ball, one of synthetic resin covered with Surlyn, a tough Dupont ionomer resin. The era of smiles is over. High-tech golf balls still find their way into the water and tall grass, however.

Billiard or pool balls used to be made of wood and then ivory. Four balls could be made from one elephant tusk. In 1869, with the popularity of pool climbing along with the cost of ivory, pool table maker Phelan and Collender decided to challenge its customers by offering $10,000 to anyone who could invent a non-ivory pool ball. John Wesley Hyatt of Albany, N.Y., combined camphor with alcohol and nitrocellulose, molding it into a spherical shape under extreme pressure. He didn't win the prize, but his creation is considered to be one of the first synthetic plastics. He continued to refine the celluloid billiard balls, but it remained a poor substitute for ivory because it was nowhere near as durable. What's worse, nitrocellulose wasn't a particularly stable substance, and on rare occasion, according to Hyatt, pool balls would explode when struck with force. In 1907, American chemist Phelan Leo Baekeland invented a new plastic-like substance called Bakelite. Balls made of Bakelite were durable, easy to produce, and wouldn't explode. By the mid-1920s, the majority of pool balls were being made out of Bakelite. Today's pool balls are usually made of acrylic or plastic resins, which are extremely durable and can be milled to exacting standards.

Billiard balls should meet seven basic criteria after going through a 13-step manufacturing process: density, balance, diameter tolerance, roundness, color precision, surface polish, and brilliance. It takes 23 days to produce, cast, cure, grind, and polish the balls. According to the World Pool-Billiard Association, a pool ball is 2.25 inches in diameter, with a tolerance of plus or minus five-thousandths of an inch.

Modern tennis balls are filled with air at two psi and are surfaced by a uniform felt-covered rubber compound. The felt delays flow separation in the boundary layer which reduces aerodynamic drag and gives the ball better flight properties. Yellow and white are the only approved colors. Most balls are a fluorescent "optic yellow," first introduced in 1972 because they were more visible on television. There are four categories: Regular Duty or All-Court, Extra Duty or Hard-Court, Grass Court, and Hi-Altitude.

The sport of lawn tennis is centuries old. In 1480, Louis XI of France forbade the filling of tennis balls with chalk, sand, sawdust, or earth, and stated that they were to be made of good leather, well-stuffed with wool. Other early tennis balls were made by Scottish craftsmen from a wool-wrapped stomach of a sheep or goat and tied with rope. Other versions used materials such as animal fur, and rope made from animal intestines and muscles. In the 18th century, strips of wool were wound tightly around a nucleus made by rolling a number of strips into a little ball. String was then tied in many directions around the ball and a white cloth covering sewn around the ball.

In the early 1870s lawn tennis arose in Britain through the pioneering efforts of Walter Clopton Wingfield and Harry Gem, using Victorian lawns laid out for croquet. Wingfield marketed tennis sets, which included rubber balls imported from Germany. After Charles Goodyear invented vulcanized rubber, the Germans were successful in developing vulcanized air-filled rubber balls. They were light and colored gray or red with no covering. John Moyer Heathcote experimented with covering the rubber ball with flannel, and by 1882 Wingfield was advertising tennis balls clad in stout cloth.

Early table tennis or ping pong balls were made of rounded wine-bottle corks, then later a 50mm wrapped cork ball. Around 1900, table tennis balls consisted of hollow celluloid spheres. In 1926, the International Table Tennis Federation (ITTF) was formed, and competition table tennis balls were standardized at 38mm in diameter and made of celluloid.

For the 2000 Olympic games in Sydney, the ITTF increased the size of the ball, from 38mm to 40mm. This was intended to make the ball easier to see on television and to slow down play to make the game more entertaining for spectators.

In 2014, the ITTF changed table tennis ball material from celluloid to a non-flammable plastic. Today, most balls are made in China of acrylonitrile butadiene styrene (ABS) and marked with one, two, or three stars (three being the highest quality and most durable).

Marbles have been played by kids of all ages for centuries. Marbles come in all sizes but commonly are a half-inch in diameter, usually made of glass. A marble can be known as a boulder, bonker, cosher, masher, plumper, popper, shooter, thumper, smasher, noogie, taw, bumbo, crock, bumboozer, bowler, tonk, tronk, godfather, tom bowler, fourer, giant, dobber, dobbert, hogger, biggie, toebreaker, peewee, or mini.

Different types and colors of marbles are aggies, alley, catseye, beachball, red devils, oily, opaque, oxblood, toothpaste, turtle, bumblebee, commie, purie, swirly, shooter, tiger, baby, and many others. Not surprisingly, marbles are very collectible.

The largest manufacturer of playing marbles is Vacor de Mexico, which makes 90 percent of the world's marbles. More than 12 million are produced daily. One mechanical technique is dropping globules of molten glass into a groove made by two interlocking parallel screws. As the screws rotate, the marble travels along them, gradually being shaped into a sphere as it cools.

What is perhaps the world's most important ball? What makes the world go round? Bearing balls. A ball bearing is a type of rolling-element bearing that uses balls to maintain the separation between the bearing races. The purpose of a ball bearing is to reduce rotational friction and support radial and axial loads. Bearing balls must be extremely hard, nearly perfectly spherical, and very smooth in order to perform well. And they must be produced in the millions, in many different sizes.

During WWII, Allied bombers targeted ball bearing plants in Germany, specifically the Kugel-Fischer plant in Schweinfurt. Nazi aircraft production required two million ball bearings per month. On Black Thursday, Oct. 14, 1943, the 8th Air Force lost 60 heavy bombers, with more than 140 others damaged, during one raid over Schweinfurt. Nearly 600 airmen, most in their 20s, were killed or captured that day, with 40 others wounded.

Bearing balls are made from steel rod cut to length on a "heading" machine and then pressed into a spherical mold with ten tons of force, at a rate faster than the eye can see, forming a raw ball. The machine can make 1,000 raw balls per minute. A flashing machine removes the burrs from the raw balls by forcing them through circular grooves cut into two heavy circular plates facing each other, one plate stationary while the other spins. The process is repeated until all the burrs are removed. The balls are then heat-treated to harden and strengthen them. They are heated to 1,490 degrees and quenched in oil to 140 degrees. The balls are heated and quenched a second time, then precision-ground in another device much like the flashing machine. Lapping removes any fine unevenness and polishes the surface to sparkling. The balls are "washed" with ultrasonic waves to remove any oil and dirt. A machine checks the size of the balls, and human inspectors look for scratches by the way light is reflected on a tray of balls. The tolerance of the steel ball is less than 0.1 micrometer. The balls are tested for strength, e.g., balls 16mm in diameter should be able to withstand a weight of 35 tons.

Sources: YouTube; various sports associations websites.

MEN BEHAVING BADLY

RIOTS, MASSACRES, FEUDS, BATTLES, TURF WARS, ASSASSINATION, MURDER, ANARCHY, GUNFIGHTS, KNIFEFIGHTS, GANGLAND VIOLENCE, SCALPING, MAYHEM, RANGE WAR, VIGILANTISM, HANGINGS

Carmack Whacked: Martyr of Political Assassination

In May 2020, a mob toppled the prominent statue which stood in front of the Tennessee State Capitol for the past 95 years. It wasn't a statue of General Jackson or President Polk or even Governor Sevier. It was a statue of white supremacist, newspaper editor, famed orator, and advocate of temperance U.S. Senator Edward Ward Carmack. The statue by sculptor Nancy Cox McCormack was erected in 1925 to celebrate Carmack's advocacy against liquor and promotion of temperance, a controversial issue at the time (Tennessee enacted Prohibition ten years before the nation as a whole). Carmack was a lawyer who served one term in the state House of Representatives. He then edited newspapers in Columbia, Nashville, and Memphis. Carmack feuded with Ida B. Wells, a writer at a black newspaper in Memphis who protested lynchings, three of which had occurred at that time in Memphis. Carmack had incited the riot which resulted in the lynchings of three black men. Then the newspaper where Wells worked was destroyed. An early civil rights activist, Wells was not in Memphis at the time and did not return to the South for the next 30 years.

Carmack became a bigshot in the dominant Democrat Party and served in the U.S. House and the U.S. Senate. In 1906, he was defeated for re-election and invited back to Nashville by Luke Lea to edit his newspaper, the *Nashville Tennessean* (at the end of World War I, as a soldier in Europe, Lea would lead an unsuccessful raid to kidnap the German Kaiser).

A man of many words, Carmack made many enemies, including Tennessee

Governor Malcolm Patterson. An essay by James Hoobler, senior curator at the Tennessee State Museum, explained: "Carmack challenged incumbent Governor Patterson for the Democratic gubernatorial nomination in 1907. When Governor Patterson, who was supported by pro-alcohol forces, won, Carmack began a print campaign against him, accusing him of 'perfidy and dishonor.' Carmack also lashed out at his old mentor at the *Nashville American,* Duncan Cooper, who had supported Patterson in the governor's race. Cooper then sent messages through personal intermediaries to Carmack, stating, 'If my name appears again, the town will not be big enough to hold us both.' Carmack refused."

Edward Ward Carmack

On Nov. 9, 1908, at the corner of Seventh and Union, not far from the Capitol, their paths met with deadly results. Carmack was making his way home when he ran into Duncan Cooper and his son Robin Cooper. When Duncan Cooper crossed the street and shouted to get Carmack's attention, the startled editor pulled his gun. Robin Cooper stepped between the men and drew his gun. Carmack fired twice, hitting Robin Cooper in the shoulder and his coat sleeve. The younger Cooper shot three times, killing Carmack instantly.

Headlines in the *Tennessean* railed: "Senator Carmack Shot Down in Cold Blood. Murder Premeditated, Deliberately Planned, and Executed in a Cold-Blooded Style."

Both Coopers were tried and convicted of murder in early 1909; they immediately appealed their convictions. The Tennessee State Supreme Court heard *Cooper v. State of Tennessee* in 1910. In a divided decision that gained national attention, the justices reversed Robin Cooper's conviction "for jury instruction errors and remanded for retrial." Robin Cooper "was put in jeopardy on remand, whereupon the prosecutor requested and the judge directed a verdict of acquittal." However, the Tennessee Supreme Court upheld the conviction of Duncan Cooper, although he never fired a single shot, on the grounds of "proximate cause," that is, that he had provoked the incident by approaching Carmack.

Within an hour of the Supreme Court's decision, Governor Patterson issued a pardon for his old friend Cooper. Prohibitionists revolted against the pardon, destroying Patterson's chances for a third term as governor and opening the way for the election of Ben W. Hooper, Tennessee's first Republican governor since Reconstruction.

Some years later in 1919, Robin Cooper's body was found facedown in Richland Creek. His skull had been bashed in with a rock, found nearby. He was a few hundred yards from his automobile, parked in Belle Meade Park. Despite an investigation, no one was ever brought to justice for his murder. Some thought it was revenge, while others thought that it was more likely a liquor deal gone bad.

Historian Hoobler wrote, "The Tennessee Woman's Christian Temperance Union (WCTU), led by Silena Moore Holman of Fayetteville, declared Carmack a prohibition martyr. She and other WCTU members astutely sensed that outrage over Carmack's death could help fuel support for outlawing alcohol. Joining with other temperance advocates, the WCTU worked to further state prohibition. In 1909, the Tennessee General Assembly passed legislation making it illegal to manufacture, sell, and use intoxicating beverages in the state. In 1909, the legislature also provided for the creation of a sculpture of Carmack by McCormack to be placed on the grounds of the Capitol. It was erected in 1927."

There were other gun battles in downtown Nashville. Perhaps the most famous happened on Sept. 4, 1813 between General Andrew Jackson and future U.S. Senator Thomas Hart Benton and their associates. Jackson and Benton were in a dispute stemming from a duel between Benton's brother Jesse and a friend of Jackson's. Jackson and Thomas Benton exchanged letters until Jackson announced he would horsewhip Benton on sight. The Benton brothers were staying in town at a hotel not frequented by Jackson to avoid "the possibility of unpleasantness." Soon, Jackson and loyalists Colonel John Coffee and Stockley Hays arrived at the Nashville Inn on the public square. All of the men carried one-shot smoothbore pistols and knives; Jackson also carried a whip.

While strolling about, Jackson saw Jesse Benton walk into the hotel and followed him. Thomas Benton was standing in the doorway of a hall leading to the rear porch. Jackson unfurled the whip and shouted to Thomas Benton, "Now defend yourself, you damned rascal!" Both reached for their pistols, but Jackson got the drop. Benton retreated and Jackson followed him step for step. Jesse Benton managed to get behind Jackson and fired his pistol. Jackson fired twice at Thomas Benton, who returned fire twice. Jackson took a ball in his left shoulder, which shattered it. Benton's sleeve bore a smouldering hole in it. Then Coffee charged at Thomas Benton, fired and missed, and frailed with the butt of the pistol. Jackson associate Alexander Donelson appeared on the scene; he and Coffee commenced to attack Thomas Benton with daggers, wounding him five times. Hays stabbed at Jesse Benton with a sword cane, which broke against a strong button. Benton then placed his last remaining pistol against Hays' chest and pulled the trigger, but the handgun misfired. Meanwhile, Thomas Benton fell down a flight of stairs. The badly stricken Jackson was carried off by friends while Thomas Benton culminated the affair by breaking Jackson's sword over his knee.

Thomas Hart Benton would leave Nashville for Missouri, which he represented as U.S. Senator for the next 30 years. Jackson recovered and gained fame by beating the British at the Battle of New Orleans in 1815. Jackson and Benton eventually became friends.

Sources: American Heritage, Elbert B. Smith, Feb. 1958; Nashville Tennessean; James Hoobler, Tennessee State Museum; Tennessee Encyclopedia of History and Culture.

....

Murder During Wartime: Three Generals Slain With Impunity

Many generals were killed during the Civil War, but three officers, one Federal and two Confederate, were murdered outside combat, and their assailants escaped without penalty. U.S. Brigadier General Jefferson Davis (no relation to the Confederate president) shot and killed Major General William "Bull" Nelson at the Galt House Hotel in Louisville, Kentucky; Confederate General Earl Van Dorn was shot and killed in Spring Hill, Tennessee by a jealous husband; and Gen. John Wharton was shot and killed in Houston in 1865 by a subordinate officer.

Bull Nelson was aptly named as he stood 6-4 tall and weighed 300 pounds. A Naval Academy graduate, he had sailed at sea and boasted a salty tongue and haughty manner. A native Kentuckian, he was passionate about keeping his home state in the Union. He established Camp Dick Robinson, where he armed and trained recruits to the Union cause. By September 1861, Bull Nelson was leading Federal troops in Kentucky. Politicians complained about Nelson's crude behavior and urged President Lincoln to send him back to the U.S. Navy. "So far as he has come into contact with citizens or soldiers in Kentucky, I think he is the most odious man I have ever known," Sen. Garrett Davis told the President. In the spring of 1862, Nelson's troops performed well at the Battle of Shiloh. In August 1862, however, Nelson's green troops were whipped at Richmond, Kentucky, in one of the most lopsided Confederate victories of the war. The inexperienced Federal troops hastily retreated after Nelson was shot in the thigh and taken out of action. The rebel invasion of Kentucky drove Nelson to Louisville to bolster that city's defenses. Nelson headquartered at the luxurious Galt House Hotel, where most of the Federal officers resided.

Nelson assigned Brig. Gen. Davis the job of organizing local men into a fighting force. A native of adjacent Indiana, Davis was a Mexican War veteran and close friend of Indiana Governor Oliver Morton, who named Davis head of the 22nd Indiana. Davis fought at the Battle of Wilson's Creek, Pea Ridge, and Corinth. Davis stood 5-9 and weighed 125 pounds; he was described by a fellow officer as "a small, sallow, blue-eyed, dyspeptic-looking man."

Davis found Nelson's orders to organize a militia beneath his dignity and basically did nothing. Hearing bad reports, Nelson called Davis to his headquarters, and soon a quarrel developed between the two generals.

There already was bad blood between Gen. Nelson and Gov. Morton. According to author Stuart Sanders, "While Nelson abhorred Morton's involvement in Army affairs, the governor despised Nelson because the Kentuckian had lost some 1,500 Indiana troops in the Federal debacle at Richmond and then blamed a Hoosier officer, Brig. Gen. Mahlon Manson, for the defeat."

The feud came to a head on Sept. 29, 1862, shortly after breakfast, in the lobby of the Galt House as Nelson confronted a group that included Davis and Morton. Davis demanded an apology from Nelson for his behavior. Nelson replied, "Go away, you damned puppy. I don't want anything to do with you." Davis crumpled up a piece a paper in his hand and flung it in Nelson's face. Nelson slapped Davis on the side of the head with his open hand. He then asked Morton if he had come to witness the insults. Nelson then walked away, telling a bystander that "I'll teach him a lesson." Davis shouted out, "I will see you again." Davis then borrowed a Tranter pistol from a friend and followed Nelson upstairs to his office.

"General Nelson, take care of yourself," Davis called. He walked to within three feet of Nelson, aimed, and fired. The bullet struck Nelson above the heart, severing an artery. Bull Nelson, unarmed, staggered away and collapsed. On the floor, Nelson told his friend, Brig. Gen. Thomas L. Crittenden, that "Tom, I am murdered." He died at 8:30 am, shortly after being baptized by an Episcopal chaplain.

Davis was put under house arrest. He claimed the pistol misfired accidentally. Davis said the shooting was not premeditated although he never expressed any regret for the killing.

At first the press reported that Confederate President Jefferson C. Davis had slipped into the hotel and murdered Bull Nelson. Then the truth emerged. Troops loyal to Nelson vowed to kill Davis in retribution. Several Federal generals wanted Davis hanged on the spot. It was widely reported that Nelson had made the first move. Within the hour, Gov. Morton was back in Indiana.

Davis was never formally charged with murder. A county grand jury charged him with manslaughter, but Davis made bail and the charge was dismissed in 1864. The whole affair was fairly quickly forgotten. Two days after the murder, Federal troops fought the Battle of Perryville and the war moved on. Davis was put back in command and fought competently the remainder of the war although he was not promoted. He was criticized for an incident at Ebenezer

Creek during Sherman's March to the Sea. Davis ordered a pontoon bridge removed from the creek, stranding several hundred freed blacks who were following the army. Many were captured by the Confederates or drowned in the creek trying to escape. Davis remained in the army after the war and died of natural causes in 1879.

Nelson's body was buried in Louisville, then moved to Camp Dick Robinson, then Maysville, his hometown.

Confederate Major General Earl Van Dorn of Mississippi was a West Point graduate, dashing cavalry commander in the Western Theater of the Civil War, and quite the ladies' man. He engineered the famous raid against U.S. Grant's logistics base at Holly Springs, Miss. In March 1863, he won the Battle of Thompson's Station in Middle Tennessee. He made his headquarters at the Martin Cheairs mansion in Spring Hill (now known as Ferguson Hall). Van Dorn, who was married, was known to keep company with a local woman, Mrs. Jesse Peters, the fourth wife of Dr. George Peters, who was often away serving in the state legislature. Mrs. Peters was 25 years younger than her husband.

Returning home on April 12, 1863, Dr. Peters was informed of his wife's dalliances with the general. On May 7th, Dr. Peters showed up at Van Dorn's headquarters and was allowed inside (Dr. Peters was well known and often visited the HQ to obtain travel passes). As Van Dorn sat working at his desk in the front room, Dr. Peters pulled out a pistol and shot Van Dorn once in the back of the head. The general died four hours later, never having gained consciousness. Dr. Peters fled the scene and was eventually arrested by Confederate authorities but never charged or tried for the murder. Dr. Peters proclaimed that Van Dorn "had violated the sanctity of my home." There was little sympathy for Van Dorn in the region due to the rumors of his extramarital affairs.

One researcher, Briget Smith, speculates that Dr. Peters murdered the general because Van Dorn was also having an affair with the teenage daughter of Dr. Peters by an earlier wife.

Confederate General John A. Wharton of Texas, an extremely competent cavalry commander, was shot and killed April 6, 1865 in front of the Fannin Hotel in Houston by Confederate Col. George W. Baylor. Wharton and Baylor had a history of antagonism regarding "an unpleasant misunderstanding over military matters." Wharton, unarmed, came into the hotel (which was Gen. Magruder's headquarters) and confronted Baylor, slapping him in the face and calling him a liar. Baylor pulled out a revolver and shot Wharton, who died instantly. He was 36. Baylor was acquitted of murder charges in 1868 and served many years as a Texas Ranger.

Sources: warfarehistorynetwork.com/daily/civil-war/the-murder-of-bull-nelson/

The Murder of Bull Nelson, Stuart W. Sanders, Dec. 20, 2018; Blog of John Banks at http://john-banks.blogspot.com/2018/10/murder-she-wrote-authors-obsession-is.html

....

Sevier vs. Tipton Feud: Battle of the Lost State of Franklin

Following the War for Independence, the territory west of the Appalachian Mountains and east of the Mississippi River was sparsely occupied by native Indian tribes who tolerated European hunters and trappers but resisted permanent white settlers. Those hearty souls who ventured over the mountains had the option of creating jurisdictions within existing states, forming new states in the union, or creating their own sovereign republics.

The state of North Carolina claimed lands that extended due west of its existing borders all the way to the Mississippi (essentially what is now the state of Tennessee). Settlers who had negotiated questionable treaties with existing tribes did not trust the North Carolina authorities to protect their interests since their coastal populations were so far away. They feared that the state might sell the land they were settling to either Spain or France.

In 1784, North Carolina voted to cede that land (four counties) to the U.S. government but then reconsidered and took back control. The settlers convened a convention to create their own state of Frankland and chose Revolutionary War hero John Sevier as their leader. On Aug. 23, 1784, roughly 50 frontiersmen signed a document in Jonesborough declaring their independence from North Carolina. The loosely organized government was headquartered in Greeneville. Due to the slow pace of communications at that time, the move was accomplished a month before the frontiersmen discovered that North Carolina had taken back the land from the U.S. government.

In the spring of 1785, Frankland petitioned the U.S. government for statehood, which angered the North Carolina authorities, who countered by forming their own overmountain administrative territory and appointed John Tipton to supervise it, headquartered in Jonesborough. Governor Alexander Martin threatened to "render the revolting territory not worth possessing."

In a bid to encourage the Congress and Benjamin Franklin to accept Frankland as the 14th state, the settlers changed the name to Franklin. Although six states voted to accept Franklin, it wasn't enough to approve statehood.

Sevier was a Virginian of French Hugenot (Protestant) descent whose family founded the town of New Market. Young Sevier married and moved overmountain to new opportunities on the Holston River. During the war, he served as lieutenant colonel of the North Carolina militia and was one of the heroes of the Battle of Kings Mountain in 1780. Sevier reared ten children by his first wife and eight children by his second. Legend claims that he fought more than 35 battles with hostile Indian warriors and won them all. Sevier was a capable, tough-minded frontiersman and statesman.

A native of Maryland, John Tipton served in Lord Dunmore's War, was a recruiting officer for the Continental Army during the Revolutionary War, and served as Colonel of the Washington County militia. He had held office in several state constitutional conventions and in several state legislatures. Tipton established an estate near present-day Johnson City, now preserved as the Tipton-Haynes State Historic Site. This was the site of the battle.

Tipton and Sevier were bitter enemies. In early 1788, Tipton ordered a North Carolina sheriff, Jonathan Pugh, to seize several slaves and livestock owned by Sevier to satisfy a court judgment. Pugh took the slaves and livestock to Tipton's estate. Sevier was outraged when he heard about the judgment. He responded by leading Franklinites to Tipton's property in present-day Washington County and attempted to reclaim the slaves. On February 27th, Governor Sevier arrived at the Tipton house leading a force of more than 100 men. He set up a perimeter and stationed sentries. He urged Tipton, who was surrounded, to surrender, but Tipton did not respond.

Meanwhile, Colonel Tipton had written his militia subordinate, Major Robert Love, and directed him to gather his Greasy Cove men and march to his house quickly. "Let no time be lost," he urged.

A company of loyalists from Washington County under the command of Captain Peter Parkinson tried to reach the Tipton house but were fired upon by Sevier's men. Three horses were killed and several prisoners taken. Then a strange thing happened, according to Tipton's later accounts. "Two young women passing by near to the still house…were fired upon from which firing one of them received a bullet through her shoulder."

On February 28th, Sevier again urged Tipton to surrender. This time Tipton responded, "To this flag I sent an answer, letting the men assembled there know that all I wanted was a submission to the laws of North Carolina, and if they would acquiesce with this proposal I would disband my troops here…" Sevier then decided to lay siege to the house. That night Major Love's "small party" arrived at the scene and managed to get to the house via a path unguarded by Sevier's men.

During a heavy snowstorm in the early morning of February 29th, Colonel George Maxwell arrived undetected with a force equivalent to Sevier's to reinforce Tipton. Which side fired the first shots is not known, but both sides fired a volley at each other. Col. Tipton decided to attack, exclaiming, "Boys, every man who is a soldier come out."

After roughly ten minutes of fighting, Gov. Sevier and his men retreated back to Jonesborough. Several men were captured and wounded on both sides. A loyalist, Dr. Taylor, stated that neither side wished to kill the other. He claimed that Colonel Tipton's men shot in the air while Sevier's men shot at the corners of the cabin. Three men were killed—two of Tipton's men and one Franklinite. The sheriff, Jonathan Pugh, was mortally wounded in the chest and died several days after the fighting. The men captured during the battle, including two of Sevier's sons, were soon released.

Tipton and his men pursued Sevier's forces and met a messenger sent from Sevier, who asked for time to consider terms. Tipton allowed Sevier until March 11th to submit to North Carolina law. Sevier and the Franklinites convened a council and sued for peace but did not submit to state law. Two days earlier, Sevier's term as governor of Franklin had expired. Hostilities continued, but the State of Franklin seemed to dissolve from lack of support.

On July 29, 1788, the North Carolina governor ordered Sevier's arrest for treason. Several months later, Tipton arrested Sevier and took him to Morganton, N.C. for trial. A group of associates and Sevier's sons retrieved him from imprisonment and took him home. Sevier was never tried.

Franklin existed as an independent state for about four years, transacted its own treaties with the Overhill Cherokee whose land it occupied, and even considered an alliance with Spain. But in the end, the leaders of Franklin decided to rejoin North Carolina in 1789. During that time, about 10,000 families moved to the territory from Virginia and North Carolina. Tennessee became the 16th state in 1796, and Sevier was appointed its first governor. He won re-election five times and died in 1815. Tipton's last political office was as Tennessee state senator from 1796-99. He died at his home in 1813.

The Franklin crisis led to a clause in the new U.S. Constitution that stipulates that while new states "may be admitted by the Congress into this Union," new states can't be formed "within the jurisdiction of any other State" or states unless the state legislatures and Congress both approve the move.

Source: Encyclopedia of Tennessee History and Culture, Tennessee Historical Society. Tipton-Hayes State Historic Site website.

....

The Black Patch War: Possum Hunters vs. Hillbillies

A hundred years ago, if you chawed tobacco or smoked a pipe, chances were the dark-fired tobacco you enjoyed came from farms in 30 counties aligned along the Kentucky-Tennessee border known as the Black Patch. Growing tobacco has always been a difficult, labor-intensive endeavor. James B. Duke and his American Tobacco Company (ATC) pioneered the industrialization and monopolization of the tobacco industry, leading to lower prices and profits for the growers, who began to suffer economic distress. On Sept. 24,

1904, five thousand tobacco growers met in Gutherie, Ky. and formed the Dark Tobacco District Planters' Protective Association of Kentucky and Tennessee (PPA) to cooperatively market their product. The PPA or the Association intended to withhold tobacco from the market until purchasing companies agreed to pay higher prices. The ATC and the Italian Regie, known collectively as the Trust, countered by paying higher prices to farmers who did not join the PPA. Leaders of the PPA tried to persuade the holdouts, called hillbillies, to join. In October 1905, members of the Robertson County (Tenn.) Branch of the PPA met at the Stainback schoolhouse and adopted the "Resolutions of the committee of the Possum Hunters Organization." The possum hunters stated their grievances against the Trust and vowed to form groups to visit hillbillies to convince them to join the PPA. Also to persuade Trust tobacco buyers to increase prices.

When those relatively benign tactics did not work, some growers turned to violence, a not uncommon occurrence in that region. Southern sociologist John Shelton Reed observed that Southerners are both the most violent and the most religious group in the United States. The Clarksville (Tenn.) *Leaf-Chronicle* newspaper called Felix Ewing, the most prominent Association leader, the Moses of the Black Patch, while referring to the Trust as "His Satanic Majesty."

Night riders, using military tactics reminiscent of the Ku Klux Klan era, paid visits to the hillbillies. The secret fraternal society was known as the Silent Brigade or the Inner Circle. According to scholar Rick Gregory, "They scraped or salted tobacco plant beds, destroyed tobacco in the fields, killed livestock, burned barns and warehouses filled with tobacco, dynamited farm machinery, and assaulted hillbillies and tobacco buyers."

The Night Riders numbered roughly 10,000 and were led by Dr. David Amoss, a physician and former drill master at Major Ferrell's Military School in Hopkinsville who applied his military training to the organization. James O. Nall, a scholar of the Black Patch War, described Amoss as a faithful member of the Christian Church at Wallonia, Caldwell County. Amoss frequently occupied the pulpit in the absence of the pastor, conducted the weekly prayer meetings, officiated at funerals, and attended to other church affairs.

On Dec. 1, 1906, raiders rode into Princeton, Ky. and attacked two of the largest tobacco warehouses in the South, destroying 75 tons of Trust tobacco.

In Hopkinsville, militia under Major Erskine Birch Bassett, the police force, and a large body of armed citizens prepared for the raiders. The night raiders were cautious and waited until Dec. 7, 1907 at 2:00 am to strike (the town defenders had dropped their guard). The masked men dismounted and marched to Main Street, where they formed six squads. Three men guarded the 7th Street bridge; others guarded downtown streets. At 9th and Main, citizens out and about were rounded up into a corral. Operators at the Cumberland Telephone office were captured before they could sound an alarm. Other raiders shot at the police station and then subdued the stunned officers inside. The fire department and railroad depot also were seized. One of the buyers for Imperial Tobacco Co. was dragged from his home and beaten. Three tobacco warehouses were burned, including one owned by John Latham and filled with tobacco grown by non-members of the PPA. The fires also destroyed several residences. Amoss, the raid leader, was accidentally shot in the head by his own men. A railroad man was shot and killed trying to save some railway property. Finally, the masked men assembled for roll call at the main intersection and marched out of town, singing "My Old Kentucky Home."

Meanwhile, Major Bassett formed a small posse and pursued the raiders. When two-thirds of the raiders separated, the posse opened fire, killing one raider and wounding another.

On Jan. 3, 1908, while militia were guarding Hopkinsville and other points, the night riders raided Russellville with 55 men and destroyed two factories. On Feb. 4, the night raiders destroyed the tobacco warehouses in two towns in Crittenden County, Ky.

The "war" forced tobacco prices up and kept them competitive from 1905 to 1914. The violence prompted Kentucky Governor A.E. Wilson to dispatch the National Guard to arrest most of the PPA leaders. The U.S. Supreme Court in 1910 ruled that the ATC was indeed a monopoly and must be dismantled, leading to higher, competitive prices. The PPA ceased to exist in 1914, when World War I closed most European markets for dark-fired tobacco.

Sources: Border States: Journal of the Kentucky-Tennessee American Studies Association, No. 9 (1993); Rick Gregory, Tennessee State University; www.westernkyhistory.org/christian/night.html.

....

The Coal Creek War: Free Miners vs. National Guard

As if coal mining wasn't dangerous enough, workers in the late 19th Century turned to open warfare to fight for their right to earn a living. The Coal Creek War of 1891-92 was fought in the hills of East Tennessee between coal miners and the mining companies that used convict-labor, and eventually against the state militia. Ironically, the war ended with the building of two new state prisons while conditions in the coal mines changed little.

By the early 1870s, the Coal Creek community in Anderson County, northwest of Knoxville, was home to 150 Welsh families who earned their living working the coal mines. In 1877, a labor dispute resulted in the first convict-laborers being brought to Coal Creek to work in the now-abandoned Knoxville Iron and Coal Company (KICC) Mine No. 1.

Prison records show that 131 convict miners died there from 1877 to 1893. Some were caught igniting methane gas at mine entrances to cook wild game over open flames.

Mining jobs were plentiful, so the miners who lost their jobs found work at mines in nearby Briceville, Fraterville, and Beech Grove. Others left the area to mine coal in Kentucky.

In 1891, the miners went on strike against the Tennessee Coal Mining Company (TCMC) over regulations having to do with the weighing of mined coal. On July 5, the company brought in convict-laborers to the company mine near Briceville. This was the beginning of the Coal Creek War, which included violent raids, negotiations, periods of truce, and use of force to protect the convict-laborers.

Since 1866, the state government had used a system by which convicts were leased out to private companies for their labor in exchange for the housing and feeding of the convicts and fees that helped pay off state debt. So-called Zebra laws resulted in the conviction of petty-crime offenders, mostly black, to man the system. Steal an apple, you end up mining coal for the man. Not surprisingly, the companies did not treat their convict-laborers well and used the system to combat striking workers and labor unions.

In 1884 the Tennessee Coal and Iron Company (TCI) leased the state penitentiary for an annual fee of $101,000. TCI not only used convict-labor themselves, but they subleased the convicts out to other coal mining companies. The TCI vice-president called the convict-laborers "an effective club to hold over the heads of free laborers."

The company tore down houses in Briceville to build a stockade for their convict-laborers. The night of July 14th about 300 armed miners surrounded the stockade. The guards surrendered and the 40 convicts were marched to the town of Coal Creek and put on a train to Knoxville. (Coal Creek later became Lake City, now Rocky Top.)

The miners called upon Governor Buck Buchanan to intervene. He agreed to talks but only after the convicts were returned to the Briceville stockade. He sent three companies of state militia to keep the peace. He called on the miners to seek justice within the court system. When miners repeated their tactics on July 20th, the governor called a special session of the state legislature, and while there was sympathy expressed for the miners, no action was taken.

On October 31st, Halloween, the miners captured the stockade again, only this time they released the 300 convicts into the woods and burned down the structure. On November 2nd, the miners conducted a raid at the Cumberland Mine in Oliver Springs, releasing 153 convicts. By the end of December, however, convicts had returned to the mines under militia guard.

The state dispatched 84 militiamen under the command of J. Keller Anderson to guard the convict stockade at Coal Creek and a small force to guard the one at Oliver Springs. Fort Anderson was built on Militia Hill in January 1892 as a base for the Tennessee National Guard to protect convict-laborers and restore order. Convicts cut trees on Militia Hill and surrounding hillsides in 1892 to open fields-of-view so the soldiers could easily spot attacking miners.

The Tennessee Coal Mining Company in Briceville dismissed convict-labor in February 1892 and sold stock in the company to miners. Subsequent attempts to convince Gov. Buchanan to remove troops from the watershed failed, so miners attacked Briceville in the summer of 1892.

On August 17th, a group of miners led by John Hatmaker attacked the TCI stockade at Oliver Springs but were beaten back by the guards. Shortly afterward, a larger group of miners reconvened at the stockade, and its guards finally surrendered. The stockade was burned, and the convicts were put on a train and sent to Nashville. The following day, militia commander Keller Anderson was captured at Coal Creek, and the miners ordered Fort Anderson's second-in-command, Lieutenant Perry Fyffe, to surrender. After Fyffe refused, the miners charged the fort, killing two militiamen, but failing to capture the fort.

Gov. Buchanan dispatched 583 militiamen under the command of General Samuel T. Carnes and ordered sheriffs to form posses. Most sheriffs ignored the order. A group of Knoxville volunteers marched to relieve besieged Fort Anderson, but as they descended Walden Ridge, they were ambushed by miners, with two volunteers killed. General Carnes arrived on August 19th, and quickly restored order and obtained Anderson's release. He then initiated a sweep of the region from Coal Creek to Jellico, arresting hundreds of miners deemed to have assisted in the insurrection. The militia used the Briceville Community Church as a temporary jail for those it arrested.

According to the Coal Creek Watershed Foundation, war correspondents from the *New York Times, Washington Post,* and *Harper's Weekly* magazine convinced soldiers to pose for photographs by standing guard over convicts during construction of the breastworks. An accidental discharge of his rifle by one of the soldiers killed a convict and put an end to the practice of posing for photographs.

Soldiers responded to attack by firing cannons into the Miners Nest encampment on Walden Ridge, located south of the Wye Gap. Soldiers also shot cans filled with mud through the Wye Gap into the town of Coal Creek to demonstrate that the town could be attacked and destroyed at any time.

In August 1892, miners in Grundy County revolted at two sites operated by the Tennessee Coal, Iron, and Railroad Company, igniting new unrest in Anderson County. When miners attacked the stockade at Oliver Springs, gunfire wounded several of the assailants. Eventually, the stockade militia surrendered and the convicts were shipped to Knoxville.

Labor unrest resulted in the defeat that November of Buchanan for re-election. The following year the state legislature voted to build two new prisons, a new state penitentiary in Nashville and the Brushy Mountain Prison near Petros, and end convict leasing when the current contracts expired in 1896. Convicts were used by the state to mine coal deposits within the Brushy Mountain prison boundaries.

Both prisons were closed late in the 20th Century. The facility in Nashville has been used in the filming of several prison movies. Brushy Mountain was famous for the 1977 escape of James Earl Ray, the assassin of Martin Luther King, Jr. Ray was captured within three days in rugged terrain eight miles away.

In 1902, an explosion at the Fraterville Mine killed 216 miners, the worst mining disaster in state history. Some believe the explosion was caused by the ghosts of convict miners once again igniting methane gas to cook wild game. In December 1911 the Cross Mountain mine explosion killed 84 miners (five were rescued).

By 1975, about 60 percent of the state's coal was strip-mined. By the early 1990s the number of coal mining establishments in Tennessee had fallen by more than two-thirds, the number of workers by three-fourths, and the value of shipments by nearly two-thirds. The major markets for Tennessee coal in recent decades have been utilities in Tennessee and neighboring states.

Sources: Coal Creek Watershed Foundation; Encyclopedia of Tennessee History and Culture.

....

The Hoo Doo War: Vigilantism Turns To Vengeful Range Warfare

What began as tensions over cattle rustling evolved into bitter feuds and finally escalated into violent vigilantism and range warfare with ethnic overtones in 1875-76 in tiny Mason County, Texas, population 650. At least a dozen ranchers, citizens, and suspected cattle thieves were killed, some by lynching. It was called the Mason County War or more commonly know as the Hoo Doo War (hoo doo meaning unlucky).

Tensions already existed within the county, which boasted a large German immigrant population. The Germans stayed loyal during the Civil War even though the state was Confederate. The Germans also purportedly owned the best land in the county. The diverse settlers stayed united against hostile native Indians until that common threat eased in the 1870s.

In 1873, the German majority appointed John Clark, an apparent stranger with little known background, as sheriff and John Wohrle as his deputy. In August 1874, Clark and a large posse of German-born supporters arrested and jailed a number of reputable ranchers, led by M.B. Thomas and Allen G. Roberts, who were rounding up cattle. They all made bail and were released. On Feb. 13, 1875, the sheriff and his posse went into McCulloch County and arrested nine men, four of whom made bail. A few days later, the body of a teenaged ranch hand was found beside the road with a note attached — "Here lies a noted cow thief."

On the night of February 18th, a mob forced the jailhouse keys from the deputy and took the five prisoners a quarter-mile down the road toward Fredericksburg to hang them from a tree.

Sheriff Clark and Captain Dan Roberts of the Frontier Battalion (Texas Rangers) chased after the mob. Two brothers were successfully hanged; one man was mortally wounded in the head; one man was saved, returned to jail and subsequently escaped; and one man went free into the night.

A local court investigated the mob murders but issued no indictments.

One member of the sheriff's posse felt threatened for speaking out against the lynchings. He rounded up 30 armed men and came to Mason to confront Sheriff Clark, who hastily left town. Clark returned on March 24 with 60 well-armed men of his own. The two groups gravitated toward the courthouse square; somehow a truce was effected.

The truce lasted two months. On May 13th, Deputy Wohrle was sent to Carl Lehmberg's ranch to speak to foreman Tim Williamson about a minor legal matter. The three men rode off toward Mason and traveled ten miles before being stopped by a dozen masked men. Accounts differ, but Williamson ended up being shot dead by Peter Bader, a German rancher.

Scott Cooley, a former Texas Ranger with a violent past, swore revenge for the death of Tim Williamson, whom he considered a father figure. He collected the names of the men he thought responsible for Williamson's death, got together a gang, including John and Mose Beard, George Gladden, and Johnny Ringo (John Ringgold), and began a ruthless retaliation that resulted in the killing of at least a dozen men.

On August 10th, Cooley shot John Wohrle in the head while he was digging a well, then scalped him. Other shootings followed, and the good citizens of Mason begged Governor Richard Coke to intervene.

Gov. Coke sent Major John B. Jones and about 40 Texas Rangers to quell the violence. On September 28th, they ran into Sheriff Clark and 20 followers at Cold Springs looking for Cooley. That same day, Cooley and three others shot Daniel Hoerster, the county cattle-brand inspector, off his horse in broad daylight as he was passing the Southern Hotel. Peter Jordan (a friend of Hoerster's) and George Gladden were wounded. During a gunfight at Keller's store on the Llano River, Clark and Keller's son wounded Mose Beard (mortally) and George Gladden. Then Johnny Ringo killed John Cheney, who had led Mose Beard into the ambush, at breakfast.

Sheriff Clark fled the county after an incident in which he took a prisoner who was never seen or heard from again.

Major Jones continued to look for Cooley and his gang with little cooperation from the local populace. He was forced to dismiss some soldiers in his command when they were found to be former friends of Cooley. Soon, the Ranger himself left Mason County.

Eventually, with all the major players dead or scattered, the deadly feuding in Mason County calmed down. No one was ever brought to trial in Mason County for any of the killings.

Gladden is said to have killed Peter Bader in Llano County. His brother, Charles Bader, was also killed at some point, supposedly because he was mistaken for Peter. Gladden was eventually tried for murder in Llano County and sentenced to 99 years (he was later pardoned). Cooley fled into Blanco County to be with friends; he died a short time later, of brain fever or poison.

Johnny Ringo spent several months in jail at the courthouse before his case was dismissed. He headed west to Tombstone, Arizona and destiny.

On the night of Jan. 21, 1877, the Mason County courthouse burned to the ground, probably due to arson, destroying all records relating to the feud.

Afternote: On the night of Feb. 4, 2021, the Mason County Courthouse was destroyed by fire. The cause was determined to be arson.

Sources: Texas State Historical Association; Allen G. Hatley, Wild West magazine, August 2005.

....

The War of the Regulation: Foreshadow of the Revolution

Lt. General William Tryon, the eighth royal governor of the North Carolina colony, needed a suitable palace in New Bern from which to govern, so he imported an architect from London and paid builders from Philadelphia to work on the project. He petitioned the colonial legislature to double the funding for the palace from £5,000 to £10,000. Finished in 1770, the royal house was "a monument of opulence and elegance extraordinary in the American colonies." His Highness and family resided in the new palace for one year prior to moving to New York but not before quelling a nasty rebellion on the frontier that foreshadowed the upcoming War of Independence.

The War of the Regulation, also known as the Regulator movement, was an uprising lasting from around 1765 to 1771, in which subjects in the western part of North Carolina took up arms against colonial officials, whom they viewed as corrupt. The colonists, already decrying excessive taxation, found Tryon's new palace unnecessary and extravagant to say the least. The rebellion was a struggle between the lower-class settlers of the backcountry and the wealthy planter elites who controlled the colonial government.

In 1768, a mob broke up the colonial court in Hillsborough, dragging officials deemed corrupt through the streets. Judge Richard Henderson adjourned court and escaped the mob during the night. The rioters destroyed and vandalized property, beat several lawyers, placed excrement on the judge's seat and a dead slave upon the lawyers' bar. After demolishing shops in town, the out-of-control mob went to the house of Edmund Fanning, a Tryon aide, drank all his alcohol, and vandalized it. The mob beat Fanning severely. They grabbed his heels, and pulled him down the stairs, banging his head on each step. They then burned Henderson's barn to the ground. Finally, they cracked the bell of the Church of England.

Many other acts of relatively minor violence took place in the western counties in the following years. The rebellion came to a climax in May 1771 at the Battle of Alamance in Orange County near present-day Burlington.

About 2,000 Regulators gathered in a show of force. Enraged, Gov. Tryon left New Bern, gathered 1,000 militia troops and funding at Hillsborough, and approached the Regulator campground late on May 15th.

Meanwhile, a loyalist force of General Hugh Waddell was en route with 236 men but was met by a large group of Regulators under the leadership of Captain Benjamin Merrill, a former loyalist officer. Realizing his force was outnumbered, Waddell fell back to Salisbury and failed to reach Alamance in time to participate in the battle.

The next morning, at about 8:00 am, Tryon's troops set out to a field about one-half mile from the Regulator camp. He formed two lines, and divided his artillery between the wings and the center of the first line. He had about 1,000 men and 150 officers. The Regulators were essentially leaderless and unprepared for a real fight, hoping to scare the militia with superior numbers.

Tryon sent a demand for surrender to "prevent an effusion of blood, as you are at this time in a state of rebellion against your King, your country, and your laws." He gave the Regulators one hour to reply but began moving his troops forward. He sent one final warning, reminding the Regulators that they had no leaders, no artillery, no ammo. "You will be defeated!" he warned.

One of the rebel leaders, Herman Husband, a Quaker, got the message and left the area. Shortly thereafter, a large group of Regulators appeared in front of the militia and dared them to open fire. One of two Regulators attempting to negotiate a truce, Robert Thompson, was retained as a prisoner by the royal governor. In a fit of pique, Tryon grabbed a musket from one of the militiamen and shot Thompson dead. Coming to his senses, Tryon sent a man forward with a white flag in an attempt to calm everybody down.

The Regulators used Indian fighting tactics to capture one of Tryon's three cannons. But they could not fire it since they had no ammunition.

Tryon sent out another white flag of truce but the flag bearer was shot and killed even as one of the Regulators called for a ceasefire. Enraged again, Tryon set his troops against the rebels and drove most of them from the field. Then he set the woods on fire. The battle had lasted about two hours.

Tryon reported his losses as nine dead and 61 wounded although others estimate up to 27 killed. The Regulators lost nine killed and up to 200 wounded. Tryon took 13 prisoners. One of them, James Few, was executed at the camp, and six others were executed later in nearby Hillsborough, including the loyalist traitor Merrill.

At the time, the Regulators were widely regarded as lawless desperadoes. But soon colonists all along the Eastern Seaboard began to resent British rule and taxation, leading to the 1775 battles in New England.

It's estimated that 90 percent of those who participated in the Regulation rebellion became Patriots during the Revolutionary War. Some officers of the

governor, such as Robert Nash, switched sides and fought as Patriots.
Sources: Encyclopedia of North Carolina; AlamanceBattleground.org.

....

Remember the Raisin! - The Battle and Massacre of River Raisin

"Remember the Raisin!" the frontier militiamen yelled as they advanced into British Canada in October 1813, defeated the King's troops and killed Tecumseh, the Shawnee chieftain and leader of the Indian confederation.

The Kentucky riflemen gained revenge for family and friends buried at Frenchtown near the River Raisin, now the site of Monroe, Michigan. At the cemetery in Monroe stands a stone monument, "Michigan's Tribute to Kentucky," that pays homage to the men slain at the Battle of the River Raisin on Jan. 22-23, 1813. In October 2010, the River Raisin became a battlefield in the National Park System.

The battle was a major defeat for the Americans and was one of the bloodiest engagements during the War of 1812. The massacre of wounded soldiers the following day shocked and enraged Americans throughout the Old Northwest Territory. The incident soon became known as "The River Raisin Massacre."

The American leader was General James Winchester, a haughty native of Maryland, unpopular with his troops for being too refined and disciplined. Winchester was a hardluck warrior, having been captured twice during the Revolutionary War. In the late 1700s he built a stone mansion named Cragfont, near Castalian Springs, Tennessee, which can be toured today.

At the beginning of the War of 1812, Winchester, who had been bypassed for command of the Army of the Northwest Territory by Gen. William Henry Harrison, was ordered to Kentucky to build an army and move upon Fort Detroit, held by the British and their Indian allies under Major General Henry Proctor. (American Gen. William Hull had disgraced himself by surrendering the fort in 1812 without putting up a fight.)

Winchester's column of 2,000 untrained regulars and volunteers, mostly from Kentucky, established a base camp at the Maumee River Rapids (today's Perrysburg, Ohio). Against Harrison's orders, but at the request of citizens, Winchester sent a relief detachment of 600 men to Frenchtown, under the command of Colonel William Lewis. On January 18th, Lewis dispersed the small force of British and Indians at Frenchtown. Two days later, Winchester's force reached the town and settled in but did not fortify their positions. Overconfident and certain that the enemy was nowhere near, Winchester decided to put up for the night in an isolated house south of the river and west of his troops, about a mile outside of Frenchtown.

British General Proctor organized a counterattack, gathering troops from Fort Malden (mostly 597 British regulars from the 41st Foot and local militiamen) and 800 Indians led by Wyandot Chief Roundhead and Walk-in-the-Water, plus six small cannons. The troops assembled the night of January 21st, five miles north of Frenchtown, ready to attack at dawn. Proctor's total force numbered perhaps as many as 1,300, compared to Winchester's 934.

The British and Indians took the Americans by surprise. Twenty minutes into the fight, the U.S. regulars on the right flank and behind a fence row retreated south to the river under intense artillery fire and flanking fire from the Indians. Winchester had been roused from his bed by the battle noise, rushed to the scene, and unsuccessfully tried to reform the regulars. He and his son and some aides were captured by the Indians and taken to Proctor. Two companies of Kentucky militiamen rushed to stabilize the regulars, but they too were overwhelmed. As the regulars retreated, Captain James C. Price and the 50 men in his Jessamine Blues sought to retrieve the American wounded but were swept away. Lieutenant Ashton Garrett and about 20 Americans were surrounded and laid down their arms. Their Indian captors then began shooting them. Garrett was the only one to escape. Another group of Americans retreated about three miles before being overtaken. About half were shot or tomahawked; only 30 escaped.

Meanwhile, the Kentucky riflemen on the left flank under Madison, Garrard, and Graves repulsed three British attacks with "coolness and intrepidity." The British were trying to occupy a large barn in front of the lines. An after-action report stated: "Ensign William O. Butler volunteered to set the barn on fire. Carrying a firebrand in the face of steady enemy gunfire, Butler raced to the barn and set it ablaze. He then returned to the barn to place more straw on the fire. By the time the ensign safely returned to his lines his clothing was riddled with bullets."

Only five of the Kentuckians were killed and 40 wounded, while one-third of the British force had been killed or wounded. At 11:00 am the artillery and shooting slackened. A white flag appeared from the British ranks. The Kentuckians were astounded to see that the flagbearer was Col. John Overton, Gen. Winchester's aide. In custody, Winchester had surrendered, claiming that he believed the Kentuckians were in a desperate situation. The riflemen exchanged heated words regarding whether to surrender, most wanting to fight to the end. Major George Madison (a distant relative of President Madison) looked to the other American officers for advice. Madison then asked Proctor if the Americans would remain safe and was told that they would. He reluctantly surrendered, knowing his forces were low on ammunition and surrounded. The Indians then began robbing the American captives and stopped only when Gen. Proctor brandished his sword.

The American wounded were placed in houses in the town where they were guarded by the British and tended by two American doctors. The main force of British and Indians withdrew back to Fort Malden in Amherstburg, Ontario, with the American captives who could walk. The British said they'd be back in the morning with sleds to transport the rest of the wounded.

American casualties totaled more than 300 killed outright, about 60 seriously wounded and more than 500 taken prisoner. Proctor reported 24 British killed and 158 wounded. There no reports of the Indian casualties.

During the night, the British guards disappeared, and in the morning 200 Indians returned to Frenchtown. The Indians then occupied the buildings, robbed the wounded captives, and took prisoners who could walk. The seriously wounded were murdered in their beds. The houses were set ablaze and any man who tried to escape was tomahawked. It was mid-afternoon before the Indians retreated with their captives to Ford Malden, killing anyone who couldn't keep up the pace. The number of Americans murdered by the Indians on January 23rd range from half a dozen to 60. Regardless of the number, the betrayal of the British and the subsequent murders became known as the River Raisin Massacre.

The River Raisin was liberated on Sept. 27, 1813, when Colonel Richard M. Johnson's Kentucky cavalry, led by men from the River Raisin, rode into the settlement. Moving on, the Kentuckians quickly pushed the British and Indians deep into Canada and decisively defeated them at the Battle of the Thames on Oct. 5, 1813. General Winchester was released by the British after a year in captivity.

Ironically, Monroe became the home of George Armstrong Custer, the victim of another famous massacre. The town honors him with a large equestrian statue.

Source: www.riverraisinbattlefield.org/the_battles.htm

....

Fort Sanders: Knoxville Campaign Ends with Debacle

Although Tennessee was a Confederate state, Knoxville and East Tennessee supported the Union, and throughout the Civil War President Lincoln wanted to protect the citizens who lived there. In September 1863, Federal Major General Ambrose Burnside redeemed himself for the disaster at Fredericksburg by occupying Knoxville with blueclad troops. Burnside had two exceptional officers in his service — cavalryman Brig. General William P. Sanders and brilliant engineer and cartographer Captain Orlando Poe. On the Tennessee River and dimpled with hills, Knoxville could be easily defended from attack. Soon the city was ringed by fortifications and artillery batteries on both sides of the river.

Following his magnificent victory at the Battle of Chickamauga, Confederate

Major General Braxton Bragg laid siege to Chattanooga and sent Lt. General James Longstreet on a campaign northeastward up the valley to recapture Knoxville. Longstreet had intrigued for Bragg's job; Bragg wanted him out of the way.

On Nov. 5, 1863, Longstreet moved up the valley and raced with Burnside's advance forces to reach the strategic crossroads of Campbell's Station (hometown of Admiral David Farragut). In an artillery duel, Burnside was able to hold the site long enough to effect a retreat back into Knoxville's fortifications but not before the gallant Gen. Sanders was killed in action. His friend Poe immediately renamed Fort Loudon, the fortification at the northwest salient of Knoxville, in his honor. Although cavalry raids by Confederate Gen. Joseph Wheeler against Fort Dickerson south of the river failed, the Confederate forces got ever closer. Poe worked his construction crews, composed mostly of contraband blacks, harder and harder, up to 18-hour workdays.

On November 17th, Longstreet moved his forces to the north and west of Knoxville and laid siege to the Federal stronghold. In planning the inevitable attack, Longstreet and his chief engineer, Brig. Gen. Danville Leadbetter, determined that Fort Sanders presented the weakest link. However, they should have worked harder at gathering the necessary intelligence about their target. As it is often noted, the battle was decided before it was begun.

The northwest bastion of Fort Sanders was manned by the 200 veterans of the fort's commander, Brig. Gen. Edward Ferraro, including the 79th New York Highlanders under Capt. William Montgomery and the 2nd U.S. Artillery under Lt. Samuel Benjamin. Shortly after the attack began, they were quickly reinforced by another 200 men.

Promptly at 6:00 am on November 29th, as the fort's standard was being raised over the ground fog, Colonel Porter Alexander's artillery guns pummeled the fortress. The barrage served as a signal for the 4,000 battle-hardened men of Major Gen. Lafayette McLaw's division to assemble and move double-time toward the fortress walls. Hard charging were the Mississippians of Brig. Gen. Benjamin Humphreys and the Georgians of Brig. Gen. William Wofford, Brig. Gen. Goode Bryan, and Brig. Gen. G.T. Anderson. Longstreet hoped to throw enough bodies at the parapets to overcome the fort's firepower and engage in hand-to-hand combat inside the breached defenses.

The attackers quickly faced three unanticipated obstacles. Around the fort, the Yankees had strung telegraph lines around the tree stumps, creating an almost invisible stumbling device. The fortress walls were much steeper than expected and covered with ice (defenders poured cistern water over them to freeze). The ditch in front of the walls was much deeper than originally thought and there were no ladders provided for climbing the walls. The Confederates began piling up in the ditch, discovering that retreating was as dangerous as advancing. The ditch quickly became a slaughter pen. The artillerist Benjamin had stuffed Hotchkiss shells with paper fuses. He lit them with a cigar, dropping the hand grenades into the ditch, yelling, "Look out, over there, some of you will get hurt!"

Highlanders Monument, Fort Sanders.

Three Confederate standard bearers bounded the parapet. One rebel yelled, "Come on, boys! The fort is ours." He was promptly pulled into the fort and clubbed to death. Two defenders, a sergeant and a private, were later awarded the Congressional Medal of Honor for capturing Confederate battle flags.

The battle was over in 20 minutes; such furious hand-to-hand combat could not last long. The ditch was filled with men on top of the wounded, gasping for air. Yankees found 98 bodies crammed within a 20-foot space. "Arms and limbs torn from their bodies lay scattered around," recalled a Yankee officer, "while at every footstep we trod in pools of blood."

The Confederates lost 813 casualties — 129 killed, 458 wounded, and 256 missing. The Federals suffered five killed and eight wounded. Fort Sanders was one of the most lopsided battles of the war.

It's hard to believe, but a second assault was considered until word was received that Sherman was en route from Chattanooga with 25,000 reinforcements. A truce was called that day to collect and bury the dead, but that night the siege recommenced.

Eventually, Longstreet retreated 65 miles up the valley to Rogersville, where he encamped for the winter. Poe rode with Sherman, engineering his March to the Sea, and after the war he engineered facilities on the Great Lakes.

Today, Fort Sanders is a trendy neighborhood bordering the University of Tennessee. The northwest bastion of Fort Sanders was located between modern-day Clinch and Laurel streets and bordered on 17th Avenue to the west. Recent research by Terry and Charles Faulkner resulted in two major discoveries — the fort was actually located a block farther to the west then previously recognized, and there are still identifiable remnants of the fortification where none were thought to exist. All else that remains today are historical markers and a monument to the Highlanders.

Sources: Hallowed Ground magazine, Joan L. Markel PhD, American Battlefield Trust; Encyclopedia of Tennessee History and Culture; Divided Loyalties: Fort Sanders and the Civil War in East Tennessee, Digby Gordon Seymour, East Tennessee Historical Society.

....

The Wabash: Greatest Indian Victory Over U.S. Army

The Battle of the Wabash, or St. Clair's Defeat, fought on Nov. 4, 1791, near present-day Fort Recovery, Ohio, was the greatest victory of American Indians over U.S. Army forces ever. Although the army soldiers fought bravely, the battle ended in a rout and a massacre.

Two years after the ratification of the U.S. Constitution, native tribes were battling settlers on the Ohio Territory frontier. President George Washington assigned one of his most trusted military officers, Major General Arthur St. Clair and his U.S. Legion army, to bring peace and order to the region beyond the Appalachian Mountains.

A native of Scotland, St. Clair, 54, served in the British army during the French and Indian War before settling in Pennsylvania. During the Revolutionary War, he rose to the rank of major general in the Continental Army. He is credited by some historians for the strategy that allowed Washington to capture Trenton, N.J., but he lost his command after a controversial retreat from Fort Ticonderoga. After the war, he served as president of the Continental Congress, which passed the Northwest Ordinance during his term. He was then made governor of the Northwest Territory in 1788.

At Fort Washington (Cincinnati) on the Ohio River, St. Clair assembled 2,300 badly trained and ill-equipped soldiers and began a torturous one-month journey northward to the headwaters of the Wabash River (near the current Ohio-Indiana border). Camp followers, women and children, were included in the expedition.

The Americans encamped in a defensive formation near the river, but they did not erect any breastworks. Kentucky militia riflemen camped across the river. St. Clair thought he was farther away from the Indian camps than he actually was.

The army soldiers formed a hollow rectangle 70 yards in depth by 350 yards wide. At this point in the campaign, St. Clair's forces numbered roughly 1,400 men. The line facing the river consisted of the battalions of Majors Thomas Butler, John Clarke, and Thomas Patterson, under the command of General Richard Butler. The second line was composed of Lt. Colonel William Darke's command — the battalions of Major Henry Gaither and Captain James Rhea, as well as the 2nd U.S. Regiment under Major Jonathan Heart.

The right flank was Captain William Faulkner's company of riflemen, and the left Captain Jonathan Snowden's troop of horsemen. Major William Ferguson apportioned his eight cannons equally to the two main lines.

The Indian forces consisted of 1,400 warriors from nine cooperating tribes, all well-led, organized into a center and right and left wings. The center consisted of Miami (Little Turtle commanding), Shawnee (Blue Jacket), and Delaware (Buckongahelas). The right wing was Wyandot (Tarhe and Roundhead), Mingo (Simon Girty), and Cherokee (John Ward). The left wing was Ottawa (Egushwa), Ojibwe (Wapacomegot), and Potawatomi (Mad Sturgeon).

Little Turtle had deployed his braves in a wide arc facing the American camp. He specifically instructed his men to target officers and artillerymen and to rapidly envelop both of the enemy's flanks. Just before dawn, the Kentuckians began shooting at Indians moving among the trees. The warriors then fired a monumental fusillade and charged en masse, raising a raucous holler heard in the main camp. The Kentuckians fled back to the main camp in wild confusion.

Major Ferguson began firing his artillery to little effect. The bursts went too high due to their placement on the river bank. Warriors specifically assigned to the task began firing upon the artillerymen, reducing their ranks rapidly. In a matter of minutes, the Indian warriors managed to kill all the sentry posts and commenced a horrendous crossfire. "Exposed to a crossfire," wrote Major Denny, "men and officers were seen falling in every direction; the distress, too, of the wounded made the scene such as can scarcely be conceived."

Despite the mayhem and his pain from gout, St. Clair and his deputy Butler commanded the army position with "cool and deliberate" instructions. Col. Darke was ordered to mount a charge with about 300 men around the Indian right flank, but although the movement was executed briskly it had little effect on the attackers. A gap weakened in the army lines, and the Indians swarmed into the center of the camp and commenced to commit atrocities almost too horrible to imagine. Men and women, both dead and alive, were scalped. The women's bodies were mutilated and set on fire. Dirt was stuffed down the mouths of corpses, signifying the Europeans' lust for land. Defenseless victims were butchered with tomahawks.

No quarter was given on either side. When Col. Darke saw one wounded Indian crawling to safety, he ran after the warrior and beheaded him.

Ordered by St. Clair to mount a bayonet attack, Major Heart's 2nd U.S. Regiment and Major Thomas Butler's levies performed the task well, but they paid a high price in casualties.

At one point, the gunfight slackened and the woods quieted down. St. Clair reasoned that the Indians had withdrawn from the fight. He was wrong. The Indians regrouped and attacked again with renewed fury. With his men now "ungovernable," St. Clair ordered a retreat at 9:30 am to save what was left of his command. By force of sheer numbers, the soldiers broke through to the trace and began the long anguishing journey back to Fort Jefferson and Fort Washington. There was no time to tend to the wounded; the Indians took their time torturing them to death.

At noon on November 8th, St. Clair finally reached Fort Washington. About 700 officers and soldiers had been killed and 300 wounded. More than 100 civilians were dead and 50 wounded. Indian casualties are not known but probably numbered one-tenth of the army's.

The U.S. Congress convened its first ever investigation into the catastrophe at the Wabash and exonerated St. Clair. Washington named another one of his war buddies, Major Gen. Anthony "Mad Anthony" Wayne, head of a newly revitalized army. On Aug. 20, 1794, nearly three years after the Wabash, Wayne exacted revenge by defeating the British and their Indian allies at the Battle of Fallen Timbers. The general built a fort there which later became the city of Fort Wayne, Indiana. In 1803, a part of the Northwest Territory became Ohio, the 17th state. In 1913, a 101-foot-tall obelisk monument was erected in Fort Recovery at the gravesite of the Wabash victims noting the "undaunted courage and patriotic devotion of the illustrious dead." A small museum opened at the site in 1938.

Sources: Wabash 1791: St. Clair's Defeat, John F. Winkler, Osprey Publishing; The Victory with No Name, Colin G. Calloway, Oxford University Press; https://armyhistory.org/the-battle-of-the-wabash-the-forgotten-disaster-of-the-indian-wars/, National Museum of the U.S. Army, The Battle of the Wabash: The Forgotten Disaster of the Indian Wars, by Patrick Feng.

SLIGHTLY IRREGULAR OFTTIMES MURDEROUS

Scoundrels, Bushwhackers, and Partisan Rangers

The Adventures of Thomas Woodward, Stovepipe Johnson, Fielding Hurst, Captain Jack Hinson, Dick McCann, Bob White, the Jackass Brigade, and George Washington Ellet and the Mississippi Marine Brigade.

Irregular warfare erupted throughout the Civil War, but nowhere in the Western Theater was it pursued with more vigor and persistence than in Middle Tennessee — the area between the Tennessee and Cumberland rivers, and Nashville, which was occupied early in the war following the joint invasion of Federal army and naval forces, the same campaign that culminated in the Battle of Shiloh. Resistance was brought to bear by Confederate cavalry chieftains such as Nathan Bedford Forrest, John Hunt Morgan, and Joseph Wheeler, but also by irregulars (known as partisan rangers), who added their resources to the campaign against Yankee aggression.

The Confederate Congress passed the Partisan Ranger Act in April 1861 to control guerrilla warfare and employ it to advantage, and to promote guerrilla warfare in the areas that were beyond the reach of the regular army. The Partisan Ranger Act led to the recruitment of irregular soldiers into the Confederate Army. Partisan rangers had the same rules, supplies, and pay as the regular soldiers of the army, but they would act independently and would be detached from the rest of the army. That was the intent at least.

Confederate guerrillas such as Dick McCann headquartered in Charlotte in Dickson County and raided Cumberland River chokepoints, north to Palmyra and east to Harpeth Shoals. Partisan rangers preyed on cargo freighters on the Tennessee River and led campaigns to capture and recapture the river port of Clarksville.

The Federals used Nashville as a logistics hub to launch military campaigns against Chattanooga in 1863 and Atlanta in 1864. Much of the materiel came south from Louisville on the Louisville & Nashville Railroad. The trestle at Murtaugh, Kentucky and the twin tunnels near Gallatin required garrisons to guard them. In August 1862, Morgan set the south tunnel on fire and disabled it for three months.

Fortifications and artillery batteries ringed Nashville, with Fort Negley the showpiece work of engineer St. Clair Morton. Fort Zollicoffer was built downstream to protect the city. Many of the fortifications were not completed until late in 1864 in preparation for Hood's invasion campaign.

Convoys of dozens of steamboats carried war goods from Cincinnati down the Ohio and up the Cumberland to the giant warehouses built in Nashville. These convoys required at least two gunboats for escort. Periodically the river became too shoal to conduct operations (wagon trains were used to carry cargo the final leg to the Tennessee capital). Due to these shortages, the Nashville & Northwestern Railroad was extended west all the way to the Tennessee River. The railroad was built by contraband black laborers who subsequently formed units of the U.S. Colored Troops and manned the redoubts and forts protecting the railway infrastructure. At the river terminus, a giant fortified depot was built to unload steamboat cargo and transfer the materiel to freight trains. The installation was named Johnsonville.

Southeast of Nashville near Murfreesboro, another gigantic fortified depot named Fortress Rosecrans was built to store all the war goods needed by Federal invasion forces. The earthen fort was so large that it encompassed portions of the Nashville Turnpike, Stones River, and the Nashville & Chattanooga railway. Numerous trestles and tunnels, guarded by soldiers in Federal redoubts, lined the railroad all the way to Chattanooga.

Confederate Colonel Adam Rankin "Stovepipe" Johnson and his 10th Kentucky Partisan Rangers attacked small garrison units in western Kentucky in July and August of 1862. Johnson earned his moniker by capturing (temporarily) the small town of Newburgh, Indiana, using a stovepipe and a charred log to fool the town's militia into thinking they were artillery pieces. Johnson joined up with Lt. Colonel Thomas Woodward of the 2nd Kentucky Cavalry to recapture the riverport of Clarksville, which was garrisoned by the 71st Ohio Regiment of Colonel Rodney Mason. Due to a misunderstanding, the Ohio unit and its leader had been wrongly labelled as cowards during the Battle of Shiloh. Mason was headquartered at Clarksville's Steward College while his men were scattered about the town.

Woodward approached from the west while Johnson swung around and tried to capture Mason. Mason and his junior officers determined that they were overwhelmed by rebel forces and surrendered. Afterwards, Mason was cashiered from the army for his "acts of cowardice."

Lt. Col. Woodward was quite a character. He was a native of Connecticut and attended West Point and Yale but was dismissed from both institutions due to drunkenness. He practiced law in Hopkinsville, Kentucky, and entered service as the captain of the Oak Grove Rangers. He obtained the rank of colonel and led the 2nd Kentucky Cavalry, assisting in the re-capture of Clarksville in 1862. He fought at Fort Donelson, Parker's Crossroads, and Perryville. Few details are known of his experiences because he failed to file after-combat reports with the War Department. Woodward was court-martialed four times, suspended from command once, and reprimanded once. On a drunken spree in August 1864, he rode into Hopkinsville, armed with a pistol in each hand, exclaiming that he was going to single-handedly take the town. He was shot off his horse and killed by a sharpshooter. He was buried at Hopkinsville.

On Aug. 2, 1862, Col. Mason met with his captor, Col. Woodward, and persuaded the Confederate to have his photograph taken with him. "I want to send it up North to my friends to let them see what a damned insignificant cuss I surrendered to," Mason said, according to witnesses. The pro-Confederate residents of Clarksville were nearly delirious with the Confederate takeover of their town. However, in September, a Federal column under Col. William W. Lowe advanced from Dover and met Woodward's rebels at Riggins Hill. The Confederate cavalry buckled under Federal artillery fire and fell back to Clarksville, which was subsequently retaken by Lowe. Despite this action, Clarksville was not permanently occupied by Federal forces until December 1862.

Confederate Major J. R. "Dick" McCann was known as the Guerrilla Chieftain. He was captured in August 1863 at Weems Springs, Tennessee, and imprisoned at Johnson's Island in Ohio. A veteran of the Mexican War, he formed the Cheatham Rifles, later Company B of the 11th Tennessee. After the war he was court clerk of Nashville until his death in 1880. One of his captors wrote of McCann: "His name has been an epitome of the seven deadly sins, and if a dastardly act were committed by a Hottentot between Knoxville and Nashville, 'Dick McCann did it.' We assure our readers that he is not the fiend he has been written and painted. He is about five feet eight inches high, 140 pounds weight, fair complexion, bright blue eyes, brilliant, polished and humorous in conversation. He was born of Irish parents at Petersburgh, Va., and came to Tennessee with his family when a mere child. He is married, having four children now in Nashville, his wife being in East Tennessee. He is not now, nor ever was for a disruption of the American Republic. He never has had but two disunionists in his command." Against secession before the war, McCann nonetheless sided with his adopted state when Tennessee became Confederate. He claimed that if Lincoln offered general amnesty to the Southerners the war could be ended quickly.

Despite their assignment to the 9th Tennessee Cavalry, McCann's Squadron continued to do independent partisan service for much of the fall and winter of 1862-63. After the war, a writer for the *Confederate Veteran* magazine stated: "It would be impossible to relate all of his numerous adventures. He was busy prowling around night and day, and rarely permitted the enemy to venture beyond the fortifications of Nashville without some evidence of his thoughtful attention."

On Jan. 13, 1863, the steamboat transport *Charter* was attacked by McCann's guerrillas at Ashland, five miles upstream from Harpeth Shoals on the Cumberland. The cargo of hay, corn, and commissary stores was destroyed and the boat burned. The crew was paroled except for six captured contraband deckhands (former slaves), who were led ashore and each executed with a shot to the head. In September 1862, McCann's unit vandalized the Louisville & Nashville Railroad between those two cities. In January 1863, in retribution, General Mitchell, commander of the Nashville garrison, ordered the houses and barns owned by McCann and an associate burned to the ground by the 85th Illinois Infantry. Up to a dozen other houses in that neighborhood were also torched that night.

In Dickson County, where Charlotte was the seat, the Federals declared martial law, arrested citizens suspected of supplying Confederates, destroyed crops, and confiscated livestock. In October 1863, Military Governor Andrew Johnson authorized the creation of "Union Guards" in Dickson County to stop "marauding gangs of Freebooters."

The village of Palmyra on the Cumberland River between Dover and Clarksville had the reputation as "one of the worst secession places on the river" and as a notorious gathering place for guerrillas and bushwhackers. Guerrilla attacks were organized at meetings held in the saloons on the court square in Charlotte. The town was equidistant from Palmyra to the north and Harpeth Shoals to the northeast. In April 1863, Palmyra would pay the price. A landing party was sent ashore under Acting Master James Fitzpatrick with orders to burn down Palmyra but not to loot. Residents of the village were given notice to evacuate immediately. One Federal officer wrote later: "It was clean work — every building was in flames and falling." U.S. Lt. Commander LeRoy Fitch reported that they had "burned the town; not a house left; a very bad hole; best to get rid of it and teach the rebels a lesson."

Captain Ellis Harper's Partisan Raiders derailed and attacked trains, burned bridges and water tanks, and attacked Federal forage and supply details wherever they could be found. Harper had been taken prisoner at Fort Donelson in 1862 and escaped prison camp. Morgan directed him to form an irregular company and assigned him as captain.

In February 1864 the Confederate Congress repealed the Partisan Ranger Act.

The Nation of Jones has been well publicized as a Union holdout in wartime Mississippi. Of lesser renown was the Hurst Nation in West Tennessee, a clan of Union supporters who saddled up to fight Confederate partisans and which proved to be more of a hindrance to Federal authorities than a help. Heading the clan was Fielding Hurst, a Union supporter and slaveholder whose family owned most of the land in McNairy County. He was imprisoned in Nashville by Confederates at the beginning of the war. Released in 1862 and back home, on his own initiative, he formed the 6th U.S. Cavalry, which included at least 23 family members. His command quickly gained a reputation for acting beyond the rules of war and settling old scores. The Federal army failed to adequately pay and equip Hurst's unit, and Hurst never failed to let Federal authorities know about it.

Hurst raided his hometown of Purdy in April 1863 and reportedly ordered the burning of the courthouse, church, and several homes. Federal officials briefly arrested Hurst.

"As Hurst's cavalry patrolled areas of West Tennessee, his men had a bad habit of leaving the regiment to go on private raids of their own," noted historian Gary Blankinship. On Jan. 11, 1864, Hurst was ordered to destroy all armed enemies of the U.S. government anywhere he met them in West Tennessee. On Feb. 12, Hurst collected more than $5,000 in ransom from the citizens of Jackson, Tennessee after threatening to burn down the town. After receiving the tribute, Hurst burned down 14 structures anyway. Confederate General Forrest, one of the fiercest warriors of the war, was outraged at the behavior of Hurst and his men. When Confederates captured and executed his nephew William, Hurst killed as many as 13 rebel prisoners (some accounts say five) in retribution. Forrest declared that he considered Hurst an "outlaw" who receive appropriate punishment if captured. Forrest also asked that the higher command deliver his reports on the atrocities committed by Hurst to the newspapers so that "such conduct should be made known to the world." On April 20th, Gen. James R. Chalmers wrote that Colonel James Neely had "drove Hurst hatless into Memphis, leaving in our hands all his wagons, ambulances, papers, and his mistresses, both black and white."

In May 1864, Hurst's men looted and burned Commerce, Mississippi. Again Forrest petitioned the Federal command for the surrender of Hurst, this time, in June, to Major General C.C. Washburn in Memphis. He complained that Hurst "…deliberately took out and killed seven Confederate soldiers, one of whom they left to die after cutting off his tongue, punching out his eyes, splitting his mouth on each side to his ears and cutting off his privates."

Hurst submitted his resignation "due to bad health" on Dec. 10, 1864. Later, he served in the state legislature and as a circuit judge. To some Unionists, Hurst provided a valuable service during the war, countering the actions of Confederate guerrillas. To some Federal officers, he was a disgrace and a pain in the ass. To most unreconstructed Confederates, Hurst was viewed as an outlaw and a murderer.

The April 26, 1863 combat on the Tennessee River between U.S. naval forces and Confederate cavalry qualifies not only as one of the strangest encounters on the Western rivers but also as one of the most successful counter-insurgency operations, albeit a minor one, of the entire war. The spirited skirmish occurred on the east bank of the Tennessee River just upstream (south) of the confluence of the Duck River. The combatants were the Mississippi Marine Brigade, a Federal counter-insurgency and escort force, facing a Texas cavalry battalion under Major Robert M. White.

The Mississippi Marine Brigade (MMB) was named for the river (its main area of operations) and not the state; it had no connection to the U.S. Marine Corps; and it was not technically a brigade. Led by Brigadier General Alfred Washington Ellet, the MMB consisted of the 1st Battalion MMB Infantry, the 1st Battalion MMB Cavalry, and Walling's Light Artillery Battery. The three gunboats in the flotilla at the time of the battle were the *Autocrat*, the *Diana*, and the *Adams*. The Mississippi Marine Brigade ranked "among the most unorthodox and controversial fighting units" of the Civil War, according to Ellet's biographer, Chester Hearn.

The story of the Mississippi Marine Brigade dates back to the beginning of the war and an energetic and enterprising 51-year-old engineer from New York named Charles Ellet Jr. (Alfred's older brother), who petitioned the Navy and War departments to adopt his unique scheme for defeating the Confederacy on the rivers. Ellet proposed the building of lightly armed but swift-moving rams. These converted civilian steamboats would be designed with reinforced hulls, extra timber in the bows, and a powerful prow that could smash the hulls of enemy boats and sink them. The usage of rams dates back all the way to the ancient Greeks and the battle of Salamis. Ellet came up with the idea after serving as an observer in the Crimean War in Russia during the 1850s. The concept was reinforced in his mind during his trans-Atlantic voyage on the liner *Arctic*, which sank after a collision with a much smaller vessel. Ellet's name carried some weight in Washington; he could boast of being the engineer of the world's longest suspension bridge, over the Ohio River at Wheeling. Ellet pestered officials with the Navy Department about his proposal and left empty-handed. But, somehow, Ellet did gain the attention of War Secretary Edwin Stanton, who approved funds for the rams.

Ellet scoured the Ohio River ports and purchased nine sidewheeler steamers that could be converted into rams. Although Ellet did not personally desire to wear a military uniform, he did intend to lead his newly formed Ram Fleet into battle. So he was appointed to the Army as a colonel in April 1862. He then recruited 15 family members into the fleet, including his two sons and his younger brother, Alfred, who served as his chief of staff. Alfred began the war as the lieutenant colonel of the 59th Illinois Infantry. The Ram Fleet was manned by men from the 59th Illinois and also from the 63rd Illinois Infantry. In essence, the Ram Fleet was a riverine force commanded by an Army officer who answered directly to the Secretary of War and not the regional commander. This unwieldy command structure would cause many problems for the Ram Fleet and its eventual successor, the Mississippi Marine Brigade, during the course of the war.

In June 1862, however, Charles Ellet's Ram Fleet performed well at the Battle of Memphis, defeating and helping to destroy the Confederate River Defense Fleet. During the battle, fought entirely on the Mississippi River, Charles Ellet was fatally wounded, and died shortly thereafter. The command of the Ram Fleet defaulted to Alfred, who eventually was promoted to brigadier general in the army.

At this point in the war, there was little use for the Ram Fleet, as it was effective only against enemy vessels and not against enemy shore batteries. Few Confederate gunboats remained on the rivers after the summer of 1862, so Ellet and his commander, Lt. Commander David D. Porter (Stanton had directed Ellet to work with the Navy commander), decided to develop a river-based counter-insurgency force, the Mississippi Marine Brigade. The swift-moving MMB would be used to conduct amphibious operations against Confederate guerrillas and partisans harassing Federal shipping on the Mississippi River.

Several new steamboats were acquired and converted expressly for MMB operations at a total cost of $350,000. According to historian Thomas E. Walker, the boats required extensive refitting. The boilers were protected with thick, heavy timbers. Two inches of solid oak along the bulwarks provided protection for the Federal riflemen, who would shoot through loopholes. The pilothouses had large sheets of boilerplate iron installed along the walls. Pulleys hanging from the forecastle were used to raise and lower a large, railed gangway, which allowed two horses to embark or disembark at the same time. This ramp facilitated the on-loading and off-loading of troops and equipment. By the start of 1863, according to Walker, the Mississippi Marine Brigade had a fleet that consisted of three sternwheelers and four sidewheelers, with three steam-powered tugs used for courier and resupply duties. Six coal barges were used to re-supply the fleet. Each of the five transports could carry 125 cavalry horses and riders and 250 infantrymen. Thus, the total strength of the MMB came to 625 cavalry and 1,250 infantrymen.

Manpower for the boat crews was lacking. Recruiters were sent to convalescent hospitals in the Midwest to entice potential signees with an appeal to their creature comforts: "No long hard marches, camping without tents or food or carrying heavy knapsacks, but good, comfortable quarters and good facilities for cooking at all times." Nevertheless, as with most riverine operations, obtaining adequate manpower was troublesome. Despite the inducements, recruitments fell short. The MMB could muster only 527 infantrymen, 368 cavalrymen, and 140 artillerymen manning six light field guns. The recruits would be known as Ellet's Scouts. Throughout the war, the MMB would be plagued with morale and disciplinary problems, the commanders having trouble controlling their men.

The brigade was mustered into service in November 1862 and participated in Sherman's assault on the Chickasaw Bluffs near Vicksburg and other operations during that campaign. Records of the MMB were lost or destroyed after the war, so details of its service are sketchy, but there was at least one occasion that the Mississippi Marine Brigade was used on the Tennessee River, as an escort for Streight's raiders.

Some background is in order. During the long hiatus following the Battle of Stones River (Murfreesboro), U.S. commanding General William Rosecrans directed one of his more ambitious subordinates, Colonel Abel Streight, to conduct a raid across northern Alabama into Georgia to destroy and disrupt the Western & Atlantic Railroad, used by Confederate forces near Chattanooga. Due to a scarcity of horses, Streight decided to mount his troopers on mules gathered from West Tennessee. Not surprisingly, the mules behaved badly, often breaking loose and forcing soldiers to scurry about the countryside and round them up. One story had Confederates tossing a beehive into the mule corral in a successful effort to create havoc among the ornery beasts. The raiders thus became known, not affectionately, as the Jackass Brigade. The Mississippi Marine Brigade under Ellet was directed to the Tennessee River to haul the mules, escort Streight's troop transports, and conduct counter-insurgency operations.

On April 17, 1863, the Mississippi Marine Brigade, along with numerous transports, shoved off from Fort Henry destined for Eastport, Mississippi, with a cargo of 1,250 mules. The flotilla consisted of the flagboat *Autocrat, Diana, Adams,* and the tug *Cleveland.* It should be noted that the U.S. Navy's Mosquito Fleet of tinclad gunboats under Lt. Commander LeRoy Fitch also participated in the operation. Fitch's fleet consisted of the tinclads *Argosy,*

Covington, and *Queen City,* and the timberclad *Lexington.*

Ellet reached Eastport on April 19th, and joined Fitch, who had been waiting impatiently. The mules mutinied while being unloaded, stampeding away in all directions and delaying the start of the raid by several days. By that time, Confederate Brig. Gen. Forrest and his cavalry command had arrived in the vicinity and given chase to Streight's raiders. Forrest caught up with Streight by May 3rd, before the Yankees could reach the railroad. Streight surrendered to Forrest after being hoodwinked into believing that Forrest outnumbered him. The raid by the Jackass Brigade turned out to be a disaster for the Federals.

Back at Eastport, the Mississippi Marine Brigade, minus the mules, began its secondary mission, that of counter-insurgency, with great zeal. During its departure, the village of Eastport burned to the ground. Ellet reported no cause for the destruction, the village having somehow mysteriously burst into flames. Beginning April 23rd and moving northward (downstream) toward Clifton, the brigade set ashore at several places, burning mills and stores and confiscating cotton, mules, and horses. Not surprisingly, the MMB earned the hatred of local residents and rebel partisans alike.

During the river operations, *Diana* accidentally ran into the tugboat *Cleveland* and sank it (perhaps evoking memories of the defunct ram fleet). The flotilla managed to raise the tug the next day. Ellet later reported inaccurately that *Diana* had run aground and that *Cleveland* had struck it.

Although the main attack occurred on April 26th between Ellet's MMB and Confederate cavalry, it was actually Navy Lt. Commander Fitch and his tinclad gunboats who first paddled into the sights of the Texas cavalry battalion led by Major Robert M. White, in a rare night fight at 2:00 am on April 24th, north of the Duck River. The riverboats were easy targets, even at night, while the naval gunners could fire only at the muzzle flashes of White's four field artillery pieces. First fired upon was the tinclad *Emma Duncan,* commanded by Acting Master William N. Griswold and manned by inexperienced sailors. One of the sailors noted that the rebels were "peppering it into us hot and heavy." One rebel shell struck the No. 1 Parrott gun portside, exploded, and mangled the arms of three sailors so badly that the three arms had to be amputated on the spot. The nighttime exchange lasted about 45 minutes before the Texans stopped firing and withdrew. The *Emma Duncan* was hulled seven times, and suffered extensive but mostly minor damage.

Two days later, on the foggy morning of April 26th, Ellet and the Mississippi Marine Brigade steamed northward on the Tennessee River toward the dangerous shoals near the confluence of the Duck River. The river was narrow at this point (the channel less than 50 yards from the east bank) and allowed for no maneuvering. At 8:30 am at the shoals, Ellet's squadron finally tangled with the Texas Rangers.

Robert M. White knew the terrain and the river well. He had been born and raised in Tennessee near the river. By the 1850s, he and his wife had moved to Bell County, Texas, where he prospered as a grocer. He served as 1st lieutenant in the Bell County Rovers, later commanding the 25 men of Bob White's Ranging Company, defending the local settlers against hostile Comanche Indians. An ardent supporter of secession, White raised a company of cavalry, which was incorporated into the Sixth Texas Cavalry, at Dallas in September 1861. The next year he was promoted to major. He and his men served in Arkansas, the Choctaw Indian Nation, Georgia, Mississippi, and Alabama. By 1865 only 18 men of the original Bell County cavalry company had survived the war.

Major White's special battalion consisted of one company from each regiment of Sullivan Ross' brigade—the 3rd, 6th, and 9th Texas cavalry and Waul's Texas Legion. White's 600 to 700 men stationed their four masked guns on the east bank opposite the shoals, where he knew the boats could not maneuver. They were expecting cargo-laden freighters and perhaps a tinclad or two.

On April 26, 1863, Ellet's flagboat, the *Autocrat,* under sailing master Samuel Henecks, led the flotilla into the narrow chute at the Duck River Shoals, unaware of any pending trouble. "The channel at this point is narrow and torturous, and the current swift, making it necessary for a steamer, when once she has entered the passage of these rapids, to go through without stopping," according to the recollections of the sailors.

The *Autocrat* was suddenly pounded with a barrage from the four-gun battery on the eastern shore, along with a flurry of lead bullets from dozens, if not hundreds, of rifles. The U.S. gunboat returned fire, as did the *Diana* and *Adams*. According to one sailor "…the river itself was quickly overhung with a dense cloud of sulpherous smoke."

Fired upon at point-blank range, the *Autocrat* was penetrated by eight shells, one hitting the upper casemate and passing through the officers' mess-room, another passing entirely through the upper structure and exploding on the other side. Many brigade members on the gunboats were wounded by wooden splinters. The pilothouse was struck with 80 rounds of bullets and canister, all the glass shattered, and only the boilerplate cladding saving the lives of the pilots. The *Diana* was struck six times and easily penetrated with cannon shells, while the grape, canister, and minié balls were stopped by the heavy oak planking of the gunboat's gunwales.

As soon as the *Autocrat* cleared the shoals, about two miles downriver, she came about and sounded her landing whistle, plowing into the riverbank, lowering her ramp, and dispensing her complement of cavalrymen. Lt. William F. Warren, the signalman atop the gunboat, worked his wigwams (signal flags), ordering the other gunboats to follow suit. Lt. Col. George Currie commanded the landing party, with Major James M. Hubbard in charge of the cavalry and Captain Daniel P. Walling in charge of the artillery units.

Major White's men, expecting to confront only transports, could hardly believe what they were witnessing—the enemy was putting ashore armed horsemen to do battle with them on land. About that time, the timberclad *Lexington,* part of Fitch's downstream force, hove into view and let loose with her big guns. That's all the persuasion the Texans needed. They quickly limbered their guns and headed eastward away from the river at a brisk pace.

Federal pursuit was slow and deliberate, according to historian Walker. "The terrain favored a defending force—a marshy, soft ground covered with thick, patchy woods and winding roads—which provided a topography with many opportunities for a defending force to ambush pursuing troops. The rapid deployment of the Mississippi Marine Brigade forced the Confederate troops to withdraw, and the only further contact came from the rebel rearguard."

Several times the Federal cavalrymen pushed far enough ahead to engage the Confederate rearguard, but they could not induce the Texans into making a stand. Eventually the chase was called off, about 12 miles inland. Casualties were light. Four Confederates were found dead on the riverbank, and four more, including a lieutenant, were killed during the pursuit. One was taken prisoner. The biggest casualty of the skirmish was the Confederate leader himself. Two to four miles inland, Major White was discovered in an abandoned house, dying of a rifle wound to the breast. He would later be taken back to Texas for burial.

The marine brigade suffered two killed (a sergeant in the infantry and a private in the cavalry) and several wounded, most from wooden splinters. The cavalryman was killed by a shell hitting the *Autocrat* which then took off the foot of another marine, and sliced off the bayonet and scabbard of a third soldier onboard. Six horses were killed while aboard the gunboats.

Of the combat, historian Hearn noted, "This marked the first time that Ellet's brigade operated exactly the way (Naval commander) Porter envisioned by landing fifteen hundred troops, with field artillery, at a moment's notice."

The April 26, 1863 skirmish was the only combat the MMB would experience on the Tennessee River. Following the skirmish at the Duck River Shoals, the Mississippi Marine Brigade was withdrawn and spent the next year operating along the Mississippi River, creating even more controversy, until the brigade was disbanded in late 1864.

Secretary of the Navy Gideon Welles noted in his diary that the Ellets were "brave, venturous, intelligent engineers, not always discreet or wise, but with many daring and excellent qualities. They had under them a set of courageous and picked men."

Perhaps the final word on the Mississippi Marine Brigade comes from U.S. Army Counterinsurgency and Contingency Operations Doctrine 1860-1941—

"Perhaps the most remarkable counter-guerrilla unit was the Mississippi Marine Brigade, an amphibious organization created in November 1862 in response to guerrilla attacks on federal shipping along the Mississippi River. Over the course of the next two years the 'marines' led an active life, skirmishing with rebel guerrillas, conducting raids, and participating in conventional operations. Although effective, the unit was troubled by morale and discipline problems and soon developed a reputation for robbery and arson as it steamed up and down the Mississippi burning towns, destroying plantations, and carting off loot. Some of the destruction was authorized in line with the Army's tough retaliatory policies, but the brigade exercised little discretion in picking its targets. Moreover, the unit's special boats were costly to maintain and considerations of economy and reputation eventually led the Army to disband the marine brigade in 1864."

No one person exemplified the deadly impact of the partisan guerrilla better than Jack Hinson, a lone sharpshooter whose vengeance against occupying Federal forces resulted in dozens of kills, according to Hinson's biographer, Tom C. McKenney, who noted, "Elements of nine regiments, both cavalry and infantry, and an amphibious task force of specially built navy boats with a special-operations Marine brigade targeted the elderly man with a growing price on his head. They never got him."

Captain Jack Hinson, as he was known, was in his late 50s when he ordered a specially made .50-caliber rifle (the gunsmith was William E. Goodman of Lewis County) and began targeting Federal officers for death. One of his favorite shooting dens was at Towhead Chute on the Tennessee River near Hurricane Creek in Benton County, Tenn. As the river flows northward through the narrow channel, the current increases significantly, and the paddlewheelers headed upstream had to work hard against the current, barely moving. A Federal officer might stand on the deck in his navy blue uniform, admiring the view. Hinson aimed between the shiny brass buttons of the victim's jacket. For each kill, he would stamp a round notch onto the octagonal barrel of his heavy rifle. By war's end, the plain-looking rifle was adorned with 36 notches (McKenney estimated that Hinson's actual kill total was close to 100).

What had motivated this lone sharpshooter to seek such vengeance? Hinson was a wealthy landowner and farmer in the area between the rivers, now known as the Land Between the Lakes. At first, he was a Unionist, opposed to secession, even though he owned slaves. The invasion and occupation of his homeland, and the increasingly harsh treatment of locals by the Yankees, forced him to change his mind. His estate was called Bubbling Springs, located three miles southwest of Dover. General U.S. Grant at one time was a guest in the house of Hinson and his wife, Elisabeth. The couple had eight sons and two daughters. One son was a Confederate soldier stationed in Virginia, who was wounded and died in 1865. Two other sons were briefly imprisoned as spies during the Battle of Fort Donelson. The eldest son, Robert, was involved with a local guerrilla group. At one point, Robert was imprisoned at the county courthouse but escaped by jumping out a second-story window. His horsemen became known as Hinson's Raiders. He was captured a second time and questioned by authorities in Nashville who never realized exactly who he was. He managed to either escape or he was paroled. On Aug. 6, 1863, Hinson's men attacked Fort Henry and seized the telegraph station.

One morning in the fall of 1862, two of Jack Hinson's younger sons were out on horseback, armed and hunting game, when set upon by a roving Federal cavalry patrol. The Hinsons, ages 17 and 22, were assumed to be spies. They were tied to trees and summarily executed by firing squad. Their lifeless bodies were put on display in the courthouse square in Dover. Then the lieutenant commander of the patrol beheaded the bodies with his saber. As the patrol made its way to Bubbling Springs to confront Jack Hinson, they placed the severed heads of his sons on the gateposts at the Hinson home. A doctor and friend of the family was able to subdue the enraged Jack Hinson and save him from being killed or imprisoned by the patrol, which eventually left the scene. At this point, Hinson, of Scots-Irish descent, determined to save his family and vowed vengeance, however long it might take. He needed time to secure his family and estate, order his custom-made sharpshooter rifle, obtain supplies, and scout shooting locations.

Hinson's first victim was the lieutenant of the patrol that killed his sons. Hiding and waiting in the woods, Hinson shot him in the saddle while leading a patrol. A short time later, Hinson was out and about and sighted a Yankee patrol which included the sergeant who had placed the boys' heads on the gateposts. On the patrol's return to base, Hinson was waiting. With cool efficiency, he shot and killed the sergeant and made his escape.

Hinson took his position at Towhead Chute and began picking off Federal naval officers on the gunboats. At one point, Hinson's shots were so devastating that the captain of one gunboat "surrendered" his vessel before realizing that there were no Confederate troops to accept his surrender.

Eventually the Hinson family was forced to abandon Bubbling Springs, which was burned to the ground by soldiers.

Jack Hinson died peacefully nine years after the war at the age of 67. Hinson's rifle is now owned by a judge in Murfreesboro, Tennessee.

Sources: The Curious Case of the 71st Ohio, Derrick Lindow, www.kentuckycivilwarauthor.com/post/the-curious-case-of-the-71st-ohio; Hoptown Chronicle, Jennifer P. Brown, Jan. 31, 2020; Clarksville Civil War Round Table, Greg Biggs; Tom C. McKenney, Jack Hinson's One-Man War: A Civil War Sniper, Pelican Publishing Co., 2014.; Encyclopedia of Tennessee History and Culture; Mark Zimmerman, Iron Maidens and the Devil's Daughters, Zimco Publications LLC.

VINCENNES
Historic Old Town on the Wabash

Home of George Rogers Clark and Clem Kadiddlehopper

Vincennes, an Indiana town on the Wabash River bordering Illinois, is one of those small towns of mythic proportions in the history of the United States that doesn't get much attention these days. The last significant event there occurred more than 200 years ago. Other such towns in Middle America include Marietta, Ohio; Harper's Ferry, West Virginia; Maysville, Kentucky; Jonesborough, Tennessee; New Bern, N.C., and Milledgeville, Georgia, just to name a few.

Founded in 1732 by French fur traders, notably François-Marie Bissot, Sieur de Vincennes, for whom the original fort was named, Vincennes is the oldest continually inhabited European settlement in Indiana and one of the oldest settlements west of the Appalachians.

Vincennes was a strategic point on the Wabash River, site of several forts occupied by various nationalities, a territorial and state capital. Today, it boasts numerous historic sites for the serious history buff and a few other attractions. Four ships of the U.S. Navy have borne the city's name.

The impressive courthouse handles the business of Knox County. The town's population of 17,000 hasn't change much, except for the comings and goings of the 4,400 on-campus students of Vincennes University, a public two-year school with a four-time national championship basketball team, the Trailblazers.

Vincennes is the hometown of Freddie the Freeloader and Clem Kadiddlehopper, the most famous incarnations of beloved comedian and entertainer Red Skelton (1913-97). Visitors to the Red Skelton Museum of American Comedy can learn about his mastery of pantomime, slapstick, pratfalls, exaggerated movement, and facial expression. He was the star of *The Red Skelton Show* (1951-71), which won three Emmy Awards, and he starred in 19 movies. His career began at age ten in a traveling medicine show. Skelton has stars on the Hollywood Walk of Fame for his work in radio and television, and also appeared in burlesque, vaudeville, films, nightclubs, and casinos, all while he pursued an entirely separate career as an artist, specializing in paintings of clowns. He is buried in California.

The city's Pyramid Mound bears evidence of prehistoric human occupation. It is a natural formation although it was first thought to have been built by Indians of the Mississippi culture. Those tribes disappeared about a thousand years ago and nobody knows why.

Along the river is the beautiful lawn of the George Rogers Clark National Historical Park, which features perhaps the most significant Classical stone edifice outside Washington, D.C. The monument, built in 1931 in classic Greek style, features an 80-foot-high granite exterior encircled by 16 columns supporting a massive round roof. Inside, a bronze statue of George Rogers Clark stands on a marble pedestal. The rest of the ceiling and rotunda walls are Indiana limestone. The floor is Tennessee marble. Seven murals depict Clark's role in winning the region west of the Appalachians. The architect was Frederick Hirons; the sculptor Hermon A. MacNeil; the painter Ezra Winter.

Outside by the river is an impressive stone statue of Italian-born Francis Vigo, a wealthy St. Louis merchant who greatly assisted Clark in his mission. On the other side of the park are the Old Cathedral Complex, dating to 1749, and the statue of Father Pierre Gibault by Albin Polasek.

The beautiful arches of the Lincoln Memorial Bridge span the Wabash River where Abraham Lincoln and his family entered Illinois in March 1830. Just across the river stands the impressive limestone and bronze Lincoln Trail

Monument by Nellie Verne Walker depicting a young Lincoln and his family, natives of Kentucky, entering the prairie state.

Vincennes served as the Indiana Territorial Capital from 1800 to 1813; Grouseland was the home of Governor William Henry Harrison, who was later elected as the country's 9th U.S. President (he died one month into his term of natural causes). The two-story red-brick house in the Federal style was completed in 1804, one of the most impressive homes on the Ohio frontier, the first brick home in the territory. John Scott Harrison was born in the home; he was the father of the country's 32nd President, Benjamin Harrison. At least five treaties with various Indian tribes were signed at Grouseland (the 11 treaties negotiated by Harrison gave settlers millions of acres to settle). In August 1810, Harrison met with Shawnee chieftain Tecumseh, who was accompanied by hundreds of braves on the lawn in front of Grouseland. The meeting lasted for eight days but ended without a treaty. Their differences were later settled in battle as part of Tecumseh's War. Harrison defeated Tenskwatawa (the Prophet), Tecumseh's brother, at the Battle of Tippecanoe in 1811, and defeated Tecumseh at Battle of the Thames in 1813. Not far from Grouseland is a tall wooden sculpture of Tecumseh dedicated in 2009. The outdoor sculpture was created by artist Peter Wolf Toth, a Hungarian immigrant who developed a deep interest in Native North American culture and history.

George Rogers Clark (1752-1818) was residing in the wilderness around Lexington in Kentucky country when the American Revolution began. At 6-2 tall, he was a larger than life character who paved the way west for colonial settlers. He built forts on the Mississippi and Ohio rivers, repelled a British-led Indian attack in the Illinois country, and led two major expeditions that destroyed the major Shawnee towns in the Ohio country.

He was the older brother of William Clark, who in the early 1800s explored the Louisiana Purchase with Meriwether Lewis.

His most famous exploits began in 1778 when he led an expedition of 150 volunteers into the frontier to protect settlers and forge an alliance with the French who lived in the British-controlled posts at Kaskaskia and Cahokia (in present-day Illinois). He was instructed to do so by Virginia Governor Patrick Henry. Clark floated 900 miles down the Ohio River to the current site of Louisville and then marched 120 miles west to Kaskaskia. He persuaded the residents to join the Patriot cause. He then journeyed east to Vincennes, site of Fort Sackville. Father Pierre Gibault, head of Kaskaskia's Roman Catholic mission, helped sway Vincenne's French inhabitants and militia to switch their allegiance to the American side. Placing Capt. Leonard Helm in command of Fort Sackville, Clark then moved west to Kaskaskia. From this base he sought and secured temporary neutrality from hostile Native tribes. In response, British Lt. Gov. Henry Hamilton headed south from Fort Detroit with a small force of British regulars and still-loyal French militia to recapture Fort Sackville. He was joined by hundreds of Indians. Capt. Helm surrendered Fort Sackville to the British in December 1778.

Clark knew his frontiersmen could not retake Fort Sackville once spring arrived and Hamilton's Indian allies returned to Vincennes from their winter homes. Clark's only hope of taking the fort lay in a surprise midwinter attack. Clark set out with 170 of his men and began a 160-mile trek across the freezing plains of southern Illinois. A midwinter thaw had set in, causing a torrent of water to come down from the north. This meant that the last 10 days of this 19-day journey were spent in icy cold water that at times reached the men's necks. Movement was difficult, to say the least, not to mention keeping their powder dry. Finally, on February 23rd, Clark and his men arrived at Vincennes, where the French inhabitants warmly treated Clark's cold, wet, starving men.

That same evening, Clark's men surrounded Fort Sackville and began to fire on it. Clark knew it would still be tricky for his small force to intimidate Hamilton into surrendering, so he employed several different strategies to strengthen his position. Clark managed to make his 170 men seem more like 500 by unfurling flags suitable to a larger number of troops and firing their rifles at a rapid rate. Meanwhile, Clark began tunneling under the fort with the intent of exploding the gunpowder stores within it. When a Indian raiding party attempted to return to the fort, Clark's men killed or captured all of them. The frontiersmen made a public show of executing five of the captive Indians with tomahawks; the gruesome exhibition frightened the British. Their subsequent surrender revealed British weakness to the local tribes, who realized they could no longer rely on the British to protect them from the Patriots.

The formal surrender of Fort Sackville by Hamilton to Clark came on Feb. 25, 1779. In 1783 the United States acquired the lands west of the Appalachians in the Treaty of Paris. Four years later, the Continental Congress established the Northwest Territory, composed of present-day Illinois, Indiana, Michigan, Ohio, Wisconsin, and eastern Minnesota.

Sources: National Park Service; HistoryNet.

SATURN V
The Most Powerful Machine On or Off Earth

Several weeks after the Soviets launched their Sputnik satellite into orbit, the Americans responded with the launch of their Vanguard rocket, which lifted off the pad three feet, then fell back and exploded into a spectacular fireball. The press labeled the event "Kaputnik." Eleven years later, a U.S. rocket of monumental proportions and power would push three men into orbit and then to the moon. Six months after that, American astronauts would be walking on the lunar surface.

The American victory in the race to the moon was a proud milestone in the Cold War between the U.S. and the Soviet Union, a triumph of capitalism over communism. To achieve that success, thousands of scientists and engineers labored to design and build the most powerful machine in the world — the Saturn V launch vehicle — the key to getting the spacecraft past Earth's gravity and into outer space.

The gleaming white Saturn V stood as tall as a 36-story building and weighed 6.5 million pounds. On top were the command module holding the astronauts, the service module, and the lunar module. The launch vehicle below consisted of three stages. The first stage (known as the S-IC) used five F-1 rocket engines generating a total of 160 million horsepower. Each F-1 engine gulped three tons of kerosene and liquid oxygen per second and blasted a tongue of flame hundreds of feet long. After three minutes of flight and at 41 miles high, the first stage would be jettisoned and the smaller second stage (S-II) would take over, using five smaller J-2 rocket engines. Then, 6.5 minutes later, the third stage (S-IVB) with one J-2 engine would send the

Test-firing an F-1 engine (inserts) at Marshall SFC.

craft into Earth orbit and subsequently propel the command-service-lunar modules to the moon.

The noise of the Saturn V lifting off the launch pad shook the ground and crackled the atmosphere, reaching the pain level of 140 decibels, equal in intensity only by a nuclear explosion. "The roar is terrific!" shouted CBS-TV announcer Walter Cronkite as the control building shook and glass windows vibrated in their frames. Wernher von Braun, the stoic German scientist and father of the beast, shouted emotionally, "Go, baby, go!" The acceleration pushed the astronauts atop the monster spacecraft back into their seats at four times the force of gravity.

The race to the moon dates back to World War II when German scientists, led by the brilliant von Braun, developed the V-2 ballistic missile (technically known as the A4) for the Third Reich. More than 3,000 of the explosive missiles were launched against England and Belgium. At the end of the war, the Americans and Soviets raced to capture German scientists and their high technology. Under Project Paperclip, von Braun surrendered to the Americans and persuaded 500 scientists and technicians to come with him to the U.S., specifically the testing grounds at Fort Bliss and White Sands, New Mexico. After the war, one hundred functional V-2s were shipped to the U.S. for testing.

In 1960, the National Aeronautic and Space Administration (NASA) chose the Redstone Arsenal at Huntsville, Alabama, as the site for the Marshall Space Flight Center (MSFC), named for General George C. Marshall, and

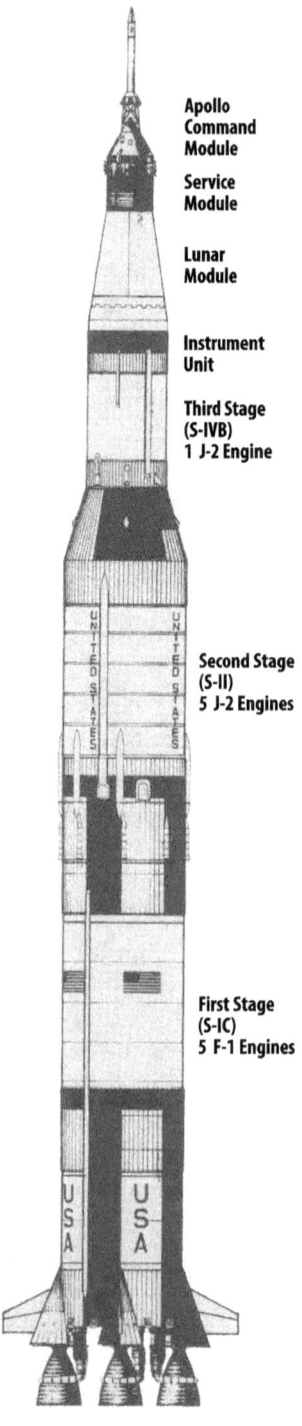

Apollo Command Module
Service Module
Lunar Module
Instrument Unit
Third Stage (S-IVB) 1 J-2 Engine
Second Stage (S-II) 5 J-2 Engines
First Stage (S-IC) 5 F-1 Engines

assigned von Braun, who had become a naturalized U.S. citizen, as director. (Wernher von Braun had been a Nazi mainly interested in rocket science although he was aware of the deadly results of the V-2s and the thousands of slave laborers who died manufacturing the rockets. In the Cold War against the Soviets, however, he was too valuable not to use his talents. American satirist Mort Sahl mocked von Braun by saying, "I aim at the stars, but sometimes I hit London.")

The primary goal of the MSFC was to produce the Saturn V launch vehicle to land a man on the moon by the end of the 1960s, as promised by President John Kennedy. Five major contractors were used: Boeing to build the S-IC or first stage; North American Aviation for the S-II or second stage; Douglas Aircraft for the S-IVB or third stage; Rocketdyne for the F-1 and J-2 rocket engines; and IBM for the instrumentation unit.

The Saturn launch vehicle had to work flawlessly each time. MSFC officials had to change the mentality of its contractors from "mass production with acceptable errors" to "craftsmanship — do it right the first time — with no errors." Prior to the Saturn V, the prototypes Saturn I and IB were also built.

Production of the main stage would be conducted at the Michoud Assembly facility outside New Orleans, which had produced Liberty ships during WWII. Testing would be performed at a Pearl River, Mississippi facility. Finished units would be barged to the launch facilities at Cape Canaveral, Florida. Saturn production commenced during the Mercury Program launches. At one critical point, in 1963, manned flight director George Meuller made a momentous decision aimed at speeding up production. Instead of building and testing the rocket stages incrementally, the entire rocket would be tested all at once, an "all-up" concept. The conservative German scientists objected, but Meuller's gutsy decision stood.

The Saturn V first stage consisted basically of two large fuel tanks, five large F-1 rocket engines, and the pumps and apparatus needed to get the fuel to the combustion chambers or nozzles. To evenly distribute the combustibles (RP-1 rocket-grade kerosene and liquid oxygen), the nozzles were designed with hundreds of flow tubes, punctured with 2,816 holes. The temperature in the chamber reached 6,000 degrees, with pressure soaring to 1,015 pounds per square inch (psi). During its first test, the F-1 rocket engine literally exploded. The combustion in the chamber was detected as being unstable. Many solutions were attempted in a trial-and-error process. Explosives were deliberately detonated inside the chamber to create instability so it could be more accurately observed and measured. Finally, after exhaustive research, the answer was reached — baffles were added to the chamber to increase stability. The baffles completely corrected the stability problem.

To adjust the rocket's trajectory, each F-1 combustion chamber or nozzle swiveled on a gimbal. To simplify movements, all of the engine's pumps and accessories were also mounted on the gimbal assembly. To save space, the two huge fuel tanks were merged into one giant tank with a wall separating them.

The Saturn I was used primarily as a research and development vehicle. Ten successful Saturn I launches in 1961-65 demonstrated engine performance and vehicle reliability. The Saturn IB was used for orbital missions with Apollo spacecraft. Its first stage was powered by eight F-1 engines.

On the Saturn V, during a typical launch, the F-1 engines begin operating 8.9 seconds before lift-off. The five engines are timed to reach full power at slightly staggered intervals to prevent a single massive shock wave from slamming into the rocket. By T-minus 0.0, the combined thrust reaches 7.5 million pounds, and four huge hold-down arms release the rocket while the upper five umbilical arms connecting the rocket to the support tower swing away. In one-third of a second the Saturn V breaks free.

Each F-1 rocket engine, so scrupulously designed and tested, was manufactured to operate for exactly 165 seconds at the beginning of the launch, then fall back to Earth and sink to the ocean floor. (In 2010, salvagers recovered from the ocean floor the remains of the centerfire F-1 engine used on the historic Apollo 11 moon mission.) Each mighty engine stood 19 feet tall by 12 feet wide and weighed over 18,000 pounds. In contrast to the F-1 engines, the J-1 rocket engines in the second and third stages were smaller and burned liquid oxygen and liquid hydrogen.

MSFC was involved in developing the Saturn vehicle's instrument unit for guidance, navigation, and control. This "brain" controlled all the ignition sequences, stage separations, guidance and control, and telemetry functions to keep the vehicle operating properly and on course. Begun as an in-house project, which evolved through several versions, the sophisticated unit eventually was contracted to IBM for final design and manufacture.

On April 16, 1965, after nearly three years and hundreds of tests, five F-1s were mounted on the Huntsville test stand and fired together for the first time. A searing yellow-white column of flame shook the ground like a sustained earthquake. All the engines worked perfectly.

The first launch of the Saturn IB, suborbital and unmanned, was in February 1966. The first launch of the Saturn V, also unmanned, was Apollo 4 in November 1967. Apollo 6 was launched in April 1968 and the performance of the Saturn V was troubling, to say the least. Two minutes into the unmanned flight, unstable pressure in the fuel tanks caused the entire rocket to oscillate in a pogo-like motion that threatened the integrity of the ship. Later, the second stage also oscillated and two of its five engines failed. A structural I-beam bent, which could have lead to a "catastrophic failure" highlighted by a huge explosion. The ship held together, and the test flight ended two hours later with splashdown. "This was a disaster," exclaimed the flight director.

As the rocket accelerated upward, it burned fuel which lightened the load—this was the secret to getting into Earth orbit. But as the load lightened, stability weakened, creating dangerous vibrations or the "pogo" effect. Something needed to be added to the fuel tanks as they emptied to create stability without increasing the weight. The solution was to add helium to the fuel tanks as they emptied. Helium weighed next to nothing.

The failure of two engines on the second stage during Apollo 6 was due literally to crossed wires, a mishap which was easily fixed. Von Braun believed the Saturn V was ready to launch men into orbit but he had to convince one man — Dieter Grau, chief of quality and reliability operations. Grau was one of the German scientists von Braun had brought with him to America. Grau ordered a total review of the spacecraft's systems and production methods and data from test burns and launches. Several unacceptable but non-critical problems were found and corrected. Finally, Grau gave his approval for launch.

In October 1968, the Saturn V took Apollo 7 into Earth orbit. Apollo 8 launched on Dec. 21, 1968, and was the second crewed spaceflight mission flown in the Apollo space program. Apollo 8 was the third flight and the first crewed launch of the Saturn V rocket, and was the first human spaceflight from the Kennedy Space Center, located adjacent to Cape Canaveral Air Force Station. Apollo 8 was the first crewed spacecraft to leave low Earth orbit and the first to reach the Moon, orbit it, and return. Its three-astronaut crew — Frank Borman, James Lovell, and William Anders — were the first humans to fly to the Moon and to witness and photograph an Earthrise.

Six months later, Apollo 11 took three men to the moon, with Neil Armstrong and Buzz Aldrin landing on the surface and walking on the moon. Kennedy's promise had been kept.

Overall, 18 Saturn V launch vehicles were produced but only 13 actually flew, all with impeccable results and no failures. The Saturn V sent two dozen astronauts to the moon (12 landed on the surface). The launch vehicle worked perfectly 13 times (excepting Apollo 6), with all vehicles lost after ocean splashdown. The total cost of producing the Saturn launch vehicles was $9.1 billion, one-third of the total program cost. In 1965-1966, MSFC reached its peak work force of 7,327 employees and budget of almost $1.7 billion.

Dr. W.R. Lucas, who became MSFC director in 1974, said, "Few of man's technological endeavors compare in scope of significance to the development of the Saturn family of launch vehicles... Saturn was an engineering masterpiece."

Sources: Power to Explore: A History of the Marshall Space Flight Center, Andrew Dunar and Stephen Waring, NASA History Series; NASA Saturn V: Owner's Workshop Manual, W. David Woods, Haynes Publishing; Apollo 8, Jeffrey Kluger, Henry Holt & Co.; Mark Carlson, Apollo's Stallions, Aviation History.

"What happens in Las Vegas is legalized gambling (known in business circles as gaming) and what stays in Vegas is your money. Also known as Lost Wages, this desert oasis is an adult wonderland built on the empty wallets of losers. One expert said there is no such thing as good luck or bad luck in Vegas: It's all based on mathematics, and the math says the house always wins, over the long run. Still, folks from all over the world journey to Vegas to vie for that royal flush, blackjack, rolling 7s and 11s, beating the spread, and especially the "big slots jackpot." As they say, you can't win if you don't play. As one Vegas visitor noted, there's no place to sit and rest in a casino without spending money.

In 2019, casinos on The Strip took in $6.6 billion in gambling revenue; downtown casinos hauled in $650 million. In the 2019 fiscal year, 169 large casinos in Las Vegas reported total revenues of nearly $22 billion. Since 1999, however, revenue generated in Vegas by non-gaming amenities has exceeded casino revenue. By 2013, the direct gaming income constituted only one-third of the total profits made by Las Vegas hotel-resort-casinos.

Of course, the Covid-19 pandemic in 2020 hit the tourism industry especially hard, and Las Vegas was no exception.

Don't think you can go to Vegas, win a fortune, and forget to pay taxes on the winnings. Anyone winning more than $1,199 is required to fill out an IRS form before receiving any cash. Vegas is a cash culture, a phenomenon of which Uncle Sam is well aware. Gambling transactions are cash only, unless one is a bigshot VIP with casino credit, comped (freebie) rooms, escorts on demand, and meal credits. If this becomes the case, you should become very, very wary.

Las Vegas (Spanish for *The Meadows*) is a place where any visitor (45 million per year) can find or secure almost anything, as long as the cash is available. There are ATMs everywhere. You can drive a Ferrari, shoot a machinegun, operate a bulldozer, zipline high above Fremont Street, party in a gondola on the world's largest Ferris wheel, eat a banana split made with a gallon of ice cream, and rent a hotel suite that includes two bowling alleys. As Mae West once said, "Too much of a good thing can be wonderful."

In the casinos, scantily clad cocktail waitresses supply gamblers with free drinks (Sinatra's favorite was Jack Daniel's). At the Montecristo cigar bar at Caesars Palace, one glass of The Macallan 40-year-old single-malt Scotch whisky will set you back $1,800, served tableside in Riedel crystal glassware.

Playing slot machines, which are more like video games these days, one can win sizable vouchers (few pay off with actual coins anymore), but everyone is seeking that ever-elusive jackpot. Senior citizens hunched over the machines, drink in one hand, cigarette dangling from their mouth, punch the square buttons in robot-like fashion (old-fashioned pull handles are still available on some machines) as the rollers spin, lights flash, and electronic background noise rumbles with a steady tingling-tangling humming. Members with player club cards can redeem accumulated points for various small appliances and knick-knacks on display. Every casino boasts a high-limit room where every push of the button on the slot machines costs $5 and up. In the corner, there's one lonely machine where each push costs you $100! At the Excalibur (the casino-hotel that looks like Disneyland), one lucky guy recently won a $39 million jackpot, beating the odds of 1 in 16.7 million. That's why folks keep coming back to Vegas.

Although it's a relatively low-key casino off The Strip, locals gamble at the Gold Coast because the pay-off odds there are reportedly better. At least, that's the rumor. Try the blackjack machine at the end of the South Bar. Not many people play roulette; the sum of all the numbers on the wheel add up to 666. Everybody wants to play craps, but apparently nobody knows how. The dice in Vegas do not have rounded corners. Sports wagering is big in Vegas, with sports books occupying large spaces in most casinos. The walls feature dozens of video screens of various sizes and tall boards of tiny red and green lights displaying the current odds and money lines. There always seems to be a horse race televised from some part of the globe.

Cigarettes and cigars can still be smoked in most casinos; vending machines are still legal here but require a lot of quarters. Beer is often served in aluminum bottles in Vegas. Some casinos contain their own full-fledged liquor stores, where bottles sport lockable theft-prevention collars.

Reportedly there's a black book of people (career criminals and/or card counters) forbidden to enter any Vegas casino; there are less than 50 names in the book. Of course, gambling can become an addiction. Many a family's life savings have been squandered at the tables or slots. Casinos heavily publicize telephone numbers of rehab centers and support services.

Back in the 1980s, workers at a Las Vegas hospital were suspended for betting on when patients would die. Too many fingers on the scales with that one. At one medical center, after the Super Bowl in 2015, a drunk performed a stand-up comedy routine for the weary occupants of the ER waiting room. He got a standing ovation.

The buffets in Vegas are legendary, featuring every type of food imaginable. Brunches feature bottomless champagne and mimosa glasses. Expensive steakhouses can be found everywhere. Even seafood. Patrons in Vegas eat 60,000 pounds of shrimp each day, more than the rest of America.

There are 30,000 professional party girls in Vegas, where prostitution is illegal. Also 2,500 exotic dancers. If you'll notice, many middle-aged men bring their "nieces" to Vegas for a good time. Ironically, the actual strip clubs in Vegas are found in special neighborhoods off The Strip.

Some folks go on vacation to shop. There are plenty of high-end stores and shops in Vegas. The Forum Shops at Caesars Palace, among others, features every high-priced, extravagant shop imaginable. At the north end of The Strip is a souvenir shop claiming to be the world's largest.

The Las Vegas Strip (Las Vegas Boulevard) is 4.2 miles long and it is not located within the city limits of Las Vegas. The airport is in Paradise. With its neon lights and LEDs, Vegas is probably the brightest spot on Earth. If you go to the top of the Strat Hotel (1,149 feet) at night you can also see some of the darkest places on Earth. Bodies are buried out there in the desert. Even without burial, bodies would mummify, it's so sunny, dry, and arid. It gets well over 100 degrees during the day in the summertime (the record is 117) but it's a dry heat, with four inches of rainfall per year and very little humidity.

Back in the day when the Mafia ran Vegas, there was an unwritten rule that a mobster wouldn't get whacked as long as he stayed in the city. However, if a button-man was told to "86" some unlucky dude, it meant to whack the guy, take him eight miles out into the desert and bury the body six feet deep. Don't worry about getting whacked in Vegas. For one thing, the Mob doesn't run Vegas anymore, much to the chagrin of long-time tourists. If you were a well-behaved visitor with money to spend, the Mob made sure you were safe and treated right. The Mob rules were simple about keeping the streets clear of bums, beggars, drunks, pimps, hookers, trick rollers, and dope peddlers. They were bad for business. Today, there's a museum downtown dedicated to the Mob.

"Nobody dies in a casino," stated Las Vegas expert Anthony Curtis. "To this day, the local media rarely reports anything about anyone who actually does die in a casino from whatever cause, and paramedics likewise don't declare someone dead till he or she is out of the casino." Violence and fist-fights are bad for business and frowned upon. There are security cameras and rent-a-cops everywhere. Most casinos operate roughly 2,000 security cameras on their premises. But only about two percent of the cameras are monitored live. There are at least 400 cameras in the valley to monitor vehicular traffic (there are no red-light or speeding cameras).

However, Vegas is also the site of the worst mass murder in history—the shooting at Mandalay Bay in 2017 that killed 60 people and wounded more than 400.

Vegas consumes huge amounts of water and electric power. Water comes from Lake Mead and power comes from Hoover Dam. The Bellagio hotel sports more than a thousand fountains that dance to music and light. The display spans more than 1,000 feet, with geysers soaring as high as 460 feet.

Party animals drive 270 miles across the desert from L.A. for the weekends, while flyers stay longer and make McCarran International Airport the seventh busiest airport in North America, with more than 600,000 take-offs and landings per year. Visitors can play slot machines inside the terminal (the machines are exactly the same as those in the casinos).

New Year's and the Super Bowl are the biggest draws in Vegas, with college basketball's March Madness close behind. Sports betting is big in Vegas, although illegal wagering still attracts more cash than legal. Bettors can legally wager on dozens of Super Bowl "propositions," such as how long the National Anthem will last and who will win the coin toss. Those who bet on an overtime game happening were consistent losers for 50 years, until 2017 (New England beat Atlanta in overtime). Sporting events are big in Vegas, which now has a pro hockey team and a pro football team. The National Finals Rodeo are held in Vegas, along with professional golf tournaments and several motor races.

There are 50 wedding chapels in Vegas, including drive-throughs, conducting 300 weddings a day. At many of them, an Elvis impersonator will conduct the ceremony. Elvis Presley was one of Vegas' biggest performers, headlining 837 consecutive sold-out shows at the Las Vegas Hilton. That's a lot of karate chops. Weighing in, Big Elvis (Pete Vallee) carries on the tradition with live shows at Harrah's. He's highly acclaimed. There are an estimated 40,000 Elvis impersonators (officially known as ETAs-Elvis Tribute Artists) in the U.S. It's a good bet many are in Las Vegas.

Although major entertainers perform in Vegas, there are also many impersonators and look-alikes (e.g., Sinatra, Johnny Cash, Lady Gaga,

Whitney Houston). Also, a lot of over-the-top architecture and attractions. The 50-ton lion outside the MGM Grand Hotel is the world's largest bronze sculpture. The Strip features a half-scale replica of the Eiffel Tower, a New York City skyline, a Roman palace, an Egyptian pyramid with the world's most powerful beam of light, a Great Sphinx of Giza bigger than the original, a simulated volcano, and a pirate lake. On West Sahara, there's a replica Statue of Liberty in front of a stripper supply house. Near downtown, visitors to the Neon Museum can wander amongst a gigantic repository of old, used casino and hotel signs, lit up bright at night. Vegas glistens and glitters with 15,000 miles of neon tubing and hundreds of millions of LED lights. The Fremont Street Experience, a pedestrian mall covered with a canopy, uses 12 million LED lights (originally 2.1 million conventional bulbs). The electric bill for the Luxor pyramid's shining light is $51 per hour. The Luxor Sky Beam is the strongest beam of light in the world, using curved mirrors and 39 xenon lamps. On a clear night, the Sky Beam (42.3 billion candela) can be seen 275 miles away.

Downtown Las Vegas is much different from The Strip; it's like drifting back in time to the late 1950s to Glitter Gulch. Kind of stuffy but still interesting. At Binion's Horseshoe, there's $1 million in cash on display (actually it's what a pile of one million dollars would look like). Back when he was alive, the notorious casino owner Benny Binion used to display $1 million consisting of one hundred $10,000 bills (the bills are now out of circulation and very rare). Downtown's Golden Gate is the oldest continuously operating hotel and casino in Las Vegas; it opened in 1906 as Hotel Nevada.

There are more than 150,000 hotel rooms in the greater Las Vegas area (20,000 meeting and conventions are held in Vegas each year), but a thousand people live in the 200 miles of drainage tunnels beneath Las Vegas. Reportedly, many of them are former Las Vegas jackpot winners.

Sources: PaySpace Magazine; Anthony Curtis' Las Vegas Advisor; Las Vegas Convention and Visitors Authority; taxi and ride-share drivers, hotel and casino personnel and a couple of yak ranchers.

EVANSVILLE
WWII Arsenal of Democracy

It's June 1944, the English Channel off Normandy, France. On the top deck of LST 532, ferrying back wounded Allies and captured Germans, a military policeman sits in a tied-down truck checking the rounds in his Colt 45 pistol magazine and glances upward at two P-47 Thunderbolt fighter planes roaring inland to attack enemy ground troops. Chances are, the light truck, the pistol ammunition, the fighter planes, and the ship itself were all manufactured in one place back in the States — Evansville, Indiana, one of the many industrial powerhouses in the U.S. arsenal of democracy.

During the war, American homeland industry quickly converted to military production and churned out two-thirds of the Allies' materietl needs, including more than 100,000 tanks and armored vehicles, 2.4 million trucks and other vehicles, 226,000 artillery pieces, more than a million machine guns, and billions of rounds of various ammunition.

At the beginning of the war, Evansville's economy was languishing despite the steady hum of the Chrysler automobile plant. Local officials took the initiative and worked diligently with the federal government to locate wartime industries in Evansville at its crook in the Ohio River. Thousands of workers, including many women and minorities, flocked to the river port in search of work and relatively high wages (up to $1 per hour) and became known as "the army left at home." Housing was a problem, with many workers housed in barracks and other temporary quarters, even tents. Bars and nightclubs such as the Blue Bar and the Trocadero attracted large crowds, and prostitution flourished. Hundreds of troops from Camp Breckenridge, Kentucky, 40 miles away, barged into town each weekend.

More importantly, industry ramped up to produce materiel for Amercian troops overseas. Thirteen plants in Evansville earned the prestigious Army-Navy "E" Award for excellence (only five percent of all industries were so honored). The city was home to 48 businesses doing war work, with $600 million in defense contracts.

Before the war, Evansville industry consisted of plants owned by Bootz, Holsclaw Brothers, Servel, Sunbeam, Briggs, Hercules, and Chrysler. In early 1942, two new manufacturing plants were begun — the Missouri Valley Bridge and Iron Company shipyard and Republic Aviation. The shipyard employed a peak of 18,000 workers and produced 167 large, flat-bottomed ships designed to deliver tanks and other war materiel during amphibious landings by grounding itself onto the beach. These behemoths were called landing ship-tanks or LSTs. They were used in the Pacific, Mediterranean, and European theaters, including the invasion of Normandy, and proved to be absolutely essential. Despite the hectic pace of production, there were never enough LSTs to go around. Most historians agree that the LST was one of the most vital pieces of equipment in the victory over fascism.

Republic Aviation produced 6,670 P-47 Thunderbolts, half of the total produced nationwide. The P-47 was a massive aircraft, nicknamed the Jug, powered by a muscular 2,500-hp radial engine and four-bladed propeller. Although it could hold its own in a dogfight against a Folke-Wolfe, the Thunderbolt was a highly effective ground-attack airplane, using machine guns, rockets, and bombs. It was also extremely rugged and could take a lot of abuse — pilots loved it because the P-47 got them back to home base alive.

From D-Day to the end of the war, Republic P-47 Thunderbolts in Europe destroyed 86,000 railroad cars, 9,000 locomotives, 68,000 motor vehicles, and 6,000 armored vehicles. They dropped 132,000 tons of bombs and expended 135 million rounds of ammo and 60,000 rockets. In 1942-45, Bolts shot down more than 3,000 enemy aircraft.

The first P-47 Thunderbolt, the *Hoosier Spirit,* went out the door at Republic Aviation, located south of the airport, soon after the last section of the assembly building was completed. Twenty months after groundbreaking, one thousand of the Juggernauts had been completed. The 5,000 workers at the plant continued to finish 14 to 30 shiny new fighters per day. The Republic plant also made modifications to the Vultec A-35 Vengeance and the Vought Corsair fighter. On April 27, 1943, President Franklin D. Roosevelt made an unannounced visit to the aircraft plant, touring the interior of the plant in his government vehicle. He met and talked with four employees who had made suggestions that increased efficiency at the plant. Then, immediately after V-J Day in August 1945, the plant was shut down. In early 1946 the facility was sold to International Harvester Company.

Before the war, the Chrysler plant was producing 275 Plymouths a day. Within five months the facility became the Evansville Ordnance Plant, which produced an astonishing 3.3 billion rounds of .45-caliber ammunition (96 percent of all produced in the U.S.). The Chrysler plant accomplished the following wartime goals with a peak workforce of 12,500 people:
- Half a billion .30-caliber rounds
- Hundreds of thousands of other special ammo
- Packed 1.5 billion rounds specially for use in the Pacific
- Reconditioned 1,662 Sherman tanks (for homeland training purposes)
- Rebuilt 4,000 Army trucks
- Delivered 800,000 tank grousers (used to increase tread traction)
- Began work on a contract for 7 million firebombs

Perhaps the most impressive work by Chrysler, in conjunction with Sunbeam Electric and Remington Arms, was to switch the ammunition casings from brass to steel, due to a nationwide shortage of brass. This was an extremely complicated problem to solve, but within a year the plant was producing more cartridges in one day than the entire U.S. smallarms industry produced in one year prior to the war.

The maker of refrigerators prewar, Servel employed 12,000 workers and produced wing panels for the P-47, 20 million 40mm shell casings and nine million 37mm casings, landing gear assemblies, field ranges, and aircraft head castings.

In addition, American Fork & Hoe manufactured bayonets; Hoosier Cardinal produced plastic domes for such iconic U.S. bombers as the B-29 Superfortress; International Steel made bridges, piers, and pontoons; Briggs Indiana manufactured wings for navy airplanes; Keller-Crescent Printing turned out military training manuals; Shane Manufacturing shipped out military trench coats; and Faultless Caster produced millions of fuses and millions of navy tracer rounds, according to historian James MacLeod.

The most celebrated product of Evansville during World War II was the LST, the first of which slid down the launchway on Halloween 1942, sideways into the Ohio River, bow facing upstream. The keel for LST 157 had been laid 129 days earlier, on June 25th. LST 157 would be sold to the British Royal Navy and end up in Asia.

The $6.3 million, 45-acre "cornfield shipyard" consisted of ten building ways, five on each side of the transfer area leading down to the launching ways at the riverbank. Theoretically, ten ships could be in production at the same time. After launching ceremonies, the ship floated to one of four

LST 325 on exhibit at Nashville wharf on the Cumberland River.

outfitting piers. Once a ship was taken out for a trial run and approved by the U.S. Navy, a broom was raised up the mast to signify "a clean sweep." Then 700 miles to the Gulf of Mexico and overseas. The shipyard operated day and night, 24/7, and by the end of the war a ship could be built and completed within 60 days.

Of the 1,051 LSTs built during the war at 16 sites, Evansville contributed 167, two dozen of which participated in the invasion of Normandy. Each LST was 328 feet long and 50 feet wide, sat six feet in the water, and carried up to 2,302 tons (usually 20 Sherman tanks). Each ship could make 12 knots on twin screws powered by a pair of General Motors diesel engines.

Dangerous fumes would accumulate inside the ship whenever tanks were loaded or unloaded. A wooden building resembling a full-scale mockup of an LST was built at nearby Fort Knox to develop methods of ventilating the interior of the ship. They decided that the best solution would be to have large overhead fans clear the entire deck of exhaust.

The LSTs bore several anti-aircraft batteries and stations because, once beached, the LSTs became Large Stationery Targets. During the Normandy landings, LSTs would ferry tanks and vehicles across the Channel from England and then take wounded soldiers and prisoners back.

While workers labored at the plants during the war, overseas 459 local Evansville men were killed serving in the U.S. military.

Women worked one of every six jobs at the shipyard, half of the 5,000 workers at the Republic aviation plant, and 60 percent of the jobs at the Chrysler ordnance plant. Mildred Osmann worked in the loft shop at the shipyard, which she said was more fun than being a stenographer. Her husband was in the army and her two brothers also worked in the yard. She was the only female member of the Boilermakers Union. There were no Rosie the Riveters at the shipyard; there were no rivets, all the joining was done by welding. Evelyn Cox was the first female welder in the yards. She said she loved her job because it never got boring. Emma Monroe followed her husband into working at the shipyard and became the first female three-position welder — flat, horizontal, and vertical-overhead. After a year of welding, she taught classes and made more money than her husband (which he didn't mind). After the war, she never worked outside her home again.

Not much of the Evansville shipyard remains today, but Evansville does boast a special WWII museum open to the public — an actual LST moored at the bend in the river. LST 325 served in three major operations during the war — the invasion of Sicily, the invasion of Salerno, Italy, and the Normandy invasion. LST 325 earned two battle stars during the war. In 1964, she was sold to Greece. In 2000, the ship was purchased by the USS LST Memorial Inc. and sailed back to the United States. A hearty crew of 28 veterans (average age 72) completed the 4,350-mile voyage and arrived in Mobile, Alabama on Jan. 10, 2001. Two years later, LST 325 arrived at Evansville for permanent display. Ironically, LST 325 was manufactured at the Philadelphia Shipyards, not Evansville.

On occasion, LST 325 meanders down the Ohio and up the Cumberland River for public tour stops at Nashville and Clarksville, Tennessee. On Oct. 1, 2012, during a blinding rainstorm and high winds, LST 325 ran aground in the mud of Lake Barkley (Cumberland River) near the Kentucky community of Buzzard Rock. The flat-bottomed behemoth, piloted by a captain with 35 years experience, was stuck fast. Two days later, after several unsuccessful attempts, the ship was floated again through the use of a 4,000-hp towboat, the ship's anchor winch and 1,800-hp engines in full reverse, the ship's Higgins boat pushing, and the filling and refilling of ballast tanks to gently rock the vessel. After a safety inspection, the museum ship sailed back to its home port in Evansville.

Sources: James MacLeod, Evansville in World War II, The History Press; Darrel E. Bigham, Evansville: The World War II Years, Arcadia Publishing; LST 325: Workhorse of the Waves & Evansville's War Machine, Evansville Courier & Press.

Utopian Dreams
~
Heaven Can Wait

Throughout history, idealists have dreamed of creating Utopian communities where men, women, and children could live in peace, prosperity, and harmony. Middle America in the 19th Century seems to have drawn its share of dreamers in pursuit of the perfect society (or the perfectly functioning company town). For Europeans coming to the New World, America seemed at first to be the shining city upon the hill, where separatists could practice their religion and way of life in peace. It wasn't that easy. Would it surprise anyone to know that none of the Utopian attempts succeeded?

Utopian communities in the heartland included Nashoba, New Harmony, the Kingdom of Paradise, the Shakers, the Ruskin Cooperative Association, Rugby, and The Farm. Other planned or "company towns" included Old Hickory, Kingsport, Oak Ridge, Harriman, Norris, and Bemis, all in Tennessee, most in the 20th Century.

Utopian communities usually center on one charismatic leader who develops plans to make his dreams come true. In contrast to totalitarian dictators, such dreams include various combinations of free love, communism, socialism, free labor, celibacy, plainness, egalitarianism, freedom, and liberty. Utopian communities usually end up colliding with reality, such as misconception and opposition from the public, punitive weather cycles, economic downturns, sickness and disease, the vagaries of human nature, and so forth.

In 1736, an educated German socialist named Christian Gottlieb Priber came to the Cherokee Nation at Grand Tellico after being kicked out of Germany, England,

and South Carolina. Well-received by the Cherokee, Priber strove for seven years to establish what he called the Kingdom of Paradise, a society where people of all races would live collectively, sharing even their children. He also strove to unite the Native American tribes into one nation. The English and the French both suspected Priber of being a spy, and in 1743 the English imprisoned him. He died in 1748. Nearly a century later, the Cherokees were forced onto the Trail of Tears to the Oklahoma Territory, although the Eastern Tribe still exists today in North Carolina.

Nashoba was a utopian community of whites and freed black slaves established in 1826 near Memphis by Scottish dreamer Frances Wright. Educated in London and living on a sizable inheritance, Fanny Wright and her sister came to America in 1818 along with the great French general Lafayette on his triumphant return. Wright suggested to Lafayette that they establish a training school for the independence of black slaves. With the help of Memphis founders Andrew Jackson and John Overton, she bought a 2,000-acre estate on the Wolf River and named it Nashoba, the Chickasaw word for wolf. In 1826, she purchased 15 slaves, recruited progressive white settlers, and began to clear land and build cabins. The goal was for the community to be self-supporting. Wright hoped to obtain support from white slave owners for her concept in which slaves would labor in the fields to repay their purchase price while receiving education to survive on their own. As a necessary compromise, Wright agreed that when slaves were freed, they would be colonized outside the United States. The next year, Fanny went to Europe to raise funds for her venture, but when she returned she found only a few individuals remaining. Sickness, internal strife, and opposition from outside critics doomed the initiative. Fanny Wright moved to New Harmony, and then moved to New York. In 1829, she returned to Nashoba and subsequently arranged for more than 30 blacks to move to Haiti, where they were welcomed. Wright intensified her role as social critic and reformer. With Robert Dale Owen, she edited and wrote for the *Free Enquirer,* the New Harmony newspaper. She and Owen founded the Working Men's Party in New York City.

In 1803, the Rappites or Harmony Society journeyed from Wurttemburg, Germany, to Butler County, Pennsylvania, and established a community called Harmony, with the Holy Bible as the sole authority. Within a decade, 700 members had built 130 houses, but in 1814 they sold out to Mennonites for $100,000 and moved to Indiana on the Wabash River. They founded New Harmony, but they sold out again in 1825 and returned to Pennsylvania. The community finally dissolved in 1905.

New Harmony, Indiana, a 20,000-acre tract, was bought by Robert Owen, a Welsh industrialist and social reformer. Owen envisioned a "New Moral

Owens' concept of a Utopian New Harmony.

World" of happiness, enlightenment, and prosperity through education, science, technology, and communal living. The experiment attracted much interest from many intellectuals but also from "crackpots, free-loaders, and adventurers." Owen went to the East Coast to recruit new members and raise funds, and returned to a "chaotic" community of 800 individuals. A constitution was adopted and a seven-person committee appointed for governance. Owen returned to Scotland to sell his textile mill and arrange for his family. His wife and two daughters chose to remain in Scotland; his four sons moved to New Harmony. The town soon became overcrowded with a dire need for adequate housing. Members quarreled over the community's credit system, and self-sufficiency was still far in the future.

The town adopted a new constitution, "The New Harmony Community of Equality," whose objective was to achieve happiness based on principles of equal rights and equality of duties.

Josiah Warren, an anarchist and one of the original founders, stated that "it appeared that it was nature's own inherent law of diversity that had conquered us... our united interests were directly at war with the individualities of persons and circumstances and the instinct of self-preservation." Owen adhered strongly to the tenets of the Enlightenment, which drove away agrarian leaders, and he attacked organized religion of any form. Also, a lack of skilled labor and supervisory management led to the failure of New Harmony two years after its founding.

A son, Robert Dale Owen, wrote that the members of New Harmony were "a heterogeneous collection of radicals, enthusiastic devotees to principle, honest latitudinarians, and lazy theorists, with a sprinkling of unprincipled sharpers thrown in," and that "a plan which remunerates all alike, will, in the present condition of society, ultimately eliminate...the skilled, efficient and industrious members, leaving an ineffective and sluggish residue, in whose hands the experiment will fail."

Another son, Richard Owen, became Indiana state geologist, an Indiana University professor, and the first president of Purdue University.

Today, the Historic New Harmony State Historic Site features 12 buildings from the early 19th Century and 20 from the mid-19th Century.

Shaker Village of Pleasant Hill, 3,000 acres in Kentucky, was home to the third largest Shaker community in the U.S. between 1805 and 1910. The Pleasant Hill Shakers are recognized for their iconic architecture, skilled craftsmanship, and profound spirituality.

In 1774, nine members of a religious sect called the United Society of Believers in Christ's Second Appearing fled England for America. They were followers of Mother Ann Lee, a child laborer in England who became a member of the Shaking Quakers, celebrants who shaked and gyrated in religious ecstasy. She claimed to have visions and a message from Christ that His second coming would be that of a woman. The sect's ultimate destination was America, where eventually 21 villages were established from Maine to Kentucky. By 1823, there were 491 Shakers at Pleasant Hill with land holdings of approximately 4,500 acres. Over a 105-year span, the Shakers constructed more than 260 structures of all kinds, including a municipal water system, one of the earliest such systems in Kentucky. The Shakers were hard-working farmers. They purchased a bull from England in conjunction with Henry Clay and owned one of America's largest herds of registered Durham Shorthorn cattle. Pleasant Hill became a leading agricultural experimental station.

The Civil War brought hard times to the Shakers, who were pacifists and did not own slaves. The Shakers believed in celibacy, which meant they had to actively recruit new members all the time. By 1910, Pleasant Hill had closed its doors as an active religious society. The last Shaker died in 1923.

Rugby was an attempt to build a model community in the wilds of Morgan County, Tennessee, based on a real estate venture founded by a company of British and American capitalists. Begun in 1880 and defunct by 1909, the experiment was termed "the last attempt at English colonization in America." The village of Rugby exists today, maintained by the Rugby Restoration Association.

Boston capitalists purchased 75,000 acres of forest land in East Tennessee, with options for another 300,000 acres. Thomas Hughes was an English social reformer, bestselling author, and an idealist who envisioned a model community formed by Americans and English "second-sons" (British custom dictated that only eldest sons inherited land). On a visit to America,

Hughes was struck by the mobility of classes, unlike the caste society in England. Hughes never resided in Rugby, but his wife and his brother did. On Oct. 5, 1880, the village of Rugby was established with about 100 residents, controlled by a Board of Aid to Land Ownership. New buildings included the Tabbard Inn, Christ Episcopal Church, a Victorian library, cottages, and boarding houses. By the next summer, the population had increased to 300, mostly Americans. Then typhoid fever killed seven residents, and many others fled in panic. The first winter had been unusually severe, followed by a lengthy drought. A promised railroad spur never materialized. Disputes over land titles delayed productive use of the land, which had to be cleared to raise crops. The mountain soil was less than satisfactory. Land sales never reached expectations, and the school never reached its potential. Most of the colonists were not used to hardships and had little experience in manual labor. Some of the younger Englishmen received funding from home and spent their time riding, shooting, playing tennis, and "just plain loafing." Rugby seemed to be thriving by the summer of 1884 due to its reputation as a health resort, but then the Tabbard Inn burned to the ground and Madame Margaret Hughes died in 1887. One major factor in Rugby's failure was the micromanagement by investors in Boston and London who didn't know the local problems. By the turn of the century many of the colonists were long gone. The English Board of Aid sold out to American interests in 1909.

Library at Rugby.

Ruskin was a utopian socialist colony operating in Tennessee City from 1894-96 and then moved to 800 acres near Dickson, Tennessee. The Ruskin Cooperative Association (RCA) was created by Julius Wayland with profits and publicity from his socialist weekly newspaper, *The Coming Nation*. RCA was named for John Ruskin, an English writer and social reformer. Members could join by buying a $500 share. The huge three-story Commonwealth House contained the press shop for the newspaper in addition to a library, dining hall, auditorium, and other shops. The RCA produced chewing gum, suspenders, coffee made from cereal, and a medicine called Ruskin Ready

Remedy. The site also included a photo gallery, steam laundry, machine shop, café, bakery, school, sawmill, cotton gin, grist mill, blacksmith shop, wagon shop, and a canning factory that operated inside a large cave. Their goods were sold in neighboring towns as well as distributed worldwide via ads in *The Coming Nation,* which had more than 60,000 subscribers.

Wayland left the colony after one year, replaced by Isaac Broome, who was to head a college which was never built. Religion was mostly ignored by members; there was no church. Although the various businesses were profitable, the Ruskin Cooperative failed due to heated disputes among its members over religion, education, free love, feminism, and more. Some saw the colony as a vehicle for social revolution while others saw it as a refuge for traditional agrarian values. Many Ruskinites, an embittered Broome later reflected, preferred to "smoke, gossip, and spit tobacco" rather than develop their minds. Although the property of the cooperative was valued at $100,000, it was sold in 1899 for a total of $12,000.

Seventy years later, a caravan of 80 school buses carrying 320 "hippie idealists" under the leadership of former college professor Stephen Gaskin arrived at The Farm near Summertown, Tennessee, a tract of 3,200 acres bought for $70 per acre. The founders were described as "free thinkers, pacifists, conscientious objectors, and mostly vegetarians." The experimental community grew to 1,200 residents before disillusionment and the 1980s economic recession forced many to leave. The "Changeover of 1983" required each adult member to contribute financially to the annual budget and operating expenses for the community. Today, The Farm is home to 200 residents (Gaskin died in 2014). Many work as independent contractors outside the community. Others work at various shops and industries on-site.

In a 2019 article in *The New Republic,* member Michael Beyer said, "We realize that there is no viable way to start a full commune within a capitalist society right now. What we can do is slowly leverage our way out of it."

Scholar Michael Gavin of Middle Tennessee State University explained, "The lack of infrastructure seriously affected the well-being and success of the communal experiment, as the large numbers of newcomers overwhelmed the meager resources. The need for adequate housing, running water, sanitation facilities, transportation, and other key necessities became acute. The recession of the early 1980s proved to be the last straw, and many residents left The Farm. In 1983 the remaining members discarded the communal system in favor of the present cooperative one, in which the land and other assets are held and maintained in common, with all residents paying a set fee for monthly dues. Under this arrangement, members retain control of their personal assets."

Today, across the U.S., there are about 170 ecovillages, co-housing settlements, residential land trusts, communes, and housing cooperatives, according to the Foundation for Intentional Community's directory.

After the Civil War, Northern capitalists recognized the potential for industrialization in the South, which offered rich deposits of coal and minerals, timberland, waterways, and cheap, non-unionized labor. Several attempts were made at creating idealized company towns to provide labor forces for industrial plants. In the late 1800s, temperance was a controversial topic, with capitalists and business owners desiring sober hard-working family men as employees. During the war, Col. Walter Harriman, a governor of New Hampshire, led his 11th Regiment through the bend in the Emory River in East Tennessee and noted its appeal. Later, his son, a lawyer and Congressman, moved his family to Tennessee and joined the East Tennessee Land Co. in Roane County in 1881. The company, formed by minister Frederick Gates, was to create a model industrial city based on temperance and attract new industry. First the town was named Fiskville, then changed to Harriman. In 1890 lots were sold in the town (buyers had to sign a pledge not to drink alcohol), an imposing brick building was erected as the company headquarters, and three subsidiaries formed to promote coal and iron mining, to develop a rail system, and to offer capital to recruit industries.

The company's early investors included 1888 Prohibition Party presidential candidate General Clinton B. Fisk, who served as the company's first president, Quaker Oats co-founder Ferdinand Schumacher, and publishers Isaac K. Funk and A.W. Wagnalls.

Unfortunately, the company, heavy in debt, went bankrupt during the economic downturn in 1893. The American Temperance University was established in 1894, and operated out of the East Tennessee Land Company's abandoned headquarters. Harriman continued to grow slowly, but the stock market crash of 1929 was a heavy blow to local industry. Today, Harriman is a town of 6,200 just off Interstate 40, and, ironically, one of the first buildings along the route into town is a liquor store.

One of the more successful attempts at a company town was Bemis in West Tennessee near Jackson which was formed in 1900 by Albert F. Bemis, a graduate of the Massachusetts Institute of Technology (MIT). His venture was based on his father's bag company. By locating the village in the middle of cotton country, building a cotton gin near the railway, and constructing decent, affordable housing for workers, Bemis succeeded in creating a model company town that thrived for nearly half a century. The 300-acre site featured about 75 houses, company stores, post office, hotel, boarding house, rail depot, schools, playgrounds, churches, auditorium, YMCA building, swimming pool, parks, bath house, and a six-hole golf course. Workers were not required to live on-site. Economic factors forced the Bemis Company to sell their mills in 1980. They closed in 1991. "Bemis remains an identifiable town with a distinctive character, but is also nationally significant as an example of American welfare capitalism," stated historian John L. Hopkins.

During World War I, the federal government built the village of Old Hickory near Nashville for workers constructing the world's largest smokeless gunpowder plant (see separate chapter). During World War II, the government built the town of Oak Ridge near Knoxville for workers whose goal was to enrich uranium for use in the atomic bomb (see separate chapter).

Around 1906, George L. Carter of the Carolina, Clinchfield & Ohio Railway envisioned a model industrial town along the Holston River in northeast Tennessee. Carter sold his holdings to John B. Dennis and Blair and Company of New York around 1914. The next year Dennis organized the Kingsport Improvement Corporation (KIC) and enlisted J. Fred Johnson, Carter's brother-in-law, as the principal promoter for the new town. Kingsport was the first economically diversified, professionally planned, and privately financed city in 20th Century America. A decade after incorporation, the town claimed ten manufacturing facilities employing 3,383 workers. Tennessee Eastman Kodak came to Kingsport during the Great Depression and during WWII received the government contract for producing RDX explosives. This led to the building of the Holston Army Ammunition Plant (Holston Ordnance Works), which became the largest manufacturing facility for explosives in the world. Also, Tennessee Eastman was chosen to operate the Y-12 uranium-enrichment plant at Oak Ridge. Today, Kingsport remains a vibrant, livable city with a sizeable industrial base. Holston Ordnance still operates outside of Kingsport as the Holston Army Ammunition Plant under the direction of the U.S. Army Materiel Command. The facility comprises 425 buildings on 6,117 acres.

Norris was built in 1933 by the Tennessee Valley Authority to house workers at its Norris Dam project. The town was thoroughly planned, with 12 housing designs available. The houses fit into the natural surroundings and all featured electric heating. Norris was the first self-contained town in the U.S. to use the greenbelt principles advocated by Ebenezer Howard. In 1948, the town was sold at public auction for $2.1 million to Henry D. Epstein, who headed a group of Philadelphia investors. They sold off all the existing houses and then in 1953 sold their remaining real estate holding to the Norris Corporation, a local corporation formed by residents. Norris has changed little in recent decades; it is the site of the Museum of Appalachia, a living mountain village.

Sources: John Egerton, Visions of Utopia, Tennessee Historical Commission; ShakerVillageKy.org; Encyclopedia of Tennessee History and Culture; RuskinVenues.com.

"Who knows what evil lurks in the hearts of men? The Shadow knows!" The Shadow was a mysterious force of good over evil, a mainstay of radio entertainment back in the 1930s and '40s before the dawn of the Age of Television. But who exactly was this shadowy figure?

With a blood-curdling laugh, the mystery man in a dark trench coat, who had the power to cloud men's minds so they could not see him, battled the gamut of evil— werewolves, vampires, psychotic murderers, gangsters, and mad scientists. His very name struck terror into the hearts of lawbreakers and criminals. At the end of each daring exploit, listeners were admonished, "The weed of crime bears bitter fruit! Crime does not pay. The Shadow knows!"

The Shadow debuted on July 31, 1930, as the mysterious narrator of the radio program *Detective Story Hour,* which was developed to boost sales of Street & Smith's monthly pulp *Detective Story Magazine.* The first issue of the pulp series *The Shadow Magazine* went on sale April 1, 1931.

On Sept. 26, 1937, *The Shadow,* a new radio drama based on the character as created by newspaperman Walter Gibson for the pulp magazine, premiered with the story "The Death House Rescue." The radio shows, some narrated by Orson Welles, lasted until 1954. Since then, six two-reel movies, a serial, and seven feature films have been based on the Shadow's exploits.

The Shadow's alter ego was actually a character named Lamont Cranston, in the same vein as Superman was really Clark Kent.

After the Shadow mopped up crime in his city, the ole vacuum-tube radio emitted the eerie sound of a creaking door and a sinister voice welcoming you into the mysterious circle of *The Inner Sanctum* (1941-52). "Pleasant dreams, hmmmmmmmm?"

MUNCIE
INDIANA

Muncie (pop. 68,000) in north-central Indiana is known for Ball State University and alum late-night talk-show host David Letterman; Jim Davis, creator of Garfield the Cat; the PBS studios used by beloved landscape painter Bob Ross; Pizza King pies; and the industry and philanthropy of the Ball brothers, manufacturers of the Mason glass jar.

Comedian Letterman hosted television talk shows for 33 years and returned to Muncie in 2007 to dedicate a college communications facility named in his honor. "If reasonable people can put my name on a $21 million building, anything is possible," he said in his speech, noting that he was at best an average student.

Sporting his signature perm hairdo, Ross painted "wet-on-wet" landscapes with little trees for 11 years on *Joy of Painting*, recorded in the studios of PBS station WIPB in Muncie. A country music fan, Ross once appeared on the Grand Ole Opry stage in Nashville, a guest of Hank Snow. He died in 1995.

Muncie was one of 11 charter members of the National Football League that formed in 1905. The Muncie Flyers played in the NFL for 20 years before going bankrupt after the 1925 season.

Muncie was known as "Little Chicago" during Prohibition because gambling, prostitution and bootleg liquor were big business in the city. In addition, gangster John Dillinger often used Muncie as a hideout whenever things got too hot in Chicago.

During the 1790s, the area was inhabited by the Delaware tribe, which had migrated west from their Middle Atlantic homelands. Muncietown, later shortened, was incorporated in 1865, became the seat of Delaware County, and attracted industry due to the advent of railroad lines and the Indiana gas boom of the 1880s.

Natural gas was first discovered in Indiana in 1876. Miners were boring a hole in search of coal.

The Ball Brothers, left to right: William Charles Ball (1852-1921), Frank Clayton Ball (1857-1943), Lucius Lorenzo Ball (seated) (1850-1932), Edmund Burke Ball (1855-1925), George Alexander Ball (1862-1955).

After they reached a depth of about 600 feet, a loud noise and a foul odor came from the hole in the ground. Frightened, the miners believed that they had breached the ceiling of Hell. They plugged the hole and did not drill any more at that location. Ten years later, Indiana's first commercial gas well was established, the Devil be damned. The Trenton Gas Field covered 5,120 square miles. Due to ignorance about oil and gas deposits, much of the natural gas was wasted, and once the gas was gone it wasn't economically feasible to tap the oil deposits, estimated to total one billion gallons.

Manufacturers moved into the area, including the Kokomo Rubber Company; Hemmingray Bottle and Insulating Glass Company; and Maring, Hart, and Company. Iron and other metal manufacturers, attracted by the cheap fuel, established factories. The natural gas deposits were a primary reason U.S. Steel chose northern Indiana for their operations.

One group that took advantage of the vast natural gas supply in Indiana was the Ball family, consisting of five brothers (Lucius, William, Edmund, Frank, and George) residing in upstate New York.

The boys' sister, Lucina, was an educator who assisted in the founding of Drexel Institute in Philadelphia, Pa., and served as its financial secretary. Their other sister, Mary Frances, married Joseph W. Mauck, who became the longtime president of Hillsdale College in Hillsdale, Mich. Their uncle, George Harvey Ball, founded Keuka College in upstate New York in 1890.

When the Ball family patriarch died, the uncle supplied financial security

Built in 1907, originally named Nebosham, this was the home of Mr. and Mrs. Edmund Burke Ball.

for the brothers. In 1880, Frank and Edmund Ball acquired the Wood Jacket Can Company of Buffalo, which manufactured tin cans in wooden jackets to hold kerosene and paints. Due to tin corrosion, the Ball brothers switched to glass containers. They soon built their own glass factory. In 1884, when the patent for Mason glass jars expired, they began manufacturing "Buffalo" glass canning jars.

(In 1858, a tinsmith in New Jersey named John Landis Mason invented and patented a screw-threaded glass jar or bottle that became known as the Mason jar. The jars were commonly used to preserve fruit, vegetables, and other commodities.)

In 1886, they incorporated as Ball Brothers Glass Manufacturing Co. When their factory burned down, the brothers began looking for alternate sites, and found Muncie with its cheap natural gas supplies more than suitable. By 1889 the Ball brothers had moved their operations and headquarters to Muncie. Despite the economic panic of 1893, the company was able to produce 22 million fruit jars for the year beginning in September 1894, and 37 million jars by 1897. By 1905 the company was producing 60 million canning jars per year. When natural gas supplies in the area began to diminish, the Ball brothers installed gas converters to use Indiana coal in their factories and continued manufacturing operations.

Made wealthy by their glass jar business, the brothers became benefactors of several Muncie institutions, including Ball State University, Ball Memorial Hospital, the YMCA, and Minnetrista. The Ball Brothers Foundation, established in 1926, continues the family's philanthropic interests. They also repaid their uncle by supporting Keuka College in New York (Ball Hall can

Beneficence (1937) is a bronze and limestone sculpture by Daniel Chester French on the Ball State University campus honoring the Ball brothers' philanthropy.

be found there).

In 1893 Frank Ball bought approximately 30 acres of land along the north bank of the White River, outside Muncie, where the Ball brothers built their homes. His sisters named the site Minnetrista.

Frank became company president in 1888 and served in that capacity for 55 years. He was president of the Muncie and Portland Traction Company, the Muncie and Western Railroad Company, and the Muncie YMCA. He also served as director of the Federal Reserve Bank of Chicago. Frank's 19-room mansion was the first Ball family home to be built on the site along Minnetrista Boulevard. The home, designed by Indianapolis architect Louis Gibson and completed in 1895, was destroyed by fire in 1967. Minnetrista, Muncie's cultural arts center, was built on the site of his former home.

George, the youngest brother, rose through the ranks from bookkeeper to chairman of the board. He partnered in several diversified businesses and served on the boards of numerous corporations. Oakhurst, the family's shingle-style residence, was built in 1895, becoming the second of the Ball brother homes to be erected on the family property in Muncie. Gibson designed the estate home. At the time of its construction the three-story residence stood on approximately two acres. George died in 1955 at the age of 92.

Lucius, the eldest brother, received a medical degree and practiced in Muncie for many years. Instead of constructing a new residence in Muncie as his brothers did, Lucius purchased an existing home and had it turned to face Minnetrista Boulevard. In the mid-1990s, following the restoration of Oakhurst, George's home, Lucius' residence was renovated to serve as an orientation center for the Oakhurst mansion and its gardens.

William was a Ball company salesman and served as the corporation's secretary. He served on many college and bank boards. His home was a red brick Georgian design named Maplewood.

Edmund served as vice president and general manager of the company, and as treasurer and secretary of the Ball brothers' corporation. In 1904 Edmund hired Marshall S. Mahurin, a Fort Wayne, Indiana, architect to design his Gothic-Revival style home, Nebosham, which was completed in 1907 and served as their residence for 50 years. Following Edmund's death in 1925, $3.3 million in assets from his estate were used to establish the Ball Brothers Foundation.

Ball State University began in 1899 as Eastern Indiana Normal University and was renamed Ball Teachers College in 1922 in recognition of the Ball brothers' support.

In 1929, Edmund Ball's wife and children commissioned Cyrus Edwin Dallin to create a bronze casting of his original Native-American sculpture, *Appeal to the Great Spirit*. The replica was erected in Muncie in 1929 and donated to the city.

In September 1937 a bronze sculpture named *Beneficence* (nicknamed Benny) was installed on the Ball State University campus to honor the Ball brothers' contributions.

Ball remained a family-owned business for more than 90 years. Renamed the Ball Brothers Co. in 1922, the business began to diversify. Ball eventually became the world's largest manufacturer of recyclable metal beverage and food containers. In the 1950s the Ball company entered the aerospace industry. Laboratories for the Ball Brothers Research Corporation were established at Boulder, Colorado, and in Muncie. The company began manufacturing aerospace equipment in 1959. Its OSO-1 (Orbiting Solar Observatory) satellite, designed and built for the National Aeronautics and Space Administration (NASA) with $1.4 million in grants, launched into space on March 7, 1962, at Cape Canaveral, Florida. Ball left the home canning business in 1993. Today, Ball-brand Mason jars and home canning supplies belong to Newell Brands. Ball is now headquartered in Colorado.

Sources: www.bsu.edu/about/history; livability.com/in/muncie/experiences-adventures/10-things-you-didnt-know-about-muncie-in; www.ball.com/na/about-ball/overview/history-timeline; www.in.gov/history/markers/550.htm.

Sycamore Shoals
Victory at Kings Mountain and the Great Leap Westward

Sycamore Shoals on the Watauga River (present-day Elizabethton, Tennessee) was the site of four historic events of major significance in the growth of a young United States — the Transylvania Purchase, the Articles of the Watauga Association, staging ground for the Kings Mountain expedition, and launching site of the Donelson voyage to the Cumberland Settlements (Nashville).

Prior to the Revolutionary War, brave souls known as the overmountain men journeyed westward over the Appalachian Mountains to hunt deer and trap beaver, and later to establish farm settlements. The first were the long hunters, who spent months in the wilderness, battling hostile Indians when necessary and trading with friendlies. One long hunter was Daniel Boone; others were Kasper Mansker, Thomas "Big Foot" Spencer, Uriah Stone, and Isaac and Abraham Bledsoe. Market prices ranged from one dollar for deerskins to as much as five dollars for otter pelts. By 1770, there were four settlements in the valleys of what would later become East Tennessee — the Watauga River, the North Holston, the Nolichucky, and Carter's Valley. The settlers negotiated a ten-year land lease with the Cherokee. This was in defiance of the colonial authorities in Virginia and North Carolina. A dissident faction of the Cherokee known as the Chickamaugans and led by Dragging Canoe also opposed the white settlements.

Confusion reigned after it was discovered that the settlements were actually in North Carolina and not in Virginia, and the land had been claimed by the Shawnee and not the Cherokee. In 1772, John Robertson, who had fled North Carolina following the Regulator Rebellion, led an effort to establish a government among the settlements. Frontier leaders signed the Articles of the Watauga Association, the earliest attempt by American-born colonists to form an independent democratic government. Five elected magistrates formed a court and conducted the business of the small government. A militia was also formed. In two years, however, the North Carolina government voided the articles and in November 1776 annexed the Watauga settlement and formed the Washington District, later Washington County.

In London, Edmund Burke warned his government that the Americans "have already topp'd the Appalachian mountains" and called attention to the settlers who had defied the King's Proclamation and were claiming land by "the robust title of Occupancy."

Dragging Canoe.

Richard Henderson, John Robertson, John Donelson, and John Sevier would all have major roles to play in the settlement and expansion of the territory that later, in 1796, would become the state of Tennessee.

Henderson was a judge in North Carolina exiled during the War of the Regulation who heard Boone's descriptions of the overmountain country and wanted to negotiate a massive land sale with the Cherokee Nation. He did business as the Transylvania ("over the mountains") Land Company. Thousands of Cherokee gathered and camped for four days at Sycamore Shoals; Carolina Dick brought in six wagonloads of English wares for trading—guns and ammo, blankets, clothing, rum. Historian Wilma Dykeman wrote: "Moving through the assembly were Oconostota, the Great Warrior, chief of all the Cherokees, tall and powerful, along with the smaller Attakullakulla, favorite of the white people who called him the Little Carpenter because of the many treaties he had cobbled together, and the gentle Old Tassel, admired for his eloquent oratory. But perhaps most commanding of all was Attakullakulla's son, Dragging Canoe, a stern, suspicious warrior, his face deeply pocked by the scourge of smallpox that had arrived with the white man's blankets. Daniel Boone, familiar to both the settlers and the Cherokees, waited awkwardly in the background."

On March 14, 1775 (about the time of the battles of Concord and Lexington), in exchange for the goods valued at about £10,000, the Cherokee sold 20 million acres of land between the Ohio and Cumberland rivers. Dragging Canoe and other young warriors objected. He declared to the whites, "You have bought a fair land, but there is a cloud hanging over it. You will find its settlement dark and bloody."

Fort Watauga.

Within four years, the Virginia legislature nullified the transaction and awarded Henderson 200,000 acres in Middle Tennessee as compensation. For years, long hunters had told tall tales about the bounty of wild game that converged at a sulphur and salt spring on bluffs near the Cumberland River. The region was unsettled, used by several Indian tribes as communal hunting grounds. Henderson was determined to settle in that region (the territory between East Tennessee and the Nashville Basin — the Cumberland Plateau — was relatively barren and inhospitable).

In May 1776, the Cherokee gave the settlers 20 days to leave or face war. The Wataugans asked for more time and used it to build Fort Watauga. In July, Old Abram of Chilowee led 300 warriors against the fort. Nancy Ward, a Cherokee married to a white man, warned the settlers of the raid. (Dragging Canoe and 400 braves attacked the Holston and Carter's Valley settlements at the same time.) Old Abram attacked Watauga at daybreak on July 21st. Women milking cows outside the fort screamed and fled for safety. John Sevier pulled one of them, Catherine "Bonny Kate" Sherrill, over the wall and into the fort (she later became his second wife). Captain James Robertson commanded 75 men and boys in the fort and possessed only six pounds of gunpowder. In a battle that lasted three hours, the Indians were repulsed. The Indians then settled into a siege. An attempt to burn the fort failed when Anne Robertson poured boiling water down onto the torchbearers. In early August, Old Abram retreated after learning that the Holston settlers had defeated Dragging Canoe at the Battle of Long Island Flats on July 20th. The Indian war would continue until 1794.

In early 1779, Robertson and a small group from Watauga journeyed north into Kentucky via Cumberland Gap and then south to the French Lick on the Cumberland River and located the site for a new settlement. Later, they returned to build housing for a much larger group of settlers yet to come.

Robertson and his group arrived on Christmas Day and drove their cattle across the frozen river. Cabins were built, along with a fort, named for Francis Nash, who had fought with Robertson in the War of the Regulation. Thus was the crude beginnings of Nashborough, later renamed Nashville. Virginia offered a bounty of 640 acres to any male citizen who would venture to the French Lick and settle.

John Donelson was an early settler in the Virginia frontier. He served in the House of Burgesses and worked as a surveyor. He became a colonel in the militia and served in campaigns against the Cherokee. Donelson was selected by Richard Henderson to lead a large group of hearty settlers along a water route to the Cumberland settlements.

Robertson and Donelson meet at French Lick.

On Dec. 22, 1779, about the time Robertson's crew reached Nashville, Donelson embarked from Fort Patrick Henry (present-day Kingsport) on the Holston River with 30 families and a flotilla of about 40 flatboats, canoes, and dugouts. Donelson's flatboat, the *Adventure,* was big enough for several families and supplies for the journey and the new settlement. The flotilla included a large number of women and children, including Donelson's 13-year-old daughter Rachel, who would later marry Andrew Jackson. Others included Robertson's wife, Charlotte, five Robertson children, and approximately 30 black slaves.

The flotilla of roughly 300 people had to navigate the Tennessee River with its swift currents and dangerous shoals and obstructions. The weather was cold and miserable. At one point, smallpox spread among the rivermen, who also had to battle hunger and exhaustion, and hostile Indians, who shot at them from the banks. During one attack, an infant was swept away by the river. Near Chattanooga, one flatboat was captured by Indians and the entire crew killed or taken prisoner. Reaching the end of the Tennessee River, the main party then had to struggle upstream on the Ohio River and then up the

Cumberland River. Some of the party quit at the Red River confluence near modern-day Clarksville.

Finally, on April 24, 1780, after traveling a harrowing thousand miles, Donelson and his flotilla reached their destination. Within a week, Henderson prepared the Cumberland Compact. Signed on May 1st by 250 men from the eight existing stations (Nashborough, Gasper, Bledsoe, Asher, Stone, Freeland, Heaton, and Ft. Union), it served as a guide for land transactions and as a simple constitutional government for settlers.

In April 1781, hostile Indians attacked settlers working outside Fort Nashborough, which was situated on a bluff over the Cumberland River. Sensing the situation, Charlotte Robertson released the hounds ("let the dogs out") from the fort. The hounds had been trained to attack Indians and "made a furious onset upon them," allowing the settlers to run back to the fort. The Indians lingered for a couple of days but then retreated, perhaps intimidated by the fort's four-pound swivel gun. Thus ended the Battle of the Bluffs. Charlotte Robertson nursed back to health one of her sons who had been scalped and left for dead. She would lose two other sons to Indian attacks. Mrs. Robertson was a frontier woman, as courageous and hearty as her husband. She would live to be 92 years old.

In 1783, North Carolina included Nashville in forming Davidson County. By 1784, one-third of the original settlers had been killed in battles with the Chickamaugans and Creeks, and only two stations remained. In 1784, Nashville was officially chartered. In 1806, Nashville was officially incorporated as a city and seat of Davidson County.

In November 1783, the Chickasaw signed the Treaty of French Lick ending their attacks against the Cumberland Settlements. Cherokee and Creek attacks, however, continued into the 1790s. One of James Robertson's children, Peyton, was killed. His head was placed on a spike in view of his home. "To see an innocent child so uncommonly massacred by people who ought to have both sense and bravery, has in a measure unmanned me," stated Robertson.

While the Robertson-Donelson expeditions were establishing Nashville, the Revolutionary War turned to its Southern campaigns in the Carolinas. Major Patrick Ferguson, a Scotsman, commanded the left wing of Lord Cornwallis' campaign northward. Ferguson commanded a force of Loyalists, trained American troops fighting for the King. Haughty, Ferguson taunted the overmountainmen, whom he disdained as savages. He claimed he would march over the mountains and "hang...western leaders and lay the country waste with fire and sword" if the frontiersmen did not swear allegiance to King George III. The overmountainmen took Ferguson seriously and decided to assemble, march to Ferguson's encampment atop Kings Mountain and attack him first. One of those men was John Sevier of Virginia. Sevier settled on the Holston in 1773 and served in the Provincial Congress of North Carolina. During the war, he was appointed lieutenant colonel of the frontier militia. Groups of armed frontiersmen gathered at Sycamore Shoals and began their march on Sept. 23, 1780. There was no overall leader of the expedition; leaders of the separate militia were Sevier, William Campbell, William Shelby, and Charles McDowell. Four days later, snow fell as the men crossed Roan Mountain, highest point on the trail. Two men deserted to warn Ferguson of the advance. On the afternoon of October 7th, the Patriots found Ferguson and his Tories atop Kings Mountain (named after a settler named King, it was a prominent hill not a mountain). The frontiersmen, armed with accurate long rifles, surrounded the hilltop, hid behind trees, and began picking off Ferguson's men. Ferguson was shot off his horse while sounding his silver whistle (he is buried atop the hill). In an hour, it was all over. The Tories suffered 120 killed with all the others captured. Ninety Patriots were shot, including 28 killed. During their return, on October 14th, the Patriots tried 30 Tories and hanged nine of them.

Many of the Patriot militia who fought at Kings Mountain returned to Cowpens on Jan. 17, 1781, to help Daniel Morgan defeat another brash young British commander, Banastre Tarleton.

Kings Mountain and Cowpens are both National Military Parks, with the expedition commemorated by the Overmountain Victory National Historic Trail.

British Commander-in-Chief Sir Henry Clinton lamented that the Battle of Kings Mountain was "the first link in a chain of evils that followed each other in regular succession until they at last ended in the total loss of America."

Along with the Battle of New Orleans, Kings Mountain is one of those hughly historic battles in America's past that are largely forgotten, along with its heroes.

John Sevier died in 1815 at age 70. His burial monument at the old courthouse in Knoxville reads: "John Sevier, pioneer, soldier, statesman, and one of the founders of the Republic; Governor of the State of Franklin; six times Governor of Tennessee; four times elected to Congress; a typical pioneer, who conquered the wilderness and fashioned the State; a protector and hero of Kings Mountain; fought thirty-five battles, won thirty-five victories; his Indian war cry, 'Here they are! Come on boys!'"

Sources: Encyclopedia of Tennessee History and Culture

the Gridiron ★ General

The greatest college football coach of all time? Many sports fans, including the experts at ESPN, would say Paul "Bear" Bryant (1913-83) of the University of Alabama. But what about the guy who taught Bear Bryant how to handle his players; who was never beaten by Bear Bryant; who had a better winning average; who was a world-class athlete at West Point; who designed his school's football stadium; and who contributed mightily to U.S. victory in World War Two?

That would be Brigadier General Robert R. Neyland III, who earned a 173-31-12 record (.829 winning pct.) over 21 years as head coach at the University of Tennessee-Knoxville. The "Gridiron General" coached from 1926 to 1952 (with stints in the U.S. Army in 1935 and 1941-45) and then served as athletic director until his death in 1962. That year, the stadium in Knoxville was named for him. Over the next decades, Neyland Stadium expanded to more than 100,000 seats, built according to engineering plans he had drawn. In 2010, a larger-than-life bronze statue of the legendary coach was installed on the west side of Neyland Stadium.

A native of Texas, Neyland (pronounced knee-lund) was a U.S. Army Corps of Engineers officer trained at West Point and the Massachusetts Institute of Technology (MIT).

On the football field, he was a genius of the defensive game. "The outstanding defensive thinker in the game," said Knute Rockne. "General Neyland's defensive theories were magnificent. All of us used them," said Bobby Dodd.

Today, the Tennessee Volunteers still learn his Eight Maxims of the game. Among others, Neyland stressed that "the team that makes the fewest mistakes will win" and "almost all close games are lost by the losers, not won by the winners." He was a strict disciplinarian, emphasized physical fitness and conditioning, and stressed the kicking game and field position.

At Knoxville, he won four national championships (Associated Press in 1951), seven Southeastern Conference (SEC) championships, and two Southern Conference championships.

He was initially hired expressly to beat Vanderbilt, which held a 17-2-2 advantage through 1926. In the next 100 years, the Vols have defeated Vandy all but about a dozen times.

Of the 216 football games Neyland coached, the Vols shut out their opponents (kept them from scoring) 109 times. From 1938 to 1940, his teams recorded an amazing 17 consecutive regular-season shutouts. In the 1939 regular season, Tennessee outscored its opposition 212-0. The Vols are the last major college football program to shut out every regular-season opponent. Neyland coached the Vols to six undefeated seasons and nine undefeated regular seasons.

Neyland was a superb student-athlete as a cadet at West Point. He won

35 games (20 consecutive) pitching for Army's baseball team, was a starting end on the Cadets' 1914 national championship football team, and was the academy's heavyweight boxing champion his final three years. He was recruited to play professional baseball by the New York Giants, Detroit Tigers, and Philadelphia Athletics, but instead went to France and served in World War I.

After the war, he served as aide-de-camp to West Point Commandant Douglas MacArthur and often quoted him, in particular — "Upon the field of friendly strife are sown the seeds that, upon other fields, on other days, will bear the fruits of victory."

In 1935, Neyland was sent overseas by the Army to supervise engineers in the Panama Canal Zone. He retired from the Army and coached from 1936-1940 but was called back to active duty during World War II. Lt. Col. Neyland was put in charge of engineering projects in the Norfolk-Chesapeake Bay area — 80 projects worth $250 million, including the Richmond Air Base, coastal defense installations to protect the Norfolk Naval Base, the Radford Ordnance Works, and Air Corps facilities at Langley Field, Virginia. Neyland's efforts were of "inestimable value in preparing the nation for war," proclaimed his superior, Lt. General Raymond Wheeler.

Next call of duty was Dallas, where he was put in charge of more than $1 billion worth of U.S. Army Corps of Engineers projects in five states. Then, in 1944, it was off to Kunming, China, to supervise the huge American supply base there. He was put in charge of obtaining military supplies from India (which had to be flown over the Himalaya Mountains) and distributing them to U.S. army and air corps units and allied Chinese units. In November 1944 a new commander replaced Neyland, now a brigadier general, with his own man, and Neyland was assigned to Calcutta, India, the port where supplies for the India-Burma theater were received and then transported to the front lines. During Neyland's tenure, the average monthly tonnage of supplies unloaded from ships increased from 75,143 long tons to 134,960 long tons. He trained his men to unload an entire ship in 44 hours. During his military career he was awarded the Distinguished Service Medal and the Legion of Merit and made a member of the Order of the British Empire. In January 1946, Neyland returned to Knoxville and his coaching job.

Before the war, Austin Shofner of Shelbyville, Tennessee, was a senior at UT-K who played guard for the Vols under Coach Neyland. As such, he learned Neyland's game maxims and his discipline. Immediately after graduating, Shofner enlisted in the U.S. Marine Corps and became a gung-ho Marine stationed in The Philippines. In 1942, he was captured by the Japanese and survived the Bataan Death March. In 1943, he and nine others escaped through the jungle from the notorious Davao prison camp. At one point, several escapees were ready to give up and surrender back to the Japanese, but Shofner persuaded them to continue. Shofner then led a Filipino guerrilla team for a year before being picked up by a U.S. submarine and taken to Australia, where he met with MacArthur, received the Distinguished Service Cross, and disclosed the details of the death march, which to that point had been a secret. These revelations led to changes in Allied strategy and tactics in the Pacific that were credited with saving the lives of thousands of servicemen. Back in the States, Shofner told his old coach Neyland that his football training (e.g., "play for the breaks") helped him survive prison camp and make his escape. Shofner retired from the USMC as a brigadier general.

At Neyland Stadium, along the southeast stands are displayed the names of four Tennessee Volunteers — Bill Nowling, Rudy Klarer, Willis Tucker, and Clyde "Ig" Fuson — who fought in WWII and did not come home alive.

Sources: Bob Gilbert, Neyland: The Gridiron General; John Painter and Matt Magill, UTSports.com.

the Great Humanitarian Blamed for the Great Depression

All Presidents carry a legacy with them, and perhaps none is so unfair and malicious as that of Herbert Hoover, America's 31st President. Unjustly blamed for the Great Depression and criticized for not being an activist President, Hoover nevertheless was a remarkably accomplished self-made man and one of history's most effective humanitarians, responsible for saving millions of lives.

Born in 1874 in West Branch, Iowa, the son of a Quaker blacksmith, Hoover was sharp enough to attend the fledgling Stanford University and turned his attention to geology and mining. Working for private companies in Australia and China as a mining engineer, Hoover was quite successful and became a wealthy man. He married Lou Henry, a college graduate who also studied geology.

When war broke out in Europe in 1914, Hoover was instrumental in a program which returned 100,000 Americans stranded in Europe. Hoover spearheaded the Commission for Relief in Belgium, where citizens were starving to death under German rule. He administered the distribution of more than two million tons of food to nine million victims of war. When the U.S. entered the war, President Woodrow Wilson appointed Hoover to lead the Food Administration, and Hoover became known as the country's "food czar." Hoover was determined to avoid rationing, instead establishing set days for people to avoid eating specified foods and saving them for soldiers' rations — meatless Mondays, wheatless Wednesdays, and "when in doubt, eat potatoes." The U.S. Food Administration was thus able to ship 23 million metric tons of food to the Allies overseas. After the war, Hoover led the American Relief Administration, which provided food to the inhabitants of Central Europe and Eastern Europe.

Hoover served as a capable Secretary of Commerce under Presidents Harding and Coolidge, and enhanced his reputation with the handling of refugees following the Great Mississippi Flood of 1927. Hoover established more than one hundred tent cities and a fleet of more than six hundred

vessels, and raised $17 million in aid. Until this catastrophe, the U.S. government tended to allow local governments to handle emergencies. In this case, the federal government was eventually forced to intervene, paving the way for the New Deal social programs under Franklin D. Roosevelt, according to some historians. Hoover was also influential in the growth of civilian aviation and the new technology of radio.

Always an ambitious man, Hoover ran as a Republican for President in 1928, beating Al Smith in a landslide, 444-87. Hoover tended to oppose governmental coercion or intervention, as he thought they infringed on the American ideals of individualism and self-reliance. Hoover made extensive use of commissions to study issues and propose solutions, and many of those commissions were sponsored by private donors rather than by the government. His wife, Lou, was an activist First Lady. The stock market crash came in September 1929, and throughout his first and only term Hoover was saddled with the reputation of not doing enough to end the economic downturn. In the 1932 election, Hoover lost to Roosevelt, 59-472, carrying only six states.

Hoover was an active critic of Roosevelt's New Deal policies and became a prominent statesman and spokesman for conservative ideals. He was appointed twice, by Presidents Truman and Eisenhower, to lead projects designed to make the federal bureaucracy more efficient and responsive.

Asked how he managed to remain active and vital despite all the criticisms against him over the years, Hoover replied, "I outlived the bastards." Hoover died in 1964 at the age of 90. His reputation has improved somewhat over the years, but Hoover is still ranked among the lower third of U.S. Presidents. Perhaps he was a far greater American and humanitarian than President.

Others: President Gerald R. Ford (1974-77) suffered from a reputation of being a klutz and uncoordinated. He stumbled down a stairway once and he had the bad habit of hitting spectators with golf balls during celebrity tournaments. All widely publicized. But as a young man, Ford was an accomplished athlete, playing football for Michigan, where he was voted MVP one year and had his jersey number retired. He was one of our most athletic presidents. Conversely, President John F. Kennedy was touted as being a virile young man full of vigor. In fact, he suffered from Addison's disease and a bad back, and took a wide variety of painkillers and medications.

Sources: Frank Freidel and Hugh Sidey, White House Historical Association; William E. Leuchenburg, Herbert Hoover, Times Books; Baltimore Sun.

Olustee

The Sunshine State's Civil War Battlefield

When you think of Civil War battlefields, Florida doesn't readily come to mind, but the state does have one battleground worth visiting—Olustee or the Battle of Ocean Pond, located between Lake City and Jacksonville. The four-hour battle, a Confederate victory, took place on Feb. 20, 1864 in an open pine barren. The battleground, created in 1919 as Florida's first state park, features a small visitor's center, monuments, cannon, a small cemetery and Union marker, trails, and interpretive signage.

During the war, Florida was a Confederate state. On Feb. 7, 1864, a Federal expedition dispatched by General Quincy Gilmore of the Department of the South and commanded by General Truman A. Seymour arrived at Jacksonville from Hilton Head, South Carolina, and easily occupied the city. Their objectives were to disrupt transportation links and deprive the Confederacy of food supplies from central Florida; capture cotton, turpentine, and timber; gain African-American recruits for the Union army; and induce Unionists in east Florida to organize a loyal state government. The Confederates were well aware of the Federal movements and feared a Federal invasion of Georgia from the south (this was months before Sherman's March to the Sea). The defense of Florida was in the hands of Confederate Brigadier General Joseph Finegan, who established a defensive position at Olustee, a small station on the Florida Atlantic & Gulf Central Railroad. He positioned his men behind earthworks between Ocean Pond, a large lake to the north, and an

impassable swamp to the south. The troops were reinforced by Brig. Gen. Alfred Colquitt's men coming from Savannah, Ga.

By this time, each side boasted about 5,500 troops. The Confederates consisted of eight Georgia regiments (1st, 6th, 19th, 23rd, 27th, 28th, 32nd, and 64th) and the 1st Florida cavalry. The Federals consisted of three New York regiments (47th, 48th, and 115th), the 1st North Carolina, 7th Connecticut, the 8th U.S. Infantry, and the famed 54th Massachusetts U.S. Colored Troops, who had fought at Fort Wagner the previous summer.

On February 20th, the Union force of 5,500 men and 16 cannon marched westward from Macclenny. Finegan sent skirmishers to draw the Union forces to Olustee, and they made contact that afternoon east of the Confederate earthworks. The battle was fought on the floor of a forest of virgin pine, free of underbrush. The Confederates were close to breaking the Union lines when they ran low on ammunition. When more ammunition arrived, the attack continued. The battle wore on for four hours, and as Finegan committed the last of his reserves, Seymour ordered a withdrawal. The battle resulted in 2,807 casualties. The Yankees marched back to Jacksonville, where they stayed until the war ended 14 months later.

After years of fundraising by the United Daughters of the Confederacy, in 1909 the Florida legislature acquired three acres to build a memorial to commemorate the event. On Oct. 23, 1912, veterans of Olustee gathered with dignitaries to dedicate the memorial and the first Florida state park. Portions of the famous 1989 movie *Glory* were filmed at Olustee park.

Florida boasts another, smaller Civil War battlefield — Natural Bridge Battlefield Historic State Park. According to the website: "During the final weeks of the Civil War, a Union flotilla landed at Apalachee Bay. The federal plan was to capture Fort Ward, located at the confluence of the St. Mark and Wakulla Rivers, and march north to the state capital. On March 3, 1865, the large union ships ran aground at Port Leon and could not make it to the fort. About 900 Union troops, including the 2nd and 99th Regiments U.S. Colored Infantry, continued to advance on Tallahassee over land. The smaller Confederate force was composed of about 600 soldiers, including old men and cadets as young as 14 from the West Florida Seminary. With a timely warning, these volunteer soldiers met the Union forces at Natural Bridge on March 6th and, after 10 hours, successfully repelled three major attacks."

There also was military activity at the beginning of the war at Federal Fort Pickens near Pensacola.

Thirty miles southeast of Olustee is Camp Blanding, a 73,000-acre training center on Kingsley Lake which serves the Florida National Guard, the Florida Army National Guard and certain ground activities of the Florida Air National Guard. During World War II, Camp Blanding (named for WWI Major General Albert Blanding) served as an infantry-replacement training center, an induction center, a German prisoner-of-war compound, and a holding center for 343 Japanese, German, and Italian immigrant residents. More than 800,000 soldiers in nine infantry divisions trained there. The camp museum and memorial park is open to the public and includes collections of artifacts related to the camp's history and outdoor displays of aircraft and armored vehicles from WWII to Operation Desert Storm.

Sources: Olustee Battlefield Historic State Park; American Battlefield Trust; Camp Blanding Museum & Memorial Park website.

THE DEEP ZONE
AND OTHER REGIONS OF THE UNDERWORLD

Near Dixon Springs, Tennessee, not too far from the abandoned cooling towers of the defunct TVA Hartsville nuclear site, sat an A-frame house that was using an abnormal amount of electricity for its occupancy. Law enforcement became suspicious, and surveillance revealed several emission "hot spots" from the 10-acre lot at night.

Long story short, in 2005, lawmen eventually discovered that the modest house sat atop one of the largest subterranean marijuana grow operations ever constructed. The owner-operator, who resided in Florida, had used his engineering expertise to construct the illegal 20,000-sq.-ft. facility within an existing cave system. The wooden floor had been cut to the contours of the cave walls, an unnecessary embellishment. The cave ceiling was covered with dozens of "grow" lights. A sophisticated system of ducting and tubing ventilated the interior and watered the plants. Workers were transported to the site blindfolded and worked weeks underground, growing and harvesting the vast crop while living and eating in cramped quarters and sleeping in bunk beds. The facility was capable of harvesting $6.8 million worth of high-quality weed per year.

The site's concrete driveway led to a large automated swinging door that led down into the cave. A vertical escape tunnel was installed at the far end of the cave, leading up to an escape hatch in the yard concealed by a rock.

The owner and two others were convicted of drug crimes, and the owner sent to federal prison. Later, the house mysteriously burned down, and the property was auctioned off by the state to a Wisconsin cheese maker.

America's heartland is covered with underground cave systems and sinkholes. Most of the bluegrass region in Kentucky and Tennessee lies on karst, which is limestone (calcium carbonate) eroded over millions of years by dissolution, producing ridges, towers, fissures, sinkholes and other characteristic landforms.

Caverns have been used ever since pre-historic time to display artwork, bury the dead, hide horses and valuables during wartime, tap the pure limestone-filtered water to make moonshine, gather bat guana to make saltpeter and gunpowder, and marvel at the fantastic rock formations.

Limestone caves are often adorned with calcium carbonate formations produced through slow precipitation. These include flowstones, stalactites (hangings from ceilings), stalagmites (formations on the floor), helictites (twiglike protrusions), soda straws, and columns. These mineral deposits in caves are called speleothems.

The Mammoth National Park cave system in central Kentucky is the longest in the world, with 367 miles of shafts and tunnels dropping to 377 feet deep. The underground site draws millions of visitors each year. More than 7,000 deep caves, those that extend beyond external light, have been recorded throughout Tennessee.

Spelunkers discovered and explored the Rumble Room, a gigantic underground chamber in Middle Tennessee, four acres in area and 350 feet tall. They kept its existence a secret until engineers publicly announced that a sewage project was to be built directly above the chamber, which would have damaged it.

Ruby Falls in Lookout Mountain near Chattanooga is the tallest cave waterfall at 145 feet. The Lost Sea near Sweetwater, Tenn., is the nation's largest underground lake. Blue Spring Cave in White County is Tennessee's longest cave at 38.4 miles and the ninth longest cave in the country. Footprints or impressions of an ancient jaguar weighing 500 pounds were found in the dark zone of the cave in 1990. The big cat lived during the Ice Age and apparently entered the cave through a now-collapsed entrance.

Cumberland Caverns near McMinnville, Tenn. is a commercial site famous for staging music concerts in the giant volcano room 333 feet below the surface, complete with giant chandelier hanging from the ceiling. The John Bell family in Adams, Tenn. was said to be haunted by the Bell Witch, who lived in a nearby cave.

Thirty-two of the 40 longest caves in the U.S. are located in the karst regions of the heartland. Limestone is the official state rock of Tennessee. Nashville, now called Music City USA, used to be called Rock City. The region has few natural lakes but many streams and springs. The limestone-filtered

THE ZONE: TRUE TALES FROM THE HEARTLAND

Blue Spring Cave. Dave Bunnell.

water is perfect for making the best whiskey in the world, as evidenced by the dozens of bourbon distilleries in Kentucky and the distilleries that produce "Tennessee whiskey." Bourbon is whiskey made mostly from corn. Tennessee whiskey takes the process a step further by charcoal filtering the distillate before being barreled. Those huge "barns" dotting the central bluegrass belt hold millions of barrels of whiskey, slowly aging and maturing. Kentucky holds an estimated 9.3 million barrels of bourbon. Jack Daniel's whiskey starts with iron-free spring water pulled from a cave near Lynchburg, Tennessee. The distillery produces 31 million gallons of whiskey per year. Back in the day, many caves were used by moonshiners to conceal their stills from federal revenue agents.

Sinkholes are kind of spooky and mysterious. Scientific surveys have located more than 54,000 sinkholes in Tennessee alone, 43 dropping 100 feet or more into the underworld. Big Sink in White County, which boasts 2,970 sinkholes and 1,169 caves, reaches down 261 feet. The Middle Tennessee counties of Robertson and Montgomery are pockmarked with more than 3,600 sinkholes.

Not far away, near Bowling Green, Ky., in 2014 in the dead of night, a 30-foot-deep sinkhole suddenly opened up directly beneath the National Corvette Museum and swallowed eight vintage Chevrolet Corvettes on display. The valuable cars were rescued and put back on display; two have been restored to their original luster. The sinkhole was studied and then filled with 4,000 tons of crushed limestone.

Near Gladeville, Tenn., a calf fell down a sinkhole and spent several days underground, just barely visible, her mother dutifully keeping watch at the rim. The poor calf was finally discovered by a farmer, pulled to safety with a tractor, and reunited with momma.

Near Gallatin, Tenn., around a hundred years ago, legend has it that a man completely disappeared near his farmhouse, in front of onlookers, without a trace. In Florida, a man sleeping in his bedroom was suddenly swallowed by a sinkhole and never seen again.

In 1989, Stefania Follini, 27, an Italian interior designer, spent 130 days of isolation in an underground room in a Carlsbad, New Mexico cave, during a scientific experiment on circadian rhythms cohosted by NASA. Her only communication with the outside world was a computer terminal. Her sense of a normal day lengthened to 48 hours, she generally felt gloomy, and lost 17 pounds. When she emerged, she guessed she had spent two months underground instead of four. She set the women's world record for longest cave isolation (now that's some sort of record).

For the most part, the ground that we stand on usually seems solid, but there are invisible forces at work down there in the underworld. Scientists warn that the time is approaching for another eruption of the New Madrid Seismic Zone (NMSZ), which extends from Cairo, Illinois, south through Missouri to Marked Tree, Arkansas. A side branch also extends into the Reelfoot Lake region of northwest Tennessee.

In fact, it is believed that Reelfoot Lake was created in the early 1800s by a series of catastrophic earthquakes which shook the earth, rearranged the landscape, and temporarily forced the Mississippi River to flow backwards. The quakes would have measured among the highest ever recorded on the modern Richter scale. Fortunately, there were few people living in the area at the time (1811-12).

"During the strongest of the quakes, great cracks and fissures opened and spewed out sand and water," according to historian Allen G. Coggins. "Gaping crevices formed, some twelve feet wide and deep and more than twenty feet in length. Low waterfalls developed at points along the Mississippi in the vicinity of New Madrid. They were short-lived, however, in the soft sediments of the river valley. Shifting currents and changing flows along the Mississippi, Ohio, Arkansas, and other rivers created and destroyed islands, sandbars, and other familiar features. The quakes caused waves to rush over river banks. Return currents washed countless limbs and even whole trees into the main channels. Massive log jams formed, making navigation even more perilous."

An earthquake as powerful as the quakes of 1811-12 may not occur for many years, according to the Memphis Archaeological and Geological Society, but scientists estimate that there is a 90 percent chance of a magnitude 6 to 7 temblor occurring in the NMSZ within the next 50 years. A repeat today of the earthquakes of 1811-12 would cause widespread loss of life and billions of dollars in damage.

Just off the 13th hole of a golf course in Middle Tennessee in someone's backyard archaeologists found the skeletons of four mastodons which roamed the earth 15,000 years ago. More importantly, remnants of stone tools and bones marred by tool marks indicate that human hunters had killed the mastodons and butchered them at the site. Many other bone fragments from horse, deer, muskrat, turtle, rodent, and large Pleistocene vertebrate were found, only about six feet below the surface.

In 1971, excavators at the site of a bank building project in downtown Nashville cut into a small cave about 30 feet below ground level. Remnants of human skeletons and animal bones were exhumed and examined by Vanderbilt University anthropologists, the Southeastern Indian Antiquities Survey, and the Carnegie Museum of Natural History. It was determined that the human remains were placed in the cave post-mortem as bones. However, the scientists also found some other interesting remains, including a large canine tooth belonging to a saber-toothed tiger (Smilodon), one of the largest specimens ever found. Carbon dating places the tiger in the area later than otherwise thought, although this dating has been disputed. The cave has been vaulted over using steel and concrete, and preserved in an artificial cavern beneath the lowest parking garage level. An access hatch (locked and secured) and ladder provides entry to the space. The skeletal animal remains, plus a skull of a Smilodon from the La Brea Tar Pits, were displayed at the bank and then at Bridgestone Arena. In 1997, the newly formed Nashville NHL hockey team chose the name Predators based on the local Smilodon, and their mascot is a saber-toothed tiger named Gnash.

Time capsules have been popular for many years. Along the eastern border of the Bicentennial Capitol Mall State Park in Nashville are time capsules from each county, which will not be opened until the state's 300th birthday on July 1, 2096.

Oglethorpe University in Brookhaven, Georgia, is home to the Crypt of Civilization, the first and most complete time capsule ever created, according to Guinness World Records. Sealed in 1940 and scheduled to be opened in AD 8113, it is located in the basement of Phoebe Hearst Hall. The crypt is a former swimming pool, measuring 20 x 10 feet. The chamber is under a stone roof seven feet thick and lies over a two-foot stone floor. The crypt is sealed with a stainless steel door welded in place. Unusual artifacts included in the crypt are seed samples, dental floss, the contents of a woman's purse, some

Artie Shaw records, an electric toaster, a pacifier, a specially sealed bottle of Budweiser beer, a typewriter, a radio, a cash register, an adding machine, a set of Lincoln Logs, and plastic toys of Donald Duck, the Lone Ranger, and a Black doll.

The Crypt of Civilization was the brainchild of Thornwell Jacobs, president of Oglethorpe University, due to his concern regarding the lack of information about ancient civilizations. He wanted people of the future to know about our civilization. He calculated the date of the start of the Egyptian calendar as 6,177 years before 1936. He added those years to 1936 to determine the opening date of AD 8113.

Set to be opened in 2025 is the world's largest time capsule in Seward, Nebraska. The vault, sealed in 1975, was the idea of local businessman Harold K. Davisson. Their claim of "world's largest" was disputed by Oglethorpe University, so Davisson built a pyramid on top of the vault to enlarge it. Among phone books and letters and 5,000 various items in the vault are a new 1975 Chevrolet Vega, a new Kawasaki motorcycle, and a leisure suit. Inside the pyramid is a beat-up 1975 Toyota automobile.

Relic hunters in the South use metal detectors to find and unearth artifacts from the Civil War such as belt buckles, bullets, buttons, and even weapons, along with a lot of beer cans, metal strapping, and other debris. Every now and then an unexploded artillery shell may be found. Unscrupulous relic hunters have been known to disturb fragile wartime earthworks and other dirt structures — that's why metal detecting is banned from national and state military parks and battlefields.

Law enforcement uses ground-penetrating radar detectors to search for the gravesites of murder victims. They haven't found Jimmy Hoffa yet. The device can be used to detect buried treasure and even buried vehicles. It is also used by historians to locate unmarked burial grounds or cemeteries.

In May 2009, the remains of a Civil War soldier were found in a shallow grave near the site of the Battle of Franklin, uncovered during a construction project. Historians could not conclusively determine whether the soldier was Federal or Confederate. Why the soldier was buried in a coffin south of Winstead Hill, away from others, has been an issue of contention. In October 2009, the unknown soldier's remains were laid to rest at Rest Haven Cemetery in Franklin following viewings and services at the antebellum St. Paul's Episcopal Church. A lengthy procession of blue and gray re-enactors and grieving women dressed in black accompanied the horse-drawn funeral carriage through the public square and into the cemetery, witnessed by hundreds of spectators and the media. After the custom-made coffin bearing the unknown soldier was lowered into the ground at the gravesite marked with stone columns from the original state capitol, representatives walked to the open grave and sprinkled soil from the 18 states which had fought at the Battle of Franklin.

In Indiana, back in the day, miners searching for coal dug a deep hole and hit a natural gas deposit. Strange noises and a foul odor sprang from the hole. Frightened, the miners thought they had broken through the ceiling of Hell. They quickly covered the hole and said a prayer.

Dead Man's Hole, Burnet Co., Texas / Nicolas Henderson-Flickr photos

Dead Man's Hole was discovered in 1821 in southern Burnet County, Texas, created by a build-up of natural gas pressure. The hole in the rock is seven feet in diameter and drops at least 150 feet. It is rumored that the bodies of at least 17 murdered men, most from the Civil War era, have been dropped down Dead Man's Hole. Maybe all the way down to Hades.

Graves aren't just for people. Near Beech Grove, Tennessee, is the decorated burial site of Old Isham, the war horse of Confederate General Benjamin F. Cheatham. Belle Meade Plantation in Nashville is the burial site of celebrated racehorse Inquirer. Behind the old hotel in Wartrace is the grave of Strolling Jim, the first champion Tennessee Walking Horse.

Artwork by ancient peoples dating back 4,000 years ago can be found in the dark zones of caves in the U.S. heartland, specifically Alabama, Kentucky, Tennessee, and Virginia. Images of religious significance are incised into rock (petroglyphs), painted (pictographs), and engraved into wet clay (mud glyphs). Pictographs are the rarest, with only a few examples known. Nearly 20 other deep art caves have been found since 1979, according to archaeologist Jan Simek of the University of Tennessee. Two caves are in Virginia, two in Kentucky, one in Alabama, and the remainder in Middle and East Tennessee.

For more recent tribes in Tennessee, caves were passageways to the underworld. "Cave art depicting serpents and winged humans may reflect a belief in the power of these dark, deep places and their role in the structure of the cosmos," wrote Simek.

About 200 million years ago a meteorite struck the earth at up to 90,000 mph and penetrated to about 2,000 feet, producing a gigantic explosion that created waves of earthquakes radiating in every direction. A crater four miles in diameter and half a mile deep was created at the impact site, now called the Wells Creek Basin in Stewart and Houston counties of Middle

Tennessee. Over many millennia the features of the crater have been eroded. The soil in the basin was found by early settlers to be better quality than the surroundings.

The center of the Wells Creek crater contains some of the finest shatter cones in the world, according to Mike Baldwin of the Memphis Archaeological and Geological Society. A shatter cone is a conical fragment of rock that is formed from the high pressure of a meteorite impact and has striations radiating from the apex of the cone. The Wells Creek shatter cones were actually formed by the shock waves that arrived before the limestone beds were tilted by the meteorite. The cones formed pointing toward the place from which the shock waves came. The Wells Creek shatter cones were formed by shock waves coming from a position which was (at the time of impact) more than 2,000 feet underground.

Sources: Memphis Archaeological and Geological Society; Encyclopedia of Tennessee History and Culture; Edward T. Luther, Our Restless Earth: Geologic Regions of Tennessee.

THE SPACE PROGRAM • THE BEATLES • GREEN BAY PACKERS • THE VIETNAM WAR

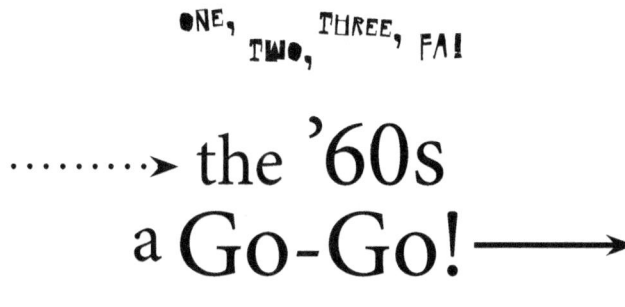

the '60s a Go-Go!
A Concise History

The Age of Eisenhower, already tainted by the "beep, beep, beep" of Sputnik, is ushered out by the youthful vigor of Camelot as Democrat John F. Kennedy defeats Republican incumbent Vice-President Richard Nixon with his energetic and photogenic television presense and a little last-minute shuffling of votes in Cook County, Illinois. First Lady Jackie commands the fashion news while the new administration calls in the best and brightest minds of the era to guide The New Frontier. The United States of America, the dominant superpower in the world, finds itself flush with affluence, with more middle-class workers buying their own homes in suburbia and sending their kids to college. Through the Peace Corps, the United Nations, and other high-minded programs, the children of the Greatest Generation, which weathered the Great Depression and sacrificed to fight and beat down fascism and the Holocaust, are determined to save the world from lingering evils. The U.S. soon finds itself dedicated to containing Communism in Southeast Asia, winning the race to land a man on the moon, and blocking the threat of nuclear annihilation from a small island 90 miles away from Key West. The Soviet Union places missiles in Cuba, and a man and then a woman in space. The U.S. is embarassed by supporting an ill-fated invasion of Cuba at the Bay of Pigs but faces down Premier Khrushchev, who removes the missiles from Fidel Castro's communist island. Meanwhile, the President's attorney general, his younger brother, launches investigations into the Teamsters and organized crime. The administration allows public employees to unionize.

1960 In January 1960, Stuart Sutcliffe, John Lennon's friend from the Liverpool College of Art, joins the Quarrymen, consisting of Lennon, Paul McCartney, and George Harrison. They change their name to the Silver Beatles. Sutcliffe will quit the band a year later, and a year after that die of a brain hemorrhage.

Black students at Fisk University stage the first sit-ins at three lunch counters in downtown Nashville, Tennessee. They are met with adversity.

In August, Pete Best joins the Beatles as drummer. The group travels to Hamburg, West Germany for the first of five trips there where they form their identity and fine-tune their sound.

On Dec. 26, 1960, the championship of the National Football League is won by the Philadelphia Eagles over the Green Bay Packers, a hardluck bunch of losers who reside in the smallest, by far, professional sports market in the nation. Their new coach, Vince Lombardi, vows to never repeat such a loss. His voice carries. "I want it understood that I'm in complete command," he says ominously upon accepting the job. One black player says that Lombardi is not prejudiced. "He treats us all like dogs."

1961

On May 5, 1961, Alan Shepard becomes the first American in space. The Mercury astronaut and Freedom 7 capsule ride atop a Redstone rocket for a 15-minute suborbital flight, three weeks after the Soviets launch the first man in space.

Three weeks later, in a speech before Congress, President Kennedy announces that an American will land on the moon and be returned safely to Earth before the end of the decade. "We choose to go to the moon," JFK declares, adding, "We shall pay any price, bear any burden, meet any hardship, support any friend, oppose any foe to assure the survival and the success of liberty."

The Beatles hire Brian Epstein as their manager.

In May, President Kennedy sends 400 American Green Berets to South Vietnam to train South Vietnamese soldiers, and then sends additional military advisors and helicopter units to transport and direct South Vietnamese troops in battle, thus involving Americans in combat operations.

On July 21st, astronaut Gus Grissom rides Liberty Bell 7 into suborbital space. The capsule sinks following splashdown and is lost.

On Oct. 27th, Saturn I, the rocket launch vehicle for the initial Apollo missions, is tested for the first time.

On the last day of 1961, the Packers rout the New York Giants, 37-0, in Green Bay for the NFL championship. Versatile player Paul "Golden Boy" Hornung, scores a record 176 points in one season (a record which stands for nearly half-a-century).

1962 On Jan. 15, 1962, President Kennedy tells the press there are no Americans in Vietnam engaged in the fighting. Two weeks later, the U.S. Military Assistance Command for Vietnam (MACV), is formed.

On Feb. 20th, former Marine John Glenn becomes the first American to orbit the Earth, landing safely despite a malfunction with the capsule's heat shield.

On March 19th, protest and folk singer Bob Dylan (Robert Zimmerman) releases his first album. He performs and records for the next 60 years.

In May, the Beatles sign their first recording contract and hire George Martin as their producer.

On May 24th, astronaut Scott Carpenter orbits the Earth in Aurora 7.

In August, Ringo Starr replaces Pete Best as the Beatles' drummer. The next month, they record their first single, "Love Me Do."

On Oct. 3rd, astronaut Wally Schirra orbits the Earth six times in Sigma 7.

In October, the first *Tonight Show with Johnny Carson* airs; the first James Bond movie is released, and the Cuban Missile Crisis is resolved.

On Dec. 21st, Vince Lombardi appears on the cover of *Time* magazine as part of the cover story on the NFL being "The Sport of the '60s." There is talk of football replacing baseball as the national pastime. Days later, on a New York City football field frozen to the hardness of concrete, Packer running back Jimmy Taylor dishes out punishment to would-be tacklers as Green Bay again defeats the Giants (Lombardi's old team), 16-7, for the NFL championship.

1963 On March 22, 1963, the Beatles release the album *Please Please Me* in Britain, where it is an instant hit. It is released in the U.S. as *Introducing the Beatles* and flops.

In April, the Golden Boy, also known to be a playboy, is suspended by the NFL for one year for betting on NFL games and associating with "undesirable persons."

In May, Gordon "Gordo" Cooper, the final Mercury 7 astronaut, stays aloft for 22 orbits.

On Nov. 4th, the Beatles perform for the Queen and the Royal Family. Later that month, their second album, *With the Beatles*, is released and stays at No. 1 for 21 weeks.

A military coup, supported by the U.S., topples the corrupt government in South

Vietnam, resulting in the assassination of President Ngo Dinh Diem. The regime is supplanted by a succession of corrupt governments that uses U.S. aid, and military advisors, to combat local guerrilla forces, the Viet Cong, and the North Vietnamese armed forces, the NVA. Meanwhile, Buddhist priests pour gasoline over their heads and immolate themselves at busy intersections in Saigon.

Three weeks later, during a trip to Dallas, Texas, President Kennedy is shot and killed by a former U.S. Marine and Communist sympathizer who is in turn shot and killed by a seedy local nightclub owner. The nation holds its breath, wondering what's going to happen next. The Vice-President, vulgar and powerful career legislator Lyndon Baines Johnson, takes over the Presidency.

Without Hornung, the Packers lose twice to the dreaded Chicago Bears, who go on to win the NFL championship.

By the end of 1963, more than 16,000 U.S. military advisors are in South Vietnam, which received $500 million in U.S. aid that year.

1964 The Beatles come to America. On Feb. 9, 1964, a record 73 million people watch the four mop-headed youngsters in matching suits on *The Ed Sullivan Show* as they perform "I Want to Hold Your Hand," "All My Loving," "Till There Was You," "She Loves You," and "I Saw Her Standing There." Teenaged girls in the audience scream so loud nobody can hear the music. Three days later, the Fab Four performs at Carnegie Hall. Fueled by the mass media, the nation experiences a sort of mass hysteria known as Beatlemania. Most adults are not amused. In April 1964, the Beatles land 14 songs on Billboard's Hot 100 singles chart. Businessmen begin to notice that the youth culture, or counterculture, can yield huge profits.

With the rocking music comes coverage of illicit drug use ("getting high") and free love (casual sex). The invention of the Pill allows women to have sex without the worries of getting pregnant (most of the time). Soon, the U.S. is invaded by British rock bands, including the Rolling Stones, who project a bad-boy image in contrast to the playful antics of the Fab Four.

Meanwhile, one of the modern wonders of the world is built in Houston, Texas — the Astrodome, a massive indoor sports stadium that uses artificial grass or turf.

On Feb. 25, 1964, in Miami, Olympic Gold Medalist Cassius Clay beats Sonny Liston for the world heavyweight boxing championship. He then changes his name to Muhammad Ali and fights until December 1981.

In 1964, a relatively harmless incident in the Gulf of Tonkin gives President Johnson the excuse to ask Congress for authorization to militarily intervene against North Vietnam without a declaration of war. U.S. aircraft begin dropping bombs on the North. Targets on the Ho Chi Minh supply trail are also hit. By the end of U.S. involvement, the U.S. will drop more bomb tonnage on Vietnam than in all of WWII.

In August, *A Hard Day's Night*, a black-and-white movie featuring the Beatles running away from female fans, opens in the U.S. and becomes an instant hit.

In November, Johnson is elected President over Republican Barry Goldwater of Arizona in a landslide victory. Goldwater is portrayed in the mass media as a right-wing nut ready to press the nuclear button. By year's end, the number of American military advisors in South Vietnam totals 23,000.

A sensation is created when Ford Motors introduces the Mustang, an all-new sportscar designed for the masses. The pony car thrives despite the longtime availability of the high-performance Chevrolet Corvette. Meanwhile, many prefer the inexpensive reliability of a cute German-made vehicle (originally authorized by Adolf Hitler) called the Volkswagen Beetle.

The Packers lose five games and finish second to Baltimore, which is beaten by Cleveland for the NFL title. Lombardi and his players vow to win the title next season.

1965

In January 1965, aides tell President Johnson that U.S. intervention in Vietnam is not succeeding and that the U.S. needs to either escalate military action or withdraw.

In March, U.S. fighter-bombers attack targets in North Vietnam as part of Operation

Rolling Thunder, which will last three years.

The Marines are the first U.S. forces to deploy large ground combat units to South Vietnam. By the end of the year, more than 38,000 Marines make up the Marine Amphibious Force.

Meanwhile, LBJ and a compliant Congress launch the Great Society, a laundry list of government social programs, including Medicare/Medicaid. Projected costs, as always, are lowballed and unrealistic.

In March, the first of the two-man space flights begins with the launch of Gemini 3. Gus Grissom becomes the first man to travel in space twice. In June, astronaut Ed White becomes the first American to walk in space, leaving his Gemini capsule and having a bit of trouble getting back inside. In August, Gemini 5 stays in space for eight days. In December, Gemini 6 and Gemini 7 rendezvous in orbit.

In July, the Beatles release *Help!*, their second movie. They are knighted by the Queen of England. In August they play Shea Stadium before a record crowd of 55,600 fans. They end the year by releasing *Rubber Soul,* a studio album showing the band turning in a new direction.

The first major race riot of the decade breaks out in the Watts section in Los Angeles.

On Oct. 16, 1965, anti-war rallies are staged in 40 American cities. Marchers in Washington, D.C. show support for the war.

In November, fighting in the Ia Drang Valley marks the first major battle between U.S. troops and North Vietnamese Army regulars (NVA) inside South Vietnam. The battle is a U.S. victory.

The day after Christmas 1965, in a rare divisional tie-breaker, the Packers beat the Baltimore Colts in overtime on a field goal in freezing temperatures. Earlier, in the fourth quarter, Green Bay tied the game with a field goal that is still disputed. The next season, the NFL increases the height of the goal-post uprights. A week later, the Packers beat the Cleveland Browns for their ninth NFL championship.

At year's end, there are 184,300 U.S. troops in South Vietnam. Half of the countryside is under some type of Viet Cong control.

1966

In February 1966, before Congress, Defense Secretary Robert McNamara states that the U.S. goal is to end North Vietnamese aggression against the South, not the defeat or destruction of North Vietnam itself.

In March, astronaut Neil Armstrong rescues Gemini 8 from a death spiral while his capsule is connected to an orbiting Agena rocket, the first docking between two orbiting spacecraft.

In April, massive B-52 bombers are used for the first time against North Vietnam. In

July, Hanoi Radio reports that captured American pilots have been paraded through the streets of Hanoi among jeering crowds. The U.S. refrains from bombing Hanoi or invading North Vietnam for fear of Communist Chinese intervention.

In July, Operation Hastings is launched by U.S. Marines and South Vietnamese troops against 10,000 NVA in Quang Tri Province, the largest combined military operation to date.

John Lennon tells the media that the Beatles are more popular than Jesus Christ, creating a furor in the U.S. and resentment against the band. The Beatles release the *Revolver* album in August. On August 29th, they perform their last live concert, at Candlestick Park in San Francisco. They barely manage to escape their manic fans, fearing for their lives.

In November, the *New York Times* reports that 40 percent of U.S. economic aid sent to Saigon is either stolen or winds up on the black market. Every night, broadcast news outlets announce the daily death toll in Vietnam.

There are 389,000 U.S. troops in Vietnam by the end of the year. Combat deaths total more than 5,000.

1967 On the first day of 1967, an end-zone interception ends the NFL championship game in Dallas and secures the second consecutive title for the Green Bay Packers. Two weeks later in Los Angeles, Lombardi's team defeats the Kansas City Chiefs, 35-10, in the NFL-AFL championship, soon to become known as the Super Bowl.

On Jan. 27, a fire rages in the pure oxygen atmosphere of the Apollo 1 capsule during a launch pad test, killing three astronauts—Gus Grissom, Ed White, and Roger Chaffee. NASA self-examines its procedures and engineering culture and makes modifications by that October.

On April 15th, anti-war demonstrations break out in New York and San Francisco involving nearly 200,000. The Rev. Martin Luther King Jr. declares that the war is undermining President Johnson's Great Society social-reform programs.

In June, the Beatles wow the world with their new album, *Sgt. Pepper's Lonely Hearts Club Band,* an intense studio concoction. It stays at No. 1 on the charts for 27 weeks.

During four days in July 1967, four die in Newark, N.J. racial violence. During five days of racial violence in Detroit, 43 die, with 5,000 buildings destroyed. City blocks burn; National Guard tanks roll through the streets.

In July, General Westmoreland requests an additional 200,000 reinforcements on top of the 475,000 soldiers already scheduled to be sent to Vietnam. President Johnson agrees only to an extra 45,000.

In August, the Beatle's manager, Brian Epstein, dies at age 32 of an accidental drug overdose.

In November, McNamara resigns as defense secretary. He has privately expressed doubts about the war strategy.

In December, the Beatles' *Magical Mystery Tour* television special is panned by critics.

On the last day of 1967, Bart Starr, the quarterback of the Green Bay Packers, sneaks the ball into the end zone to win the "Ice Bowl" and defeat the Cowboys for the team's third consecutive NFL title. It is 13 degrees below zero in Green Bay. Two weeks later, in much warmer Miami, the Packers beat the Oakland Raiders, 33-14, for their second Super Bowl win. Two weeks later, Lombardi steps down as head coach but remains as general manager. He has won five NFL championships in nine years.

By year's end, U.S. troop levels in Vietnam have reached 463,000, with 16,000 combat deaths to date.

1968 On Jan. 21, 1968, 20,000 NVA troops under the command of Gen. Giap attack the American air base at Khe Sanh, manned by 5,000 Marines, and begin a 77-day siege.

Ten days later, 84,000 Viet Cong guerrillas aided by NVA troops launch the Tet Offensive, attacking a hundred villages throughout South Vietnam. An attack against the U.S. Embassy in Saigon is fended off. A massive battle for the city of Huế commences. The month-long battle, which involves street-to-street fighting, ends with the U.S. retaking the city.

The Tet Offensive is a huge defeat for North Vietnam, with the Viet Cong virtually wiped out. However, due to massive and controversial media coverage, support for the war begins to wane on the part of the American public and Congress.

In early 1968, the Beatles spend time in India with the Maharishi Mahesh Yogi; George Harrison learns the ins and outs of Indian music. In May, the Beatles form

Apple Corps to support new musical artists. The company, badly mismanaged, will eventually hemorrhage money.

In March, Johnson stuns the country by announcing that he will not run for re-election. He calls a halt to the bombing, and in May peace talks begin in Paris.

In April, civil rights activist the Rev. Dr. Martin Luther King Jr. is shot and killed in Memphis by James Earl Ray, setting off riots and violence in more than 100 cities.

On April 23rd, anti-war activists at Columbia University seize five college buildings.

On June 5th, Robert F. Kennedy, brother of the slain President, is shot and killed by a Palestinian in Los Angeles after Kennedy wins the California Democratic Party primary.

On July 1st, General Westmoreland is replaced as U.S. commander in Vietnam by General Creighton W. Abrams.

In August, during the Democratic Party national convention in Chicago, 10,000 anti-war protesters gather on downtown streets and are confronted by 26,000 police and national guardsmen.

In October, Apollo 7, the first manned Apollo mission, launches on a Saturn I for an 11-day mission in Earth orbit, featuring the first live TV broadcast of humans in space. In December, Apollo 8 becomes the first manned mission to orbit the moon and capture the famous "Earthrise" photo.

In November, the Beatles release the two-disc *White Album,* full of self-indulgent creativity that highlights the growing divisions among members of the band.

In one of the greatest political comebacks of all time, Richard Nixon wins the 1968 presidential election over Democrat Hubert Humphrey. Nixon pledges "peace with honor" in Vietnam. Alabama governor and segregationist George Wallace runs for President on the American Independent Party and wins 10 million votes, five states, and 46 electoral votes.

Harvard professor Henry Kissinger becomes Nixon's National Security Advisor.

1969 On a cold afternoon in January 1969, the Beatles perform their last live concert, on the rooftop of Apple Corps in London.

On January 12th, the New York Jets of the AFL upset the Baltimore Colts of the NFL in Super Bowl III in Miami. In their first year without Coach Lombardi, the Packers miss the playoffs with a losing record.

In February, Vince Lombardi leaves the Packers to become part-owner and head coach of the Washington Redskins. In September of the next year, Lombardi dies of cancer at the age of 57. Grown men, tough guys, openly weep at his funeral. The Tiffany trophy awarded to the Super Bowl winner is renamed the Lombardi Trophy. The Packers bring home the trophy two more times since then. In 2003, a 14-foot-tall bronze statue of Coach Lombardi is dedicated at Lambeau Field (along with a statue of Curly Lambeau).

In March 1969, John Lennon marries avant garde artist Yoko Ono. They honeymoon in Gibraltar, holding press conferences in bed to promote world peace.

Rumors circulate that Paul McCartney was killed in a car accident and replaced with a look-alike. Fans scour their songs and interviews for clues — "Paul is dead" and "the Walrus is Paul."

In May, the *New York Times* breaks the news of the secret bombing of Cambodia. As a result, Nixon orders FBI wiretaps to determine the source of the news leak.

In Vietnam, 46 men of the 101st Airborne Division die during a fierce ten-day battle at Hamburger Hill in the A Shau Valley near Huế. 400 others are wounded. After the hill is taken, the troops are then ordered by their commander to abandon it. NVA then move in and take back the hill unopposed.

On June 8th, President Nixon meets South Vietnam's President Nguyen Van Thieu at Midway Island and informs him that U.S. troop levels are going to be sharply reduced. During a press briefing with Thieu, Nixon announces "Vietnamization" of the war and a U.S. troop withdrawal of 25,000 men.

On July 20th, Neil Armstrong and Buzz Aldrin land and walk on the moon while Mike Collins orbits in the Apollo 11 capsule. Armstong says, "One small step for a man, one giant leap for mankind," as he steps onto the lunar surface. Armstrong subsequently refuses to capitalize on his fame as the first human to walk on the moon.

In August, Kissinger conducts his first secret meeting in Paris with representatives from Hanoi. The Viet Cong begin a new offensive, attacking 150 targets throughout South Vietnam.

On Aug. 15-18th, 400,000 young people attend the Woodstock music festival in upstate New York. Thirty-two acts perform, but not the Beatles.

On Sept. 2, Ho Chi Minh dies of a heart attack at age 79.

In September, John Lennon decides to leave the Beatles. *Abbey Road*, their last studio album, is released and goes straight to No. 1.

In October, the New York Mets, baseball's most hapless team, win the World Series, 4-1, over the Baltimore Orioles in an upset comparable to Hell freezing over.

By year's end, America's fighting strength in Vietnam has been reduced by 115,000 men. 40,024 Americans have now been killed in Vietnam.

1970

In January 1970, Paul McCartney announces he has left the Beatles. In April, he releases his first solo album, *McCartney*.

On April 30th, President Nixon stuns America by announcing the U.S. and South Vietnamese incursion into Cambodia. The announcement generates a tidal wave of protest by politicians, the press, students, professors, clergy members, business leaders, and many average Americans against Nixon and the Vietnam War.

In April, an explosion ruptures the service module of Apollo 13, days after launch and within reach of the moon. Abandoning the mission to land on the moon, the astronauts climb into the Lunar Module and slingshot around the Moon to speed their safe return back to Earth.

Weeks later, Communist China launches its first satellite, Dong Fang Hong-1, on a Long March 1 rocket, becoming the fifth nation capable of launching satellites into space.

In May, the Beatles album *Let It Be*, recorded before *Abbey Road*, is released. The documentary *Let It Be* premieres in London with none of the Beatles in attendance.

On May 2, 1970, American college campuses erupt in protest over the invasion of Cambodia. Two days later, at Kent State University in Ohio, National Guardsmen shoot and kill four student protesters and wound nine.

In response to the killings, 400 colleges and universities across America shut down. In Washington, nearly 100,000 protesters surround various government buildings, including the White House and historical monuments. On an impulse, President Nixon exits the White House and pays a late-night surprise visit to the Lincoln Memorial and chats with young protesters.

By year's end, American troop levels in Vietnam drop to 280,000. The U.S. death toll there has reached 54,909.

H.R.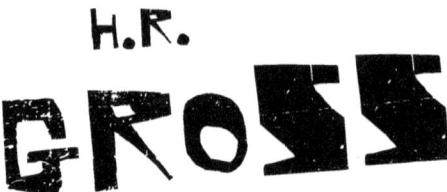

The Congressman Who Didn't Want to Spend Money

"A billion here, a billion there, and pretty soon you're talking about real money," lamented Republican Senator Everett Dirksen of Illinois back in the 1960s. He was commenting on the proclivity of Congress to spend money the country didn't have on new federal programs. Their solution was to raise taxes on hard-working citizens. The U.S. Congress seems even more hell-bent than ever these days on bankrupting the Treasury, passing a $1.9 trillion Covid-19 aid bill of which only 10 percent was actually Covid-19 aid.

As of January 2021, the U.S. national debt totaled roughly $27.6 trillion, or $220,748 per U.S. taxpayer. The U.S. federal debt to GDP ratio is now 130 percent, up from 53 percent in 1960. The total amount of unfunded federal liabilities is $158 trillion.

One former member of the House of Representatives must be rolling over in his grave. Known as "the useful pest," Harold Royce "H.R." Gross of Iowa was a Republican who served 13 terms in the House, retiring in 1974. He fought against government spending in nearly all of its manifestations.

Gross was well-known for his frugality, independence, and persistence. "He had an ascetic appearance, thinning hair, glasses, a penetrating stare and a perpetually worried expression. He also had a bass voice that would resonate through the House chamber," wrote commentator Fred Barnes.

He was fearless, rarely missed a roll call, and personally read all the details of every spending bill. Instead of attending social events at night, he stayed at home with his wife and two children, pouring over legislation or watching professional wrestling on TV.

Despite his role as pest and curmudgeon, he was widely admired and beloved by most members of Congress.

Gross was born in rural Iowa and attended public schools. He served in the Army in WWI in France and attended the Missouri School of Journalism. He began his radio career at WHO-AM in Des Moines. He read the news; a young guy named Ronald Reagan did the sports. He had "the fastest tongue on radio." He won his first House race in 1948.

Rep. Gross denounced an extension of the Marshall Plan, the United Nations, the funeral of President John F. Kennedy, the size of the White House security detail, the Peace Corps, the U.S. Space Program, federal pension "double-dipping," and foreign aid. He refused to go on congressional junkets, exclaiming, "Why should the taxpayers pay for my vacations?"

He opposed the Uniform Monday Holiday Act in 1968 and he opposed the Peace Corps because it was a haven for draft dodgers (members were exempt from the military draft). He was a vocal critic of the Kennedy Administration's foreign policy. He tried to block the sale of grain to the Soviet Union. He appeared on national television with four other legislators demanding stronger measures to get Russian troops out of Cuba.

His mission was to cut spending from every piece of legislation, and save the country from financial bankruptcy. His war cry was "How much will this boondoggle cost?"

Often he opposed stands by his own party. Under pressure to toe the party line, he quipped, "I took my last marching orders in 1916-19." He opposed spending by either party. Despite his seniority, he was never appointed to a position of leadership or committee office. Minority Leader Gerald Ford said, "There are three parties in the House — Democrats, Republicans and H.R. Gross."

Critics called him out for "the single most curmudgeonly act in the history of Congress." Gross had argued against an "eternal flame" at JFK's gravesite because the gas to keep it burning would cost too much.

Gross admitted to having only one regret about his entire career — voting "present" rather than "nay" on the Gulf of Tonkin Resolution, explaining that the Vietnam War cost too much. H.R. Gross died in 1987 at the age of 88.

"His commitment and tenacity earned him a legendary reputation as watchdog of the Treasury," said Senator Charles E. Grassley, Republican of Iowa, who succeeded Gross.

"He was clever, knowledgeable, focused, and tireless in ways no other congressman could match or even tried to," said Barnes.

Sources: https://www.usdebtclock.org; Biographical Directory of the U.S. Congress; New York Times; Washington Post; Fred Barnes, Washington Examiner; Ed Rollins, CNN.

Where Are They Now?
Historic Ships, Aircraft & Spacecraft

Historic ships, aircraft, and spacecraft can be viewed at museums across the nation. You can come aboard some ships and walk around. Some aircraft, including warbirds, you can buy a ride into the wild blue yonder. Here's a list (nowhere near comprehensive) of museum ships and crafts open to the public. Check websites for specific tourist information.

Historic Ships

1700s and 1800s:
USS Constitution, "Old Ironsides," Charlestown Navy Yard, Massachusetts
USS Constellation, Baltimore Harbor, Maryland
USS Monitor, Mariners' Museum and Park, Newport News, Virginia
CSA H.L. Hunley, Warren Lasch Conservation Center, North Charleston, South Carolina
USS Cairo, Vicksburg National Military Park, Mississippi

Battleships:
USS Alabama, Mobile, Alabama
USS Arizona, Pearl Harbor National Memorial, Hawaii
USS Iowa, Port of Los Angeles, California
USS Missouri, Pearl Harbor, Hawaii
USS Massachusetts, Fall River, Massachusetts
USS New Jersey, Camden, New Jersey
USS North Carolina, Wilmington, North Carolina
USS Olympia, Independence Seaport Museum, Philadelphia
USS Texas, San Jacinto Battleground State Historic Site, La Porte, Texas
USS Wisconsin, Norfolk, Virginia

Aircraft Carriers:
USS Hornet, Alameda, California
USS Intrepid, Intrepid Sea, Air & Space Museum, NYC
USS Lexington, Corpus Christi, Texas
USS Midway, San Diego, California
USS Yorktown, Patriots Point, Mount Pleasant, South Carolina

Submarines:
Trieste, National Museum of the US Navy, Washington, DC Navy Yard

THE ZONE: TRUE TALES FROM THE HEARTLAND

USS Nautilus, Naval Submarine Base, New London, Connecticut
USS Cod, Cleveland, Ohio
USS Bowfin, Pearl Harbor National Memorial, Hawaii
USS Growler, Intrepid Sea, Air & Space Museum, NYC

Miscellaneous:
LST 325, USS LST Memorial, Evansville, Indiana
U-505 IXC German U-boat, Museum of Science and Industry, Chicago
PT 305, National WWII Museum, New Orleans

Historic Aircraft

National Air and Space Museum, Washington, D.C.
"Spirit of St. Louis" Ryan NYP (Charles Lindbergh)
Bell XP-59A Airacomet
"Glamorous Glennis" Bell X-1 (Chuck Yeager)
Rutan Model 76 Voyager
Wright Brothers Flyer-1903

Steven F. Udvar-Hazy Center, Chantilly, Va.
Air France Concorde
"Enola Gay" Boeing B-29 Superfortress
"Flak Bait" Martin B-26B Marauder
North American Rockwell Shrike Commander 500S (Bob Hoover)

National Museum of the US Air Force, Dayton, Ohio
Air Force One-Boeing VC-137C SAM 26000
"Memphis Belle" Boeing B-17 Flying Fortress
"Bockscar" Boeing B-29 Superfortress
"Hanoi Taxi" Lockheed C-141C Starlifter
North American XB-70 Valkyrie
Boeing B-1B Lancer
Lockheed F-117A Nighthawk
Lockheed SR-71A Blackbird
Lockheed U-2A

National Naval Aviation Museum, Pensacola, Florida
McDonnell Douglas F/A-18A Hornet-Blue Angels Navy Flight Demonstration Squadron
Northrup SBD Dauntless BuNo 2106 (Battle of Midway)
NC4 Flying Boat-1919

Spruce Goose (Howard Hughes) Evergreen Aviation and Space Museum, McMinnville, Oregon
Beechcraft Staggerwing, Beechcraft Heritage Museum, Tullahoma, Tennessee

Organizations that offer flights for purchase:

Commemorative Air Force
"Fifi" Boeing B-29 Superfortress
"Diamond Lil" Consolidated B-24 Liberator
and 24 other WWII aircraft

Collings Foundation
"Witchcraft" Consolidated B-24J Liberator
"Tondelayo" North American B-25 Mitchell
"Nine O Nine" Boeing B-17 Flying Fortress

EAA-Oshkosh, Wisconsin
"Aluminum Overcast" Boeing B-17 Flying Fortress
"Tin Goose" 1929 Ford Tri-Motor
"Bonzo" 1934 Steve Wittman D-12

The Spirit of St. Louis

Apollo 11 Command Module

USS North Carolina

Spacecraft

Mercury capsules:
Freedom 7	JFK Library and Museum, Boston
Liberty Bell 7	Kansas Cosmosphere and Space Center, Hutchinson
Friendship 7	National Air and Space Museum, Washington, D.C.
Aurora 7	Museum of Science and Industry, Chicago
Sigma 7	US Astronaut Hall of Fame, Kennedy Space Center
Faith 7	Johnson Space Center, NASA, Houston

Gemini capsules:
Gemini 2	Air Force Space and Missile Museum, Cape Canaveral Air Force Station
Gemini III	Grissom Memorial, Spring Mill State Park, Mitchell, Ind.
Gemini IV	National Air and Space Museum, Washington, D.C.
Gemini V	Johnson Space Center, NASA, Houston
Gemini VI	Stafford Air & Space Museum, Weatherford, Okla.
Gemini VII	Steven F. Udvar-Hazy Center, Chantilly, Va.
Gemini VIII	Armstrong Air and Space Museum, Wapakoneta, Ohio
Gemini IX	Kennedy Space Center, NASA, Merritt Island, Fla.
Gemini X	Kansas Cosmosphere and Space Center, Hutchinson
Gemini XI	California Museum of Science and Industry, Los Angeles
Gemini XII	Adler Planetarium, Chicago

Apollo Command Modules:
Apollo 1	NASA Langley Research Center, Hampton
Apollo 7	Frontiers of Flight Museum, Dallas
Apollo 8	Museum of Science and Industry, Chicago
Apollo 9 "Gumdrop"	San Diego Air & Space Museum
Apollo 11 "Columbia"	National Air and Space Museum, Washington, D.C.
Apollo 12 "Yankee Clipper"	Virginia Air & Space Center, Hampton
Apollo 13 "Odyssey"	Kansas Cosmosphere and Space Center
Apollo 14 "Kitty Hawk"	Kennedy Space Center, Florida
Apollo 15 "Endeavour"	National Museum of the US Air Force, Dayton, Ohio
Apollo 16 "Casper"	US Space & Rocket Center, Huntsville
Apollo 17 "America"	Johnson Space Center, Houston

Shuttle Atlantis	Kennedy Space Center Visitor Complex
Shuttle Discovery	Steven F. Udvar-Hazy Center, Chantilly, Va.
Shuttle Endeavour	California Science Center
Shuttle Enterprise	Intrepid Sea, Air & Space Museum, NYC

SpaceShipOne (Rutan) National Air and Space Museum, Washington, D.C.
Lunar Module LM-2 National Air and Space Museum, Washington, D.C.
Saturn I and Saturn V (mock-up) rockets, US Space & Rocket Center, Huntsville, Ala.

Four Top Ten Boomer Rankings
Go ahead. Disagree with me. I double-dog dare you.

TOP TEN ALBUMS
1. Waiting For Columbus • Little Feat
2. Aja • Steely Dan
3. Abbey Road • The Beatles
4. Live in Hollywood • Linda Ronstadt
5. Layla & Other Assorted Love Songs • Derek & the Dominos
6. Led Zeppelin 4 • Led Zeppelin
7. Live at Leeds • The Who
8. Sticky Fingers • The Rolling Stones
9. Live at Fillmore East • The Allman Brothers Band
10. Speaking in Tongues • Talking Heads

Honorable Mention: Abraxas, Santana; Shades of Deep Purple, Deep Purple; Take-Offs and Put-Ons, George Carlin; Indianola Watermelon Seeds, B.B. King; Briefcase Full of Blues, The Blues Brothers; Hotel California, The Eagles; The Nightfly, Donald Fagan; The Koln Concert, Keith Jarrett; Live Bullet, Bob Seeger and the Silver Bullet Band; Goodbye to Yellow Brick Road, Elton John; The Jealous Kind, Delbert McClinton; Will the Circle Be Unbroken, Nitty Gritty Dirt Band; Lost Dogs and Mixed Blessings, John Prine; Shoot Out at the Fantasy Factory, Traffic; Tres Hombres, Z.Z. Top; The Doors, The Doors.

TOP TEN MOVIES
1. The Wizard of Oz (1939)
2. The Godfather (1972)
3. The French Connection (1971)
4. Patton (1970)
5. Raiders of the Lost Ark (1981)
6. Cool Hand Luke (1967)
7. Christmas Story (1983)
8. Blazing Saddles (1974)
9. Bladerunner (1982)
10. Das Boot (1981)

Honorable Mention: The Big Lebowski (1998), Star Wars (1977), Psycho (1960), Sunset Boulevard (1950), Apollo 13 (1995), Rocky (1976), Goodfellas (1990), Fargo (1996), American Grafitti (1973), Alien (1979), Die Hard (1998), The Great Escape (1963), 2001: A Space Odyssey (1968), North by Northwest (1959), MASH (1970), Bullitt (1968), Airplane (1980), Serpico (1973), Nobody's Fool (1995).

TOP TEN BOOKS
1. Washington: A Life • Ron Chernow
2. Churchill: Walking With Destiny • Andrew Roberts
3. The Underground Man • Ross MacDonald
4. Polar Star • Martin Cruz Smith
5. 1776 • David McCullough
6. When the Sacred Ginmill Closes • Lawrence Block
7. The Liberation Trilogy • Rick Atkinson
8. The Martian Chronicles • Ray Bradbury
9. Mere Christianity • C.S. Lewis
10. The Civil War: A Narrative • Shelby Foote

The Deep Blue Good-By, John D. MacDonald; The Looming Tower, Lawrence Wright; Parliament of Whores, PJ O'Rourke; Fear and Loathing in Las Vegas, Hunter Thompson; The First Deadly Sin, Lawrence Sanders; The Eiger Sanction, Trevanian; Lindbergh, A. Scott Berg; Leonardo da Vinci, Walter Isaacson; Hue 1968, Mark Bowden; Matterhorn, Karl Marlantes; The Visual Display of Quantitative Information, Edward R. Tufte; Stalingrad, Antony Beevor; Monuments, Judith Dupree; The Glorious Cause, Robert Middlekauff; Normandy '44, James Holland.

TOP TEN TELEVISION
1. The Bob Newhart Show
2. Lonesome Dove
3. Band of Brothers
4. The Dick Van Dyke Show
5. Last Man Standing
6. Everybody Loves Raymond
7. Bosch
8. Breaking Bad
9. Better Call Saul
10. Law and Order

Honorable Mention: Get Smart, The Middle, The Twilight Zone, Star Trek, Cheers, Columbo, Sanford & Son, The Andy Griffith Show, Monty Python's Flying Circus, NYPD Blue, St. Elsewhere, Rockford Files, The Avengers, The Fugitive, Homicide: Life on the Street; Rowan and Martin's Laugh-In; Saturday Night Live.

Albums limited to one per group/performer; no Greatest Hits compilations. Books limited to one per author. Television includes series and mini-series.

www.ingramcontent.com/pod-product-compliance
Lightning Source LLC
Chambersburg PA
CBHW071858290426
44110CB00013B/1199